WITHDRAWN
NDSU

Behavior Modification
Principles and Clinical Applications

Behavior Modification
Principles and Clinical Applications
Second Edition

Edited by
W. Stewart Agras, M.D.
Professor of Psychiatry
Stanford University School of Medicine
Stanford, California

Little, Brown and Company
Boston

Copyright © 1978 by Little, Brown and Company (Inc.)

Second Edition

Previous edition copyright © 1972 by Little, Brown and Company (Inc.)

All rights reserved. No part of this book may be reproduced in any form or by any electronic or mechanical means, including information storage and retrieval systems, without permission in writing from the publisher, except by a reviewer who may quote brief passages in a review.

Library of Congress Catalog Card No. 77-81503

ISBN 0-316-02031-1

Printed in the United States of America

BF
637
B4
B44
1978

Contributing Authors

W. Stewart Agras, M.D.
Professor of Psychiatry,
Stanford University School of Medicine,
Stanford, California

David H. Barlow, Ph.D.
Professor of Psychiatry and Psychology,
Brown University Program in Medicine
and Butler Hospital, Providence

Gary R. Birchler, Ph.D.
Assistant Professor, Department of Psychiatry,
University of California, San Diego,
School of Medicine, La Jolla

James M. Ferguson, M.D.
Assistant Professor, Department of Psychiatry,
University of California, San Diego,
School of Medicine, La Jolla

Isaac M. Marks, M.D.
Senior Lecturer, Institute of Psychiatry
(University of London); Consultant Psychiatrist,
Maudsley Hospital, London, England

Craig Barr Taylor, M.D.
Assistant Professor, Department of Psychiatry,
Stanford University School of Medicine,
Stanford, California

Preface

This book provides an overview of findings from the behavioral sciences that have application to clinical problems and presents selected descriptions of behavior therapy techniques. For this second edition, two new chapters have been added, one discussing the effects of relaxation-training procedures on various psychosomatic conditions and the other describing three multicomponent or packaged therapies. In addition, each of the chapters in the previous edition has been revised and several rewritten to reflect changes that have occurred in the field during the past five years. It is hoped that the book will continue to be used in advanced undergraduate courses and by clinicians and clinicians-in-training, who would find an overview of the field of behavior therapy useful.

As in the first edition, a short account of the behavior therapies can be obtained by reading the editor's introduction to each chapter, together with the pages referred to therein. These introductions do not comment on much of the experimental and theoretic material, concentrating instead on therapeutic techniques, their indications, and a brief review of their efficacy. Finally, the annotated therapeutic index serves to recommend therapeutic approaches for particular clinical problems.

This book was prepared during a year in residence at the Center for Advanced Study in the Behavioral Sciences, an environment that, under the able direction of Dr. Gardner Lindzey and with the support of the excellent staff, is particularly conducive to such work. The contributing authors also acknowledge the assistance of journal editors and publishing companies who have allowed reproduction of figures originally published elsewhere by them. Specifically, Figure 3 (by W. S. Agras) is reproduced by permission of the editor of the *Archives of General Psychiatry* (30:279, 1974) and the American Medical Association; Figure 11 (by J. M. Ferguson) is reproduced by permission of Bull Publishing Company, Palo Alto, California, from their book *Learning to Eat* (1975). Thanks also to Brunner-Mazel, New York, and to Benjamin J. Williams et al., authors of *Obesity Behavioral Approaches to Dietary Management* (1976), for permission to reproduce Figure 12.

W. S. A.

Contents

Contributing Authors   v

Preface   vii

Outline of Behavior Disorders   xi

1. **The Behavior Therapies: An Introduction**   1
   W. Stewart Agras

2. **The Behavior Therapies:
   Underlying Principles and Procedures**   15
   W. Stewart Agras

3. **Reinforcement and Extinction Procedures**   36
   W. Stewart Agras

4. **The Token Economy**   64
   W. Stewart Agras

5. **Aversive Procedures**   86
   David H. Barlow

6. **Relaxation Training and Related Techniques**   134
   C. Barr Taylor

7. **Exposure Treatments: Conceptual Issues**   163
   Isaac Marks

8. **Exposure Treatments: Clinical Applications**   204
   Isaac Marks

9. **Therapeutic Packages: Tools for Change**   243
   James M. Ferguson and Gary R. Birchler

Annotated Therapeutic Index   293

Subject Index   302

Outline of Behavior Disorders

I. Adult Disorders
   Neurotic Behavior
      Phobia
         Analogue and animal studies   163
         Clinical studies   204
      Compulsive behavior   218
      Hysterical reaction   48
      Depression   45, 217
   Psychotic Behavior
      Delusional speech   43, 52
      Chronic psychosis   69
   Psychosomatic Disorders
      Hypertension   151
      Headache   154
      Asthma   155
   Sexual Problems   103
   Obesity   113, 255
   Cigarette Smoking   110
   Interpersonal Problems
      Assertiveness training   268
II. Disorders of Childhood and Adolescence
   Classroom Behavior   45, 56, 78
   Delinquent Behavior   75
   Self-injurious Behavior   114
   Enuresis   248

1. The Behavior Therapies: An Introduction
W. Stewart Agras

Editor's Introduction

In the beginning, some 20 years ago, behavior therapy was largely characterized by opposition to psychoanalytic theory and practice, an opposition engendered in part by the lack of demonstrated efficacy of psychoanalytic practice, and in part by the growing discrepancy between the practices of psychoanalysis and those suggested by the findings of experimental psychology. At present, the field is characterized by a sizable body of research, a fruitful interaction between the experimental behavioral sciences and the clinic, and a developing therapeutic technology. Behavior is viewed as being more affected by current events in the social environment than was formerly believed. Treatment procedures are well specified and therefore easily transmittable, and directed at specific behavior problems. This offers an important contract to the broad-gauge, less specific approach of the traditional therapies.

Two major influences that gave birth to the field can still be discerned. The first was the development of an alternative mode of therapy, systematic desensitization [26], using a mediational approach, in which the treatment of anxiety is hypothesized to lead to behavior change. By contrast, in the second development, the application of the operant approach to clinical problems, behavior is changed directly by altering events in the social environment that influence performance. Although there are exceptions and a marked tendency toward a merging of interests, workers in the first tradition have tended to focus upon the problems encountered in adult outpatient populations and to use between-group experimental designs; while those in the second tradition have tended to work with the problems of children and institutionalized adults, and to use within-subject experimental designs.

Thus, the field today is one of the major arenas of psychotherapy research, which one hopes will lead to the discovery of new principles underlying therapeutic behavior change and to the development of new and more effective therapeutic techniques. Moreover, it is by no means as narrowly focused a venture as earlier critics supposed. Indeed, the range of conditions to which the behavior therapies have been applied, as the reader of this volume will discover, is probably broader than that covered by the traditional psychotherapies. The relationship between the experi-

mental behavioral sciences, on the one hand, and endeavors in the clinic, on the other, is as it should be, and augurs well for the future.

W. S. A.

The rise of behavior therapy has stimulated both conflict and research. Early developers often attacked the traditional psychotherapies, producing a strong defensive reaction and a rejection and criticism of behavior therapy. Such antagonism is unfortunate, since it diverts attention from the contribution that the experimental behavioral sciences can make to practice and research in psychotherapy. These sciences contribute experimental methods and suggest new therapeutic possibilities that may strengthen the efficacy of traditional psychotherapies and lead to the development of new and more effective forms of therapy. This should be welcomed by therapists of all persuasions, none of whom can be satisfied with the results of present-day techniques.

Naturally, the viewpoint of the experimental behavioral scientist differs from that of the clinician. Overt measurable behavior is emphasized while thinking and feeling tend to be deemphasized, a point of view often opposite to that of the clinician. Yet this new emphasis may shed light upon aspects of behavior that have been neglected. Similarly, different concepts are used by the behavioral scientist, who emphasizes the environmental antecedents or consequences of behavior rather than explanatory internal concepts such as defense mechanisms or ego structure. Again, the fresh viewpoint may stimulate new thinking and creative insight.

Early Development

Most historians of the behavior therapies point to scattered empiric use in the past of concepts and techniques similar to those of present-day behavior therapy. In the nineteenth century, the era of moral therapy, rehabilitation toward normal behavior was stressed. Thus, Dr. John S. Butler is described [2] as relying on positive attention to build up desired behaviors: if a patient tore at her clothing, he provided her with a new dress and took every opportunity to compliment her on her appearance—a nice example of the use of social reinforcement! Later, Simmel [19] used procedures such as banishing patients to their rooms if they showed undesirable behaviors, a procedure now more technically known as "time-out" from reinforcement. Such techniques made no impact on the field of psychotherapy, partly as a result of the demise of moral therapy, but chiefly because of the lack of an experimental or theoretic framework.

Psychotherapeutic techniques, in fact, developed as an extension of the case history method of data collection and analysis. This approach is shared with other medical specialties and has shaped the thinking and practice of psychiatry and clinical psychology. To an internist the patient complains of a symptom, which is viewed as secondary to organic dysfunction. To a psychiatrist the patient, or his relatives, complain of a change in behavior (although this may be phrased as change in feeling or thinking). Sharing the viewpoint of medicine, psychiatry came to regard abnormal behavior as being secondary to internal changes.

This view was incorporated in the most important theoretic system to predate the behavioral approach, namely, psychoanalysis. However, many notions about behavior are shared by the two schools of thought, including the view that the history of an individual is important in understanding present behavior, that maladaptive behavior is largely acquired through learning in a social environment, and that the basic scientific aim is to understand the factors that influence abnormal behavior so as to modify it more effectively. Freud developed psychoanalysis without reference to psychology because psychology, in its infancy at the turn of the century, was unable to investigate complex human behavior. The first attempts to integrate the developing knowledge about learning with psychoanalytic theory consisted of translating one set of concepts into the other [7]. Later translations were more sophisticated [3] but did not change the research tactics or therapeutic procedures of psychiatry or clinical psychology.

More important were the clinical applications of behavioral techniques based on Pavlov's work. In an early and, by today's standards, somewhat crude experiment, Watson [25] produced a phobia in an infant by pairing a noxious stimulus (noise) with a neutral stimulus (a white rat). After a few pairings, crying and avoidance of the rat occurred, as well as avoidance of other animals, such as a rabbit, and materials such as fur, and to a lesser extent, cotton and wool. Soon afterward, Jones [10] described several direct techniques that eliminated children's fears. These included gradual approach to the feared object, and social imitation, in which a child was exposed to children who were not afraid of the same object, and who thus modeled normal approach behavior for the child.

More therapeutic applications were those of Kantorovich [11] in alcoholism and Max [17] in the case of a homosexual. Both paired electric shock with the problem behavior. However, these isolated usages made little or no difference to treatment methods. Indeed, the only treatment based on learning theory that had gained some acceptance by the mid-forties was aversion therapy for the treatment of alcoholism [14], in which the taste and smell of alcohol were paired with nausea induced by the injection of apomorphine.

Later Development
Recent developments in the behavioral therapies derive from two sources: dissatisfaction with the results of the verbal psychotherapies and the growth of alternative approaches to treatment, particularly Wolpe's systematic desensitization [26] and extensions of Skinner's experimental work [20] from the laboratory to the clinic.

Dissatisfaction with the results of verbal psychotherapy grew slowly, since there was little research on the efficacy of such therapy. Eysenck's review articles [4,5] highlighting this problem produced an unfortunate furor, and his later writings on behavior therapy were interpreted as being antagonistic to psychoanalytic psychotherapy, placing proponents of such therapies in a defensive position. Nevertheless, Eysenck's position that psychotherapy had not been shown to be more effective than no treatment was solidly based. His critics identified many of the methodologic difficulties in evaluating the effects of psychotherapy but could not rebut his main conclusion. Later, Bergin [1], in a reanalysis of the data of controlled-outcome studies of psychotherapy, found that patients treated with psychotherapy show both negative and positive change when compared with untreated control subjects, who show slight improvement and cluster about the mean. This evidence suggests that behavior change does occur during psychotherapy but is masked in group studies, where the positive and negative effects cancel out. Moreover, in a recent review [16] of reasonably well-controlled comparisons of psychotherapy with no treatment or minimal treatment, psychotherapy was found to be better in 20 studies and of no benefit in 13, again suggesting that psychotherapy produces therapeutic behavior change in some circumstances.

Nonetheless, the realization that verbal psychotherapy has uncertain effects left an opening for new forms of therapy. One such form was described by Wolpe in his book *Psychotherapy by Reciprocal Inhibition* [26]. Wolpe, an enthusiastic developer of new ideas, based this therapy on observations derived from an animal experiment, in which he successfully used feeding to reduce learned avoidance behavior in cats that by this means were gradually led to approach a feared situation. He hypothesized that "if a response incompatible with anxiety can be made to occur in the presence of anxiety-evoking stimuli, it will weaken the bond between the stimuli and the anxiety response." Instead of using feeding to inhibit anxiety in humans, Wolpe found that relaxation was seemingly as good. Thus, patients with neurotic avoidance behavior imagine a series of gradually more fear-arousing scenes while deeply relaxed. Supposedly, anxiety will be inhibited by relaxation as patients are progressively able to approach their feared object, first in their imagination and then in reality.

The second class of new therapies derives from B. F. Skinner's experimental analysis of behavior [20]. Skinner and his associates were able to gain precise control of certain aspects of animal behavior in the laboratory by varying the consequences of behavior. One of the first applications to the clinic was that of Fuller [9], who shaped a simple arm-raising response in a "vegetative idiot" by making a sugar-milk solution contingent on successively nearer approximations to this behavior. Later, Lindsley [15] used the techniques of operant conditioning to investigate the behavior of schizophrenics, after which a rapid expansion to various kinds of behaviors in children and adults occurred (see Chapters 2 to 5).

Since then, several other techniques, such as implosion, flooding, assertiveness training, and relaxation training, have been included within the behavior therapies, because they are either based on procedures derived from experimental psychology or are aimed at direct behavior change. At this point it can be seen that a number of forces have influenced the development of behavior therapy and that some way of defining the field is necessary.

Definition

There are two ways to define the behavioral therapies. One is to list the therapeutic procedures that purport to be derived from experiments in learning. Such a list includes:

1. Systematic desensitization
2. Shaping by positive reinforcement, including token economies
3. Aversive therapies
   a. Punishment
   b. Escape and avoidance conditioning
   c. Classic Conditioning
   d. Covert sensitization
4. Implosion-flooding
5. Modeling
6. Assertiveness training
7. Relaxation therapy
8. Paradoxical intent

This technique-oriented approach has the disadvantage of making behavior therapy a "school" of psychotherapy parallel with, but divorced from, other schools of therapy.

An alternative is to define the field as the use of the techniques of the experimental behavioral sciences to tease out the principles underlying therapeutic behavior change. At first, it would seem wise to determine the therapeutic efficacy of variables known to affect normal behavior. Later, discoveries unique to the modification of deviant behavior will doubtless be made. As effective variables are identified, they may be combined into therapeutic procedures testable in controlled-outcome studies. Unfortunately, the behavioral sciences are not advanced enough to allow a comprehensive compilation of the variables that cause behavior change. For the time being, then, it is necessary to blend these two approaches, moving from therapeutic technique to experiments analyzing the effective ingredients of such techniques, and from variables that affect behavior to new therapies.

Relationship to Psychoanalytic Psychotherapy

As noted earlier, psychoanalysis followed the theories of medicine by hypothesizing that internal events explain disturbed behavior. Constructs such as ego, id, and superego, and hypothetical energy such as libido are used in a series of somewhat loosely arranged hypotheses to explain behavior. The experimental behavioral sciences, on the other hand, consider behavior to be maintained largely by current environmental events. Skinner [21] objects to the use of inner constructs to explain behavior on the ground that such constructs can be misleading. Thus, while a functional analysis of behavior is interested in the direct effect of punishment on behavior, a mental psychology views punishment as inducing anxiety, which in turn causes behavioral change. The danger in such a formula is that there is a tendency to view anxiety as causing the behavior change, and to forget to specify what caused the anxiety in the first place. The more complex the internal hypotheses, the more likely this is to happen. Skinner therefore argues for the simpler approach, in which the environmental factors prompting and maintaining abnormal behavior are defined and their effects analyzed experimentally.

Psychoanalytic psychotherapies usually assume that the following factors are essential to change symptoms: emotional and intellectual understanding or insight, resolution of the conflict underlying the symptom, and the use of transference behavior to achieve the first two aims. These assumptions have been essentially untested; however, they derive from psychoanalytic observations and hypotheses. The aims of psychoanalytic therapy, according to Knight [12], are:

1. Disappearance of presenting symptoms
2. Real improvement of mental functioning, for example,
    a. The acquisition of insight, intellectual and emotional, into the childhood sources of conflict, the part played by precipitating and other reality factors, and the methods of defense against anxiety that have produced the type of personality and the specific character of the morbid process
    b. Development of tolerance, without anxiety, of the instinctual drives
3. Improved reality adjustment, for example,
    a. More consistent and loyal interpersonal relationships with well-chosen objects
    b. Free functioning of abilities in productive work

The main drawback to this list is that, with the exception of change in symptoms, most of the aims are unmeasurable. Particularly difficult to measure are aims such as development of tolerance of instinctual drives, which are based on hypotheses concerning inner mental events.

The behavior therapies, on the other hand, assume that problem behavior is maintained by its consequences. Thus, to change behavior it is necessary to change those consequences and to arrange an environment in which appropriate new behavior can be learned. The aims of behavior therapy, therefore, are to:

1. Eliminate problem behavior (symptoms) directly, either in the life situation in which it occurs or in a specially designed artificial situation
2. Build up desired behaviors in small, progressive steps in a specially designed program.

These aims, together with the theoretic and experimental predilections of the behavior therapies, have implications both for the design of therapy and for the evaluation of outcome. Treatment should be aimed at a well-delineated problem and should consist of specific and replicable procedures, rather than poorly defined treatment for global problems. Assessment of change should involve direct measurement of the target behavior and not global ratings, which depend so much on recall and are considerably influenced by the demand characteristics of the measurement situation.

Example of Procedure
A simple example of the differences in procedure between the psychoanalytic psychotherapies and a behavior therapy is illustrated by a case of agoraphobia in a married woman aged 23 years. She had not been able to leave her home alone for more than one year and had associated fears of crowds, choking, and dying. Her past history revealed a brief episode of fear of choking and dying in childhood. At that time her mother was in hospital having a thyroid operation, and the patient, who was "very close to her," recalled thinking that her mother might die. Her agoraphobia started shortly after marriage and progressively worsened.

Psychoanalytically oriented treatment would aim at elucidating the conflicts underlying her symptom, using verbal interchange and the transference relationship to enable the patient to gain insight into her problem. An initial hypothesis might be that the patient was overdependent upon her mother and that separation through marriage replicated the frightening situation in childhood when her mother deserted her and was in danger of dying. Further therapy might involve exploration of ambivalent feelings and fantasies toward her parents and her husband. Change in symptoms would be expected to occur as insight developed, to be reflected in changes in interpersonal relationships and in the therapeutic transference.

From a behavioral viewpoint, the first problem to be dealt with was that of not being able to leave home alone, which was the patient's presenting problem. Several approaches were possible. One possibility was to identify factors in her environment that maintained the problem behavior, such as attention given to the patient by her mother and husband for not leaving home. Gradual removal of such attention might lead to a reduction in phobic behavior.

The approach decided on, however, was to teach the patient to leave a safe situation (in this case, the hospital) by herself. As a first step, an objective measure of agoraphobia was devised. Since the central symptomatic behavior was the patient's difficulty in leaving a dependent situation, the distance walked from the hospital alone was used as a measure. A course was laid out from the hospital to downtown, and landmarks were agreed upon by patient and staff at about 25-yard intervals for more than one mile. The patient was asked to stay on the course and to note the point at which she turned back. Two 30-minute treatment sessions were held each day. At the end of each attempted walk the patient reported how far she had gone. Since much of the course was observable, checks were made that confirmed the accuracy of the patient's report.

The second step was to determine her initial level of behavior by having her attempt to walk alone over the course for a few sessions, after which treatment was begun. This simply consisted of praising the patient and commenting enthusiastically about her progress each time she met the reinforcement criterion. This was determined as follows: if the patient was praised for walking 100 yards alone in one trial and then she walked 120 yards in the next, the criterion for reinforcement became 110 yards, that is, the mean value between the previous criterion and the next trial in excess of it. The patient now had to meet, or exceed, 110 yards to receive praise.

As can be seen in Figure 1, the patient was able to walk farther alone during each session during reinforced practice in the first phase. Although it is not essential clinically to test whether the treatment being used is responsible for the behavior change, it is, nevertheless, useful to do so. Thus, for the next few days the therapist no longer praised the patient for improvements in performance. After a brief spurt, her performance declined and picked up again only after further reinforcement during the final phase. At this point the patient was able to walk downtown alone, and she was then encouraged to walk elsewhere, which she found she could do. In addi-

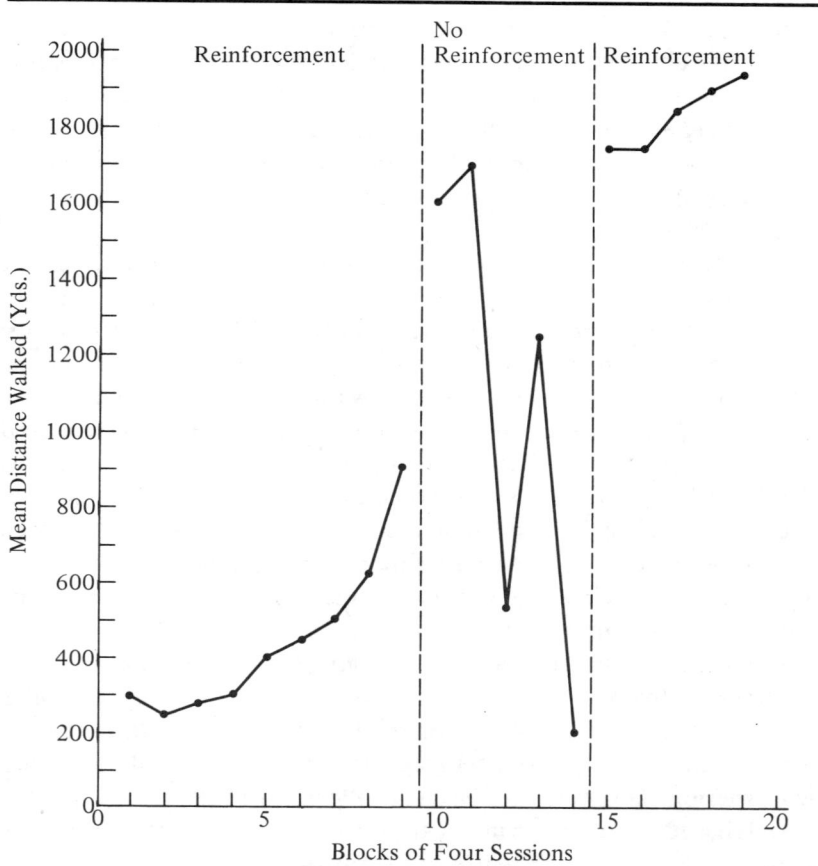

Figure 1. *Partial data from the experimental treatment of an agoraphobic patient, showing the effect of introducing, removing, and reintroducing praise, given contingent on walking alone. That reinforcement was responsible for improved performance is demonstrated by worsening in the middle phase, when it was withdrawn.*

tion, her associated fears of crowds, choking, and dying also decreased. Follow-up two years later showed her to be symptom-free and also revealed that her family life had improved considerably, probably as a result of losing her incapacitating phobic behavior.

Although in this instance little further therapy was needed, in other cases fears of choking and dying might well have required separate treatment. In addition, problems in the agoraphobic woman's relationship with her husband and mother might well have needed attention. For example, she might have been in need of assistance to assert herself and to be generally less dependent upon them (see Chapter 9 for details of assertiveness training). Successful treatment of the presenting problem often reveals many residual problems of living that require attention before therapy can be concluded.

Comparison of Behavior Therapies and Insight-Oriented Therapy
The major difference, then, between insight-oriented therapy and the behavior therapies is that the former first changes attitudes and feelings as expressed in a verbal interchange, expecting life behavior to alter later; while the latter first change behavior, expecting that changes in attitudes and feelings will follow. Until recently, little experimental work had been done to determine which is the more effective approach to behavior change, or which combination of attitude, insight, and emotional and behavioral change is most effective. However, these issues are presently being subjected to close experimental scrutiny as increased attention is given to the cognitive aspects of behavior change.

Some evidence suggests that the insight and behavior psychotherapies do not differ in practice as much as appears on the surface. In both, a relationship exists between patient and therapist, the quality of which in certain contexts affects the outcome of therapy. Also in both, therapeutic instructions and suggestion that improvement will occur are given. Frank [6] has shown that persuasion is an effective ingredient in verbal psychotherapy, while more recent work [13, 18] suggests that the same holds true for the behavior therapies. Positive reinforcement has also been found to occur within a verbal psychotherapy, namely, Rogerian therapy. Truax [23] analyzed tape recordings of a single long-term case treated by Rogers. He unexpectedly found that the therapist responded differentially to five of the nine behaviors studied and that the rate of emission of four of these behaviors increased during therapy, demonstrating the presence of selective social reinforcement. This appears to be the only study of the influence of social reinforcement within a verbal psychotherapy, although a number of authors have examined this question in analogues of verbal psychotherapy [24], again finding a definite effect of contingent social attention.

Finally, a quotation from Freud's collected papers [8], in which he discusses the psychoanalytic treatment of agoraphobia, suggests that insight is not enough and that the therapist must pay attention to direct behavior change. "One can hardly ever master a phobia if one waits till the patient lets the analysis influence him to give it up. . . . One succeeds only when one can induce them . . . to go about alone and to struggle with their anxiety while they make the attempt." Similarly, Terhune [22], in his description of an apparently successful form of psychotherapy, considers that direct approach to the feared object or situation in reality is of great importance and benefit. Undoubtedly, both Freud and Terhune paid attention to, and praised, their patients' progress, and their ideas are echoed in Chapters 7 and 8.

If there are procedures common to the verbal and behavioral psychotherapies, then the scientific problem becomes the identification of those processes that lead to therapeutic behavior change. Research has already led to the discovery of several variables that alter both normal and deviant behavior. These will be described in the next chapter. Although the coverage will not be complete, it will form an introduction to those subsequent chapters describing application of the procedures in the form of the behavior therapies.

Summary and Overview
As noted, the behavior therapies developed out of the coincidence of a growing dissatisfaction with the efficacy of the prevailing verbal psychotherapies, the introduction of a new therapy—systematic desensitization—and the increasing relevance of the experimental behavioral sciences to the clinic. Some of the techniques, such as the application of selective positive reinforcement and extinction, are direct applications of procedures that have been investigated in experimental psychology laboratories, often with a wide range of organisms. Others that appear to have been derived from animal experiment, such as systematic desensitization, have been radically altered in the transition from animal to human so that the relationship to the original experiment appears strained. Yet others, such as implosive therapy, in which patients are exposed to intensely imagined fear-arousing situations, have an even looser connection with the findings of the experimental behavioral sciences. The task in such therapies as desensitization

and implosion is first to assess their effectiveness and then, if they are effective, to find out how they work.

Doubtless, there are many commonalities between the more traditional psychotherapies and the behavioral therapies. In both there is a relationship between therapist and patient, and the therapist influences the patient by behaving in a certain way. Yet, as we shall see in subsequent chapters, the behavioral approach offers a set of specific procedures to influence behavior change in particular ways. This increase in therapeutic precision should lead to more effective and, equally important, more cost-effective treatment. Beyond this, one hopes that the field of psychotherapy will become one in which findings from the basic sciences will be tested in an applied setting, fostering an interaction that will be mutually beneficial.

References

1. Bergin, A. E. The effects of psychotherapy: Negative results revisited. *Journal of Counseling Psychology* 10:244, 1963.
2. Bockhoven, J. S. *Moral Treatment in American Psychiatry*. New York: Springer Publishing Co., 1963.
3. Dollard, J., and Miller, N. E. *Personality and Psychotherapy*. New York: McGraw-Hill, 1950.
4. Eysenck, H. J. The effects of psychotherapy: An evaluation. *Journal of Consulting Psychology* 16:319, 1952.
5. Eysenck, H. J. *The Effects of Psychotherapy*. New York: International Science Press, 1966.
6. Frank, J. D. *Persuasion and Healing*. Baltimore: Johns Hopkins Press, 1961.
7. French, P. M. Relations between psychoanalysis and the experimental work of Pavlov. *American Journal of Psychiatry* 12:1165, 1933.
8. Freud, S. Turnings in the ways of psychoanalytic therapy. In *Collected Papers,* Vol. 2. New York: Basic Books, 1959.
9. Fuller, P. R. Operant conditioning of a vegetative human organism. *American Journal of Psychology* 62:587, 1949.
10. Jones, M. C. Elimination of children's fears. *Journal of Experimental Psychology* 7:382, 1924.
11. Kantorovich, N. V. An attempt at associative reflex therapy in alcoholism. *Novoe v Refleksologii i Fiziologii* 3:436, 1929.
12. Knight, R. P. Evaluation of the results of psychoanalytic therapy. *American Journal of Psychiatry* 98:434, 1941.
13. Leitenberg, H., Agras, W. S., Barlow, D. H., and Oliveau, D. C. Contributions of selective positive reinforcement and therapeutic instructions to systematic desensitization therapy. *Journal of Abnormal Psychology* 74:113, 1969.
14. Lemere, F., and Voegtlin, W. L. An evaluation of the aversion treatment of alcoholism. *Quarterly Journal of Studies on Alcohol* 11:199, 1950.

15. Lindsley, O. R.   Operant conditioning methods applied to research in chronic schizophrenia. *Psychiatric Research Reports* 5:118, 1956.
16. Luborsky, L., Singer, B., and Luborsky, L.   Comparative studies of psychotherapies. *Archives of General Psychiatry* 32:995, 1975.
17. Max, L. W.   Breaking up a homosexual fixation by the conditioned reaction technique: A case study. *Psychological Bulletin* 32:723, 1935.
18. Oliveau, D. C., Agras, W. S., Leitenberg, H., Moore, R. C., and Wright, D. E.   Systematic desensitization, therapeutically oriented instructions and selective positive reinforcement. *Behavior Research and Therapy* 7:27, 1969.
19. Simmel, E.   Psychoanalytic treatment in a sanatorium. *International Journal of Psychoanalysis* 10:70, 1929.
20. Skinner, B. F.   *The Behavior of Organisms*. New York: Appleton-Century-Crofts, 1938.
21. Skinner, B. F.   Behaviorism at Fifty. In T. W. Wann (Ed.), *Behaviorism and Phenomenology*. Chicago: University of Chicago Press, 1964.
22. Terhune, W. B.   The phobic syndrome. *Archives of Neurology and Psychiatry* 62:162, 1949.
23. Truax, C. B.   Reinforcement and nonreinforcement in Rogerian psychotherapy. *Journal of Abnormal Psychology* 71:1, 1966.
24. Ullman, L. P., Krasner, L., and Collins, B. J.   Modification of behavior through verbal conditioning: Effects in group therapy. *Journal of Abnormal and Social Psychology* 62:128, 1961.
25. Watson, J. B., and Rayner, P.   Conditioned emotional reactions. *Journal of Experimental Psychology* 3:1, 1920.
26. Wolpe, J.   *Psychotherapy by Reciprocal Inhibition*. Stanford: Stanford University Press, 1958.

2. The Behavior Therapies: Underlying Principles and Procedures

W. Stewart Agras

Editor's Introduction

The clinician interested in using a new therapeutic procedure requires an adequate description of the technique, an elucidation of underlying principles, in order to use the therapy flexibly, and an evaluation of its effectiveness. The major principles underlying therapeutic behavior change are described in this chapter and are amplified in subsequent chapters, where their relationship to particular therapeutic procedures is discussed.

The immediately surrounding events that most affect behavior can be classified into those occurring before a particular behavior and those occurring after. In the first category are procedures such as therapeutic instructions, modeling, and setting events or stimulus control, while in the second category, among a variety of procedures, are reinforcement and feedback. To reflect the growing interest of the field of behavior therapy in cognitive variables that affect behavior, there is discussion of self-instruction, monitoring, and self-reinforcement.

It should be emphasized that these events and procedures affecting behavior have been isolated by research, both in the laboratory and in the field, and our understanding of them will doubtless change as new findings are made. Such research is an excellent antidote to the distressing tendency of applied fields to become overly dogmatic in the transmission of ideas and procedures from one generation of practitioners to the next.

It is in this spirit that the contributors to this volume have reviewed the available research, in order to shed light on the mode of action and efficacy of the behavior therapies. As noted previously, two main lines of research exist. The first is the single-case experiment, in which subjects are used as their own control. In such studies the relatively immediate effect of a particular therapeutic variable can be assessed. Experiments of this nature can be used to sort out effective procedures from ineffective ones and to discover how a therapy works. Effective procedures can then be embodied in a therapeutic package or program, which must be tested, either against no treatment or against a standard therapy. As a result of this research and an evolving understanding of the process of behavior change, it seems likely that an increasing number of well-specified therapeutic procedures for particular behavior problems will become available.

W. S. A.

As noted in the previous chapter, a large body of experimental work suggests that environmental events, particularly those of the social environment, influence behavior. This is fortunate, since such events can often be altered, resulting in therapeutic behavior change. These environmental influences can be roughly classified into those occurring before a particular behavior, such as therapeutic instructions, and those occurring as a consequence of behavior, such as reinforcement.

Behavioral Antecedents

Events that occur before a behavioral sequence influence subsequent performance. Such events fall into two broad classes. First, there is stimulus control—for example, the traffic light. When it is green, the traffic moves; when it is red, the traffic stops. The color change leads to quite complex behavior change on the part of both pedestrians and drivers. Then there is behavioral demonstration—often called modeling—in which a performance sequence is demonstrated and the client then carries out successively closer approximations to the correct performance. Intermediate between these two classes are procedures such as therapeutic instructions, which in part act as signals to perform in a certain way, and in part verbally outline expected performance.

The first example of stimulus control of behavior is classical or respondent conditioning, in which learning appears to occur by repeatedly associating an environmental event and a behavior, usually visceral or autonomic behavior.

Respondent Conditioning

Respondent conditioning is important because it deals with autonomic responses that often form part of neurotic behavior. The basic notions of the conditional reflex are familiar enough; certain inborn responses are regularly elicited by certain stimuli. For example, food in the mouth (uncontitional stimulus) induces salivation (unconditional response). If another stimulus is paired with the presentation of food, e.g., a buzzer (conditional stimulus), it will, after a number of pairings, come to elicit salivation (conditional response).

It seems possible that various kinds of environmental stimuli initially paired with frightening events could come to elicit a rapid heart rate or other visceral responses characteristic of anxiety. Moreover, in humans capable of symbol formation, words can become conditional stimuli and may elicit the same responses. Thus, punishment by overly strict parents might evoke a cardiovascular response in a child, while associated stimuli such as the sights or sounds of quarreling, authority figures, or even words with aggressive connotations may later elicit the same, and now inappropriate, response. This phenomenon is known as stimulus generalization; the further the stimulus is removed from the original conditioned reflex, the less the autonomic response.

Extinction of a conditional response occurs if the conditional stimulus is presented a number of times without being followed by the unconditional stimulus. After an interval, presentation of the conditional stimulus will once more elicit the conditional response in a weaker form, a phenomenon known as spontaneous recovery. Thus, repeated exposure to a fear-arousing stimulus either in reality or in imagination leads to a decline in heart rate.

While extinction is one example of the therapeutic use of classical conditioning techniques, others, such as conditioning an aversive response, have been used more frequently. Thus, apomorphine, which elicits nausea, has been paired with the smell and taste of alcohol; approach to alcohol then elicits nausea and avoidance behavior (see Chapter 4, pages 97–99). Similar notions led Mowrer [28] to propose the "bell and pad" method of treating enuresis, in which a buzzer wakes the child as soon as urination begins, and which is a successful approach to this difficult problem if used correctly.

Another therapeutic use of classical conditioning has been to increase sexual arousal to heterosexual stimuli in homosexuals who wish to extend their range of sexual experience [17]. Using short movie clips of homosexual activities as the unconditional stimulus, and slides of a potential heterosexual partner as the conditional stimulus, researchers found that two out of three male homosexuals showed increased heterosexual arousal after the conditioning procedure, but not after a backward conditioning, in which no pairing took place. In one of the cases, however, the timing of the stimulus pairing had to be altered by presenting the conditional and unconditional stimuli simultaneously rather than in sequence.

Finally, a recent report [44] demonstrated the use of classical conditioning to produce changes in systolic blood pressure. A buzzer (the conditional stimulus) was followed by tilting a table to lower blood pressure. After a few pairings the buzzer alone came to elicit small decreases in systolic blood pressure. Like so much of the work in the autonomic area, this finding has no immediate applied significance; however, such a procedure might be used to lower further the reduced blood pressure brought about by the use of feedback or relaxation procedures (see Chapter 6).

While repeated pairing of stimulus and behavior in the classical conditioning procedure leads to a stimulus controlling the onset of a particular (often autonomic) behavior, stimulus control may be acquired in other ways. Thus, if behavior is reinforced only in the presence of a particular stimulus, then it will occur only under such conditions in the future. This is known as discrimination or discriminative control of behavior. To take a clinical example, phobic behavior can be viewed as a form of stimulus control, in which avoidance occurs only in the presence of a particular object or situation, or of course, symbolic representations of the situation in pictures or thoughts. Since the etiology of phobia is not known, Marks (see Chapters 7 and 8) prefers to use the more descriptive term *evoking stimuli*.

Discriminative Stimuli

Less attention has been paid to the therapeutic use of discriminative stimuli than to the use of procedures such as reinforcement. Yet in some circumstances such stimuli may exert more powerful effects on behavior than reinforcement. Thus, in a study in which children were taught to imitate simple movements [32], reinforcement made little difference to the frequency of imitated responses; however, when the experimenter left the room after telling the children what to do, the number of imitations dropped dramatically. When he returned imitative behavior strengthened again. Here, the experimenter was the stimulus condition exerting strong effects on behavior.

It is, of course, important to identify which stimuli control what behavior. In a particularly exciting experiment Rincover and Koegel [36] found that autistic children may not attend to the obvious stimulus in a learning situation. When teaching such children simple tasks, these workers found that no generalization from a training session to other situations occurred, even when the original therapist was present. The experimenters noted, however, that when instructing a child to perform a behavior ("Touch your chin") the therapist made a gesture toward his own chin. When a stranger told the child to touch his chin *and* made the hand movement, then the child performed the behavior. It was the movement, not the verbal instruction, that was controlling the child's behavior. Of course, the reverse could occur. Someone might make such a gesture and the child would touch his chin (a nice example of the "disturbed posturing" of such children). Similar examples of unusual stimulus control were found in other autistic children.

Symbolic representations can also control behavior. Some sexual problems, for example, can be conceived of as disorders of stimulus control. The fetishist is sexually aroused by a nonsexual stimulus, e.g., a shoe. In the absence of such a stimulus little or no arousal occurs. Fantasying the stimulus or listening to an audiotaped description of the situation also produces sexual arousal. Abel and his colleagues [1] used audiotapes with differing descriptions of sexual situations, in conjunction with direct measurement of penile arousal. In one case a patient described himself as aroused only by women's sandals. However, it turned out that he was, in fact, aroused by women's feet, not by the sandals, and only if the woman was responsive to him. Obviously, such findings have important diagnostic and therapeutic implications.

Fading
Stimulus control can be altered by a procedure known as fading. This technique can be illustrated by its use in teaching children to read. Pictures of an object known to a child can slowly be dimmed while the printed word remains illuminated, thus teaching the meaning and use of the word [14]. More complex stimulus control can be changed in the same way. As noted earlier, sexual behavior can often be viewed as an example of stimulus control. The heterosexual responds to an attractive person of the opposite sex, while the complex stimulus controlling sexual arousal of the homosexual is a person of the same sex. In one therapeutic experiment [7], fading was used to alter sexual arousal patterns in male homosexuals by slowly increasing the illumination of a nonarousing slide of a woman and dimming an arousing slide of a male. By starting with 100 percent illumination of the male and increasing the visibility of the female very slowly while arousal (monitored by penile measurement) was kept constant, increasing heterosexual arousal was obtained. Moreover, the heterosexual arousal generalized into the real world, allowing new relationships to be established.

Therapeutic Instructions
The initial contact between therapist and client (or student and teacher) consists of an explanation of what to expect during the course of therapy or teaching, and enunciation of the rules that obtain. These instructions interact with the pupils' or clients' prior experience with physicians, therapists, or teachers, and influence subsequent behavior. For example, the effectiveness of placebo administration presumably depends upon these factors. Thus, a group of outpatients who had reached maximum improvement with brief psychotherapy showed further improvement following a course of inert medication given with instructions suggesting that improvement was to be expected [16]. In another study of neurotic outpatients Hoehn-Saric, Frank, Imber, Nash, Stone, and Battle [18] found that patients given a brief prepsychotherapy interview, in which the goals of therapy were outlined, improved more following subsequent psychotherapy than did a group of patients who were not given the interview.

Moreover, therapeutic instructions are as important to the outcome of a behavior therapy such as systematic desensitization as they are to the outcome of the verbal psychotherapies. Leitenberg, Agras, Barlow, and Oliveau [20] treated two groups of snake-fearful young women with systematic desensitization, varying only the instructions given them, so that the women in one group thought they were taking part in an experiment on visualizing snake fears while those in the other group believed they were being treated for their fears. Only the latter group improved more than untreated controls.

Therapeutic instructions, however, produce different responses in different persons. Figure 2 shows the data for three agoraphobic patients who were given instructions suggesting that they should steadily improve simply by practicing in their phobic situation. There were three patterns of behavior; no effect (S1), a transient effect (S2), and steady improvement (S3). The most common patterns seem to be the first and second, which have now been observed in a number of patients with severe neurotic disorders. Overall, the findings suggest that therapeutic instructions are beneficial, although individual responses will vary considerably. There is also evidence that instructions lead to greater and longer-lasting changes in less severe behavior problems, e.g., snake fears, than in more severe problems, such as phobias.

Intriguingly, therapeutic instructions seem to influence autonomic as

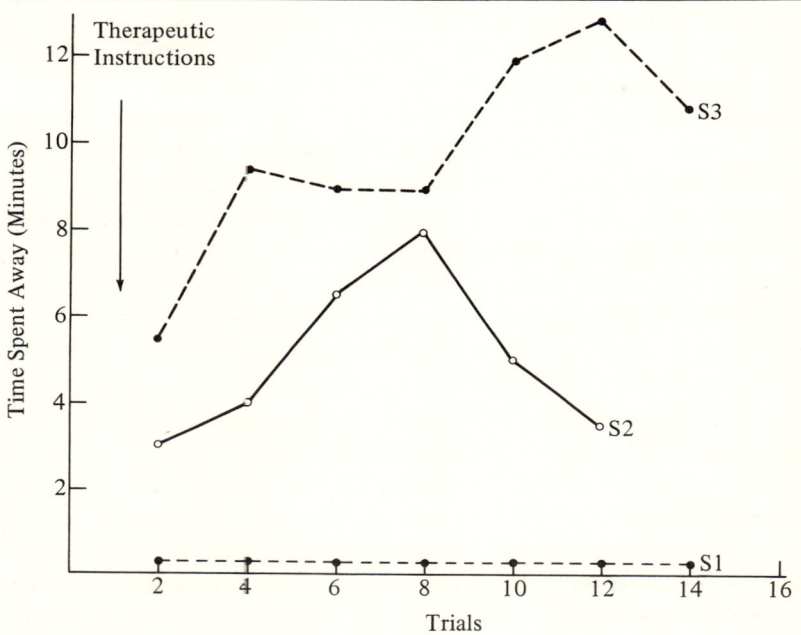

Figure 2. *The effect of therapeutic instructions on the ability of three agoraphobic subjects to walk alone as measured by time spent away on each trial. As can be seen, three different patterns occur; no effect (S1), a transient effect (S2), and steady improvement (S3).*

well as voluntary behavior. Thus, Redmond, Gaylor, and McDonald [35], in a laboratory experiment with six hypertensives, demonstrated that asking subjects to raise and lower their blood pressure led to substantial changes. On average, blood pressure was lowered by 7.7 per 2.5 millimeters of mercury (mm Hg). Interviews suggested that subjects used mental imagery to try to bring about the desired change, visualizing themselves in such relaxing situations as lying on a beach.

A variant or subcomponent of therapeutic instructions is the *prompting* of a particular behavior. Thus, a teacher might remind a pupil to complete a piece of work, or a therapist might ask a patient to practice a new behavior. Kindergarten children being taught to read, for example, imitated more words when the teacher stressed those words by saying them louder

[37]. Naturally, behavior initiated by prompting or therapeutic instructions should be strengthened and maintained by feedback and reinforcement.

Self-instruction

Luria [23] has suggested that children's behavior is at first regulated by instructions and promptings from adults, and later the child's own speech, in the form of telling oneself what to do, comes to exert control over behavior; finally, thought or inner speech takes over. Thus, an external stimulus governing behavior—a command or instruction—fades into an internal stimulus exerting discriminative control. Working with this hypothetical chain of events, a number of investigators have developed a therapeutic strategy to alter what clients say to themselves.

One of the earliest studies [26] was directed toward helping impulsive children alter their behavior. In a series of classroom tasks the experimenter first demonstrated a self-instructional process by saing: "Okay, what is it I have to do? You want me to copy the picture with the different lines. I have to go slowly and carefully. Okay, draw the line down, down, good. . . . " Children first repeated these instructions aloud while working, then whispered them, and finally were told to say them silently. Children treated in this way performed significantly better than a group who practiced the tasks without self-instructions on seveal paper-and-pencil tests.

In a later study Bornstein and Quevillon [9] found that a self-instructional procedure with three overactive preschool boys produced an immediate and powerful effect on attending behavior in the classroom. Unlike the procedure in the previous study, direct measurement of classroom behavior was made, and follow-up for about three months showed good maintenance of improvement. Meichenbaum [27] now considers that self-instructional procedures can be introduced most easily to children in the context of play and with the instruction to think aloud. Once they have been successfully used in play, practice in other situations can be started.

Self-instructional procedures have also been used with phobic-like conditions such as anxiety about speaking in public. In one experiment the efficacy of self-instruction was compared with that of systematic desensitization, the latter having been shown by Paul [31] to be more effective than verbal psychotherapy in the treatment of that condition. In the self-instructional procedure [25] clients identified self-defeating instructions in public-speaking contexts, and practiced supportive self-talk in a group situation.

This procedure was as effective as desensitization, and the data suggested that self-instruction was more effective with subjects who showed more generalized patterns of anxiety. This suggestion, that self-instruction may mediate generalization of therapeutic effect, is quite plausible, since subjects might be supposed to carry around their own set of discriminative stimuli. Unfortunately, no critical examination of this notion has yet appeared in the literature. Moreover, at present one may conclude only that a procedure to teach self-instruction has certain effects, and not that self-instructions are, in fact, used in everyday life and are responsible for the therapeutic effect. It is possible, for example, that self-instructional clients may practice new behavior more frequently than do clients treated in other ways, which could account for the greater therapeutic efficacy of this technique.

Modeling
The final procedure to be discussed in this section is modeling, which leads to learning by imitation. One of the techniques most frequently used to induce behavior change is to show people how to do things. Learning can occur in a variety of ways with this technique. Subjects can observe both the modeled behavior and its consequences, describe it verbally, or practice the behavior, which then comes under the control of its consequences.

Bandura and his colleagues have investigated a number of aspects of the modeling process, particularly as it applies to the elimination of fearful behavior. In one study [4] children who showed severe fear of dogs on a behavioral approach test were divided into several differently treated groups. Two groups observed a fearless child approach a dog during some eight sessions, in either an enjoyable context—a party—or a neutral context. Both groups improved considerably more than two other groups, who simply saw a dog or saw the party without a dog. Sixty-seven percent of the children in the modeling group were able to remain alone in a room with a dog, while very few of the children in the control group were able to do so.

The ability to imitate is notably deficient in some types of behavioral disorders, such as childhood autism. However, it has been shown [3] that imitative responses can be shaped and that the newly developed class of behavior, i.e., a tendency to imitate, can be used to generate new responses. Exposure to a model may more effectively build up complex repertoires of behavior in some circumstances than shaping each piece of the repertoire item by item. Thus, college students [22] who had not been able to acquire a complex sequence of behavior when it was taught by differential reinforcement of correct and incorrect responses rapidly acquired the behavior when exposed to models.

This form of learning probably occurs in the verbal psychotherapies. Although therapists restrict the range of their behavior during psychotherapy, they do offer model solutions to problems in verbal form, especially in the more directive supportive therapies and in the later phases of psychoanalytic psychotherapy, where identification with the therapist may become important. The concepts of identification and imitation are related, identification usually referring to behaviors performed in the absence of the model and restricted to the class of interpersonal behaviors.

Other forms of psychotherapy use imitative learning in a more planned way. Role-playing techniques are an excellent example of this; the therapist and patient enact problem situations, the therapist sometimes exchanging roles with the patient to demonstrate more adaptive ways of behaving. Assertiveness training is one example of the systematic use of modeling by means of role-playing (see Chapter 9). Similarly, Mowrer [29], in integrity therapy, consistently models more straightforward and more adaptive ways of behaving, described as self-disclosure and personal accountability.

Behavioral Consequences

The first set of behavioral consequences, often colloquially referred to as rewards, strengthen behavior. More correctly, they are referred to as reinforcers, which in turn are classified into two varieties, positive and negative reinforcers, and two procedures, positive and negative reinforcement.

An event is considered to be a *positive reinforcer* if the behavior that precedes it is found to have an increased probability of occurring. Many events positively reinforce human behavior, although it is important to remember that what is reinforcing for one person may not be for another. Food, water, sexual activity, and warmth are all positive reinforcers. Social attention, praise, grades, and money are also reinforcers, and many others have been described in clinical studies—for example, candies, cigarettes, treats of various kinds, and access to a psychotherapist. *Negative reinforcers* are usually defined in a slightly different way; namely, that when they are removed, the behavior that preceded them tends to have an increased probability of occurring. Generally, painful stimuli such as excessive heat, blows, electric shock, noise, and social criticism are negative reinforcers.

Given the observed relationships between behavior and certain kinds of environmental events, it obviously becomes possible to produce behavior change by making such events contingent on behavior, i.e., *operant conditioning*, which includes procedures such as shaping, extinction, and aversive control.

Shaping

Shaping has clear relevance for therapeutic behavior change, since it involves building up desired behavior by applying selective positive reinforcement. It is necessary that the subject exhibit some initial behavior, which is then built up by reinforcing closer and closer approximations to the desired final response. This is achieved by waiting for—or by prompting— the first reponse and immediately following it with positive reinforcement. The response probability is thereby increased and is also likely to overshoot—that is, to come nearer the final desired behavior as a result of variations in the amplitude of response. By reinforcing sufficiently often to maintain a suitable response rate, and by increasing the criterion for reinforcement, the desired behavior is slowly built up. (This technique is described in detail in Chapter 3 in the section on the procedure of positive reinforcement.) During shaping, reinforcement is given for most responses that meet the slowly changing criterion. Once a pattern has been established, the frequency of reinforcement is changed to one that is sufficient to maintain behavior of the desired strength.

Self-reinforcement

In the uses of reinforcement so far described, another person, for example, a therapist or family member, controls the delivery of reinforcement, be it a material consequence such as tokens or money, or a social consequence such as attention or praise. However, in some circumstances persons can administer reinforcement to themselves. This requires the existence of three conditions: (1) individuals must have access to reinforcers so that (2) they can make delivery of reinforcement contingent upon completion of a particular performance, which implies (3) the ability to define and maintain standards of performance. If successfully used, this kind of reinforcement procedure is extremely useful therapeutically, especially in helping individuals to maintain self-control over long periods of time.

At present, there seems to be no doubt that both animals [6, 24] and human beings [3, 15] can learn to use self-reinforcement procedures, although some form of externally imposed contingency is necessary to ensure maintenance of the use of self-reinforcement. In particular, occasional punishment for the use of noncontingent self-reward [5, 6] seems to facilitate the continued accurate use of the procedure. But why should humans continue to use self-reinforcement strategies? the answer seems to lie in two areas: how well standard-setting and self-denial are learned, and what social factors facilitate their continued use. Bandura [6] points out that upholding high standards is promoted by "a vast system of rewards, including praise, social recognition, and awards, whereas few accolades are bestowed on people for self-rewarding mediocre performances." Moreover, some behaviors carry their own negative consequences. "To those burdened with excessive weight, for example, the discomforts, maladies, and social cost of obesity create inducements to control overeating. Such negative consequences can, of course, be brought to the forefront by the therapist or may occur to the patient as worrying thoughts, which in turn may serve as cues or inducements to maintain self-control."

Reinforcement of Autonomic Responses

For many years it was thought that reinforcement affected only voluntary behavior. However, recent work suggests that reinforcement affects autonomic responses; thus, it has been shown that operant procedures affect such responses as heart rate [10, 41, 42], blood pressure [8, 38], gastric acid secretion [43], and salivation [12]. Since we are not able to observe such behavior accurately, the procedures often include some form of display of the response being worked with—biological feedback. This subject will be discussed in greater detail in the next section and also in Chapter 6.

Extinction

While desirable behavior can be encouraged by shaping, it is often necessary to eliminate unwanted behavior. One way to do this is to determine what reinforcer is maintaining such behavior and then to remove that reinforcer. This procedure is called extinction. Upon removal of reinforcement the behavior will weaken and finally disappear. At times, however, the behavior will strengthen before falling off. This is shown in Figure 1 (page 10) during the middle phase, in which praise for walking farther was withheld. The patient at first walked twice as far before showing a decline in this behavior. Examples of the therapeutic use of extinction are to be found in Chapters 2 and 3.

Aversive Procedures

Another way to reduce the frequency of unwanted behavior is to use aversive procedures in one of three main arrangements: escape, avoidance training, and punishment. In an escape procedure the individual can stop an ongoing aversive event by performing an action. In an avoidance paradigm the individual prevents the onset of an aversive event by making a response. Both arrangements strengthen the escape or avoidance behavior. In the clinical use of these procedures the escape or avoidance behavior is usually incompatible with the behavior to be reduced. Thus, the alcoholic might be taught to spit out alcohol, or push away an alcoholic beverage and sip a soft drink.

Avoidance behavior can be extremely persistent, since by its very nature the organism can never discover that the aversive stimulus has been discontinued—i.e., the behavior is 100 percent successful in avoiding an aversive consequence and is therefore maintained in the total absence of such reinforcement. Many persistent neurotic behaviors may be the product of avoidance training. Thus, ritualistic behavior, which may be aimed at avoiding an unwanted consequence, by its very continuance prevents the discovery that the avoided contingency will no longer occur. Hence, a person whose handwashing ritual is aimed at preventing infection and death is constantly reassured by the absence of such events, as long as the handwashing continues. Moreover, if an infection occurs, handwashing is increased!

The third method of reducing the frequency of unwanted behavior, punishment, refers to the procedure of making an unpleasant event contingent upon behavior. This has the effect of reducing the frequency of the unwanted behavior, often very rapidly. It is therefore a useful procedure when it is important to gain quick control of a subject's behavior; e.g., unruly or aggressive behavior in children. However, it has some drawbacks. First, behavior is only temporarily suppressed; remove the punishment and the behavior recurs. This can be overcome by reinforcing behavior incompatible with the punished behavior; thus, aggressive behavior might be punished and more cooperative behavior reinforced at the same time. Second, the subject can learn an avoidance response that is just as undesirable as that which was punished. Punishing stealing might lead to a person's hiding crime more efficiently to prevent discovery and avoid punishment. Third, excessive punishment can produce unwanted side effects such as general social withdrawal, fear responses, and aggressive behavior. Nonetheless, punishment can be a useful clinical procedure, particularly when other methods, such as reinforcement and extinction, are unsuccessful (see Chapters 3–5).

Information Feedback
Behavior not only produces reinforcing consequences but also provides information as to the extent of action. This is most obvious in activities such as throwing a ball, where the results of one throw alter the next. Unfortunately, the information generated by our more complex behavior is not always clear, and may not, therefore, assist in modulation of the activity. Experiments with augmented information feedback have shown such feedback to be important in the acquisition of motor skills [45] and in programmed instruction [34], and more recently as a therapeutic variable. Feedback may be provided by oneself, i.e., self-monitoring; by a therapist; or by a device, as is most often the case with biofeedback.

SELF-MONITORING. Recording and collation of aspects of one's own behavior may come to exert control over that behavior in a relatively weak and transient way. Occasionally, however, it has quite powerful effects. Broden and her colleagues [11] investigated the effect of self-monitoring with two eighth-grade students, using a reversal design. Study time in one case and talking out in the other case were the problem behaviors within a classroom setting. In the first case the addition of reinforcement led to maintenance of improvement, while in the second case, in which no reinforcement was used, the positive gains deteriorated over time. This is similar to Stuart's [39] finding with overweight persons. Self-monitoring alone led to small changes that disappeared without the addition of other elements of the treatment program. In another interesting, perhaps unique, case, self-recording using a wrist counter led to a dramatic reduction in the frequency of several different tics exhibited by a patient [40]. The frequency of each tic was reduced only when the self-recording procedure was introduced. Clearly then, self-monitoring should comprise an aspect of many treatment programs, thus actively including clients in their own treatment and facilitating goal setting.

THERAPIST FEEDBACK. Quantitative information concerning behavior change provided by a therapist facilitates therapeutic progress. In one of the first studies of this issue [19] information about the length of time spent confronting a phobic situation was found to facilitate progress. Adding contingent praise did not enhance the effect of feedback. A later extension of this work [21] examined the reverse sequence in five phobic patients to determine whether feedback would add anything to ongoing therapist praise. The addition of precise performance feedback led to a dramatic increase in time spent approaching the phobic object or situation. However, when feedback was removed the new rate of gain was maintained by praise alone. It seems, then, that feedback might be particularly important in the initial phase of a therapeutic program.

A slightly different finding was made in the treatment of anorexia nervosa [2]. As is shown in Figure 3, reinforcement, consisting of extra privileges made contingent upon weight gain, had little effect upon either caloric intake or weight. The addition of feedback, provided partly by the therapist (calories eaten each day and weight gain) and partly by the patient (a count of the number of mouthfuls eaten at each meal) led to a remarkable increase in food consumption and weight gained. However, unlike the case of phobia, contingent privileges alone had little effect upon weight gain. A therapeutic package consisting of reinforcement, feedback, and large meals, each of which was shown to have a therapeutic effect in a series of controlled experiments, appears to lead to consistent weight gain of about 1.5 kg per week (a useful addition to the treatment of this puzzling disorder).

Information feedback also facilitates therapist behavior. In one study psychiatric aides were ranked [33] according to the progress of their patients. This led to improvement in their clinical skills, as measured by increased appropriate behavior of their patients. In a similar study Panyan, Boozer, and Morris [30] found that the number of therapeutic sessions conducted by aides increased threefold when they were given feedback as to the number of sessions they had conducted. An interesting aspect of both these studies is that the feedback was publicly displayed, so that all aides could

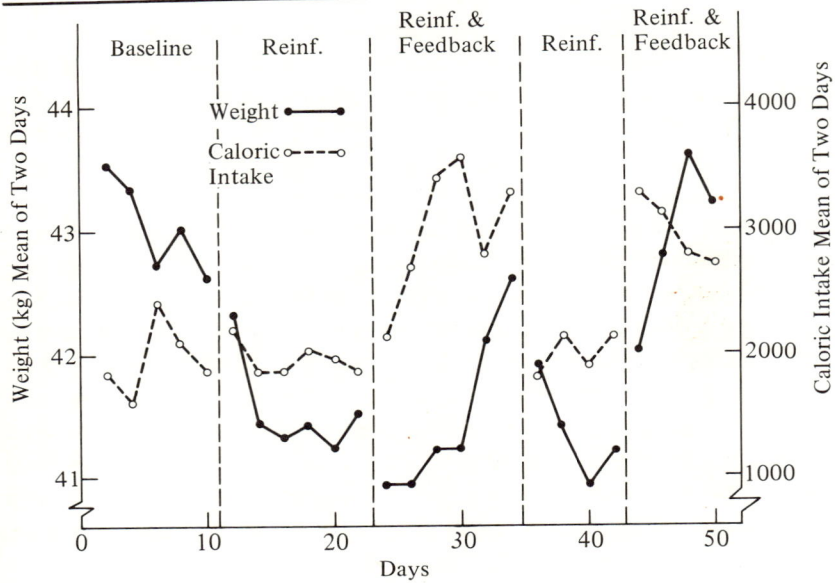

Figure 3. *Information feedback added to reinforcement resulted in marked increases in caloric intake and weight (phases 3 and 5) as compared with the effect of reinforcement alone (phases 2 and 4) in a patient with anorexia nervosa.*

view not only their own but others' performances. Presumably, such a method provides more motivation than the private display of progress.

BIOFEEDBACK. There is no doubt that biofeedback is an idea whose day has come. Unfortunately, widespread coverage in the popular press and the fascination of the American public with technology has thoroughly obfuscated what biofeedback can and cannot do. Many studies fail to separate the effects of feedback from reinforcement, while in others there is an absence of an appropriate experimental design. To date, the main work has been with the cardiovascular system, particularly with altering heart rate and rhythm, and blood pressure, and with the enhancement of states of relaxation using electromyographic feedback (see Chapter 6).

There appears to be no doubt that electromyographic feedback enhances muscle quietude. Whether this is of clinical significance is not yet established, since the precise relationship between muscular tension and the experience of relaxation is obscure (see Chapter 6, pages 139-144, for a detailed discussion of this issue). In uncontrolled studies, frontalis feedback has led to fewer complaints of tension headache [13], suggesting that one use of electromyographic feedback might be in the treatment of localized muscle spasm.

Many other physiologic responses are affected by feedback (usually combined with reinforcement); for example, salivation [12] and gastric secretion [43]. In the latter case, three of four normal subjects were able to raise and lower their rates of gastric secretion. Again, these findings are of much clinical interest, but more work is needed before they can be considered of clinical import. There is no doubt that behavior change occasioned by biofeedback and reinforcement procedures occurs, but many technical problems—particularly those involved in providing a sensitive, ongoing measure of the behavior—need to be solved. Until such solutions are found, the obtained changes are likely to be too small to allow for widespread use.

Summary and Overview

That the immediately surrounding events in part determine behavior has been amply demonstrated in this chapter, and will continue to form the theme of the remaining chapters. Since such events can often be changed either by the persons themselves or by direct intervention—for example, changing the interaction of family members, or reorganizing a classroom or a ward—then therapeutic behavior change becomes possible. Moreover, adaptive skills can be directly taught and the opportunity to practice them afforded.

While therapeutic experiments often attempt to isolate the effect of a single variable, sometimes imparting an air of therapeutic naiveté, effective procedures are combined into therapeutic packages in clinical practice (see Chapter 9). All therapies make use of instructions, prompts, and some form of social encouragement and reinforcement; and more specific techniques are always embedded in this matrix, which itself depends upon an adequate relationship between therapist and client.

Nonetheless, the behavior therapies go beyond the relatively nonspecific approaches of the more traditional psychotherapies, adding focused behavior change procedures. There is also increasing evidence that this approach is at least as effective as, and often more economical than, the verbal psychotherapies, while in some instances behavioral therapies are more effective. Thus, in the treatment of moderately severe clinical phobias (see Chapter 8), in obesity (see Chapter 9), and perhaps in the treatment of hypertension and cardiac arrhythmias (see Chapter 6), behavior therapies have increased the effectiveness of treatment. In the management of inpatient settings, the less specific techniques of milieu therapy have been extended by the application of reinforcement procedures through the token economy (see Chapter 4). Even in more complex disorders with multiple determinants—for example, delinquency—encouraging results are being obtained (see Chapter 3).

Naturally, problems remain. Many behavior change procedures have immediate and circumscribed effects. Generalization of therapeutic change over time and across different settings is often weak, and more basic understanding of the processes of stimulus control and generalization is needed. Moreover, identical behaviors may have different causes and may be maintained by different environmental events. Thus, the effect of a particular treatment may be different, even in similar disorders.

All this suggests that the field of psychotherapy is changing, and that as therapeutic experiments continue, increasingly effective therapies for well-defined conditions will emerge. This implies a need to increase the precision of diagnostic procedures, to develop better clinical monitoring systems, and to offer training to allow therapists to update their skills. The following pages introduce therapists to the use of the various procedures (which have been briefly described in this chapter) in clinical situations.

References

1. Abel, G. G., Blanchard, E. B., Barlow, D. H., and Mavissakalian, M. Identifying specific erotic cues in sexual deviations by audiotaped descriptions. *Journal of Applied Behavior Analysis* 8:235, 1975.
2. Agras, W. S., Barlow, D. H., Chapin, H. N., Abel, G. G., and Leitenberg, H. Behavior modification of anorexia nervosa. *Archives of General Psychiatry* 30:279, 1974.
3. Bandura, A., and Kupers, C. J. The transmission of patterns of self-reinforcement through modeling. *Journal of Abnormal and Social Psychology* 69, 1964.
4. Bandura, A., Grusec, J. E., and Menlove, F. L. Vicarious extinction of avoidance behavior. *Journal of Personality and Social Psychology* 5:16, 1967.
5. Bandura, A., and Mahoney, M. J. Maintenance and transfer of self-reinforcement functions. *Behavior Research and Therapy* 12:89, 1974.
6. Bandura, A. Self-reinforcement: Theoretical and methodological considera-

tions. *Behaviorism*. In press.
7. Barlow, D. H., and Agras, W. S. Fading to increase heterosexual responsiveness in homosexuals. *Journal of Applied Behavior Analysis* 6:355, 1973.
8. Benson, H., Shapiro, D., Tursky, B., and Schwartz, G. E. Decreased systolic blood pressure through operant conditioning techniques in patients with essential hypertension. *Science* 173:740, 1971.
9. Bornstein, P. H., and Quevillon, R. P. The effects of a self-instructional package on overactive pre-school boys. *Journal of Applied Behavior Analysis* 9:179, 1976.
10. Brener, J., Kleinman, R. A., and Goesling, W. J. The effects of different exposures to augmented sensory feedback on the control of heart rate. *Psychophysiology* 5:510, 1969.
11. Broden, M., Hall, V., and Mitts, B. The effect of self-recording on the classroom behavior of two eighth grade students. *Journal of Applied Behavior Analysis* 4:191, 1971.
12. Brown, C. C., and Katz, R. A. Operant salivary conditioning in man. *Psychophysiology* 4:156, 1967.
13. Budzynski, R., Stoyva, J., and Adler, C. Feedback induced muscle relaxation: Application to tension headache. *Behavior Therapy and Experimental Psychiatry* 1:205, 1970.
14. Corey, J. R., and Shamow, J. C. W. The effects of fading on the acquisition and retention of oral reading. *Journal of Applied Behavior Analysis* 5:311, 1972.
15. Felixbrod, J. A., and O'Leary, K. D. Effects of reinforcement on children's academic behavior as a function of self-determined and externally imposed contingencies. *Journal of Applied Behavior Analysis* 6:241, 1973.
16. Gliedman, L. H., Nash, E. H., Imber, S. D., Stone, A. R., and Frank, J. D. Reduction of symptoms by pharmacologically inert substances and by short-term psychotherapy. *Archives of Neurology and Psychiatry* 79:345, 1958.
17. Herman, S. H., Barlow, D. H., and Agras, W. S. An experimental analysis of classical conditioning as a method of increasing heterosexual arousal in homosexuals. *Behavior Therapy* 5:33, 1974.
18. Hoehn-Saric, R., Frank, J. D., Imber, S. D., Nash, E. H., Stone, A. R., and Battle, C. Systematic preparation of patients for psychotherapy. I. Effects on therapy behavior and outcome. *Journal of Psychiatric Research* 2:267, 1964.
19. Leitenberg, H., Agras, W. S., Thompson, L. E., and Wright, D. E. Feedback in behavior modification: An experimental analysis in two phobic cases. *Journal of Applied Behavior Analysis* 1:131, 1968.
20. Leitenberg, H., Agras, W. S., Barlow, D. H., and Oliveau, D. C. Contribution of selective positive reinforcement and therapeutic instructions to systematic desensitization therapy. *Journal of Abnormal Psychology* 74:113, 1969.
21. Leitenberg, H., Agras, W. S., Allen, R., Butz, R., and Edwards, J. Feedback and therapist praise during treatment of phobia. *Journal of Consulting and Clinical Psychology*, 43:396, 1975.
22. Luchins, A. S., and Luchins, E. H. Learning a complex ritualized social role. *Psychological Record* 16:177, 1966.
23. Luria, A. R. *The Role of Speech in the Regulation of Normal and Abnormal Behavior*. New York: Liveright, 1961.

24. Mahoney, M. J., and Bandura, A.   Self-reinforcement in pigeons. *Learning and Motivation* 3:293, 1972.
25. Meichenbaum, D., Gilmore, J., and Fedoravicius, A.   Group insight vs. group desensitization training in treating speech anxiety. *Journal of Consulting and Clinical Psychology* 36:410, 1971.
26. Meichenbaum, D., and Goodman, J.   Training impulsive children to talk to themselves: A means for developing self-control. *Journal of Abnormal Psychology* 77:115, 1971.
27. Meichenbaum, D.   *Cognitive Behavior Modification.* Morristown, N.J.: General Learning Press, 1974.
28. Mowrer, O. H.   Apparatus for the study and treatment of enuresis. *American Journal of Psychology* 51:163, 1938.
29. Mowrer, O. H.   Integrity therapy: A self-help approach. *Psychotherapy Theory Practice and Research* 3:114, 1966.
30. Panyon, M., Boozer, H., and Morris, N.   Feedback to attendants as a reinforcer for applying operant techniques. *Journal of Applied Behavior Analysis* 3:1, 1970.
31. Paul, G. L.   *Insight Versus Desensitization in Psychotherapy.* Stanford: Stanford University Press, 1965.
32. Peterson, R. F., and Whitehurst, G.   A variable influencing the performance of generalized imitative behaviors. *Journal of Applied Behavior Analysis* 4:1, 1971.
33. Pomerleau, O., Bobrove, R. H., and Smith, R. H.   Recording psychiatric aides' performance for the behavioral improvement of assigned patients. *Journal of Applied Behavior Analysis* 6:383, 1973.
34. Pressey, S. S.   Development and appraisal of devices providing immediate scoring of objective tests and concommitant self-instruction. *Journal of Psychology* 29:417, 1950.
35. Redmond, O. P., Gaylor, M. S., and McDonald, R. H.   Blood pressure and heart rate response to verbal instruction and relaxation in hypertension. *Psychosomatic Medicine* 36:285, 1974.
36. Rincover, A., and Koegel, R. L.   Setting and stimulus control in autistic children. *Journal of Applied Behavior Analysis* 8:235, 1975.
37. Risley, T. R., and Reynolds, N. J.   Emphasis as a prompt for verbal imitation. *Journal of Applied Behavior Analysis* 8:235, 1975.
38. Shapiro, D., Tursky, B., Gershon, E., and Stern, M.   Effects of feedback and reinforcement on the control of human systolic blood pressure. *Science* 163:586, 1969.
39. Stuart, R. B.   A three-dimensional program for the treatment of obesity. *Behavior Research and Therapy* 9:177, 1971.
40. Thomas, E. J., Abrams, K. S., and Johnson, J. B.   Self-monitoring and reciprocal inhibition in the modification of multiple tics of Gilles de la Tourette's syndrome. *Behavior Therapy and Experimental Psychiatry* 2:159, 1971.
41. Weiss, T., and Engel, B. T.   Operant conditioning of heart rate in patients with cardiac arrythmias. *Psychophysiology* 6:636, 1970.
42. Weiss, T., and Engel, B. T.   Operant conditioning of heart rate in patients with premature ventricular contractions. *Psychosomatic Medicine* 33:301, 1971.
43. Whitehead, W. E., Renault, P. F., and Goldiamond, I.   Modification of hu-

man gastric acid secretion with operant conditioning procedures. *Journal of Applied Behavior Analysis* 8:147, 1975.
44. Whitehead, W. E., Lurie, E., and Blackwell, B. Classical conditioning of decreases in human systolic blood pressure. *Journal of Applied Behavior Analysis*. In press.
45. Wolfle, D. Training. In S. S. Stevens (Ed.), *Handbook of Experimental Psychology*. New York: Wiley, 1951.

3. Reinforcement and Extinction Procedures
W. Stewart Agras

Editor's Introduction
The psychotherapeutic application of the procedures of positive reinforcement and extinction is one of the clearest demonstrations of the relevance of the experimental behavioral sciences to the clinic. To use such procedures the behavior to be changed must be accurately defined and, preferably, measured. Thus, in the case described on pages 38–42, withdrawal and its desired opposite, socialization, were not discussed; rather, the latter was defined as the amount of time the patient spent talking to the nursing staff at certain times of day. This was measured by timing the amount of such conversation. Once the baseline rate of conversation was established, then an environmental event hypothesized to be reinforcing could be made contingent upon conversing; in this case tokens that gave the patient an opportunity to do things he enjoyed were given for every two minutes he talked to a nurse. Conversely, he could not engage in such activities without earning them by talking. By keeping an ongoing measure, the effect of the contingent application of tokens could be followed, permitting continuous assessment of the efficacy of therapy.

Extinction simply means the removal of a reinforcing event. In the clinic this implies that an adequate behavior analysis can be made so that the events reinforcing the behavior to be changed can be defined. Although this can be done from the history on occasion, it is much better to observe the problem behavior directly and to see what the consequences of the behavior are. Usually, these turn out to be attention of one kind or another. What might appear to the observer to be undesirable attention may, in fact, be reinforcing. The hypothesis is tested by measuring the behavior to be changed and observing the effect of removing the hypothesized reinforcer; for example, instructing a mother not to attend to unwanted behavior. A practical point to note is that following removal of the reinforcer the unwelcome behavior may first increase in frequency before it decreases.

In practice other procedures such as therapeutic instructions, modeling, and information feedback are often combined with reinforcement and extinction. However, the opportunity to develop and practice new and adaptive skills is of paramount importance.

All this is very different from the more traditional role with which many therapists feel comfortable. It is a different way of thinking about and observing behavior and involves a more active therapeutic role. Failure and success are immediately apparent from the ongoing measures. Are reinforcement and extinction practical therapies? Seemingly so, if the therapist is willing to work with the staff of institutions and with family members, for they often become the therapists, making the measures and applying the therapeutic procedures while the professional therapist supervises progress and makes changes to carry out the overall therapeutic plan, which, of course, has been evolved in discussion with the patient and family.

The applications of these procedures are many: from psychosis to neurosis; in children and adults; in institutions and the home. If it is correct that much deviant behavior is learned in the natural environment, namely, the home, and is maintained by that or other environments, then the logical place to work is in those environments or with that part of the environment that can be brought to the therapist. Working with family members, enabling them to change their behavior toward the patient, is exemplified by the recent work on depression described on pages 45–47.

The evidence that reinforcement and extinction procedures are effective is derived mainly from single, case-controlled studies. There is no doubt that very severe problem behaviors such as delusional talk and phobic and depressive behavior have been dramatically altered as a result of applying such procedures. In addition academic and social problems in the classroom have been ameliorated by combined applications of reinforcement and extinction.

However, several problems exist. The use of behavioral measures has revealed that most patients or clients have a cluster of loosely related behavior disorders. Altering one may not alter others. Altering behavior in one environment may not ensure transfer to another. This remarkable specificity of behavior, which has been largely ignored up to the present by nonbehavioral therapists, reveals the need to add procedures to all therapeutic attempts, in order to ensure generalization. This is described on pages 49–50. Finally, the long-term effects of the use of reinforcement and extinction techniques are still uncertain. Few controlled-outcome studies of the application of selective reinforcement procedures in clinical disorders (token economies excepted) have been done. Preliminary evidence suggests that long-term benefits do occur, but this has yet to be confirmed.

W. S. A.

The application of the procedures of positive reinforcement and extinction to effect behavior change is one of the clearest illustrations of the relevance of the experimental behavioral sciences to the clinic. There have been many demonstrations, with a wide variety of organisms, that the probability of a behavior occurring is increased when it is followed by certain events [27]. These events are known as positive reinforcers and the procedure as selective positive reinforcement. Behaviors such as the infant's smile [14] or crying [24] can be altered by selective attention from other persons, as can verbal behavior. Simply saying "Right" or "Wrong" was shown by Thorndike [52] in 1933 to influence the emission of verbalizations. Later, it was found that responses such as "Mm-hm" influenced the frequency of certain choices of words [21, 55], and an analysis of one of Carl Rogers' psychotherapeutic sessions [53] suggested that what patients talk about in nondirective therapy is much influenced by the selective responses (verbal reinforcement) of the therapist.

When behavior is no longer followed by a reinforcing event, its occurrence becomes less probable [27, 32], a procedure and effect known as extinction. Although the procedures of positive reinforcement and extinction are often combined in practice, they will be discussed separately in this chapter for the sake of clarity. Token economies, which are applications of positive reinforcement to an environment such as a psychiatric ward, a classroom, or a halfway house using a token exchange system, will be described in Chapter 4.

The Procedure of Positive Reinforcement
To illustrate the steps involved in applying positive reinforcement, the treatment of a 21-year-old male inpatient with severe behavior problems will be described [4]. This young man had been hospitalized almost continuously for four years and his behavior had shown a steadily worsening trend. He spent most of his time in his room or in solitary occupations, rarely approached others or initiated conversation, and answered questions tersely but logically. Following the slightest criticism or physical hurt, he would walk off the ward and start to swear, always following a particular pattern. Treatment, including psychotherapy, drugs, and electroconvulsive therapy, had not helped. Diagnosed as displaying a severe obsessive-compulsive disorder, his behavior appeared to be an effort to avoid the slightest physical hurt or social rebuff.

Behavioral Definition

In the face of a complex behavior disorder, the first task for both patient and therapist is to choose a problem to work on. In the case just described, the first problem chosen was the patient's avoidance of social interaction, since it was agreed that solving this would facilitate all subsequent therapy. Next, it is necessary to define the problem behavior precisely, so that the occasion for reinforcement is clear and, preferably, so that the behavior can be measured to assess the effect of reinforcement. In this case, the target behavior was defined as self-initiated conversation with a designated member of the nursing staff outside the patient's room and during three scheduled 90-minute sessions each day. The nursing staff was instructed not to start a conversation with the patient but to respond appropriately to attempts to talk with them. An ongoing measure of the behavior was made by having the nurses time the duration of each of his conversations with them.

Selecting Reinforcers

Once the behavior has been defined, the second step is to find a reinforcer. In the case of hospitalized patients, the opportunity to engage in extra social or recreational activities, to watch television, or to spend extra time with staff may function as a reinforcing event. Similarly, the opportunity to earn and spend money and to spend extra time with a therapist have been used to strengthen behavior. However, different types of reinforcers may be more or less effective with different individuals; therefore, individualization of the reinforcers is important. To do this, a reinforcer survey may be used, in which persons rate various events as attractive or unattractive [16], or, better still, what persons do may be used as a guide in the selection of reinforcing events.

In this case, talking with and observing the patient revealed that he enjoyed sitting in the hospital lobby "watching the world go by," listening to music on the radio, and watching television. The opportunity to do these things was therefore used as a reinforcer, and a simple token exchange was devised. Since the patient had already agreed that he would like to learn to talk more easily with others, it was suggested to him that he should consider this as work, and that like others he could earn his pleasures. Then, he was told that for every two minutes he talked with a nurse during the three daily sessions, he would earn a token exchangeable for five minutes of any of the above-mentioned activities. Naturally, he was unable to engage in these activities without tokens.

Prompting

Before beginning a reinforcement regimen, behavior must exist so that reinforcement can be made contingent upon it. If the behavior does not occur, increasingly similar behaviors can be reinforced or the behavior can be demonstrated to the patient, who is asked to imitate it (see page 23). Most simply, the patient can be instructed or reminded (prompted) to perform the behavior, as in the present case. At the beginning of each 90-minute session the patient was asked to talk with the nursing staff as much as possible. As can be seen in Figure 4, (Baseline) this prompted a low level of conversation, which showed no sign of increasing over a 10-day period.

Reinforcement

Once a behavior is elicited—in this case conversing with nurses—the next step is to follow the behavior with a reinforcing event. At first each instance of behavior is reinforced, but usually this is quickly changed to an intermittent *schedule* of reinforcement, which leads to behavior more resistant to extinction. In the present case, a *fixed-ratio schedule* of reinforcement was used, in which the nursing staff gave the patient a token for a fixed amount of conversation; namely, talking for two minutes. This procedure led to an increase (see Figure 4) in conversation from less than five minutes to more than 20 minutes each day. The usefulness of an ongoing behavioral measure is well demonstrated here, since it is clear that during the instruction-only phase no progress was made, and that only after reinforcement was begun did the patient start to talk increasingly longer with the nurses.

To test whether reinforcement was responsible for the therapeutic effect, a control period was instituted for the next few days. This is not absolutely necessary in clinical practice but can give valuable information if the results seem to be unusual in any way. During this period the patient was given 25 tokens (the highest number he had earned) every morning; that is, no response was required from him in order to obtain reinforcement. As can be seen in Figure 4, after a brief spurt his conversational ability showed a steady decline during this phase. Then, in the final phase the original reinforcement procedure was reinstated, giving rise to a further

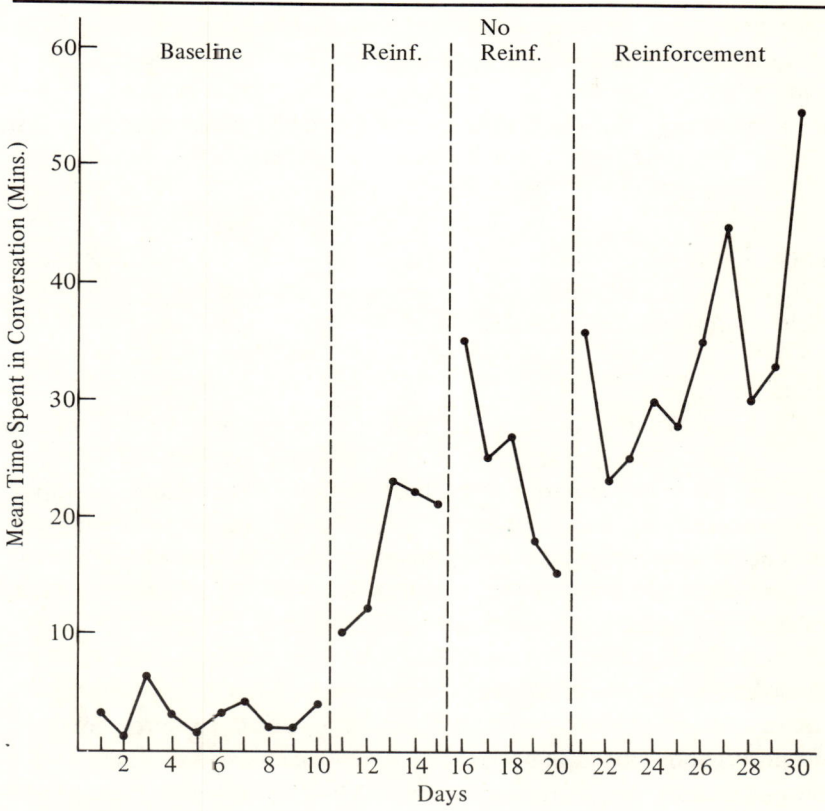

Figure 4. *The effect of positive reinforcement on the conversational ability of a severely withdrawn compulsive patient. The introduction of contingent tokens led to a gain in conversational ability, removal (noncontingent tokens) to a decline in conversation, and reintroduction to a steady gain.*

increase in conversational ability. This conclusively demonstrates that reinforcement was responsible for the therapeutic effect.

Generalization Training

Once a behavior is firmly established in one setting—in this case, talking in the nurses' station with particular individuals—steps must be taken to ensure generalization to other settings and to thin out "artificial" reinforcement, allowing natural reinforcers to maintain the behavior. Thus, both the schedule and the site of reinforcement were changed. Instead of holding sessions, the nursing staff observed the patient at randomly chosen times throughout the day. These times averaged 20 minutes from the last reinforcement and varied between 5 and 35 minutes—an example of a *variable interval schedule* (VI 20) that leads to high rates of behavior. If the patient was seen talking either to staff or to other patients at one of these times, he was given tokens, regardless of where the talking took place. Slowly, the intervals between reinforcement were lengthened, and finally token reinforcement for conversing was withdrawn. At this point no decline in talking was noted, suggesting that talking had become reinforcing in itself.

This was, of course, only the first step in treatment, which later included treating the patient's fears of injury by reinforcing increasingly direct exposure to his feared situation (see Chapters 1 and 8 for detailed examples of this procedure), and teaching a series of prosocial behaviors ranging from better grooming and dressing habits to job interview skills. Finally, he was able to be transferred to, and benefit from, a rehabilitation center, which had not been able to help him previously.

Positive Reinforcement: Application to the Psychoses
The vast majority of individual applications of positive reinforcement to psychotic conditions have been with patients diagnosed schizophrenic. A study of Gelfand, Gelfand, and Dobson [20] of social reinforcement patterns upon a psychiatric ward serves as an excellent introduction to the rationale for this use of positive reinforcement (and extinction). The behavior of six schizophrenic patients hospitalized at a Veterans Administration Center for 7 to 19 years was observed, together with the behavior of the nurses, aides, and other patients toward them. It was found that appropriate patient behavior was attended to by the nursing staff 68 percent of the time, by other patients 56 percent, and by aides 44 percent. This latter low rate may be particularly serious, since aides spend more time with patients than do nurses. When inappropriate patient behavior was observed, it was found that nurses attended to it 39 percent of the time, aides 30 percent of the time, and other patients 12 percent. Thus, the nursing staff was attending to, and, therefore, presumably reinforcing, both adaptive and maladaptive behavior rather indiscriminately. What is needed is dif-

ferential attention; high rates to prosocial behavior, and no attention to maladaptive behavior. This is the meaning of *selective positive reinforcement*.

The first clinical studies with schizophrenic patients involved attempts to change some of the more severe behaviors of so-called profoundly regressed individuals. Thus, Isaacs, Thomas, and Goldiamond [28] worked with two catatonic schizophrenics, who had been mute for 14 and 19 years. The treatment of the first of these patients illustrates the method of *shaping* by means of successive approximation of the desired behavior, using chewing gum as a reinforcer. The therapist noticed that when he held out a piece of gum, the patient briefly looked at it. This movement was first reinforced by giving the patient gum contingent upon the eye movement, followed by reinforcement of face and lip movements, and finally a croak. To promote speech the therapist then modeled and prompted the patient to say "gum." After several sessions the patient said "gum, please," after which he responded to questions in both individual and group sessions. He also exhibited spontaneous speech. Generalization training was conducted by having a nurse, to whom the patient eventually spoke, attend the individual sessions, and later by having ward personnel react only to verbal requests of the patient. Unfortunately, not all staff did this and may thus have prevented full recovery. Several replications of this case study [48, 49, 29] confirm that shaping can reinstate speech in mute or near-mute chronic schizophrenic patients and that modeling and prompting speech are components of the treatment package.

Delusional Speech
The other major use of positive reinforcement with schizophrenic patients has been in the modification of delusional speech, again in patients hospitalized for many years. In the first controlled study, Ayllon and Haughton [9] treated a 47-year-old woman diagnosed as chronic schizophrenic, who made frequent references to the British Royal family. For example, statements such as "I am the Queen" had been noted in her record for 14 years. Nursing staff recorded her behavior, classifying verbalizations into delusional and neutral. Following a baseline condition, delusional talk was reinforced by attention, and neutral talk was ignored. Under these conditions the patient became increasingly delusional. When the contingencies of reinforcement were reversed, delusional talk dropped to a very low level,

normal conversational interchange taking its place.

The next study [64] replicated and extended Ayllon and Haughton's work, this time with 10 schizophrenics who had been hospitalized an average of 12 years. Each had a different set of delusional utterances; e.g., "Mr. Bean is torturing me," or "I have a radio in my head," and each had been, and continued to be, treated adequately with phenothiazine medication. Two procedures were used, feedback in individual sessions as to whether responses to questions were delusional or not, and reinforcement using tokens exchangeable for a variety of privileges. Reinforcement for normal talk was given both in individual sessions and on the ward by nurses. A "bonus" condition was used for some patients to produce low rates of delusional behavior. Here, extra tokens were given if delusions occurred in less than a fixed percentage (e.g., 10 percent) of all talk.

A single-case experimental design was used; in five cases feedback was followed by reinforcement, and in the other five the sequence was reversed. Seven of 10 patients showed less than 10 percent delusional behavior on the ward during the last two days of the treatment phase; six out of 10 showed less than 5 percent; and in three cases delusional speech was eliminated. The effect of feedback was less strong than that of reinforcement, although one patient's delusional speech was practically eliminated by the use of feedback alone. There is a suggestion in the data that feedback followed by reinforcement was more effective—all five patients showed less than 19 percent delusional speech on the ward—while with the reverse sequence only two patients showed such a reduction.

These results are quite striking, again suggesting that reinforcement procedures may be a useful adjunct to the psychopharmacologic treatment of schizophrenia, especially in the chronically delusional patient. However, generalization of the therapeutic effect from one situation to another was limited, emphasizing the need for generalization training as a part of any reinforcement procedure. Such an approach was used by Patterson and Teigen [44] with a patient who had shown limited generalization from a previous reinforcement procedure. An individually arranged token reinforcement program was used to decrease the frequency of delusional answers to direct questions. Training was continued after the patient was discharged from hospital to a residential convalescent home and reasonable generalization, as measured by spontaneous talk and two visits from a social worker, was found. Overall, the patient tended to answer provocative questions from strangers in a guarded but nondelusional way.

Positive Reinforcement: Application to the Neuroses
Positive reinforcement has been successfully used with a number of behavior disorders classified as neurotic, including phobia and other anxiety states [25, 35], conversion paralyses such as astasia-abasia [3], depression [39, 47, 26, 43], and anorexia nervosa [5, 12, 36].

Phobia
Direct reinforcement of approach to the feared or phobic situation rather than use of imaginal procedures, as in desensitization or implosion, appears to be useful. However, since the topic of phobia is treated in detail in Chapters 7 and 8, only a summary of the work will be presented here.

With the method of reinforced practice it is necessary first to arrange an opportunity for the patient to approach the feared and avoided situation. For the agoraphobic patient described in Chapter 1 (pages 8–11), a course over which she could walk increasingly far from a "safe" place was provided; with the social fear described earlier in this chapter, an opportunity to converse with nursing staff sufficed. Although considerable ingenuity may be necessary in devising such situations, many of the most common phobic situations can be reproduced to provide a graded approach, e.g., claustrophobia [35], animal phobias [61], fears of injury [3, 29], and, by using tape recordings, fears of thunderstorms [18]. Once the approach situation is arranged, therapeutic instructions, modeling, or prompts are used to initiate approach to the feared situation, which is then strengthened using social or other types of reinforcement. Evidence from both single-case [2, 4, 35, 37] and group-outcome [18] studies suggests that shaping (also termed successive approximation or reinforced practice) is a superior treatment to either desensitization or implosion. However, the main element responsible for therapeutic effectiveness appears to be exposure to, and practice in, the feared situation, rather than reinforcement, which is simply one means of achieving exposure.

Depression
This prevalent disorder may be the result of insufficient reinforcement of established behavior, i.e., extinction, a thesis similar to that of psycho-

analytic theory, which hypothesizes loss to be an event central to the etiology of depression. It is also probable that relatives and friends of the depressed person attend to depressive behavior such as somatic complaints and statements concerning loneliness or sadness, thus increasing the frequency of such behavior. Finally, as prosocial behavior is extinguished, the depressive is able to elicit less and less reinforcement from the environment, as has been demonstrated by Libet and Lewinsohn [40]. Cognitive changes also occur, with patients viewing themselves as worthless, inadequate, or weak.

If this view of depression is correct, treatment should consist of altering the reinforcement contingencies in the depressed person's social environment by working with the involved family, and aiding the patient to recognize distorted cognitions. In the latter case Lewinsohn [38] suggests that the feeling of dysphoria is difficult for the depressed person to label accurately, and is liable to be explained as "I am sick," leading to an increase in the expression of somatic complaints, or as "I am weak, inadequate, or no good," or "I am unlikable." If depressed persons can be brought to relabel their feeling state successfully, as, for example, "I am feeling bad because something is wrong with my environment," then such persons may be better able to cope.

In one of the first experimental approaches to this problem, Liberman and Raskin [39] treated a 37-year-old woman who had been depressed since the recent death of her mother. The patient was observed at home by the therapist, and instances of behavior such as crying, complaining, and withdrawal were recorded, as was adaptive behavior. Her family was noted to be responding mostly to depressive behaviors. Family members were then taught to ignore depressive behavior and to attend to adaptive behavior, following which the latter behavior increased and depressive behavior sharply decreased. When the family stopped doing this in the third phase of the experiment, the patient once more became depressed, a state of affairs that was finally reversed in the last treatment phase. Follow-up one year later showed the patient to be "continuing to function well without depressive symptoms." This study is of interest from two viewpoints. First, it confirms that family members tend to respond to depressive rather than adaptive behaviors, suggesting that at least one aspect of the reinforcement hypothesis concerning the etiology of depression is correct. Second, reversal of this state of affairs is demonstrated to be therapeutic.

Confirmation of the importance of reinforcement techniques was provided by Reisinger [47], who treated an institutionalized patient by directly modifying crying and smiling. In this study the patient was given tokens (later backed up by social reinforcement) when she smiled and lost tokens when she cried. In this way the frequency of smiling was increased and crying was eliminated. That this change was attributable to the procedures used was demonstrated by reversing the contingencies, which caused smiling to decrease and crying to increase. The patient was discharged at the end of therapy and 14 months later appeared well.

The most direct evidence of the beneficial use of reinforcing adaptive behavior was offered by a study of the effect of a token economy upon depressive behavior [26]. In this instance tokens were earned by patients on a psychiatric unit for adaptive behaviors such as working at jobs off the ward. The experiment consisted of a baseline period, in which tokens with no extrinsic value were given contingently; a reinforcement period, when tokens were exchangeable for privileges; and a return to baseline. Each of the three patients worked more during the reinforcement condition than during baseline. Moreover, their depression, measured behaviorally [63], improved only during the reinforcement phase.

These studies, taken together, strongly suggest that the reinforcement of adaptive behavior, either by altering patterns of social attention within the family or by providing reinforcement such as tokens, is an excellent treatment for the nonpsychotic depressed patient. In practice such a treatment would be combined with extinction of depressive behavior, as defined by somatic complaints, withdrawal, and so on. While there has been no controlled-outcome study of a pure reinforcement approach to depression, one study of a combination treatment is pertinent [43]. In this experiment 20 depressed outpatients were randomly assigned to a behavioral counseling procedure or to routine treatment involving various elements of medication and group or individual psychotherapy. Behavioral counseling consisted of training the family to provide more healthy reinforcement patterns, as previously described, together with a feedback procedure, in which partners could inform each other as to whether a particular interaction was pleasant or unpleasant. Behavioral counseling produced superior results to routine treatment on all measures after eight weeks of treatment and at three-month follow-up. Thus, the evidence for the superior efficiency of behavioral counseling over other therapeutic strategies commonly used in treating depression is beginning to accumulate.

Conversion Paralyses
Several experimental studies of individual patients demonstrate the effectiveness of reinforcement in treating conversion symptoms such as astasia-abasia (paralysis of the lower extremities) [3] and "hysterical" blindness [22]. In one such study [3] the patient was a young woman who had not walked normally for five years and who when treatment was begun could only crawl. A shaping procedure was used, with the patient first sitting in a chair and unable to put her feet on the floor. Both praise and exchangeable tokens were used to shape putting her feet upon the ground, then standing for increasing periods, and finally walking holding a nurse's hand. The patient was then told that she was going to be helped to use a walker, and specific instructions and prompts were combined with contingent social attention both for distance walked and for the form of walking. Both instructions and reinforcement were found to modify walking, and the combination of these two procedures was most effective. Finally, the patient was taught to dispense with the walker.

With chronic cases such as this, the generalization of improvement depends largely upon the family. A recent case report [30] demonstrated this fact in the treatment of a 42-year-old man with astasia-abasia. Following successful treatment with reinforcement, he recovered the ability to walk, but four weeks later he relapsed. A videotape of his interaction with family members showed them to be ignoring his positive initiatives. The family was then taught to reinforce adaptive behaviors and ignore complaints, leading to more successful maintenance of walking. Even broader interventions may be needed in some cases. Patients who have been disabled for some time may lack the skills needed to cope successfully with their environment and may need to be taught assertive skills (see Chapter 9) or job-finding and work skills. Thus, a proper behavioral assessment must go well beyond the presenting problem in order to develop a well-organized treatment program leading to personal growth, defined by an increase in adaptive social skills, with the ultimate aim of enhancing enjoyment of life.

Classroom Behavior
Numerous studies have demonstrated the efficacy of positive reinforcement procedures in modifying social and academic problems in the classroom. Since many involve the use of the token economy, they will be considered

in the following chapter (see also page 56). One study, however, merits special attention, because it affords a controlled comparison between a relationship therapy with and without the use of positive reinforcement [19]. Forty-two adolescents referred for social and academic difficulties, including truancy, were randomly assigned to four differently treated groups. One group received no treatment, while the others were treated with relationship therapy, contingent social attention, or contingent attention, supplemented by monetary reinforcement ($10 per month supplied noncontingently).

The major finding was that truancy declined from about 50 percent time absent to 20 percent in the two groups receiving reinforcement; but it was unaffected in the group receiving a relationship therapy alone. Moreover, when the latter group was treated with reinforcement in a second phase of the experiment, truancy declined to about 20 percent. Other behaviors showed similar trends. It is also interesting to note that monetary reinforcement added nothing to the effect of social reinforcement, a comforting note in our money-minded society.

Generalization of Improvement
Although generalization of behavior change, either from one environment to another or from one behavioral class to another in the same person, does not usually occur without specific training, some intriguing exceptions to this rule have been described. For example, Wahler, Sperling, Thomas, and Teeter [58] found that stuttering in two boys improved when their oppositional behavior was successfully reduced. Similarly, Twardosz and Sajwaj [54] found that increasing sitting in a hyperactive child resulted in replicable increases in the child's use of toys and nearness to other children, as well as in a decrease in posturing.

These are important and challenging findings; they suggest that extra therapeutic benefits can occur unexpectedly, thus increasing the efficiency of therapy. Simple explanations may account for some of these changes. For example, one behavior may be incompatible with another, so that increasing one results in a decline of the other. Working and being depressed may be examples of such incompatible behaviors. Alternatively, in some cases other behaviors may be reinforced accidentally if they occur concurrently with the behavior being treated. Again, extinguishing one behavior—for example, overactivity—might lead to greater opportunity to engage in more positive behaviors, such as playing with toys. Reinforcing a skill such as imitation may increase a child's capacity to learn and lead to increases in a number of unrelated behaviors. Finally, behavior change in a group setting has beneficial effects on those who observe reinforcement being delivered [51, 15], which may account for some of the surprising changes in behavior consistently seen by most therapists. This phenomenon, termed vicarious reinforcement [13], may be one of the variables involved in successful group therapy. Several studies have demonstrated the existence of this effect, whereby improvement spread from reinforced to nonreinforced peers. In one such study [51], treating one child produced a modest change in peer behavior, while treating two and then three children produced additional and large changes affecting the whole classroom. This effect should obviously be used systematically by those working in group settings.

Although explanations such as these may account for some unexpected instances of generalization, recent work by Wahler [57] points to the possibility that rather dissimilar behaviors may be strongly associated. While treating two boys for some three years and measuring their behavior both at home and at school, Wahler observed that certain behaviors appeared in clusters before treatment, and that modification of one of these behaviors was associated with diminution (or increase) in others. These clusters seemed to be idiosyncratic to each child and did not generalize as clusters from one environment to another. Moreover, with the exception of the behavior treated, no changes in the social environment could be detected that might be responsible for the observed effects. The clusters of behavior are something of a mystery, having no obvious explanation. Nevertheless, their identification may be useful, since it may be possible to modify one element of a cluster and thus indirectly influence a problem behavior.

The Procedure of Extinction

The term *extinction* refers both to a procedure—removal of an event or events reinforcing a behavior—and to an effect—a decline in the frequency of the behavior. One of the most common sources of reinforcement for human behavior is contingent social attention and interaction. As we have seen, such attention can reinforce problem behaviors, such as the delusional utterances of a schizophrenic or depression. Identification and removal of such events constitute the most common application of the procedure of extinction. But this is not always easy. Identification of reinforcing events often requires direct observation of the patient and family interacting. Moreover, some events may occur infrequently and thus be difficult to identify. Removing the reinforcing events in an extinction procedure often requires family, attendants, or nursing staff to change their behavior and may necessitate extensive persuasion and training of such persons. Moreover, the procedure of extinction often leads to a startling but temporary effect, known as an extinction burst (see Figure 1, page 10), in which the frequency of the unwanted behavior first increases. This effect may be difficult for both family and institutional staff to tolerate. Finally, the rate of extinction may differ depending upon the schedule of reinforcement-maintaining behavior. For example, partial reinforcement has been shown to result in slowing of extinction [30]. Furthermore, in the natural environment it is very likely that behavior will be maintained on a partial reinforcement schedule.

Nevertheless, extinction has been used successfully with a number of problem behaviors and is often combined with reinforcement and punishment procedures. Reinforcers are of two kinds, positive and negative (see Chapter 2, pages 24–26). When negative reinforcement is maintaining a behavior the person's "symptom" serves to avoid an aversive event. As with positive reinforcement, such aversive events are likely to be social in nature—parental censure, social failure, marital conflict, and unwelcome tasks. The extinction of negatively reinforced behavior is apt to be slow, as an animal experiment demonstrates. Solomon and Wynne [50] trained dogs to jump a barrier in order to avoid an electric shock. When the shock was turned off the dogs continued to jump in response to the signal for shock. In other words, once having learned to avoid shock by jumping, they did not wait to see if the shock was present. It was safer to jump. This may be the situation for persons with phobias and compulsions. The original aversive stimulus has long gone, but patients continue to avoid situations that are associated with the original aversive events, or situations symbolically similar to the original site of learning.

To extinguish such avoidance behavior it is necessary to prevent it occurring, so that the person can find out that there is no longer anything painful to avoid. This is one way of conceptualizing the effects of desensitization, implosion, flooding, reinforced practice, and response prevention, all of which result in exposure to feared and avoided situations. These techniques are further discussed in Chapters 7 and 8; the remaining discussion here will be restricted to extinction of positively reinforced behaviors.

Applications of Extinction

Application to the Psychoses

As with positive reinforcement, most applications of extinction to the psychoses have been aimed at eliminating one or another behavior of individuals diagnosed as schizophrenic. However, in the case chosen to illustrate the procedure, the patient was diagnosed as having an involutional depression [9]. Although electroconvulsive therapy had been helpful during a long hospitalization, the patient, a middle-aged woman, continued to complain interminably about various body functions.

Nursing personnel recorded each instance of somatic complaint made to them, and these were numerous during the baseline period. When the hypothesized source of reinforcement, namely, attention from the nursing staff, was removed, the frequency of somatic complaints declined. This was accomplished by teaching the nursing staff not to give sympathy or attention to somatic complaints. In the next phase of the experiment somatic complaints were once more attended to and were found to increase in frequency, disappearing only in the final phase, when extinction was once more in effect. This experiment not only demonstrates the therapeutic effect of extinction but again shows that the hospital environment can inadvertently reinforce unwanted behavior, resulting in unnecessary prolongation of hospitalization. It is also to be noted that the effect of extinction was slow, taking nearly 100 days for hypochondriacal conversation to diminish to acceptable levels, possibly as a result of uncontrolled reinforcement of the patient's complaints by other patients and visitors. Nevertheless, the program was successful, and the patient was able to leave the hospital.

The same authors report a similar instance of a patient diagnosed as chronic schizophrenic, whose incessant somatic complaints were improved by an extinction procedure. Other behaviors of schizophrenic patients treated successfully with extinction include reduction of interference with ward management by a patient who persistently entered the nurse's office [11]; reduction of delusional behavior [9]; and reinstatement of self-feeding patterns [10]. In one case report [1] a patient who believed he was the Antichrist would eat very little for fear that he would burn up. This behavior had led to a 50-pound weight loss. Members of the nursing staff were noted continually hovering over the patient persuading him to eat. When this attention, which was hypothesized to reinforce "not eating," was stopped, and the patient was told that he would be able to eat only in the dining room at mealtimes, his intake increased from 500 to 1800 calories per day over one month. Thus, an apparently delusionally based behavior was, in fact, being maintained by social reinforcement and not by the delusional belief.

Finally, Lovaas and Simmons [41] describe the use of extinction with two severely retarded institutionalized children, one eight and the other 11 years old. Both had to be physically restrained to prevent self-injury and were scarred from their self-abuse. During a daily session lasting 90 minutes, all attention for self-injury was stopped, resulting at first in a very high rate of self-injury—possibly caused by an extinction burst—and then in lower rates. One child showed almost no tendency to injure himself at the end of 10 days, while the other showed a diminished but still existent tendency. No generalization to other situations was noted. The authors describe replications of these results with other children, noting a slow diminution of self-injury in each case, with particularly high rates at first. It seems reasonable to ask whether such a slow procedure, accompanied by such suffering, is in fact humane when compared with the rapid results obtained with aversive therapy (see Chapter 5).

Application to Neuroses
Since extinction is usually combined with other procedures, such as positive reinforcement, examples of its exclusive use in neurotic conditions are not common, although the theme of controlling self-injury persists. Thus, in the case of a 20-year-old woman with intractable neurodermatitis, Walton [60] noticed that scratching appeared to be reinforced by the solicitous attention of family members, including daubing ointment upon the sores. When the family was told to discontinue such attention, scratching slowly declined over a two-week period and within three months the patient's skin was normal. A four-year follow-up revealed no relapse. Similarly, [7] a five-year-old child was also treated successfully by stopping her mother's attention to the picking and scratching. In this case much of the mother's behavior was critical, in that she scolded the child for scratching; yet when this was stopped the child's scratching and picking also declined. Not all social reinforcement need be pleasant! Criticism is, after all, attention,

and may suffice to reinforce the very behavior it is aimed at suppressing.

Other examples of the use of extinction with minor yet still troublesome behavior problems come from work reported with children. Thus, Williams [62] reported a simple treatment for a 21-month-old child whose prolonged tantrums when he was put to bed were a considerable problem to his parents. These tantrums seemed to have developed as a result of his prolonged illness as an infant, which naturally resulted in a great deal of attention and care. Reasoning that the child was gaining parental attention by means of the tantrums, Williams advised the parents to put the child to bed and immediately leave the room. On the first night the tantrum lasted 45 minutes, on the second no tantrum occurred, and by the end of a week all crying had stopped. Unfortunately, a relative then put the child to bed and reinforced crying once more; this necessitated a second course of extinction, which was again successful. A similar experiment [24] demonstrated that crying in nursery school was correspondingly reinforced by teacher attention, and that removal of such attention quickly reduced such crying. Another type of behavior also occurring in nursery school, social isolation, was found to be susceptible to extinction [8]. Teachers were noted to approach the child only "to find out what was bothering her." When the child played with others she received no attention. On reversal of this pattern of attention, playing with others increased dramatically, and time spent alone or with adults decreased. Again, several reversals of the contingencies demonstrated the effectiveness of the extinction procedure.

Finally, Alford, Blanchard, and Buckley [6] treated an adolescent girl whose pattern of vomiting after every meal had lasted for many years. Removal of social attention for vomiting led to rapid cessation of this behavior, which recurred briefly during the treatment program only when accidentally reinforced by other patients. Again, the results strongly suggest not only that extinction is a useful procedure, but that social reinforcement plays an important role in the maintenance of maladaptive behavior and by implication may play an important role in the genesis of abnormal behavior.

Reinforcement and Extinction Combined
In practice, as noted in the beginning of this chapter, reinforcement and extinction procedures are used in combination; indeed, in many of the cases already described the separation has been somewhat artificial. An

example of the combined use of extinction and reinforcement is reported by Wolf, Birnbrauer, William, and Lawlor [65], who treated a nine-year-old retardate, Laura, who was removed to a residential school and thereafter began to vomit in class. After three months she was sick almost every day and was usually sent back to her dormitory. Since no physiologic cause for her vomiting was evident and drug therapy had failed, the authors reasoned that missing class might be reinforcing her vomiting. They therefore suggested the use of an extinction procedure to the teacher; namely, that Laura stay in class whether or not she vomited. In addition she was given attention and candy for appropriate classroom work, thus reinforcing behavior competitive with vomiting and incompatible with leaving class. With the introduction of these procedures, vomiting slowly declined until it stopped. During the next school year, however, the child vomited once again and was immediately sent to her dormitory; as we might expect, vomiting increased in frequency. When extinction and reinforcement were restarted, vomiting once more ceased.

In an important extension of the combined use of reinforcement and extinction procedures, Wahler, Winkel, Peterson, and Morrison [56] taught parents to manage their children's behavior problems at first in a laboratory setting and then at home. The children exhibited a range of behaviors including refusal to comply with parental commands, inattention, and whining or outright temper tantrums. The parents were taught how to ignore problem behaviors and attend to desired behaviors. In each case feedback as to progress, based on measurement of parental attention, was given to the parents, either during interaction with their children or afterward.

In some children, this combination of extinction and reinforcement produced decreases in oppositional behavior and increases in cooperative behavior. However, in others, even though parents used the procedures correctly, no behavior change was observed [57]. In these cases a punishment procedure, time-out (from positive reinforcement), was used (see pages 93–94) contingent upon oppositional behavior, with very successful results. Thus, it appears that although with some problems, such as oppositional behavior, or, as was seen earlier in this chapter, self-injury, a combination of reinforcement and extinction should first be used, punishment may be necessary to reduce the undesirable behavior to manageable rates.

One of the most thorough evaluations of the combined use of reinforcement and extinction, aimed at children with social and academic problems in the classroom, was reported by Kent and O'Leary [31]. In an attempt to duplicate the realities of the clinical situation, they accepted referrals from 53 classrooms. Treatment consisted of behavioral assessment, school and home intervention, and, finally, a systematic withdrawal of treatment, the whole program taking some 20 hours. The core of the intervention was the use of extinction and reinforcement by teachers and parents.

One hundred and four children were randomly assigned either to this treatment program or to no treatment. When therapy had been completed, both direct observational measures and teachers' reports of classroom problems and academic achievement showed that the treated group had improved more than the untreated group. Disappointingly, however, at nine-month follow-up the untreated group had caught up with the treated group as far as classroom behavior was concerned. However, the treated group now showed greater improvement in grades.

One might argue that the effects seen in this experiment were attributable simply to the extra attention received by the treated group and not to the specific procedures used. This may indeed be so. However, in the classroom study of reinforcement described earlier in this chapter (see page 49), extra attention provided no benefit over no treatment, while the addition of reinforcement produced considerable change. Thus, it seems likely that the specific procedures used by Kent and O'Leary did in fact produce the changes in behavior observed.

While combinations of reinforcement and extinction, otherwise known as differential attention, have been successfully used with a variety of children's behaviors, a further limitation upon the general applicability of the technique was noted by a group of workers in two different centers [25]. Four of six children with rather severe oppositional behaviors became worse when differential parental attention was started. Moreover, when the mothers went back to their old habit of inconsistent attention, their children's behavior improved, a pattern that continued over several reversals of the treatment condition.

Why did this happen? The authors speculated that it might have been caused by a prolonged extinction burst. But they also noted that the absolute amount of parental attention to the child was less during the differential attention procedure than during inconsistent attention, a possible factor in the unexpected deterioration of behavior. No matter what the cause, these findings suggest that while differential attention is a useful treatment procedure in children with oppositional behavior, complications may occur. When using such procedures, therapists should carefully monitor the child's behavior, and be ready to change therapeutic tactics should behavioral worsening persist.

Training the Reinforcing Agent
As we have seen, parents can be trained to reinforce their children's behavior more effectively. Similarly, teachers or ward personnel can be trained more correctly to reinforce their pupils or patients with beneficial results. Thus, Hall, Panyen, Rabon, and Broden [23] provided practical help for a teacher who was beginning to lose control of her class. As is the case with many teachers, she was selectively attending to problems in the class and thus increasing the frequency of such disruptive behavior. During a baseline period students in her classroom were observed to be studying some 40 percent of the time, but with a more experienced teacher they studied 90 percent of the time. Despite conferences with the principal, this lamentable state of affairs continued. The teacher was then taught to attend to study behavior and to ignore inappropriate or problem behaviors. As a result, she was able to raise from 5 percent to 20 percent her attention to positive pupil behavior, which itself increased to 70 percent. To confirm this effect, the teacher was instructed to resume her old behavior, with a corresponding decline in studying. Reinstating the new techniques led to a stable study rate of about 80 percent—about the same level obtained by the experienced teacher. This is a simple experimental demonstration of the effects of teaching classroom management skills and of the relative ineffectiveness of principal counseling.

In a study with psychiatric aides [48] general consultation about their patients—a technique often used on psychiatric wards—did not help either the aides or their patients. On the other hand, supervision of observed aide-patient interaction did help, as did quantitative, publicly displayed feedback as to how their patients were doing, and reinforcement in the form of bonus payments contingent upon patient improvement.

Since the latter contingency is not allowable in most institutions, bonus payments may not be a practical approach to the enhancement of staff performance. Nevertheless, several less problematic techniques may help, such as teaching skills by breaking helping behaviors into easily manageable subcomponents, and letting staff practice new skills while affording social approval. Kirigin and her colleagues [33] demonstrated the effectiveness of this type of "workshop" in training teaching parents, showing that persons taking the workshops were more skillful than those not attending. On the other hand, the usual kind of didactic workshop rarely leads to improvements in skills, although it may generate substantial enthusiasm. Quilitch [46], for example, demonstrated that such workshops produced no improvement in staff management of retarded inmates as measured by levels of patient activity. However, a second technique, which has been repeatedly shown to increase performance, namely, feedback of patient performance to staff, led to substantial improvement. Specific intervention does improve performance!

Overview

Just as positive reinforcement influences the behavior of everyday life, so it also influences problem behavior. There is evidence that the social environment, whether it be the family, school, or hospital, can unwittingly strengthen and maintain depressive behaviors [39], delusional speech, and other problem behaviors of schizophrenic patients [1, 9, 10, 11, 27, 63], as well as oppositional behavior or tantrums [9, 57, 58]. Such environments can be altered to become more therapeutic [23, 45], and a variety of psychotic, neurotic, and other problem behaviors can be beneficially influenced by the separate or combined use of reinforcement and extinction. More recent research has demonstrated further extension of the use of reinforcement procedures to different populations, such as nursing home residents, by providing incentives for increased social participation [42], and to new problems, such as maintaining a cleaner environment by reducing littering [17] or using less electricity in the home [34].

Reinforcement and extinction procedures are, as we have seen, usually combined with a series of other necessary but less powerful behavior change procedures, such as therapeutic instructions, prompts, modeling, and information feedback (see Chapter 2), into what might be called a therapeutic package. Both the therapeutic and environmental uses of reinforcement alone and combined with other procedures have been demonstrated to be effective, not only in uncontrolled case studies but also in controlled experiments. To date, most of these experiments have used intensive designs with reversals of contingencies. Thus, we can be sure that the techniques work, at least in their immediate outcome. There are, however, fewer group-outcome studies, so that a less strong statement can be made about wider applicability and longer-term outcome.

Some limitations of the use of reinforcement and extinction techniques are apparent. First, generalization to other behaviors and to new environments does not often occur spontaneously. This means that generalization training—application of the same therapeutic procedures in different environments and with various behaviors—must form a part of the behavior change plan. Second, some classes of behavior, most notably self-injury and severe tantrums, do not readily respond to reinforcement and extinction procedures. Here the use of punishment procedures as described in chapter 5 seems most humane.

Finally, ongoing research is opening up some fascinating work, which promises to enhance our understanding of behavior. The discovery that behaviors tend to appear and disappear in conjunction with other dissimilar behaviors is one such advance, which has both basic and applied implications [59]. The advantages and disadvantages of applying reinforcement to individuals within a group, or to the behavior of the group as a whole, is another area of active research, with important implications for schools and other institutions.

Thus, we can expect continuing development of our understanding of the multiple uses of reinforcement and presumably, therefore, the possibility of continued improvement of therapeutic techniques. In the next chapter we shall examine one such area of developing reinforcement technology, the token economy.

References

1. Agras, W. S. Behavior therapy in the management of chronic schizophrenia. *American Journal of Psychiatry* 124:240, 1967.
2. Agras, W. S., Leitenberg, H., and Barlow, D. H. Social reinforcement in the modification of agoraphobia. *Archives of General Psychiatry* 19:423, 1968.
3. Agras, W. S., Leitenberg, H., Barlow, D. H., and Thomson, L. E. Instructions and reinforcement in the modification of neurotic behavior. *American Journal of Psychiatry* 125:1435, 1969.
4. Agras, W. S., Leitenberg, H., Wincze, J. P., Butz, R. A., and Callahan, E. J. Comparison of the effects of instructions and reinforcement in the treatment of a neurotic avoidance response: A single case experiment. *Journal of Behavior Therapy and Experimental Psychiatry* 1:53, 1970.

5. Agras, W. S., Barlow, D. H., Chapin, H., Abel, G. G., and Leitenberg, H. Behavior modification of anorexia nervosa. *Archives of General Psychiatry* 30:279, 1974.
6. Alford, G. S., Blanchard, E. B., and Buckley, T. M. Treatment of hysterial vomiting by modification of social contingencies: A case study. *Behavior Therapy and Experimental Psychiatry* 3:209, 1972.
7. Allen, E. K., and Harris, F. R. Elimination of a child's excessive scratching by training the mother in reinforcement procedures. *Behavior Research and Therapy* 4:79, 1966.
8. Allen, E. K., Hart, B. M., Buell, J. S., Harris, F. R., and Wolf, M. M. Effects of social reinforcement on isolate behavior of a nursery school child. *Child Development* 35:511, 1964.
9. Ayllon, T., and Haughton, E. Modification of symptomatic verbal behavior of mental patients. *Behavior Research and Therapy* 2:87, 1964.
10. Ayllon, T., and Haughton, E. Control of the behavior of schizophrenic patients by food. *Journal of the Experimental Analysis of Behavior* 5:343, 1962.
11. Ayllon, T. and Michael, J. The psychiatric nurse as a behavioral engineer. *Journal of the Experimental Analysis of Behavior* 2:323, 1959.
12. Bachrach, A. J., Erwin, W. J., and Mohr, P. J. The Control of Eating Behavior in an Anorexic by Operant Conditioning Techniques. In L. P. Ullman, and L. Krasner (Eds.), *Case Studies in Behavior Modification*. New York: Holt, Rinehart & Winston, 1965.
13. Bandura, A. Vicarious and Self-reinforcement Processes. In Glaser, R. (Ed.), *The Nature of Reinforcement*. New York: Academic Press, 1971.
14. Brackbill, Y. Extinction of the smiling response in infants as a function of reinforcement schedule. *Child Development* 29:115, 1958.
15. Broden, M., Bruce, M., Mitchell, M., Carter, V., and Hall, R. V. Effects of teacher attention on attending behavior of two boys at adjacent desks. *Journal of Applied Behavior Analysis* 3:199, 1970.
16. Cautela, J. R., and Tastenbaum, R. A. A reinforcement survey schedule for use in therapy, training, and research. *Psychological Reports* 20:1115, 1967.
17. Clark, R. N., Burgess, R. L., and Hendee, J. C. The development of antilitter behavior in a forest campground. *Journal of Applied Behavior Analysis* 5:1, 1972.
18. Crowe, M., Marks, I. M., Agras, W. S., and Leitenberg, H. Time-limited desensitization, implosion and shaping for phobic patients: A crossover study. *Behavior Research and Therapy* 10:319, 1972.
19. Fo, W. S. O., and O'Donnell, C. R. The buddy system: Relationship and contingency conditions in a community intervention program for youths with nonprofessionals as behavior change agents. *Journal of Consulting and Clinical Psychology* 42:163, 1974.
20. Gelfand, D. M., Gelfand, S., and Dobson, W. Unprogrammed reinforcements of patients' behavior in a mental hospital. *Behavior Research and Therapy* 5:201, 1967.
21. Greenspoon, J. Verbal Conditioning and Clinical Psychology. In A. J. Bachrach (Ed.), *Experimental Foundations of Clinical Psychology*. New York: Basic Books, 1962.
22. Grosz, H. J., and Zimmerman, J. Experimental analysis of hysterical blind-

ness: a follow up report and new experimental data. *Archives of General Psychiatry* 13:255, 1965.
23. Hall, R. V., Panyen, M., Rabon, D., and Broden, M. Instructing beginning teachers in reinforcement procedures which improve classroom control. *Journal of Applied Behavior Analysis* 1:315, 1968.
24. Hart, B. M., Allen, T. E., Buell, J. S., Harris, F. R., and Wolf, M. M. Effects of social reinforcement on crying. *Journal of Experimental Child Psychology* 1:145, 1964.
25. Herbert, E. W., Pinkston, E. M., Hayden, M. L., Sajwaj, T. E., Pinkston, S., Cordua, G., and Jackson, C. Adverse effects of differential parental attention. *Journal of Applied Behavior Analysis* 6:15, 1973.
26. Hersen, M., Eisler, R. M., Alford, G., and Agras, W. S. Effects of a token economy on neurotic depression: An experimental analysis. *Behavior Therapy* 4:392, 1973.
27. Honig, W. K. (Ed.) *Operant Behavior: Areas of Research and Application*. New York: Appleton-Century-Crofts, 1966.
28. Isaacs, W., Thomas, J., and Goldiamond, I. Applications of operant conditioning to reinstate verbal behavior in psychotics. *Journal of Speech and Hearing Disorders* 25:8, 1960.
29. Kale, R. J., Kaye, J. H., Whelan, P. A., and Hopkins, B. L. The effects of reinforcement on the modification, maintenance, and generalization of social responses of mental patients. *Journal of Applied Behavior Analysis* 1:315, 1968.
30. Kallman, W., Hersen, M., and O'Toole, D. H. The use of social reinforcement in a case of conversion reaction. *Behavior Therapy* 6:411, 1975.
31. Kent, R. N., and O'Leary, K. D. A controlled evaluation of behavior modification with conduct problem children. *Journal of Consulting and Clinical Psychology* 44:586, 1976.
32. Kimble, G. A. *Hilgard and Marquis' Conditioning and Learning*. New York: Appleton-Century-Crofts, 1961.
33. Kirigin, K. A., Ayela, H. E., Brautman, C. J., Brown, W. G., Minkin, N., Phillips, E. L., Fixsen, D. L., and Wolf, M. M. Training Teaching-parents: An Evaluation of Workshop Training Procedures. In E. Ramp, and G. Semb (Eds.), *Behavior Analysis Areas of Research and Application*. Englewood Cliffs, N.J.: Prentice-Hall, 1975.
34. Kohlenberg, R., Phillips, T., and Proctor, W. A behavioral analysis of peaking in residential electrical energy consumers. *Journal of Applied Behavior Analysis* 9:13, 1976.
35. Leitenberg, H., Agras, W. S., Edwards, J. A., Thomson, L. E., and Wincze, J. P. Practice as a psychotherapeutic variable. *Journal of Psychiatric Research* 7:215, 1970.
36. Leitenberg, H., Agras, W. S., and Thomson, L. E. A sequential analysis of the effect of selective positive reinforcement in modifying anorexia nervosa. *Behavior Research and Therapy* 6:211, 1968.
37. Leitenberg, H., Agras, W. S., Thomsen, L. E., and Wright, D. E. Feedback in behavior modification: An experimental analysis in two phobic cases. *Journal of Applied Behavior Analysis* 1:131, 1968.
38. Lewinsohn, P. M. The Behavioral Study and Treatment of Depression. In M. Hersen, R. M. Eisler, and P. M. Miller (Eds.), *Progress in Behavior Mod-*

ification, vol. 1. New York: Academic Press, 1975.
39. Liberman, R. P., and Raskin, D. E. Depression: A behavioral formulation. *Archives of General Psychiatry* 24:515, 1971.
40. Libet, J., and Lewinsohn, P. M. The concept of social skill with special reference to the behavior of depressed persons. *Journal of Consulting and Clinical Psychology* 40:304, 1973.
41. Lovaas, O. I., and Simmons, J. Q. Manipulation of self-destruction in three retarded children. *Journal of Applied Behavior Analysis* 3:143, 1969.
42. McClannahan, L. E., and Risley, T. E. Design of living environments for nursing home residents: Increasing participation in recreation activities. *Journal of Applied Behavior Analysis* 8:261, 1975.
43. McClean, P. D., Ogsden, K., and Grover, L. A behavioral approach to the treatment of depression. *Behavior Therapy and Experimental Psychiatry* 4:323, 1973.
44. Patterson, R. L., and Teigen, J. R. Conditioning and post-hospital generalization of non-delusional responses in a chronic psychotic patient. *Journal of Applied Behavior Analysis* 6:65, 1973.
45. Pomerleau, O. F., Bobrove, P. H., and Smith, R. H. Rewarding psychiatric aides for the behavioral improvement of assigned patients. *Journal of Applied Behavior Analysis* 6:383, 1973.
46. Quilitch, H. R. A comparison of three staff management procedures. *Journal of Applied Behavior Analysis* 8:59, 1975.
47. Reisinger, J. J. The treatment of "anxiety-depression" via positive reinforcement and response cost. *Journal of Applied Behavior Analysis* 5:125, 1972.
48. Sherman, J. A. Reinstatement of verbal behavior in a psychotic by reinforcement methods. *Journal of Speech and Hearing Disorders* 28:398, 1963.
49. Sherman, J. A. Use of reinforcement and imitation to reinstate verbal behavior in mute psychotics. *Journal of Abnormal Psychology* 70:155, 1965.
50. Solomon, R. L., and Wynne, L. C. Traumatic avoidance learning: The principle of anxiety conservation and partial irreversibility. *Psychological Review* 61:353, 1954.
51. Strain, P. S., Shores, R. E., and Abraham, M. M. An experimental analysis of "spillover" effects on the social interaction of behaviorally handicapped preschool children. *Journal of Applied Behavior Analysis* 9:31, 1976.
52. Thorndike, E. L. An experimental study of rewards. *Teachers College Contributions to Education*, No. 680. New York: Teachers College, 1933.
53. Truax, C. B. Reinforcement and non-reinforcement in Rogerian psychotherapy. *Journal of Abnormal Psychology* 71:1, 1966.
54. Twardosz, S., and Sajwaj, T. Multiple effects of a procedure to increase sitting in a hyperactive, retarded boy. *Journal of Applied Behavior Analysis* 5:73, 1972.
55. Ullman, L. P., Krasner, L., and Collins, B. J. Modification of behavior through verbal conditioning effects in group psychotherapy. *Journal of Abnormal Psychology* 62:128, 1961.
56. Wahler, R. G., Winkel, G. H., Peterson, R. F., and Morrison, D. C. Mothers as behavior therapists for their own children. *Behavior Research and Therapy* 3:113, 1965.
57. Wahler, R. G. Oppositional children: A quest for parental reinforcement

control. *Journal of Applied Behavior Analysis* 2:159, 1969.
58. Wahler, R. G., Sperling, K. A., Thomas, M. R., Teeter, N. C., and Luper, H. T. The modification of childhood stuttering: Some response-response relationships. *Journal of Experimental Child Psychology* 9:411, 1970.
59. Wahler, R. G. Some structural aspects of deviant child behavior. *Journal of Applied Behavior Analysis* 8:27, 1975.
60. Walton, D. The Application of Learning Theory to the Treatment of a Case of Neurodermatitis. In H. J. Eysenck (Ed.), *Behavior Therapy and the Neuroses*. London: Pergamon, 1960.
61. Watson, J. P., Gaind, R., and Marks, I. M. Prolonged exposure: A rapid treatment for phobias. *British Medical Journal* 1:13, 1971.
62. Williams, C. D. the elimination of tantrum behavior by extinction procedures. *Journal of Abnormal and Social Psychology* 59:269, 1959.
63. Williams, J. G., Barlow, D. H., and Agras, W. S. Behavioral measurement of severe depression. *Archives of General Psychiatry* 72:330, 1972.
64. Wincze, J. P., Leitenberg, H., and Agras, W. S. The effects of token reinforcement and feedback on the delusional verbal behavior of chronic paranoid schizophrenics. *Journal of Applied Behavior Analysis* 5:247, 1972.
65. Wolf, M. M., Birnbrauer, J. S., William, T., and Lawlor, J. A Note on Apparent Extinction of Vomiting Behavior of a Retarded Child. In L. P. Ullman, and L. Krasner (Eds.), *Case Studies in Behavior Modification*. New York: Holt, Rinehart & Winston, 1965.

4. The Token Economy
W. Stewart Agras

Editor's Introduction
The token economy is a special case of the application of reinforcement and extinction procedures. Exactly the same principles apply; namely, definition of the behavior to be changed, contingent application of a hypothesized rewarding event, and monitoring of the effect through performance measures. Instead of using reinforcers directly, tokens that can later be exchanged for a variety of consumer goods and pleasurable activities are used. Also, instead of being applied to an individual, the procedure is applied to a group in a whole environment: a ward, a home for delinquents, or a classroom. Adaptive behaviors are built up by reinforcement with tokens and, if necessary, undesirable behaviors are eliminated by using the technique of response cost, namely, the contingent loss of tokens.

Psychotherapists tend to limit their activities, preferring to treat the verbal, the intelligent, and the less handicapped. Ninety-eight percent of private patients seen by members of the American Psychoanalytic Association are white, and 78 percent have at least a college education [15]. State hospitals have many unfilled positions, both for psychiatrists and psychologists. The token economy may be an antidote to this trend. The role of the professional therapist is altered more drastically than with other applications of reinforcement procedures. The main therapy is provided continuously by aides, nurses, guards, teachers, houseparents, or even fellow patients. The professional therapist designs the economy, teaches the staff, supervises the results by way of ongoing, objective behavioral measures, and makes changes based on these observations. Experiments can be conducted to achieve maximum cost efficiency and to evaluate the overall effectiveness of the program.

Instituting such an economy implies environmental control. If privileges are used as reinforcers, then they must be obtainable only by way of a token exchange. This means that the hospital or school administration must agree with the aims of the project and take the necessary administrative measures to allow for such control. Moreover, staff at all levels must be educated in the use of the token system and be convinced enough of its advantages to work willingly within it. Thus, the first steps in starting a token economy are to seek administrative support and to educate the staff. Many of the problems that beset such programs are described on pages 67–69. However, newcomers to the field are advised to seek consultation with someone who has directed such a program or to visit an operating token economy to familiarize themselves with the myriad of small operational details that can make or break such an endeavor. The mere giving of tokens is not a token economy. Properly done, the token economy is a complex motivating environment.

Once maximum performance is achieved within a token economy, the problem of generalization to the natural environment occurs. Ideally, a series of environments, each more closely approximating the terminal environment, should be available, all run along the same lines, perhaps with money gradually replacing tokens. For the back ward patient, a series of more open wards, a halfway house, and an independent group living situation might be considered. Again, the family is a natural group for the application of variants of token economy, particularly for the disturbed child or adolescent. In such instances a behavioral contract is often drawn up between parents and child(ren), forming a vehicle for the exact specification of desired and undesired behaviors and the reinforcers and punishments. This technique appears to help families to reorganize themselves and to communicate better, allowing positive behaviors (and therefore feelings) more chance to be manifested.

As in the case of reinforcement and extinction procedures, abundant experimental data demonstrate the immediate powerful effects of the contingent application of tokens with a variety of problems, including those of the long-term mental hospital patient (pages 69–73), those related to delinquency (pages 75–78), and social and academic problems in the classroom (page 79). Moreover, a beginning series of controlled-outcome studies suggests that longer-term benefits also occur. It also seems that aspects of the social environment, such as the provision of extra social reinforcement engendered by the use of tokens, are important contributors to the effectiveness of the token economy. This should remind us that such programs are not automated sterile endeavors, but that, as in all other therapy, the relationship between the various participants is of critical importance.

W. S. A.

The token economy is a special case of the application of reinforcement and extinction. Exactly the same principles apply, but instead of using reinforcers directly, tokens that can later be exchanged for a variety of consumer goods and pleasurable activities are used. Also, instead of being applied to an individual, the procedure is applied to a group in a defined environment—a hospital ward, an institution for delinquents, or a classroom.

That tokens can acquire reinforcing properties even in animals was shown in experiments by Wolf [41] and Cowles [10]. Chimpanzees were successively taught to push tokens into a slot to obtain grapes, then to press a lever for tokens, and finally to collect a number of tokens before exchanging them for grapes. Subsequently, new behaviors were taught by using tokens only as reinforcers. However, for the human such demonstrations are unnecessary, since a multitude of natural experiments have demonstrated the reinforcing value of that ubiquitous token—money. The token economy is simply a monetary economy, with all the attendant advantages and disadvantages of such a system.

The first organized token economies were introduced in 1961 by Ayllon and Azrin [4] in the mental hospital, and by Staats and his colleagues [35] in the classroom. As was noted in the previous chapter, institutional staff, whether in the mental hospital or the classroom, tend to reinforce both undesirable and desirable behavior. The token economy is an antidote to this trend. When properly used, it allows shorthanded staff to attain the basic goals of their program and leaves them more time to work on the individual and unique problems of their students, clients, or patients.

Four levels of organizational complexity exist. In the first, tokens are used solely for management purposes. Thus, in a mental hospital ward the main aim would be to combat the apathetic behavior so often seen in such settings. Behaviors such as rising on time, dressing and grooming neatly, ward housekeeping, and taking medication regularly and on time might be developed and strengthened. At the next level of organization, staff are taught to use social reinforcement and extinction procedures in addition to dispensing tokens. Such a step—more complex than a token management system—is a necessary stage in the development of more active intervention. At the third level, individual token and social reinforcement programs are added to the basic token economy. This is the best form of token economy but needs more and better-trained staff. Finally, individual programs within an institution can be brought together under one system with institution-wide exchange rates and a central commissary, thus allowing a wider variety of goods and services to be exchanged for tokens. Patients can move from ward to ward through a series of environments, each more closely resembling the real world. In the last stages of rehabilitation, money might replace tokens and a halfway house or a less supervised living arrangement might replace the ward.

Tokens come in a variety of shapes and sizes. The simplest are round plastic discs or cardboard squares, usually imprinted with a design to prevent forgery. However, points can also be used; these are tabulated on a card carried by the patient, each addition being signed by a staff member or marked with a paper punch of a particular design. Finally, a credit card system has been used, complete with weekly statements to each patient [20]. All systems should allow for the tabulation of both the amount earned by each patient and the behavior reinforced, so that the patient's progress can be monitored.

Operational Problems
Since token economies depend upon an institution for their continuance and are complex environments requiring trained and cooperative staff, they are prone to develop problems, to break down, and even to be discontinued. Thus, Stegner and Peck [36] found that eight of 35 programs in Veterans Administration Hospitals had been discontinued at the time of their survey. Hall and Baker [14], in their view of 28 British hospital-based token systems, provide an interesting analysis of the main problems, which involve patient selection, staff problems, administrative problems, and community reaction.

The Patients
Only 45 percent of the token economies sampled by Hall and Baker were able to select patients for their programs; yet there is evidence (see page 70) that not all patients are suitable for, or responsive to, such programs. All too often, rejects from other wards are sent to the newly established token program, which cannot cope with a diverse set of difficult management problems.

In addition, patients test the limits of the program in many ways. Forgery of tokens is not unknown, nor is stealing from staff or other patients, or borrowing, with or without coercion. Thus, Ayllon and Azrin [3] found that patients with the highest earnings spent more tokens than they had earned, while those with the lowest earnings spent fewer. Other patients go into business and lend, charging interest, or sell items at a profit when the commissary is closed. Careful monitoring is needed to minimize such activities so that some patients will not be exploited by others.

Staff
Only 24 percent of the token economies sampled by Hall and Baker were able to select staff. This is unfortunate, for some staff are unreliable and a few are hostile. In addition, one or two staff members who do not accurately reinforce behavior can seriously disrupt a token program. Training and continued close supervision of staff can minimize these problems, but transfer of staff who are not able to function in such a system is often necessary. Staff on the evening or night shift present a special problem, since communication between shifts is not always clear, supervision is often less adequate, and training may not be as extensive. Faulty reinforcement on the evening shift may lead to an increase in less desirable behavior, which in turn stresses the often less-than-adequate staff on such shifts. Special precautions, such as rotation of staff through the different shifts, evening visits by the supervising psychologist or psychiatrist, and extra training for the evening staff, can help correct such problems.

Careful supervision of the functioning of the economy by a well-trained professional is essential, yet only 53 percent of the token economies in Hall and Baker's sample had a psychologist who devoted a major portion of his time to the program, while 29 percent of programs had no supervising psychologist. Without supervision, token economies are liable to lose their effectiveness and, worse still, may lead to increasingly used punitive rather than reinforcing procedures. Ongoing staff training, involving systematic staff reinforcement (see page 57), is essential even in the least complex of programs.

Administration and the Community
Continued support by both administrators and the community is essential, although token economies in schools may be particularly susceptible to the lack of such support. In the hospital, nursing administration can cause problems by too frequent removal of well-trained nursing staff from programs, or by not maintaining optimal levels of staff. Physicians may refer unsuitable patients, and hospital administrators may not support the use of material reinforcers. Such problems can be minimized by communicative

education of administrators and by the development of close working relationships between the supervisor of the economy and the administration.

Finally, patients' relatives or the parents of schoolchildren may object to the use of a token economy and have been known to sabotage such programs. Education, even in the form of explanatory brochures, may help in such cases, while a successful program will eventually attract much support. On a more mundane level, patients' relatives may smuggle goods into token economy wards, thus weakening the effect of available reinforcement.

While such problems are not insurmountable, the newcomer to the field is advised to seek consultation with someone who has directed such a program or to visit an operating token economy in order to become familiar with the myriad of small operational details that can make or break such an endeavor. The mere giving of tokens is not a token economy. Properly done, the token economy is a complex motivating environment that can be helpful with a variety of behavior problems.

The Token Economy: Application to the Psychoses

Attempts to improve the social functioning of the back ward patient, particularly by providing the opportunity to work, are by no means new. However, systematic research on the effects of such reinforcement on the long-stay mental hospital patient was stimulated by publication of the pioneering work at Anna State Hospital [2-4]. The aim of this project was to develop behaviors relevant to life, both within and outside the hospital; thus, work was chosen as the target behavior, on the assumption that working is incompatible with the display of many psychotic behaviors.

In a series of experiments, Ayllon and Azrin [4] demonstrated that the work output of severely disabled patients was enhanced by the use of tokens. For example, with tokens a group of patients worked for a total of about 45 hours each day, but when tokens were stopped, work output dropped to 10 hours each day. Freely available ward privileges did not maintain the more desirable performance of these patients—quite the contrary. During this period the patients lost interest in working and began to develop the apathetic behavior so "typical" of the chronic psychotic.

Many replications and extensions of this work have now appeared. Winkler [39], working in a locked "refractory" women's ward, found that various adaptive behaviors increased substantially with token reinforcement. These included getting up, dressing and making the bed, attending morning exercises and meals, and doing various tasks, among them occupational therapy. Free (noncontingent) tokens led to a falloff in performance similar in extent to that noted by Ayllon and Azrin. Violent and noisy incidents were treated by contingent loss of tokens (fines or response cost; see Chapter 5), which led to a diminution of such activities. Interestingly, staff morale improved considerably as a result of working in the token economy; absenteeism dropped by 24 percent in the token ward, compared with only 3 percent in a comparable nontoken ward.

Similar changes among patients and staff were found by McReynolds and Coleman [25] working in one of the oldest state hospitals in the United States. Token economy ward staff felt that 80 percent of their patients would benefit from further treatment, while the staff of a comparison nontoken unit thought that only 50 percent of their patients would improve. Such a change in expectation might well be correlated with beneficial changes in behavior toward patients. Whether these changes are attributable to the token economy or simply to the introduction of a novel approach to treatment cannot be decided from these experiments.

Not all patients on a token economy ward improve, and some continue to perform adequately without this form of external reinforcement. Lloyd and Abel [22], working with a chronic schizophrenic population, noted that 21 of their 52 patients were nonresponders. Similarly, Allen and Magaro [1] found that 16 of 39 patients did not attend occupational therapy sessions when tokens were made contingent on attendance, while nine patients attended without reinforcement. Finally, Ayllon and Azrin [4] found eight of 44 patients to be nonresponders, while 10 continued to work satisfactorily, but less actively, when tokens were removed. These data suggest that about one-quarter of back ward patients respond satisfactorily to a structured program alone and that the use of tokens confers little additional benefit, while 20 to 40 percent do not respond. Thus, correct selection of patients based on a trial in a token economy ward seems essential.

Another approach is to enhance the performance of those who do not respond to the usual token economy. One method [3] is *reinforcer sampling*, in which patients are briefly exposed to elements of the reinforcer—a method similar to the free sample often used by advertisers. Thus, patients were assembled out of doors and then asked if they would like to spend tokens for a walk. This brief exposure to the open air resulted in a marked increase in the number of patients who did so. Of 20 patients who had never walked, 14 now participated. Moreover, five continued to take part even when reinforcer sampling was stopped.

A different procedure was used by Mitchell and Stoffelmayr [26] employing *Premack's principle* [31], which states that opportunity to engage in a higher-frequency behavior can be used to strengthen the occurrence of a lower-frequency behavior. Working with two very inactive back ward patients, these investigators used the opportunity to sit down and not work (a high-frequency behavior), to reinforce working at a specific task. Moreover, they gradually shaped and strengthened the desired behavior. By varying the reinforcement conditions, they demonstrated the effectiveness of this procedure.

In one of the most interesting attempts to strengthen the working habits of chronic schizophrenic patients, Wing and Freudenberg [38] studied the effect of adding social reinforcement, modeling, and prompts to an ongoing monetary economy. In the baseline condition (see Figure 5) the work output of two groups of patients who were paid according to the number of completed tasks (coil stripping) was measured. As can be seen, the output of both groups slowly increased. In the next phase one group was given extra social attention for working (reinforcement, modeling, and prompts), while both groups continued to be paid. Patients in group B, who received extra attention, showed a marked improvement in output, while group A's performance remained stable. Removal of the extra atention led to a decline in performance for group B, and reinstatement for both groups led to a marked increase in output in both groups. Finally, the social reinforcement for group B only was removed, at which point this group's performance fell below that of group A. The authors note that 11 of the patients who had the lowest output in the baseline conditions accounted for 60 percent of the improvement in performance. Thus, an intensive, specifically directed social relationship can add much to an ongoing monetary (or token) economy.

Controlled-Outcome Studies
The studies described so far strongly suggest that useful adaptive behaviors can be taught to long-term residents of back wards. But, we may ask,

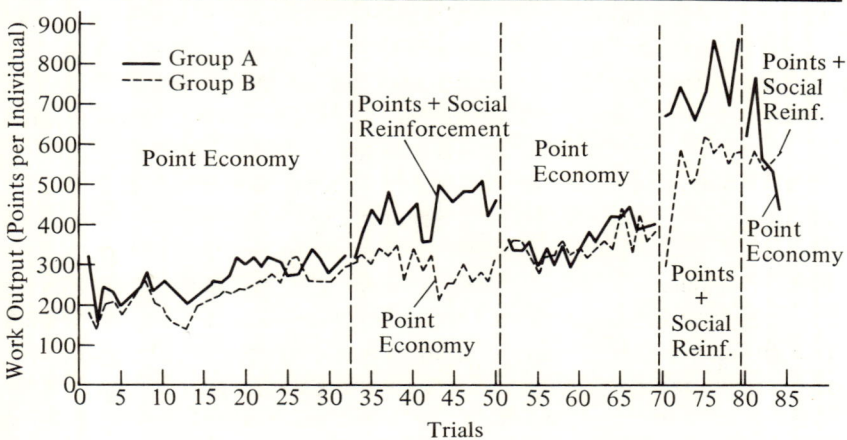

Figure 5. *The effect of adding and removing social reinforcement upon the work output of patients in a point or token economy. Redrawn from data presented by Wing and Freudenberg [38].*

does this benefit these patients in any other way? Are they able to leave the hospital and to function in the community? Do they show less psychotic behavior? The few controlled-outcome studies, comparing the token economy with more traditional treatment, begin to answer these questions.

In the first of these studies [6], patients discharged from a token economy and two traditional psychiatric wards were compared in a nonrandomized design on several variables. The most important finding was that patients discharged from the token economy had been in hospital longer (15.8 years) than those on the other wards (2.1 years), yet there were no differences in this variable within the wards before treatment started. This is an encouraging and logical finding, suggesting that the token economy particularly aids in the rehabilitation of the more disabled patient.

A similar study [13] compared the behavior of matched patients before and after treatment on a token economy and a more traditional ward. Major differences in favor of the token economy were found, including lessening of such psychotic behaviors as thinking disorders and depression, as well as changes in grooming and social behavior. A third study [33] again compared matched groups of patients. Once more, similar differences in mood, cooperative behavior, communication, and social contact were found, each of these variables being measured by ward ratings. What was perhaps more important, 27 patients from the token economy ward were referred to vocational rehabilitation, as compared with four from the control ward; patients on the token economy were also prescribed less medication and spent more time out of hospital on passes.

While these experiments suggest that the token economy is an efficient method of rehabilitating the back ward patient and that it is more effective than traditional methods of ward management, some reservations in the interpretation of results are worth noting. None of these studies was controlled for the effects of nonspecific or placebo factors. As noted earlier, any new program enhances the enthusiasm of members of staff and may change their behavior toward patients. A more adequate control is to compare the token economy with an active alternative program, such as milieu therapy. Moreover, in at least some of the studies the token economy ward has been somewhat better staffed than the control ward. Nonetheless, there is more evidence for the efficacy of the token economy than for any comparable system, such as milieu therapy; thus, while awaiting further experimental evidence, its use for the chronic psychotic can be strongly recommended.

Application to the Neuroses

The token economy has been used infrequently with those diagnosed neurotic, although reinforcement has been delivered in the form of tokens to some individual patients with phobia, anorexia nervosa, astasia-abasia, and depression [17], as noted in the previous chapter. One problem, particularly in cases of anxiety or depression, is the taking of unnecessary pills, especially the minor tranquilizers such as meprobamate, or pain relievers such as aspirin. Usually, administration of such medication starts or continues during hospitalization and medicine is often given when the patient complains of fear, an ache, or a pain. Such contingent administration presumably reinforces the tendency to complain, to the detriment of both patient and staff. One token economy was arranged to decrease this vicious cycle [28]. Patients could buy their *unnecessary* medicine with tokens. Under this condition the number of such medications taken decreased from 170 to 20 per week for women and from 60 to two for men. The following interchange dramatizes the effect: *Patient:* "I have a headache, nurse; can I have some medicine for it?" *Nurse*: "Certainly, but it will cost you four tokens." *Patient*: "Forget it. It doesn't hurt that badly!"

Two other neurotic behaviors have been treated with token systems in hospital settings—stuttering and that constellation of behaviors, the hysterical personality. In the treatment of stuttering small groups of patients were exposed to intensive therapy for some 21 days, in order to increase the rate of speech and decrease the number of stuttered syllables [18]. Tokens exchangeable for basic commodities and privileges were given contingent upon progressive improvement both in speech rate and in number of syllables stuttered during nine 45-minute sessions each day. Delayed auditory feedback was incorporated into the treatment, and in the last stage tape recordings of patients interacting with strangers, sales clerks, and prospective employers were also rated and reinforced. A series of experiments demonstrated that tokens were effective in changing speech patterns, and 65 percent of patients were found to be free of stuttering at one-year follow-up.

The evidence for benefit in the case of hysterical personality is less strong, since no controls were used in the assessment of effects [19]. Five young women, four of whom had attempted suicide, were treated as a subgroup within an ongoing milieu program. Hysteria was defined as a maladaptive set of behaviors including breaking rules, inappropriate anger outbursts and tantrums, suicidal threats, somatic complaints, and unassertive behavior (e.g., opportunities to speak or act were not taken, or were not effectively carried out). The basic program revolved on a required schedule of activities from 7:00 A.M. to 11:00 P.M. Failure to adhere to the schedule resulted in loss of privileges, which were individually defined. Thus, smokers could not smoke, hearty eaters were denied second helpings, and fastidious groomers, which included all the patients, were deprived of makeup and other toiletries. Other maladaptive behaviors were treated with positive or negative verbal feedback from patients and staff.

This is, of course, a relatively primitive reinforcer exchange program. However, more sophisticated adaptations are possible, and at present it remains the only attempt to treat complex and faulty interaction styles on an inpatient basis. While the authors present no data to demonstrate the efficacy of the program, they note that four of the five patients had a reasonably good outcome.

Application to Delinquent Behavior
Therapeutic approaches to the steadily worsening problem of delinquency have not been favored with much success. However, two approaches that use aspects of the token economy point the way toward a more successful future. These methods are: *Improving academic or work skills*, with the rationale that delinquent behavior occurs because individuals lack the skills to gain enjoyment in more adaptive ways, and *increasing the frequency of prosocial behavior* within institutional settings. A third approach, which focuses upon family intervention and which is not based upon the use of tokens, is similar in method to the procedures used for oppositional children described in the previous chapter.

Academic and Work Skills
In one of the earliest and still most impressive studies, Schwitzgebel and Kolb [32] paid delinquent youths to talk into a tape recorder "to find out how teenagers feel about things." After making initial contact in the street or at poolhalls, the delinquents' attendance and promptness at future meetings was shaped with natural reinforcers, such as a 25-cent bonus or a sandwich in a nearby cafe. At first reinforcement was continuous, but later it was intermittent.

With this procedure, attendance and promptness became excellent; slowly, the boys began to value their contact with the therapist. Finally, after about 20 sessions, subjects would usually take a part-time job, and slowly cease to attend. A matched-control group of delinquent boys was selected from state correctional records and the progress of each group was compared three years after termination of therapy. Treated subjects accumulated an average of 2.4 arrests and 3.5 months in prison, compared with 4.7 arrests and 6.9 months for the control group. This is one of the few studies with a modest but definite long-term success in the treatment of delinquency.

Turning to the enhancement of academic skills, two studies stand out. The first was carried out at the National Training School for Boys with a set of delinquents arrested and incarcerated for relatively serious offenses [7]. A point system that allowed the selected group of 41 boys a maximum of choice was instituted. Points were earned by completing schoolwork and could be spent on extra privileges. A marked improvement in grade level and IQ occurred, and what was more important, one year after release the recidivism rate for this group was two-thirds that of the training school as a whole. Unfortunately, by the third year the benefit had vanished. Such a decline in effect is not astonishing, since no maintenance program was attempted. Quite possibly, an employment program similar to that of Schwitzgebel and Kolb might have produced longer-term benefits.

The second program aimed at enhancing academic achievement is the most comprehensive approach yet developed, and it is partially preventive in nature. Called PREP (Preparation through Responsive Educational Program), it was carried out in a junior high school with students considered to be disruptive, in need of academic help, or both [8]. English and mathematics were chosen as the academic areas to be worked on; in addition, interpersonal skills useful both at school and at home were taught and encouraged. The basic motivating system was the use of points, which were exchangeable for candy, soft drinks, high-interest games, and time to "goof off." Thirty students exposed to the program for one year were compared with a matched group of the same size. The experimental group improved significantly more than the control group did in almost all academic subject areas. Moreover, administrative referrals fell off in the experimental group but not in the control group.

These studies, taken as a group, suggest that delinquents' academic and work skills can be substantially improved, leading to short-term reduction of delinquent acts. However, problems with experimental design suggest that a conservative interpretation of the data is appropriate. In the Schwitzgebel and Kolb study, only boys who agreed to participate were treated. Such boys may be those most likely to do well, unlike the control group chosen from state files. Similar reservations exist for the National Training School experiment, while in the case of the final study, no evidence exists at this time to suggest that enhanced academic achievement affected the delinquent careers of the treated subjects.

Prosocial Behavior
That small, homelike settings with well-designed motivating environments can offer a useful alternative to the larger institution is strongly supported by the experimental work emanating from Achievement Place [5, 9, 29, 30]. This series of houses was started by Montrose Wolf and his colleagues at the University of Kansas with youths referred from a juvenile court. Each house manages eight boys or girls at a time, the young people being looked

after by two well-trained houseparents.

The main element of the therapeutic program is a point economy, in which many behaviors earn or lose points. Once earned, points are exchanged for snacks, games, time away from home, a money allowance, and shopping trips. Newcomers to the program start with a daily exchange of points and then move on to a weekly system. Later, some privileges become noncontingent, and if behavior is maintained the youth begins to spend increasing amounts of time at home, while parents are worked with in individual counseling sessions to deal with problems brought about by the youths' home visits. There is no doubt that this well-arranged environment allows a positive relationship to develop between the youths and their houseparents, leading to an atmosphere of warm social approval and support.

In a series of controlled studies using reversal designs, many of the elements in the Achievement Place program have been shown to change behavior effectively. Thus, the point system reduced aggressive behavior, increased prompt attendance at meals and tidiness, and even raised knowledge of current events [29, 30]. At a later stage of research, school performance was investigated using feedback from the teacher to the home [5]. The teacher would simply mark a card "Yes" or "No" for two categories: "Obeyed classroom rules," and "Studied the whole period," and points were given at Achievement Place for "Yes" cards. This combination of feedback and reinforcement effectively changed the youths' classroom behavior.

In addition to prosocial and classroom behavior, interpersonal problems may be responsible for continued delinquency. Thus, one study from the Achievement Place group [9] focused on the conversational skills of delinquent girls. The investigators first identified the appropriate use of questions, positive feedback, and the amount of time spent talking as components of skillful conversational ability, and validated these findings by having community members rank videotapes of conversations as to excellence. Then, four girls with deficient skills were trained to increase these aspects of conversation using instructions, demonstration, and practice, with videotaped conversations. Before training the girls were rated worse conversationalists than a group of junior high school girls. After training they were rated better than such girls, adding yet another component to the Achievement Place program.

Houses similar to Achievement Place are now being operated successfully in many parts of the country, and one systematic replication of some of the original research has been reported from California [21]. The houseparents had less training and the boys were of Mexican-American background. Some differences were noted. For example, lateness at meal times was not a problem for these boys, and, despite the use of contingent points, they would not save money. Although the reinforcement system was demonstrated to change behavior effectively, once changed, behavior remained improved by instructions, prompts, and even threats of fines. Social interaction and reinforcement may be more important in the California house than in Achievement Place, perhaps due to the different ethnic background of the California youths, or the social aspects of the environment may have been underestimated in the original research.

While these studies demonstrate the effectiveness of the token reinforcement program with a variety of important behaviors, they do not estimate the long-term effects of the approach. Unfortunately, no controlled-outcome studies exist; however, a matched sample of boys assigned to the Kansas School for Boys was compared on a variety of outcome measures with a group of boys from the Achievement Place program [37]. Two years after discharge, recidivism was 19 percent for Achievement Place and 53 percent for the boys' school, while the school attendance figures were 90 percent and nine percent, respectively. Moreover, the differences in cost for the two programs are startling. The more individualized Achievement Place program cost only half as much per boy as the standard institutional program, while the initial costs (construction, etc.) were one-quarter those of institutions. Since the Achievement Place program at the very least produces no worse results than those of the larger institution, the cost estimates argue strongly that the smaller house should replace the larger, more impersonal institution.

Classroom Applications

One of the most frequent sites of application of the token economy, particularly for children with academic and disruptive or other problem behaviors, has been the classroom. As described in the previous sections, both academic and disruptive behavior of delinquents has been modified using a token economy, with backup reinforcers being dispensed at home. In the usual application, however, reinforcement is dispensed at school within a token or point economy, with relatively inexpensive material goods or various kinds of privileges as backup reinforcers.

Thus, O'Leary and his colleagues [27] demonstrated in a convincing reversal design that tokens were more effective than rule setting or social attention in decreasing the amount of disruptive behavior of seven children in a classroom. That academic activities can be similarly modified over long periods of time was shown in another study [24], in which assignment completion was the target behavior. Without tokens, assignments were finished and handed in 64 to 94 percent of the time. The use of tokens increased this to nearly 100 percent for all assignments, the increase being maintained over a complete academic year.

Within the classroom, as in other settings, the interesting question now is not whether behavior can be changed, but what the mechanism of change is within a token economy. Mandelkar, Brigham, and Bushell [23] measured the number of social contacts between teacher and child in two groups of children to whom the teacher alternately dispensed tokens contingently and noncontingently. During each contingent application of tokens the number of social contacts doubled. The use of a token economy changes teachers' behavior in a more positive direction, and at least a part of the effect of the economy is attributable to such changes. Obviously, teachers (and other workers) in a point system or token economy learn to observe behavior more accurately; they also learn when to attend to or ignore behavior, perhaps making them more likely to become effective social reinforcers. In addition, the giving of tangible rewards in the form of tokens or points is likely to increase the value of that person's social interaction.

Another explanation is also likely—that improvement in children's behavior leads teachers to give them more attention, and that the token economy initiates and maintains positive social feedback. Sherman and Cormier [34] systematically reduced two students' disruptive classroom behavior without the teacher's being aware that such changes were being made. The teacher's attention was found to increase as the behavior improved and to decrease when the students' behavior worsened. Similar changes are very likely to occur within a token economy, and, as was seen in the psychiatric ward, the introduction of an economy enhances the social atmosphere of the classroom, increasing the amount of positive interaction.

One problem with the token economy, as with other reinforcement procedures, is the relatively small amount of generalization of improvement to periods when the token economy is not in effect. One innovative way to enhance generalization is to teach students aspects of self-control, including accurate self-evaluation. This was achieved in one study of disruptive youngsters [11] by rewarding them with tokens for accurately matching teachers' evaluation of their work; i.e., by awarding themselves the same number of points as the teacher. Using this method, students continued to show low levels of disruptive behavior even when the token economy was not in effect.

Token Economics
Token systems are economic systems in miniature. In the planning and operation of a token economy, it is important, therefore, to consider economic factors as they bear upon treatment goals. Winkler [40], for example, examined the spending patterns of patients in a token system and found that such patterns follow general economic laws. As income (token earnings) increased, patients spent an increasing proportion of their tokens upon luxuries (goods available in a shop). Thus, to enhance the effect of tokens, it is important as behavior improves, and earnings therefore increase, to provide a wide range of backup reinforcers, especially nonessential items. If new spending is not fostered, the reinforcing value of tokens will diminish. Moreover, patients will be able to save tokens and will be less likely to earn them. In some token systems the problem of savings is dealt with by canceling such savings at regular intervals; for example, by changing the color of tokens each week, or by not carrying forward balances of points from one week to another. This both increases the tendency to spend and allows for a more consistent reinforcement effect.

Another method used to enhance performance is to raise prices. In so doing it is important to take into account the elasticity of demand. Winkler found that spending on cigarettes was very elastic while spending on food items was inelastic. Thus, prices should be raised on essential items rather than upon luxury items, since in inflationary times spending on luxury items diminishes, while spending on essential items is continued. So managers of token economies should test the effects of various economic changes in their system over short periods of time before deciding upon final adjustments in the prices of consumer goods.

Overview

As we have seen, the token economy is a complex motivating environment requiring skilled direction, monitoring of the client's progress, and continual modification based upon the degree of achievement of programmatic goals. The economy is particularly adaptable to institutions such as the psychiatric hospital, the home for delinquents, or the schoolroom. Nevertheless, it can be used in other contexts. Thus, Everett and his colleagues [12] demonstrated that the number of riders on a campus bus could be increased by giving tokens to those boarding. Tokens were redeemable at local stores for a variety of goods. This system is, of course, reminiscent of "S & H Green Stamps," itself a practical variant of the token economy.

The main ingredients of a token economy are identifiable target behaviors and a wide range of goods or privileges that can be earned. The choice of target behaviors should be based upon the needs of the clientele and not solely upon those of the institution. Thus, keeping order *may* be a necessary first step in the operation of a token or point system, but it should not be the only goal. Choice of reinforcers will depend on the circumstances of the clientele and may often be naturally occurring aspects of the environment. In the classroom, for example, a reinforcing event may be the opportunity to do as one wishes for a few minutes, or on the ward the chance for an extra walk. But there must always be a sufficiently wide range of reinforcers available, both to lower the chance of satiation and to cater to individual tastes.

Given these essential ingredients, does the token economy work? As we have seen, not everyone responds to the system. At least in the psychiatric ward, and probably in the schoolroom, there are those who do not respond, although specially designed subprograms can increase responsiveness. The majority of controlled studies of the efficacy of the token or point system have used a sequential design with alternating baseline (no treatment) and token or point conditions and have shown the remarkable advantage of introducing such a treatment into a wide variety of situations and with many different behavior problems. Fewer studies use the more sophisticated control of giving nonredeemable tokens contingently. This controls for staff attention to behavior problems. Again, redeemable tokens have been shown to confer large benefits.

These studies unfortunately tell us nothing about the long-term benefits of using a token or point system. To answer this question, controlled-outcome studies are needed. Most outcome studies come from the psychiatric ward and compare a treated with an untreated or traditionally treated group. Again, the token economy turns out to confer substantial benefits to patients, but this simple comparison does not provide adequate control for nonspecific therapeutic effects [16]. Introducing a new treatment leads to increased staff enthusiasm, which may transmit substantial benefits to patients. Such clinical trials need to be done, but we may conclude that there is more evidence that a token system will confer benefit, especially within the psychiatric ward, than there is for any comparable treatment approach, such as milieu therapy.

Given some evidence for therapeutic effectiveness, the next question is how does the token economy work? Is the effect solely attributable to the reinforcing effect of tokens? Or is it a result of other factors? The majority of sequential studies strongly suggest that the contingent application of tokens backed up by a wide range of goods and privileges is the main component. Factors such as goal setting do not, in themselves, seem to contribute much. However, a secondary effect seems to be the response of staff to the improvement of patients or pupils. In the studies emanating from the psychiatric ward, marked improvement of staff morale was noted. In the classroom, Sherman and Cormier's demonstration [34] that teachers respond with increased social attention to students' improvements, coupled with the observation [23] that teachers' social attention increases during contingent application of tokens, suggests that increased social reinforcement from staff, secondary to improvement in their charges, is an important factor in the efficacy of the token economy.

Finally, a word of warning. A token economy is *not* the mere giving of tokens contingent upon a few obvious target behaviors, such as getting up on time or attending to schoolwork. It is *not* a fixed economic system set up once and for all. It must be constantly adjusted in order to maximize motivation, learning, and growth and must be altered to fit the needs of those whose behavior is being changed. The administration of a token economy is not for the amateur. The newcomer to the field is advised to seek consultation with someone who has directed a token or point economy, or to visit an operating token economy to become familiar with the myriad of small operational details that can make or break such an endeavor.

References
1. Allen, D. J., and Magaro, P. A. Measures of change in token economy programs. *Behavior Research and Therapy* 9:311, 1971.
2. Ayllon, T., and Azrin, N. H. The measurement and reinforcement of behavior of psychotics. *Journal of the Experimental Analysis of Behavior* 8:357, 1965.
3. Ayllon, T., and Azrin, N. H. Reinforcer sampling: A technique for increasing the behavior of mental patients. *Journal of Applied Behavior Analysis* 1:13, 1968.
4. Ayllon T., and Azrin, N. H. *The Token Economy: A Motivational System for Therapy and Rehabilitation.* New York: Appleton-Century-Crofts, 1968.
5. Bailey, J. S., Wolf, M. M., and Phillips, E. L. Home based reinforcement and the modification of pre-delinquents' classroom behavior. *Journal of Applied Behavior Analysis* 3:223, 1970.
6. Birky, H. J., Chambliss, J. E., and Wasden, R. A comparison of residents discharged from a token economy and two traditional psychiatric programs. *Behavior Therapy* 2:46, 1971.
7. Cohen, H. L., and Filipczak, J. *A new learning environment.* San Francisco: Jossey-Bass, 1971.
8. Cohen, H. L., Filipczak, J., Boren, J., Golding, I., Storm, R., Bishop, R. M., and Breiling, J. *Academic and Social Behavior Change in a Public School Setting.* Maryland: Educational Facility Press, 1974.
9. Minkin, N., Braukmann, G. J., Minkin, B. L., Timbers, G. D., Timbers, B. J., Fixsen, D. L., Phillips, E. L., and Wolf, M. M. The social validation and training of conversational skills. *Journal of Applied Behavior Analysis* 9:127, 1976.
10. Cowles, J. T. Food tokens as incentives for learning by champanzees. *Comparative Psychology Monograph* 5:14, 1937.
11. Drabman, R. S., Spitalnik, R., and O'Leary, K. D. Teaching self-control to disruptive children. *Journal of Abnormal Psychology* 82:10, 1973.
12. Everett, P. B., Hayward, S. C., and Meyers, A. W. The effects of a token reinforcement procedure on bus ridership. *Journal of Applied Behavior Analysis* 7:1, 1974.
13. Gripp, R. F. and Magaro, P. A. A token economy program evaluation with untreated control ward comparisons. *Behavior Research and Therapy* 9:137, 1971.
14. Hall, J., and Baker, R. Token economy systems: Breakdown and control. *Behavior Research and Therapy* 11:253, 1973.
15. Hamburg, D. A. Report of ad hoc committee on central fact-gathering data of the American Psychoanalytic Association. *Journal of the American Psychoanalytical Association* 15:841, 1967.
16. Hersen, M., and Eisler, R. M. Comments on Heap, Boblitt, Moore, and Hord's "Behavior-Milieu Therapy" with chronic neuropsychiatric patients. *Psychological Reports* 29:583, 1971.
17. Hersen, M., Eisler, R. M., Alford, G. S., and Agras, W. S. Effects of token economy on neurotic depression: An experimental analysis. *Behavior Therapy* 4:392, 1973.

18. Ingham, R. J., and Andrews, G.   An analysis of a token economy in stuttering therapy. *Journal of Applied Behavior Analysis* 6:219, 1973.
19. Kass, D. J., Silvers, F. M., and Abroms, G. M.   Behavioral group treatment of hysteria. *Archives of General Psychiatry* 26:42, 1972.
20. Lehrer, P., Schiff, L., and Kris, A.   The use of a credit card in a token economy. *Journal of Applied Behavior Analysis* 3:289, 1970.
21. Liberman, R. P., Ferris, C., Salgado, P., and Salgado, J.   Replication of the Achievement Place model in California. *Journal of Applied Behavior Analysis* 8:287, 1975.
22. Lloyd, K. E., and Abel, L.   Performance on a token economy psychiatric ward: A two year summary. *Behavior Research and Therapy* 8:1, 1970.
23. Mandelkar, A. V., Brigham, R. A., and Bushell, D.   The effects of token procedures on a teacher's social contacts with her students. *Journal of Applied Behavior Analysis* 3:169, 1970.
24. McLaughlin, T. F., and Malaby, J.   Intrinsic reinforcers in a classroom token economy. *Journal of Applied Behavior Analysis* 5:263, 1972.
25. McReynolds, W. T., and Coleman, J.   Token economy: Patient and staff changes. *Behavior Research and Therapy* 10:29, 1972.
26. Mitchell, W. S., and Stoffelmayr, B. E.   Application of the Premack principle to the behavioral control of extremely inactive schizophrenics. *Journal of Applied Behavior Analysis* 6:419, 1973.
27. O'Leary, K. D., Becker, W. C., Evans, M. B., and Saudargas, R. A.   A token reinforcement program in a public school: A replication and systematic analysis. *Journal of Applied Behavior Analysis* 2:3, 1969.
28. Parrino, J. J., George, L., and Daniels, A. C.   Token control of pill-taking behavior in a psychiatric ward. *Journal of Behavior Therapy and Experimental Psychiatry* 2:181, 1971.
29. Phillips, E. L.   Achievement Place: Token reinforcement procedures in a home-style rehabilitation setting for "pre-delinquent" boys. *Journal of Applied Behavior Analysis* 1:213, 1968.
30. Phillips, E. L., Phillips, E., Fixsen, D. L., and Wolf, M. M.   Achievement Place: Modification of the behaviors of pre-delinquent boys within a token economy. *Journal of Applied Behavior Analysis* 4:45, 1971.
31. Premack, D.   Toward empirical behavior laws. 1. Positive reinforcement. *Psychological Review* 66:219, 1959.
32. Schwitzgebel, R., and Kolb, D. A.   Inducing behavior change in adolescent delinquents. *Behavior Research and Therapy* 1:297, 1964.
33. Shean, G. D., and Zeidberg, Z.   Token reinforcement therapy: A comparison of matched groups. *Behavior Therapy and Experimental Psychiatry* 2:95, 1971.
34. Sherman, T. M., and Cormier, W. H.   An investigation of the influence of student behavior on teacher behavior. *Journal of Applied Behavior Analysis* 7:11, 1974.
35. Staats, A., Finley, J., Minke, K. A., Wolf, M., and Brooks, C.   A reinforcer system and experimental procedure for the laboratory study of reading acquisition. *Child Development* 35:209, 1964.
36. Stegner, C. A., and Peck, C. P.   Token economy programs in the Veterans Administration. *Hospital and Community Psychiatry* 21:371, 1970.

37. Trotter, R. J. Behavior modification: Here, there, and everywhere. *Science News* 103:260, 1973.
38. Wing, J. K., and Freudenberg, R. K. The response of severely ill chronic schizophrenic patients to social stimulation. *American Journal of Psychiatry* 311, 1961.
39. Winkler, R. C. Management of chronic psychiatric patients by a token reinforcement system. *Journal of Applied Behavior Analysis* 3:47, 1970.
40. Winkler, R. C. The relevance of economic theory and technology to token reinforcement systems. *Behavior Research and Therapy* 9:81, 1971.
41. Wolf, J. F. Effectiveness of token rewards for chimpanzees. *Comparative Psychology Monograph* 5:11, 1936.

5. Aversive Procedures
David H. Barlow

Editor's Introduction
As noted in the preceding chapters, some maladaptive behaviors can be reduced in frequency or eliminated altogether by either reinforcing competing adaptive behaviors or using extinction procedures. However, it is not always possible to identify or remove the reinforcer or to identify a competitive behavior. At other times, as in the case of self-destructive behavior, it is necessary to bring behavior rapidly under control, which is not usually possible with reinforcement or extinction procedures. In such cases aversive procedures are applicable.

Three main paradigms for their use exist. The first is classic conditioning, in which a stimulus eliciting the maladaptive behavior is paired with a noxious stimulus. In the case of an alcoholic the sight or smell of alcohol might be paired with painful electric shock. Theoretically, anxiety or fear comes to be associated with the once-pleasurable stimulus. The second paradigm is punishment. Here a behavior—for example, drinking alcohol—is followed by the noxious stimulus. This procedure also contains elements of classic conditioning, since the smell or taste of alcohol is automatically paired with the noxious stimulus in a punishment paradigm. The third procedure is avoidance training, in which the subject avoids punishment, for example, by pushing away a glass of alcohol within a certain time limit.

There are many aversive stimuli: electric shock, chemical substances such as apomorphine that produce nausea and vomiting, and even noxious odors. More recently, verbal aversion, consisting of descriptions of disturbing scenes, has been used in the procedure known as covert sensitization. Here, scenes of the behavior to be eliminated are paired with the aversive scenes. Finally, as noted earlier, response cost or fines within a token economy can be used, as can time-out from positive reinforcement. In the latter procedure, which is particularly useful with children, a short period of isolation is used, thus removing reinforcement during that time.

The application of a particular aversive stimulus within one of the three paradigms described earlier constitutes the aversive therapies. Again, the same principles of behavior change apply; namely, precise definition of behavior and continuing measurement to allow for ongoing analysis of the efficacy of the procedure. This is especially necessary when strong aversive stimuli are being used in a punishment paradigm. Such a procedure should be quickly effective and should be discontinued if it does not work, so that undue pain is not inflicted. The aversive therapies raise a number of ethical issues that must be faced squarely by every therapist using them. Naturally, no aversive stimulus that causes tissue damage should be used. As with all therapies, the informed consent of the patient, or parents in the case of a minor, should be obtained. This should entail a discussion of the aversive stimulus and procedure, the side effects of the procedure, the chance of success, and the methods used to evaluate the efficacy of therapy. Application within captive populations raises special problems. Here, the informed consent of the director of the institution is necessary; but, in addition, the formation of an advisory committee, which should include nonprofessionals to monitor the use of such therapies, should be considered.

The aversive therapies have a number of applications, the more important of which are for the severely oppositional or self-destructive child, the alcoholic, and some subjects exhibiting sexual behavior problems. In the chapter that follows, Barlow insists that aversive procedures form only part of a therapeutic program and that attention should be directed toward building up behaviors to replace the suppressed behavior—heterosexual behavior in the case of homosexuals, more successful coping with social and work problems for the alcoholic, and cooperative, constructive behaviors for the oppositional child.

In the case of alcoholism, chemical aversion (pages 97-99) appears to be potentially the most useful therapy, giving in clinical series a one-year abstinence rate of 60 percent, and with the use of periodic booster sessions, 95 percent abstinence. With sexual deviation (pages 103-110) electrical aversion in a punishment or avoidance paradigm has been used most frequently, punishing both deviant fantasies and, where possible, actual sexual behavior, as in the case of cross-dressing. However, the evidence suggests that covert sensitization may be equally effective, and thus should perhaps be used first in these behavior disorders. The oppositional or self-destructive child has been dealt with by using time-out and electrical aversion (pages 114-119). Many studies have included control procedures in a single-case analysis demonstrating the immediate effectiveness of the aversive procedure, but, again, no long-term controlled-outcome studies exist. However, this is less critical in the case of such children, since immediate management is often the most difficult problem, one with which aversive procedures are effective.

Once behavior is brought under control in a treatment setting, the prob-

lem of transfer to other environments is again raised. Barlow suggests that there is a difference between voluntary and nonvoluntary patients in this regard. Transfer is rarely found in the captive subject but is often seen in the case of the voluntary patient, raising the possibility that the motivated patients may use the effects of the procedure to control their behavior. Thus, in the presence of the stimulus eliciting the deviant behavior a patient might imagine the unpleasant effects of the aversive procedure, thus controlling a tendency toward deviant behavior. This is an interesting hypothesis, worthy of further study. It is of direct clinical relevance, since patients can be instructed to maximize the efficacy of aversive therapy by using the procedure for self-control.

W. S. A.

We have all had personal experience with aversive procedures designed to change our behavior. As Kazdin [82] notes, " . . . aversive techniques are deeply enmeshed in many social institutions including government and law (e.g., fines and imprisonment), education (e.g., failing grades on exams, expulsion, and probation), religion (e.g., damnation), international relations (e.g., military coercion), and normal social intercourse (e.g., discrimination, disapproval, humiliation, and social stigma). Routine interactions of most individuals with both physical and social environments result in aversive events ranging from a burn on a hot stove to verbal abuse from an acquaintance."

A more recent development has been a systematic extension of these techniques, emanating from basic research on behavior, to the clinic. Aversive techniques are now being used to treat an increasing variety of behavior disorders, such as alcoholism, sexual deviation, shoplifting, ruminative vomiting, hallucinations, depressive thoughts, and violent or aggressive behaviors. Concurrent with this growth in use, there has been a growing public confusion as to the definition of aversive techniques, which some equate with torture. Unquestionably, there has been misuse of aversive procedures. In some cases this is the result of well-intentioned therapists not being familiar with the basic principles underlying the use of aversive procedures. Where abuses do exist, the development and dissemination of clear ethical guidelines for the use of aversive procedures should make abuses apparent to professional societies, governmental agencies, and the public, thereby decreasing or eliminating these abuses. With these developments, the full therapeutic benefits of these procedures will be available to relieve suffering and enhance human functioning.

The Major Aversive Paradigms
The assumption underlying the use of aversive techniques, as with other behavior modification procedures, is that therapy consists of unlearning inappropriate responses, thoughts, and feelings, and learning more appropriate behavior. Several different ways in which aversive stimuli can be used to facilitate learning have been discovered in the laboratory and applied to maladaptive behavior. These paradigms and examples of their use are described below.

Classic Fear Conditioning
This procedure, developed by Pavlov, involves pairing two stimuli, the conditioned stimulus (CS) and the unconditioned stimulus (UCS). For example, in treating pedophilia (sexual attraction to young children), the pedophilic stimulus (CS)—usually a picture or slide—is presented to the patient, followed immediately by an aversive stimulus (UCS) such as a brief electric shock. Theoretically, after repeated pairings of the two stimuli the patient will develop a similar feeling to the pedophilic image as that experienced in response to shock, often described as "anxiety." If the conditioned response is strong enough, the patient will avoid these feelings of anxiety, now associated with pedophilia, by avoiding situations in which pedophilic behavior occurs. Another possible explanation is that the attractive stimulus is devalued, so that the patient perceives the stimulus as less attractive.

Punishment
In punishment the aversive stimulus follows the occurrence of a clearly defined *behavior*. This differs from classic fear conditioning, where no behavioral response is required. For example, in treating alcoholism using a punishment paradigm, the patient pours whiskey, picks up the glass, and begins to drink before receiving a shock. In classic fear conditioning, the sight and smell of alcohol would be paired with the shock, without the occurrence of a behavioral response. These two procedures are often confused and are, in fact, difficult to separate, since during punishment classic

conditioning also occurs. Each time a response is punished, the sensory cues associated with the behavior are being paired with the aversive stimulus. If drinking a glass of whiskey is punished by shock, then seeing and smelling whiskey are also paired with the aversive stimuli.

Avoidance and Escape Learning
A third procedure allows the patient to avoid the aversive stimulus. For example, an alcoholic beverage might be placed in front of an alcoholic, with shock programmed to follow 10 seconds later. If the patient pushes the drink away, however, no shock is received. This is called avoidance conditioning. The notion is that with repeated trials the patient will develop a habit of actively avoiding alcohol. A variant of this procedure is escape conditioning, where the subject can terminate the aversive stimulus by engaging in a more adaptive behavior. This paradigm has been little used in the clinic.

Aversion Relief
The cessation of an aversive stimulus such as shock produces a period of "relief," subjectively reported as pleasant. If a formerly neutral or undesirable object is associated with this relief, the object hypothetically picks up pleasurable qualities and becomes more attractive. For example, the offset of shock has been associated with heterosexual slides to increase heterosexual responsiveness. Since this paradigm involves simple pairing of a pleasant state (relief from shock) with a formerly neutral stimulus, it is essentially a classic conditioning paradigm. Furthermore, the purpose is not to suppress an undesirable behavior but rather to strengthen a desired behavior. Thus, this paradigm uses an aversive stimulus in a different way.

The Aversive Stimuli
A variety of stimuli have been employed in aversive therapy, including nausea-inducing chemicals and painful electrical stimuli as well as covert sensitization, in which upsetting scenes are described and vividly imagined by the patient. Milder aversive stimuli, such as removal of positive reinforcement, have also been used.

Chemical Aversion
Usually, this refers to the use of drugs such as apomorphine hydrochloride

or emetine hydrochloride that induce nausea and vomiting. In a typical procedure, the patient drinks 20 ounces of lukewarm saline solution containing 1.5 grains of oral emetine. This fluid is easily regurgitated. The patient is then given an injection of 3.25 grains of emetine hydrochloride, 1.65 grains of pilocarpine hydrochloride to produce sweating and salivation, and 1.5 grains of ephedrine sulfate to prevent a fall in blood pressure. Emesis occurs in about 10 minutes, and the dosage has to be adjusted as sessions continue. The usual dosage for apomorphine is 5 mg subcutaneously, which produces emesis in approximately 10 minutes. However, Raymond [127] has successfully used smaller doses, starting with 0.05 grain and increasing to 0.1 grain, with nausea and not emesis the desired response.

Chemical aversion has some disadvantages: (1) It is very unpleasant and may lead to refusal or premature termination of treatment. (2) The onset of nausea and vomiting does not always occur at the desired time. Since it seems important that the sight or drinking of alcohol occur *just before* nausea or vomiting, the unpredictability of the emetics may cause improper pairings and retard learning. (3) The patient develops tolerance to apomorphine. (4) Serious cardiovascular effects may occur, and extensive vomiting may lead to dehydration or, occasionally, gastrointestinal hemorrhage. (5) Since medical and nursing surveillance is necessary, the treatment is expensive and time-consuming.

Another chemical aversion agent is the drug succinylcholine chloride dehydrate. This drug, usually administered in an intravenous infusion, produces respiratory paralysis in humans through a curarizing effect at the motor end-plates of the efferent neurons serving the skeletal muscles. this is extremely aversive, and continuous medical supervision by an anesthesiologist is required during administration. Moreover, patients should be fully informed as to the unpleasant effects of this substance, and they will undoubtedly have to be very highly motivated to complete treatment.

Electrical Aversion
Nonconvulsive electric shock is currently the most widely used aversive stimulus. It can be administered through two electrodes about half an inch in diameter, usually placed on the forearm, calf, or fingertips and held in place by snap fasteners or elastic cloth strips. Electrode jelly is sometimes

used. A safer and more effective means is the electrode described by Tursky, Watson, and O'Connell [150]. This device consists of two rings of aluminum recessed in a plastic casing. The electrodes are covered with a sponge that makes contact with the skin. This electrode was developed in order to: (1) delineate precisely the area of stimulation, (2) cause minimal interference with the mobility of the subject, (3) prevent skin irritation and burning, and (4) reduce muscle involvement as a secondary concomitant of shock stimulation [154].

The intensity of shock is individually determined for each subject through verbal report or by its effect on the inappropriate behavior. The desired intensity, as subjectively reported by the subject, can be from painful to a point just beyond that reported to be tolerable. A behavioral index of the appropriate intensity is the withdrawal or flinch reaction. Since most patients adapt to shock, the intensity must be increased from session to session in order to maintain a sufficient level of aversive stimulation. Shock is usually generated from batteries, and recently small portable devices have been used. Precautions must always be taken to prevent inadvertent passage of current through the chest. *In addition, a usual precaution exercised in our laboratory is self-administration by the therapist of all levels of shock to be used with a patient.* Certain patients are unsuitable for electrical aversion; for example, those with peripheral neuropathy. For a thorough review of the administration of electric shock, see Tursky [149].

Shock shares with chemical aversion the problem of unpleasantness to the patient, resulting in occasional refusal or termination of treatment.

Covert Sensitization
In this procedure vivid descriptions of noxious scenes, such as vomiting and nausea, are described to the patient in conjunction with descriptions of the undesirable behavior [32]. For example, in the treatment of unwanted homosexual arousal, the following scene of the patient approaching his boyfriend was described: "As you get closer to the door you notice a queasy feeling in the pit of your stomach. You open the door and see Bill lying on the bed naked and you can sense that puke is filling up your stomach and forcing its way up to your throat. You walk over to Bill and you can see him clearly. As you reach out for him you can taste the puke, bitter and sticky and acidy on your tongue, you start gagging and retching

and chunks of vomit are coming out of your mouth and nose, dropping onto your shirt and all over Bill's skin."

The description of the nauseous scene often lasts for one to two minutes. The particular choice of adjectives is individualized to create optimal aversion. These scenes are most effective if some of the sensations or stimuli described actually occur during the undesirable behavior or if the actual aversive consequences of the deviant behavior (occurring too long after the behavior to inhibit it) are added. Examples from exhibitionism would be the guilt and fear of being caught and the negative reactions of relatives and friends. A recent development [73] is the construction of several aversive scenes, from which the patient chooses at the beginning of each session, and the increased self-administration of these scenes. Maletzky [101] and Blanchard, Libet, and Young [22] have successfully added noxious odors to aversive images.

Covert sensitization is becoming increasingly popular and has the advantage of administration totally in the imagination, which results in flexibility in the choice of aversive images and facilitates self-administration of the technique outside the therapist's office. Furthermore, the scenes can be tape-recorded to save therapist time. It also seems less unpleasant than chemically or electrically aversive stimuli and may be less likely to cause termination of treatment.

Time-out

Time-out from positive reinforcement refers to a procedure in which an individual earning reinforcement is prevented from doing so. The procedure is often used with institutionalized patients or with children at home or in the classroom. In a typical example, a disruptive child or patient is removed, contingent upon disruptive behavior, from a situation where reinforcers such as other people or entertainment are present. The time-out interval is usually 2 to 10 minutes, with release dependent on the absence of any undesired behavior, for example, crying. Longer periods of time-out have the disadvantage of reducing the number of times the behavior is punished, thus lengthening the time necessary for the patient to learn to suppress the behavior, as well as reducing the number of potential reinforcements for behaving more appropriately. Time-out seems less aversive than other techniques but requires careful attention and consistency from the responsible attendant, such as a parent, teacher, or hospital aide.

Overcorrection
This is the term for a procedure developed by Foxx and Azrin [61, 62]. Most often applied to disruptive behavior of children or institutionalized adults (nonvoluntary populations), this treatment package contains several components including *restitution*, in which the patient restores certain aspects of his environment to a better condition than they were in before disruption, and *positive practice*, in which those behaviors involved in restitution are extended beyond the point of simple correction. For example, a child who overturns a table might first be required to restore the table to its original position and to dust and wax it. Second, the child might be required to "practice" the behavior on all the tables in the room. Since a component analysis of the package has not been carried out, it is not clear if this is mainly a punishment procedure or something else, such as reinforcing incompatible behavior. But most investigators consider it a punishment procedure [53], and it will be treated as such in this chapter.

Miscellaneous Aversive Stimuli
White noise or tones have been used most often, for example, by Flanagan, Goldiamond, and Azrin [58]; but other variations include use of a bicycle horn [131], which proved effective in suppressing disruptive behavior. The optimal range for any of the above noises is 100 to 120 decibels (db). Another less frequently used aversive stimulus is a noxious odor in the form of sulfureted potash or some related substance that has, for example, been used to treat obesity [3]. Colson [36] reports that of three substances, ammonium sulfide, butyric acid, and aromatic ammonia (smelling salts), smelling salts was the most effective in one case. A very popular technique in clinical settings is the use of a rubber band [108]. Usually, the patient is instructed to wear the rubber band on one wrist and snap it contingent on unwanted thoughts or urges. Finally, in situations where control of positive reinforcement is possible, such as token economies in institutions, a system of fines, technically known as response cost [83], can be imposed contingent on undesirable behaviors.

Which Aversive Stimulus?
The choice of an aversive stimulus is usually based on the therapist's familiarity with a particular method. The tendency has been to choose one stimulus—for example, chemical aversion in the early sixties, and apply it

to every disorder. If this type of aversion proved to have shortcomings, as chemical aversion did, then researchers would suggest a wholesale switch to a "better" type, such as electrical aversion. Recently, guides for choosing a particular aversive stimulus to treat a particular disorder have emerged, based partly on clinical experience and partly on principles derived from general experimental psychology.

Briefly, it may be that the effectiveness of aversive stimuli varies depending on the sensory modalities involved in a particular disorder. For instance, obesity and alcoholism, which involve mostly olfactory and gustatory sensory modes, would be more effectively treated with aversive stimuli in these two modalities. Such aversive stimuli might include nausea produced by drugs or imaginally, perhaps in conjunction with noxious odors. This notion is based on the well-known "bait shyness" work, in which animals rapidly learn to avoid food on the basis of olfactory and gustatory cues if the food previously led to a toxic reaction [66, 67]. Based on this and other work, Seligman [137] has proposed the notion of "preparedness," which states that lower organisms and, perhaps, humans are prepared by virtue of evolutionary adaptation to learn certain associations very easily. Thus, the wild rat that survives ingesting poisoned food and learns to avoid the taste of that food will survive, as will a predisposition to make that association. A similar phenomenon may exist in humans. Extending these principles to clinical settings, Wilson and Davison [158] and Elkins [49] have suggested that nausea is biologically more appropriate than shock in aversive therapy for alcoholism. If one follows this line of speculation, self-destructive behavior or any disorder involving tactile stimulation may be best treated by electric shock; auditory hallucinations by aversive noise; and cigarette smoking by smoke satiation. This notion has yet to be evaluated experimentally but it may provide important leads on the choice of aversive procedures in clinical populations.

Side Effects of Aversive Procedures
Both positive and negative side effects result from the application of aversive techniques. Many negative side effects were first noticed in experimental laboratories during work with lower organisms. However, not all of these have been observed in clinical settings. The most obvious side effect is the tendency to avoid the setting in which aversive stimuli are used [23]. This leads to the loss of some voluntary patients, who find

aversive stimulation more frightening than the thought of continuing their undesirable behavior. A supportive relationship and reiteration of the benefits of treatment help overcome this complication.

In lower organisms aversion stimulation often elicits aggression. This has recently been confirmed with humans in an analogue laboratory situation [124]. With nonvoluntary patients, an aversive stimulus that involves close physical proximity, such as leading a disruptive child to an isolation room (time-out), affords an opportunity for aggression. Bandura and Walters [10] also note that children imitate behavior that they observe in adults. If one is attempting to control a disruptive child's behavior through physical punishment, the child may in turn control the behavior of peers or parents with aggressive or punishing behavior. If this pattern develops, one should reinforce more appropriate social behavior.

A further side effect observed only in clinical settings, namely, depression, sometimes occurs in patients who are attempting to control maladaptive behavior that is intrinsically pleasurable, such as overeating, sexual deviation, or alcoholism. Such patients find it pleasing to visualize themsleves without their problem. Only rarely do they realize the amount of pleasure gained from their behavior, and when this behavior begins to diminish during treatment emotional reactions of ambivalence, frustration, a sense of loss, and occasionally depression develop. These behaviors or emotions are not a result of the aversive stimulus per se but are related to the accompanying loss of positive reinforcement. *This points to a need to replace highly reinforcing problem behavior with alternative behaviors from which the patient will derive equal pleasure. Encouragement of alternative behaviors in conjunction with the use of aversive techniques will be a recurrent theme in this chapter.*

Although the negative side effects of the application of aversive stimuli have rightly been emphasized, more positive effects have also been observed. Some investigators have noted that as the target maladaptive behavior decreases, other maladaptive behaviors also decrease and more appropriate behaviors increase. This has been noted in both psychotic children [53, 128] and voluntary adult patients [15].

Clinical Applications
The clinical application of aversive procedures will be discussed separately for each of the major behavioral problems for which such treatment has been used and seems to be indicated.

Alcohol and Drug Abuse
Although aversive procedures of some kind play an important role in the treatment of alcoholism and drug abuse, it is becoming accepted that the most successful programs are comprehensive in scope and attempt to achieve three goals [120]: (1) To decrease the immediate reinforcing properties of alcohol or drug ingestion; (2) to teach the client alternative behaviors incompatible with alcohol or drug abuse, such as appropriate social skills; and (3) to rearrange the client's environment to facilitate a nonsubstance abuse life-style (see refs. [77, 119, 139, 140] and Chapter 9). Aversion procedures are relevant to the first goal, and each of the major aversive stimuli—chemical, electrical, and verbal—as well as time-out and response cost, have been used to treat alcohol or drug abuse.

CHEMICAL AVERSION. The most extensive application has been that of Voegtlin and his colleagues [152], who treated more than 4,000 cases of alcoholism at the Shadel Sanitorium in Seattle using emetic drugs as the aversive stimulus in a punishment paradigm with the usual classic fear-conditioning aspects present. Although apomorphine was employed with early cases, emetine was later used to avoid the sedative effect of apomorphine, which was hypothesized to interfere with conditioning.

In the typical procedure [92] the patient was instructed that liquor is intrinsically obnoxious to the body and that the injections to be given were to *sensitize* the nervous system so that the true obnoxious characteristics of liquor would be more apparent. Patients were also told that after treatment they must *never* taste or experiment with liquor. Just before nausea and vomiting occurred, the patient was asked to take a glass containing one ounce of whiskey and to smell, taste, and swallow it. He was encouraged to swirl the liquor around in his mouth in order to appreciate fully the gustatory sensations. Two or three trials were held per session, and each session lasted about 45 minutes, usually being carried out on alternate days. The average number of sessions was four to six, so that the course of therapy lasted about 10 days. Counseling and practical advice on work and family stresses were also offered.

Lemere and Voegtlin [91] obtained follow-up data on 4,096 of their patients, with some patients followed for 10 to 13 years after treatment. One year after treatment, a remarkable rate of 60 percent total abstinence was found. Over the 13-year period, 50 percent of those treated were totally abstinent, including patients who relapsed but who were then successfully retreated. The abstinence rate was significantly improved by booster sessions following treatment. Patients who received two or more booster sessions during the year after initial treatment had a greatly improved chance of remaining abstinent for the full year [152]. Ninety-five percent of 84 patients remained abstinent, whereas the abstinence of a comparable group of 88 patients who did not receive booster sessions was 73 percent. Weins, Montague, Monaugh, and English [156] have reported a very close replication of these results, noting 63 percent of 261 patients abstinent after one year. Eight percent of the patients could not be contacted and were included in the failures.

This procedure has also been applied within a group therapy context, where it was found that the gagging and retching of one member of the group facilitated nausea and vomiting by other members whether they received an emetic or simply a placebo. Using this technique, Miller, Dvorak, and Turner [117] found 18 of 20 patients abstinent at eight-month follow-up. With a similar procedure, Zvonikov [168] reported 66.5 percent total abstinence one year after treatment and claimed that his results were the best obtained in Russia to that date.

These are high rates of success. It is possible that group procedures facilitate conditioning, both by reinforcing participation in therapy and by acting as an incentive to remain sober after treatment, as is the case with Alcoholics Anonymous groups. Furthermore, when therapy takes place in a group setting, it is possible that aversion is learned not only to the narrow stimulus situation consisting of a glass of whiskey but also to the social setting in which others are drinking. Since much drinking occurs in social situations, this learning may transfer more easily to the environment. Successful use of chemical aversion has also been reported in case studies of drug addiction [94, 127].

The importance of a comprehensive program is underlined when one examines the social and environmental factors that predict treatment success in aversion therapy. In Lemere and Voegtlin's extensive series, 71 percent of patients with stable employment records remained abstinent, while the rate for those who were unemployed or only sporadically employed was 21 percent. Abstinence, however, did not vary with the type of work. Of those patients who formed new friendships by joining abstinence clubs, 87 percent remained abstinent. On the other hand, continued association with "drinking buddies" was a major cause of relapse. This point is dramatically illustrated in several reports of patients who would force down the first several drinks despite the presence of nausea or even vomiting. For these patients the reinforcing value of relief from life stresses was prepotent over a conditioned aversion to alcohol.

A second chemical aversive stimulus is succinylcholine. Overall, the results of this stimulus have been disappointing with alcoholics [35, 55]. However, with heroin addiction, Thomason and Rathod [147] report a procedure in which the addict prepares a "fix" and as he is about to "shoot up" he receives injected succinylcholine. On the basis of urine analysis, 8 of 10 patients were drug-free up to five months later. Although no control group was available, it is interesting to note that this procedure, consisting of injection of a "drug," is in the same sensory modality and indeed is very close in form to the undesired behavior. While patients must obviously be highly motivated, the procedure deserves further investigation. Success with this procedure has also been reported in a case of long-standing severe addiction to hydrocarbon inhalation in which covert sensitization had failed [22].

ELECTRICAL AVERSION. This aversive stimulus was first used in 1928 by Kantorovich [80] who treated 20 alcoholics in a punishment paradigm for 5 to 20 sessions. Seventeen of the 20 patients acquired stable aversion reactions to alcohol. After a follow-up ranging from three weeks to 20 months, 14 (70 percent) of the treatment group remained abstinent. On the other hand, seven out of a control group of 10 patients receiving hypnotic suggestion or medication reverted to their drinking pattern a few days after release from hospital. With the development of more sophisticated measures, the results of electrical aversion have been less encouraging, abstinence rates seldom exceeding 50 percent for short follow-up periods and often being zero [21, 42, 70, 76, 100, 121, 160]. In a well-controlled study, Miller, Hersen, Eisler, and Hemphill [122] found that electrical aversion and a placebo treatment both reduced drinking by 36 percent and they concluded that all results were due to placebo effects.

The development of seminaturalistic living environments where the drinking behavior of alcoholics can be studied has permitted a closer look at the effects of aversion on drinking [42, 160, 161]. The most interesting finding to emerge is that the success of treatment is related more closely to the length of time that the contingencies remain in effect in the patient's environment, rather than to the type of aversive stimulus or paradigm used. Thus, Wilson and Tracey [161] punished drinking whenever alcohol was available, instead of the more usual frequency of one or two half-hour sessions per day [42]. Shock was administered either by the therapist or by the patient himself, with little difference in effect. The authors concluded that results of aversion are meaningful only if the contingencies remain in effect. This point will be raised again below.

A few case studies have examined the effects of electrical aversion on drug addiction [93, 166]. In light of Wilson and Tracey's study, Wolpe's procedure [166] is relevant, since the addict carried a portable shocker with him. In an interesting variation, Blackly [20] treated the well-known tendency of drug addicts to continue injecting themselves with nondrug solutions after stopping drug use. Presumably, this tendency is attributable to the conditioned reinforcing properties the injecting ritual acquires after repeated association with heroin. Blackly's method consisted of a patient's beginning to inject himself in front of a group of addicts but receiving a shock from an "electric needle" upon contact. Injection compulsion reportedly decreases with this procedure.

COVERT SENSITIZATION. Covert sensitization is the third major stimulus used in the aversion therapy of alcoholism and drug abuse. Typically, scenes leading up to drinking for alcoholics are vividly described. There are detailed descriptions of events or thoughts leading to drinking, details of the setting in which drinking occurs, and descriptions of drinking companions and of the typical beverages imbibed. At every approach point aversive scenes are introduced, so that aversion is connected not only with the actual drinking but with all aspects of behavior leading up to drinking (e.g., walking into the bar, sitting down, ordering a drink). Alternated randomly are scenes where the patient begins the chain of behavior but decides to avoid it and feels relieved and relaxed for having done so. Ten to 20 scenes are presented during each session, and Cautela [32] recommends biweekly sessions for several months. Emphasis is placed on the use of the procedure to strengthen self-control; thus, patients are instructed to practice their scenes between sessions and to use them to dampen any urges to drink that might occur.

Miller [118] combined hypnosis with aversive scenes that sometimes produced vomiting in the office. In some cases only one session was administered. He reports 93 percent of 24 patients completely abstinent at nine-month follow-up. In the one controlled study testing the effects of covert sensitization in the treatment of alcoholism, Ashem and Donner [4] administered six sessions of covert sensitization, in which a total of 35 scenes were presented. At six-month follow-up, 6 out of 15, or 40 percent, of the treated subjects were abstinent, while none of eight no-contact control subjects was abstinent. The findings indicate a clear effect from treatment, but the percentage remaining abstinent is modest. Covert sensitization has also been reported successful with individual cases of alcoholism [32, 42] and with heroin addicts [125, 164].

Electric shock to images of drinking was recently compared with the usual covert sensitization procedure, each administered twice a day [161]. There was little difference in effectiveness but a clear preference for the less aversive covert sensitization was demonstrated by a much higher dropout rate from the shock condition. However, the results were not clinically impressive in either condition. Drinking in this analogue situation was suppressed far less than with a shock procedure in a punishment paradigm that was in effect at all times drinking was available.

TIME-OUT. In light of these findings, one of the more exciting developments in recent years is the introduction of mildly aversive procedures into patients' environment as part of a comprehensive program. Thus, Bigelow, Liebson, and Griffiths [18] imposed a 15-minute physical and social isolation on alcoholics in an analogue setting in a hospital and reduced drinking by 50 percent over baseline. Hunt and Azrin [77] instructed relatives and friends to provide social interaction and activities *only* during periods of sobriety. Any evidence of intoxication resulted in a temporary loss of these reinforcers (time-out from positive reinforcement). This procedure was part of a comprehensive program meeting all three treatment goals mentioned above: the treatment group significantly exceeded the performance of a control group receiving usual hospital care on a number of drug, social, and work variables.

Miller [119], in a very clever study, devised a program for the most difficult population of all, the chronic public drunk. Required goods and services (e.g., meals, clothing, cigarettes, and shelter) provided by charitable agencies were suspended for five days contingent on drinking as assessed by random breath-analyzer tests and direct observation. A group of 10 alcoholics in this condition was compared with a control group of 10 that continued to receive these services noncontingently. The number of arrests dropped from a mean of 1.70 in the two months preceding treatment to 0.30 in the two months following treatment. No change was noted in the control group. The number of days employed also rose for the treatment group, but not for the control group. Blood alcohol levels decreased considerably in the treatment group. The limitation of a two-month follow-up makes replication important.

Little work has been reported with drug addicts, but along the same lines Boudin [24] successfully employed a contingency-contracting procedure, in which $50 of a black amphetamine addict's money held in an account was forwarded to the Ku Klux Klan, contingent on drug taking. This response cost procedure was highly aversive to the patient, who remained drug-free for 15 months.

Implications of Data

Because of the low remission rate of alcoholism, percentage of success, when described in a firm and verifiable manner such as total abstinence, can be meaningful. This is further buttressed by the few reports of "spontaneous" abstinence in untreated alcoholics over a period of time. Of 62 untreated alcoholics followed for a mean of 6.7 years by Kendell and Staton [84], only one became abstinent. Thus, the 60 percent one-year abstinence rate reported by Lemere and Voegtlin [91] and by Wiens, Montague, Manaugh, and English [156] with chemical aversion and the higher rate (95 percent) reported when patients participated in two or more booster sessions are impressive.

A review of the experimental and clinical evidence thus far indicates that nausea induced by chemical aversion and perhaps by covert sensitization (this awaits further inquiry) is the more effective stimulus if one is treating alcoholism in a time-limited manner; for example, one or two sessions a day. Although considerably less evidence is available for drug addicts, the best reported results are with succinylcholine [22, 147], which, despite its extreme aversiveness, cannot be ruled out for the drug addict willing to undergo the procedure. The similarity between the treatments is that they are in the same sensory modality as the undesired behavior and thus follow the hypothetical guidelines on the "biologically appropriate stimuli" discussed above. Elkins [50] suggests combining chemical aversion and images of nausea in a covert sensitization paradigm. Conditioned aversion established in the biologically appropriate sensory modality may facilitate the self-use of this treatment in highly motivated patients after termination of treatment. There is little or no evidence for the utility of electric shock used in this manner. An extension of aversive contingencies into the patient's natural environment [77, 119] would seem proper and useful. Obviously, a combination of the two procedures might be superior to either one administered independently.

Finally, the relationship between the use of the drug Antabuse and aversion therapy must be considered in the treatment of alcoholism. Theoretically, Antabuse is an aversion treatment, since drinking is suppressed by the threat of the nausea, vomiting, and vasodilation that occurs when even a small amount of alcohol is consumed. The major differences between aversion therapy and treatment by Antabuse, however, lie in the attitude of the patient. After successful aversion therapy, the patient is no longer attracted to alcohol, although some weak temptations may arise and become progressively stronger if no booster sessions are used. If aversive procedures are extended to the natural environment, urges to drink are presumably weakened more permanently. With Antabuse treatment alcohol is just as attractive to the patient, who is simply restrained from drinking by the threat of the Antabuse reaction. Thus, aversion therapy and Antabuse might be effectively combined so that the attractiveness of alcohol would be neutralized by aversion therapy, and any weak temptation that arose would be suppressed by the feared effects of Antabuse. Under this condition, patients might be more disposed to continue taking Antabuse.

Sexual Deviation
As in the treatment of alcohol and drug abuse, there is a growing realization that the use of aversive procedures must be part of a comprehensive treatment package for sexual deviation. There are at least four possible treatment goals for sexual deviation: (1) reducing deviant arousal, (2) increasing heterosexual arousal, (3) increasing heterosexual social skills, and (4) modifying gender role deviation or the degree to which one maladaptively identifies with the opposite sex [11, 12, 159]. In fact, several recent reports have indicated that increasing heterosexual arousal alone results in less deviant arousal in some cases, thereby avoiding the unpleasantness of

aversion [13]. Yet, as Davison and Wilson [45] point out, after sampling opinions from members of behavior therapy associations, aversion therapy is viewed as the treatment of choice for sexual deviation.

Several clinical trials illustrate the importance of a comprehensive treatment package. Feldman and MacCulloch [57], in their well-known study of aversion therapy for homosexuality, found prior or current heterosexual experience, or both, to be one of the best predictors of successful treatment, a finding also reported by Bancroft [7]. In a later important study, Bancroft [8] found that suppression of deviant arousal by electrical aversion was not related to later therapeutic success. Increases in heterosexual arousal during treatment were the only important predictors of success. Paradoxically, aversion therapy is sometimes seen to increase heterosexual arousal, although there is no obvious reason why this should happen [8, 12, 143]. Marks, Gelder, and Bancroft [105] noted that simple transvestism without accompanying gender role problems responded well to aversion therapy alone, but in patients with gender role deviations aversion was ineffective (see below).

Nevertheless, aversion procedures are likely to remain an important component of an overall treatment package based on a thorough behavioral analysis. It is, therefore, heartening that some aversive procedures seem effective and that what is perhaps the least aversive of all treatments, covert sensitization, may be the most effective. With sexual deviation (as with alcoholism and drug abuse) chemical, electrical, and verbal aversive stimuli have been used. Unlike substance abuse, however, the most popular and seemingly most effective stimuli are electrical and verbal rather than chemical.

HOMOSEXUALITY. Although some therapists question whether homosexuals should be treated at all [44] and most are screening requests very carefully, many people with homosexual arousal patterns decide that they wish to decrease the strength of their arousal. But the effects of treatment for homosexual patterns are not overwhelmingly convincing. The extensive series of homosexuals treated by Freund [65] with chemical aversion in Czechoslovakia aroused interest in the application of aversive techniques to this population despite the relatively poor results obtained (40 percent heterosexual after treatment, dropping to 25 percent after three years).

Since that report, several series of cases and some controlled research have been reported on the application of aversive techniques to homosexuality. Feldman and MacCulloch [56] administered electric shock in an avoidance conditioning paradigm in which patients could avoid some of the shocks by switching off a homosexual slide. In addition, an attempt was made to increase heterosexual responsiveness by flashing on a slide of a female when shock was turned off in an aversion relief paradigm. The results demonstrated that 58 percent of 43 homosexuals were exclusively heterosexual at the end of treatment and remained that way for at least one year. In the most ambitious study on aversion therapy to date, Feldman and MacCulloch [57] compared an avoidance paradigm with classic conditioning and found no difference, with approximately 60 percent success in both paradigms. Since the avoidance paradigm contains classic conditioning features (that is, a pairing of shock with the sexually deviant stimulus, with no response required on the part of the patient), it seems likely that the classic conditioning component is responsible for success. These two treatments were superior to a third condition consisting of psychotherapy, after which treatment only 20 percent of homosexuals changed their sexual preference. Feldman and MacCulloch also looked for predictors of success in their treatment. In addition to heterosexual experiences, described above, youth (below age 30) and absence of other behavior problems predicted positive outcome.

More recent results with electrical aversion have been less encouraging. In a pilot study with 10 homosexuals, Bancroft [7] made shock contingent upon penile erection to homosexual slides in a punishment paradigm. Three of the patients were also shocked for homosexual fantasies. Seven patients showed changes in sexual interest as measured by an attitude scale, but only three maintained their gains over one to three years. In a later study of methods to increase heterosexual responsiveness, Bancroft [8] compared the effects of electrical aversion administered to 15 homosexuals with those of systematic desensitization in a second group of 15. In the aversion group only five were rated as improved at a follow-up ranging from one year to three years later, but it is interesting to note that the one factor predicting success at six-month follow-up was the occurrence of, or increase in, heterosexual arousal during electrical aversive treatment, rather than a decrease in homosexual arousal. This "paradoxical" effect of aversion in sexual deviation has now been replicated in laboratories around the world [12, 27].

Birk, Huddleston, Miller, and Cohler [19] treated eight homosexuals with a combination of electrical aversion and group therapy aimed at increasing heterosexual social responsiveness. They found this treatment clearly superior to a no-treatment control, with five patients much improved after treatment. After two years, however, only two patients remained exclusively heterosexual. Three relapsed as a result of an "inability to establish a good object relationship with a woman."

In a series of studies, McConaghy [109–112] has examined the effects of aversive therapy in some detail. Although McConaghy [109] found no difference between chemical and electrical aversion, both groups did better than a control group, based on reports of deviant sexual behavior. However, the improvement rate was only 33 percent. McConaghy and Barr [112] compared aversion delivered in a classic conditioning paradigm with an avoidance paradigm and backward conditioning. All groups improved, with 50 percent of the combined treatment group showing some improvement, and 25 percent substantial improvement.

In the best study to date from that laboratory, McConaghy [111] demonstrated electrical aversion to be superior to a positive conditioning treatment consisting of an attempt to condition sexual arousal classically to pictures of females. While the technique to increase heterosexual arousal can be faulted on procedural grounds (as the author points out), it makes for a good placebo conditon. Once again, aversion was superior at one-year follow-up based on reports of homosexual urges and behavior, with a percentage of success similar to that in McConaghy and Barr's study. Interestingly, aversion produced a trend of increased heterosexual arousal over and above the positive conditioning techniques. This study again demonstrates that aversion is effective, although the percentage of success is not remarkable.

Some other recent uncontrolled studies support these findings. Hallam and Rachman [69], in a paper orientated toward theory, reported four successes out of seven with electrical aversion in a follow-up of less than one year. Tanner [143, 144] applied electrical aversion exclusively, with modest success, but Canton-Dutari [31], using electrical aversion as part of an innovative treatment package, reports that 91 percent of 54 homosexuals could control homosexual arousal after treatment; 50 percent of those followed up were exclusively heterosexual after 3½ years.

Numerous case studies have recently been reported using covert sensitization to treat sexual deviation (cf. [26]). In one study of the mechanism of action of aversion therapy in homosexuality, Barlow, Leitenberg, and Agras [15] demonstrated that a verbal aversive stimulus was responsible for decreases in homosexual responsiveness. With single cases of homosexuality and pedophilia, respectively, a sequential experiment was carried out in which noxious scenes were paired with the homosexual scene in the first phase, the sexual scenes were presented alone in the second phase (while the patient was told to expect continued therapeutic improvement), and the noxious scenes were reinstated in the third phase. Despite positive expectations on the part of the patients throughout the experiment, homosexual responsiveness declined only during the pairing, indicating that this factor was responsible for improvement. In a replication and extension of this experiment, Barlow, Agras, Leitenberg, Callahan, and Moore [14] demonstrated that these changes occurred even if it was suggested that deviant arousal would increase during covert sensitization. In a well-controlled study, Callahan and Leitenberg [30] compared electrical aversion with covert sensitization in six sexual deviates. They found the treatments were roughly equal in suppression of penile erections, but covert sensitization was more successful at helping patients suppress homosexual urges. Since patients disliked shock, with some refusing subsequent sessions—a finding also noted with alcoholism [161]—the evidence appears to point to the superiority of covert sensitization in treating deviant arousal patterns. Nevertheless, it is seldom that any aversive technique can be used alone, since a functional analysis of other aspects of homosexuality may reveal more important target behaviors for treatment [12]. This probably accounts for the relatively modest percentages of success in studies concentrating solely on aversive treatment for homosexuality.

TRANSVESTISM, FETISHISM, AND SADOMASOCHISM. Numerous case studies point to the efficacy of treating these disorders with aversive procedures [104, 107]. Davison [43] used covert sensitization successfully to treat sadistic fantasies, and Marks, Rachman, and Gelder [106] treated a masochist with electrical aversion. Interestingly, masochism does not contraindicate the use of aversion, presumably because of the very specific nature of masochistic stimuli. There is no evidence of a generalized "love of pain."

The best paper to date on these disorders, in terms of information yielded, was published by Marks, Gelder, and Bancroft [105]. In their procedure the patient is treated intensively for two weeks and receives two one-hour aversion therapy sessions per day. The aversive stimulus is electric shock to the arm or leg. For the first few sessions the transvestite or fetishist is asked to imagine his cross-dressing or his fetishistic object. When the patient reports a clear image of this fantasy by raising his finger, one or two shocks are delivered to suppress the images. The patient is told that the purpose of the procedure is to ensure that the fantasies are not pleasurable. Next, the patient is asked to carry out the deviant behavior, that is, a transvestite would begin to cross-dress. At variable intervals a warning signal is given followed by one to three shocks that stop when the clothes are removed. Sometimes the patient can avoid shock completely by undressing quickly. For several months thereafter, booster sessions are held at gradually increasing intervals (from weekly to monthly). In the series described by Marks and his colleagues [105], 12 transvestites and fetishists, five sadomasochists, and seven transsexuals were treated. At the end of treatment 16 of the 17 transvestites, fetishists, and sadomasochists, but no transsexuals, were greatly improved. Two years later, 13 remained greatly improved. A small untreated group of transvestites showed considerably less improvement. Similar results with sadistic and transvestite behavior were reported in an experiment by Brownell and Barlow [27].

The failure of aversion in transsexuals with multiple problems is consistent with the need for a comprehensive experimental analysis of the problem [12]. In one reported success in the treatment of transsexualism [16], aversion for deviant arousal was effective only after multiple other aspects of the patient's disorder were treated.

EXHIBITIONISM. Evans [54] reported the use of an avoidance paradigm in a series of 10 patients who had been exhibiting themselves an average of 2.5 times per month. Cards with printed words on them signaling either an aspect of the patient's exhibitionistic behavior or normal sexual activities were randomly projected on a screen, and the patient was instructed to imagine the behavior being cued. During each session, 20 exhibitionistic words and 40 "normal" words were shown. Each exhibitionistic word was followed by a shock that the patient could avoid by quickly advancing to the next slide. One session was administered each week for 20 weeks followed by one session every two weeks for two months, and finally one session a month. By the end of six months all the patients had reported a cessation of urges to exhibit as well as any exhibitionistic behavior. These encouraging results with exhibitionists have been replicated in a number of case studies and, more recently, in an extended series of cases. Maletzky [101] treated 10 exhibitionists with "assisted" covert sensitization (aversive images combined with noxious odors). All aspects of exhibitionism, including fantasies, had been eliminated in all 10 patients at one-year follow-up as determined by reports, checks with relatives and friends, and client records. Rooth and Marks [129] treated severe exhibitionists with electrical aversion and self-control procedures. Although four patients experienced some relapses and reexposed themselves, all were much improved at one year and continued to receive booster sessions.

Finally, in a remarkable series, Wickramasekera [155], employing a procedure called aversive behavior rehearsal, previously described by Serber [138] and by Stevenson and Jones [142], reports success with a series of 20 exhibitionists. In this procedure the patient exposes himself and is encouraged to verbalize his fantasies and follow his usual behavior in front of a small group of four or five women for about 20 minutes; later he may be shown a videotape of the procedure. The women either react neutrally or ask clinical questions (e.g., "Why are you doing this?"). Wickramasekera notes that this is extremely aversive to the patient and may be contraindicated for anyone physically susceptible to acute stress. If patients refuse to go through with the treatment they may choose a less aversive procedure, in which they watch a videotape of someone else exposing himself. Up to four sessions have been administered, but usually one session is sufficient. In follow-ups at three months to seven years, no patient has exhibited himself and all are reported well. In view of the reported aversiveness of this procedure and the seeming effectiveness of covert sensitization, a logical sequence of treatment might be covert sensitization followed by aversive behavior rehearsal, if covert sensitization alone is ineffective.

Implications of Data

A number of general procedural points concerning the treatment of sexual deviates with aversion therapy should be noted. Sexual deviation consists of a chain of behaviors culminating in the sexual act. It was noted earlier that Marks, Gelder, and Bancroft [105] treated both fantasies and behavior, thereby pairing aversion with several aspects of the chain of events leading to the sexually deviant act. Evans [54] also apparently shocked fantasies of each event in the deviant chain. This may be particularly important in light of recent data from our laboratory indicating that behavior early in the homosexual chain, such as meeting and gaining consent from a prospective partner while cruising, is *more* pleasurable than engaging in sex. This may account for the oft-noted promiscuity of some homosexuals who seek out several different partners a night rather than remain with the first partner.

Generally, the results of aversive procedures with sexual deviation, particularly when included in a comprehensive treatment package, are more encouraging than results obtained with alcoholics. Although there have been no experimental attempts to extend aversive contingencies into the natural environment, as with alcoholics (e.g., [119]), a reasonable percentage of success is still obtained. Few properly controlled studies have been done; nevertheless, aversive procedures seem most effective in "simple" cases of excess arousal, where alternative social and sexual behaviors are firmly in place. Results are less encouraging with homosexuality and still less encouraging with transsexualism, conditions where increasing degrees of complexity require multifaceted intervention.

In both direct [30] and indirect comparisons [54, 101], covert sensitization seems at least as effective as electrical aversion and should thus be used pending evidence to the contrary. However, in refractory cases, aversive procedures applied in settings more closely approximating the real world [105, 155] and employing naturally occurring aversive consequences similar to the biologically appropriate aversive stimuli used in alcoholism might be more effective. Wickramasekera's procedure [155] accomplishes both of these goals. But covert sensitization is a particularly flexible method for presenting personalized aversive consequences (being discovered by family, authorities, etc.), if only in imagination, which may account for much of its success.

Other Consummatory Behaviors

CIGARETTE SMOKING. The uncontrolled results of aversive treatment for cigarette smoking appear encouraging, since smoking rates decline substantially. However, placebo controls also substantially reduce smoking, suggesting that factors other than aversive control are at play. Furthermore, the attained reduction is short-lived. One reason for this may be the ubiquity and high frequency of smoking. Since smoking is associated with an infinite variety of activities during a typical day, cues that prompt smoking are numerous as contrasted with sexual deviation, where the behavior occurs infrequently and in specific circumstances. Additionally, a smoker is not usually overwhelmed by the urge for a single cigarette, making smoking subject to self-control for periods of days and giving many smokers the illusion that they can stop any time they desire. However, since smokers cannot avoid, and are constantly confronted with, situations where smoking frequently occurs, the probability of relapse is high (see ref. [78]).

In several studies [86, 90, 123, 141, 153, 154], groups receiving electrical or verbal aversion, administered either by themselves or by therapists, have been compared with groups receiving other treatments or attention placebo. No differences have been found. In some cases there were slight advantages to groups receiving covert sensitization [154] or electrical aversion [141] rather than placebo shortly after treatment, but nonspecific factors clearly accounted for most of the change [113]. This finding was replicated in a large-scale study comparing the effects of electrical aversion on heavy smoking with several placebo conditions [130]. In view of these data, the recent results obtained by Dericco, Brigham, and Garlington [47] are surprising, since electrical aversion alone completely suppressed smoking in eight subjects and no relapses had occurred at six-month follow-up. Using a multiple baseline across subjects design, the effect of nonspecific factors was ruled out. The authors note that, unlike the procedure in previous studies, shock was continued until total suppression was achieved after 20 sessions or more. Further, shock was more intense than in previous studies, and subjects received several sessions after they had stopped smoking.

Elliott and Tighe [52] reported an interesting technique based on response cost, in which a sizable amount of money ($65) was placed in escrow, portions being paid back as the smoker completed various periods of abstinence. With this regimen, 94 percent of 25 subjects remained abstinent. Fifteen to 17 months after treatment, five of the 11 patients in the group being followed were still abstinent. Unfortunately, no control group was provided. Using a similar contingency-contracting procedure to ensure attendance at sessions, Chapman, Smith, and Layden [34] obtained 55 percent abstinence at one-year follow-up combining electrical aversion with self-control procedures. In most cases smoking was eliminated during treatment sessions. The therapist closely monitored results for 11 weeks after treatment and offered booster sessions during follow-up. Close monitoring by the therapist and the contingency-contracting to ensure attendance at treatment sessions were undoubtedly contributory; but, as in the study by Dericco, Brigham, and Garlington [47], the amount and intensity of electrical aversion were greater than in other studies.

What seems to be the most promising aversive technique for smoking was first suggested by Wilde [157]. In this treatment hot, smoky air is blown into the patient's face as the patient smokes cigarettes at a much higher frequency than normal. This stimulus has the possible advantage of sharing the same sensory modality as the undesired behavior and magnifies some of the mildly aversive properties that are naturally present in the smoker's environment. A similar technique has been used on a large series of smokers by Lublin and Joslyn [99] and by Lichtenstein [95]. Lublin's apparatus consisted of a pistol-type hair dryer enclosed in a box with a lighted cigarette burning near the air intake. While the smokers puffed on a cigarette every three seconds, as cued by a metronome, the blower was turned on until the situation was intolerable. At this point the smoker would extinguish the cigarette, and a fan would then blow a refreshing stream of mentholated or pine-scented air toward the patient. The patient was asked to pick up a cigarette as soon as possible after the trial (usually half an hour) and repeat the procedure.

Two major studies attest to the effectiveness of this procedure [96, 135]. In one of these [135], subjects followed the standard procedure of inhaling every six seconds until they could no longer tolerate further smoke inhalation. As soon as the subject could inhale once again, another trial was begun. Trials were continued until the subject reported that smoking produced dizziness, nausea, or choking. This procedure was administered initially for three consecutive days, and "impromptu" sessions were held at less frequent intervals until smoking was eliminated, averaging seven sessions for each subject. A contingency-contracting procedure similar to that used by Chapman, Smith, and Layden [34] encouraged completion of treatment.

There were three treatment regimens—rapid smoking alone; warm, smoky air blown in the subject's face alone; and a combination of the two—and they did not differ from each other in their effectiveness, producing 60 percent abstinence at six-month follow-up. A well-constructed placebo condition also reduced smoking after treatment, but this group had largely relapsed at follow-up. Significantly, the therapist continued to monitor progress periodically by telephone during follow-up. While this procedure obviously did not help the control group, it may have contributed to the successful maintenance in the treatment groups.

It is encouraging that any treatment is successful with such a difficult and dangerous problem as smoking. This is particularly so since the major difficulty is maintenance of gains, almost any procedure being able initially to eliminate smoking. Nevertheless, with proper maintenance procedures, such as a contracting procedure or frequent contact during the critical three months after stopping, both shock and rapid smoking seem effective, with rapid smoking having the strongest empiric support at this time. Rapid smoking, of course, provides an aversive stimulus in exactly the same sensory modality as that provided by normal cigarette smoking, thus building it on the naturally occurring aversive consequences that all smokers occasionally experience. But both treatments are extremely aversive. It seems that shock must be used for long periods at high intensity to effect change, and rapid smoking raises heart rate and blood carboxyhemoglobin [46, 72]. Although Danaher, Lichtenstein, and Sullivan [40] report that the effects are not dangerous to healthy young adults, careful screening for cardiovascular and respiratory diseases should be undertaken before administering the rapid smoking procedure.

Many research reports on smoking have administered very few treatment sessions, often as few as one or two, and seldom more than 10. Prevention of relapse may depend on the consistent administration of treatment sessions beyond the point where the smoker stops smoking. More prolonged treatment and the combination of aversive techniques such as use of hot, smoky air with behavioral contracts that set up both negative and positive consequences for smoking in the natural environment, in the manner of Elliott and Tighe [52], might well lead to greater success in the treatment of this condition.

OVEREATING. Overeating presents an even more difficult problem than smoking if one is considering the exclusive use of aversive techniques, since occasions for eating are almost as numerous as those for smoking, and the goal of treatment is to reduce, not eliminate, eating. Like smoking, overeating has, on occasion, been successfully treated by a number of procedures, suggesting once again that placebo factors and "will power" or, more accurately, self-control techniques may play a significant role. Although a few case studies report successful use of aversive techniques [32, 115], most recent controlled studies, usually testing covert sensitization, failed to discover any significant benefit when compared with control groups [48, 51, 59, 79].

Clinicians who have treated severe cases of obesity in a hospital setting have often observed a complete loss of appetite by the patient and a concomitant loss of weight. Usually, however, weight is quickly regained when the patient leaves hospital. This phenomenon may be an example of Schachter's [134] findings that environmental cues, such as the sight of tempting food or situations in which eating formerly occurred, determine eating in the obese. In treating obesity, therefore, it is imperative to take the treatment to the environment by developing self-control. The most promising programs are those that involve a total package of self-control procedures (see Chapter 9, page 255). Within the package aversive procedures may play a role if particular foods are difficult to resist for individual patients. Administration of covert sensitization [31] or noxious odors [3, 60] would seem particularly appropriate. More powerful contingencies within the environment, such as a response-cost procedure, in which the patient deposits money that is then sent to a disliked charity contingent on weight gain or failure to lose weight, may also be a useful adjunct [102, 103].

Self-Injurious Behavior
One of the most dramatic results of aversive techniques is in their application to the self-injurious behavior of mentally retarded or psychotic children. As already noted in Chapters 3 and 4, reinforcement and extinction procedures may not be sufficient to eliminate problems of this type. In an early example of the use of time-out, Wolf, Risley, and Mees [165] treated head banging, face slapping, self-scratching, and hair pulling in a 3½-year-old child. These behaviors occurred in high-frequency tantrums, causing the child to be bruised and bleeding. Sedation, tranquilizers, and

restraints had been tried without success. The attendants were instructed to put the child in an isolation room when two or more of these behaviors occurred simultaneously until the behavior ceased. Later, a minimum time of 10 minutes in isolation was established. Self-destructive behavior steadily diminished in severity and was eliminated after four months. A six-month follow-up revealed no tantrums at home.

In another example of the application of aversive procedures to self-destructive behavior, Lovaas and Simmons [98] described the case of a 16-year-old retarded girl with psychotic features who, when removed from restraints, would bite her hands severely (one finger had previously been amputated), remove her nails by their roots with her teeth, and bang her head (her scalp was covered with scar tissue as a result of this). A total of five one-second shocks contingent on these behaviors eliminated the problem. However, generalization to other situations is not always complete, and the patient may have to be shocked in other situations; however, if the command "No" is paired with the shock, then the word itself often becomes sufficient to suppress further behavior. A remarkably consistent finding in cases of this nature is the appearance of more desirable behavior, such as smiling, playing, and not avoiding adults after the elimination of self-destructive behavior.

Tate and Baroff [146] described a case where both time-out and shock were successfully used to suppress different self-destructive behaviors. The patient was a blind, mentally retarded nine-year-old boy whose self-injurious behavior began at age four and consisted of slapping or punching his face and head, hitting his head on floors and other hard objects, butting his shoulder with his chin, and kicking himself. These behaviors were severe enough to have resulted in detached retinas. When left free the patient hit himself about twice a minute; thus, most of the time he was restrained in bed. It was also noted that physical contact seemed quite pleasurable to him. During daily 20-minute sessions, two therapists walked with the patient, each holding one hand, allowing chin-to-shoulder hits that were ignored. After five sessions, the therapists withdrew their hands whenever he hit himself. Hits were reduced from six per minute to zero. During a five-session control period, when physical contact was not withdrawn, hits returned, only to be suppressed again by reinstatement of the punishment procedure. This suggests that the punishment procedure was responsible for the declines in this behavior.

The procedure described above could not be used with head banging, since it would take too long, possibly endangering the child. Thus, the child was instructed that if he continued to hit himself he would be shocked and that the shock would hurt. Self-injurious behavior was then punished by a portable shocker, which quickly decreased the behavior. The patient was allowed freedom for increasing periods of time and was given attention by the attendant when he did not hurt himself. Punishment was continued, and after six months no self-injurious behavior had occurred for 20 days. In addition, appropriate social behavior and smiling emerged, and recreational activities and occupational therapy became possible.

Similarly successful case studies have been reported by Corte, Wolf and Locke [37], who suppressed eye poking and hair pulling, among other behaviors, in a 14-year-old male, and by Scholander [136], who suppressed a choking response in a 14-year-old male. Merbaum [114] eliminated severe self-slapping in a psychotic boy in two hours. These and other cases (e.g., [145]) demonstrate clear and immediate effects of shock. To test the necessity of arranging shock in a contingent fashion, Wincze and Bachman [162] conducted a series of single-case experiments in two self-injurious retarded adults and found that although noncontingent shock somewhat reduced this behavior, contingent shock was superior. A recent case of severe self-destructive behavior suppressed by covert sensitization [33] also should encourage investigation of this procedure, although it would not seem applicable to severely retarded or psychotic populations. Finally, Harris and Romanczyk [71] described successful application of overcorrection to head banging and suggested it as a possible alternative to shock in severe cases.

Lang and Melamed [89] described a dramatic study of a nine-month-old infant who began vomiting at the age of five months following meals. The vomiting and rumination had worsened so that food was regurgitated within 10 to 15 minutes, and small amounts were brought up continually. All medical and dietary approaches had failed, and the child's life was considered in danger. Sessions were held immediately after eating and lasted about one hour. Electromyogram recordings and observation determined the beginning of regurgitation. Shock was administered through electrodes placed on the infant's calf until vomiting stopped. The infant reacted to the shock by crying or cessation of vomiting. After two sessions very few shocks were needed. By the sixth session vomiting was eliminated during the sessions. Sessions were held at different times of day and under different conditions, such as while the infant was lying in bed or being held, to ensure transfer of effects. Several days after the sessions were discontinued, a brief relapse occurred, and treatment was resumed for three more sessions. Other more normal social behaviors increased along with weight, and a one-year follow-up revealed a perfectly healthy child.

This case study has been replicated in equally dramatic fashion by the use of shock by Kohlenberg [87] with a 21-year-old retarded female; by Toister, Condron, Worley, and Arthur [148] with a 7½-month-old infant; and by Cunningham and Linscheid [39] with a 9½-month-old infant, among others. In an innovative experimental case, Sajwaj, Libet, and Agras [132] eliminated ruminative vomiting in a seven-month-old infant with lemon juice. Noting that rumination was preceded by vigorous tongue movements, 5 to 10 cc of lemon juice was squirted into the infant's mouth as soon as tongue movements were detected. If rumination persisted after 60 seconds, lemon juice was reapplied. After 16 feedings, lemon juice was withdrawn for two feedings and then reintroduced. Rumination decreased, increased slightly during withdrawal of lemon juice, and decreased again when treatment was reinstituted. As in all the cases cited above, the harmful behavior showed no recurrence in follow-ups over several years.

The experimental manipulation reported in some of the studies mentioned [98, 132, 146, 162] demonstrates that the aversive stimulus is responsible for treatment success. The rapidity with which electric shock eliminates self-destructive behavior supports the use of this stimulus, since less aversive procedures may allow irrevocable injury to occur before the behavior is suppressed. However, at least in cases of infant rumination, lemon juice would seem a less aversive alternative.

Since most of the patients described in the preceding section and some of those to be described in the following section cannot voluntarily leave treatment, the aversive stimulus, particularly if it is shock, must be applied under carefully specified conditions. First, the inappropriate behavior must be clearly defined, so that the occasion for the aversive stimulus is clear; every occurrence of the behavior should be punished, and the procedure, if carried out by an aide or parent, should be closely supervised. If no improvement is noted after two or three sessions, the procedure should be reassessed, with changes in the aversive stimulus or termination of punishment as possible alternatives. It is also important to reinforce alternative behaviors during treatment to help ensure the continued absence of self-destructive behaviors, particularly if social attention maintained the self-destructive behavior in the first place.

Socially Disruptive Behavior

Most socially disruptive behavior referred for consultation occurs in nonvoluntary patients, such as psychotic adults or children. The referring agents are usually the nursing personnel on a psychiatric ward or the parents of an unruly child. By contrast, the socially disruptive behavior of nonpsychotic adults is usually handled through legal rather than medical channels. At least three procedures are frequently used: time-out, response cost, and overcorrection.

TIME-OUT. Tyler and Brown [151] reported the use of time-out procedures to control disruptive behaviors in 15 delinquent boys during recreational periods in a training school. Misbehavior around the pool table, such as throwing the balls, striking someone with the cues, or breaking the rules of the game, resulted in placement in isolation for 15 minutes. No warnings were given, and the procedure was carried out in a matter-of-fact way. Under these conditions disruptive behavior was nearly eliminated. To test if this procedure was, in fact, responsible for the success, it was removed, and the staff returned to their old methods of warning and reprimanding the boys contingent on disruptive behavior. The behavior quickly returned to a high rate. Reinstatement of the time-out condition reduced the behavior once again. Calhoun and Matherne [29] tested for schedule effects of time-out and found that contingent application after every wrong response was more effective than after every second or fifth response in an aggressive retarded female.

RESPONSE COST. Kazdin [81] has reviewed this area and notes several applications of the procedure to disruptive behavior. For example, Winkler [163], in the context of a token economy, successfully suppressed aggressive behavior and loud noises with a system of token fines. Most examples of this procedure occur in a token economy setting, where it is particularly convenient to apply. In a well-controlled single-case study, Burchard and Barrera [28] compared time-out and response cost in suppressing antisocial behavior in mildly retarded adolescents in a token economy. Although no differences were noted between the two procedures, higher levels of punishment (e.g., 30 tokens lost or 30 minutes of time-out) were more effective than five tokens or five minutes, and the suppressing effect of the greater punishment increased over time, while the lesser punishment decreased in effectiveness. The authors note that response cost, contrary to time-out, has the advantage of not removing the subject from the ongoing social situation, thus giving him more time to learn.

OVERCORRECTION. The overcorrection procedure described above has been applied to socially disruptive behaviors in a number of settings and to behavior problems such as physical assault, screaming, and biting in retarded and brain-damaged patients [61], and pica eating with copophragy (ingesting fecal material) [63]. In one interesting example, Azrin and Wesolowski [5] applied overcorrection to 34 institutionalized retarded residents who were stealing each other's food and clothing. Overcorrection involved not only returning the item but presenting the victim with one of the subject's own items. This procedure eliminated stealing.

As in the treatment of self-destructive behavior, the aversive stimuli are applied in the environment when the disruptive behavior occurs and initially they are successful only when in effect (i.e., removal of the stimulus leads to recovery of the disruptive behavior). To decrease disruptive behavior permanently, it is necessary to remove positive reinforcers that may have been maintaining the behavior, build up alternative behaviors during the time of behavioral suppression, or do both.

OTHER PROCEDURES. In the majority of cases, aversive techniques have been applied to adult disruptive behavior in institutionalized nonvoluntary patients. There are, however, some cases where patients have sought treatment to gain control of their disruptive behavior. Such an example was reported by Agras [1] in the case of a 25-year-old schizophrenic who was participating in a rehabilitation program but who suffered from occasional episodes of glass breaking that necessitated physical restraints and recommitment to a state hospital. Twenty series of contingent shocks eliminated the behavior.

In another example, Kellam [83] treated a 48-year-old housewife who was threatening suicide after her tenth apprehension for shoplifting over a 16-year period. There was no economic motive for her behavior, since she could readily buy any of the items. For five weeks the patient watched a film of herself entering a store, shoplifting, and being watched by disapproving faces. Shock was administered on an intermittent basis to coincide with the disapproving faces. At this point the patient reported a fear of shops and a sensation of being watched whenever she entered one. After three months she had not stolen again, but she reported several urges to steal, at which point faces would loom before her eyes and she would feel that everyone in the store was watching her. The urge then quickly disappeared. The aversive stimulus of social disapproval is a very appropriate one for shoplifting, since it is a natural consequence of the behavior in the environment. A similar case was recently treated with covert sensitization [68].

Aversive Procedures: An Overview
The preceding descriptions of behavior disorders in which aversive techniques have been used are by no means complete. Aversive therapies have also been used to treat speech dysfunctions such as stuttering [25, 58, 116], tics [167], and writer's cramp [97]. Others have applied the techniques to gambling [55], nail biting [41], and chronic cough [2]. Of particular interest is success in cases of repetitive disruptive thinking, such as suicidal thoughts [88] and hallucinations [74, 75].

Effectiveness Outside Treatment
In recent years it has become apparent that aversive control is far more effective if it is programmed into the environment [119, 161]. In these situations the aversive stimulus ideally is always contingent on the unwanted or disruptive behavior. As noted in the beginning of this chapter, this general approach is used by governments, however imperfectly, through systems of fines and imprisonments. But, much of the work in this chapter describes the application of aversive stimuli for only a few sessions, often in an outpatient setting. Suppression of behavior is expected to generalize to the rest of the client's life. One of the most puzzling aspects of aversive control is why it is effective outside the treatment situation where the aversive stimulus is no longer present.
  This problem, and the solutions that have been proposed, illustrate a case where evidence from animal experiments can be misleading when applied to human behavior. On the basis of work with animals, many in-

vestigators proposed that an avoidance paradigm should be employed in treatment, since this leads to greater resistance to extinction or, in other words, to longer-lasting effects. The notion here was that organisms would continue to avoid the stimulus or the undesired behavior long after learning trials were over because they would not test reality or take a chance on receiving shock by performing the undesired behavior. This does not apply, however, to patients in a therapeutic setting, who are well aware of the presence or absence of electrodes or emetic drugs. Thus, the active-learning paradigm in aversive control, as Rachman and Teasdale [126] note, seems most often to be punishment, classic fear conditioning, or, as is usually the case in therapeutic situations, a combination of the two. This conclusion leaves unanswered the question of permanency of effect.

How Aversion Works
But permanency of effect does not occur in all patients. A notable exception is in the case of nonvoluntary patients, for example, psychotic adults and children, where aversive control is not completely programmed into the environment. In several case studies involving this population, therapeutic effects did not generalize outside the treatment situation and therapy had to be reapplied in each new setting. However, voluntary patients, such as alcoholics or sexual deviates, often report transfer of therapeutic effects from the treatment setting to the environment, even after one session. At the basis of this theoretic issue is the question: Does aversive therapy produce an automatic conditioned response irrespective of the patient's motivation, or does a general attitude change account for improvement [64, 69]?

In some cases of alcoholism or sexual deviation, it seems that a conditioned fear response is acquired, in which a patient will not approach a drink or an attractive male even if he "wants to." Moreover, aversion often has a very specific effect (e.g., an alcoholic treated in an aversive paradigm for drinking whiskey will not drink whiskey but will drink beer), suggesting the presence of a conditioned response. However, most patients voluntarily undergoing treatment do not report this phenomenon. Most highly motivated patients report immediately after treatment some lessening of attraction for the stimulus or behavior, which they potentiate by cognitively rehearsing or "remembering and practicing" the aversive stimulus whenever they are in a "tempting" situation. The oft-noted quick extinction of an emotional or "automatic" response [64] and a considerable number of clinical observations [57] support this interpretation. Although controversy will exist until the research results are in, this reviewer would agree with Bandura [9] that time-limited aversive therapy with voluntary patients may temporarily devalue the behavior or stimulus, giving the highly motivated patient an opportunity to apply the contingencies in a "self-control" fashion through cognitive rehearsal.

The clinical implications of these notions are as follows: (1) It is desirable to program the aversive control into the natural environment, through contingency contracting if necessary; (2) a biologically appropriate or "prepared" aversive stimulus should be used if available, preferably one that is in the same sensory modality as the behavior, or that is a naturally occurring consequence of the behavior; (3) the patient should be taught to use the learned associations in a "self-control" fashion.

Concluding Considerations

The necessity of building up viable alternative behaviors has been stressed throughout this chapter. Whether these be new ways to deal with stress, new ways to achieve gratification, or positive reinforcement from the environment, evidence supporting the importance of this concept is found in both voluntary and nonvoluntary patients. The results of aversive therapy in alcoholism correlate directly with the presence of social and occupational skills. In homosexuality, results correlate directly with the presence of heterosexual responsiveness. Disruptive behavior in psychotic adults and children is more easily eliminated if alternative social behaviors are available. The implication is that aversive techniques should seldom be used in the absence of procedures designed to develop alternative behaviors.

Lastly, it should be noted that behavior usually occurs in a chain with a beginning and an end. Administering aversive techniques to the final behavior in the chain, such as sexual acts in homosexuality or tasting whiskey in alcoholism, and subsequent "cognitive rehearsal" of this step in a self-control fashion may not be adequate. As noted earlier, evidence from our research in homosexuality indicated that behavior early in the homosexual chain, such as meeting and gaining consent from a prospective partner while cruising, may be *more* pleasurable than engaging in sex. Similarly, drug addicts, when deprived of drugs, will sometimes inject themselves with tap water to derive the acquired pleasure from the act of injecting. If aversion is applied only to the end of the chain, then the performance of preliminary behavior outside treatment may set the occasion for recurrence of undesirable behavior. Some of the more successful aversive procedures (e.g., [104]) therefore include the administration of aversion to all aspects of behavior, including the initial fantasies or urges that presumably begin the chain.

Ethical Considerations

One cannot describe the use of aversive procedures without discussing the ethical context of their use. While most psychotherapists, particularly behavior therapists, have been grappling with the ethics of an increasingly effective technology of late (cf. [17] for a detailed discussion of this issue), the use of aversive procedures is particularly salient in the eyes of the public. Ethical issues are most important when severely painful stimuli are applied to nonvoluntary, institutionalized patients. In instances when relatively nonaversive procedures such as covert sensitization are applied to voluntary outpatients, ethical issues are less pressing. However, prompted by Burgess' nightmarish *A Clockwork Orange*, the public has been sensitized to accounts of inflicting pain on unsuspecting patients, such as retarded children. And yet, as Baer [6] points out, to refuse to use aversive measures because of preconceived biases could relegate otherwise treatable patients to a lifetime of maladjustment. Put another way, the consequences of *not* using aversive procedures in cases of severe self-injurious behavior would be such that one might question the judgment and the ethics of making such a decision.

Therapeutic procedures involving pain, or at least unpleasantness, are a part of all our lives. What parents would not feel guilty if they neglected to send their children to the dentist, where they will be subject to pain-inflicting needles and drills, in order to achieve widely agreed-upon positive consequences? As Begelman [17] puts it, ". . . The argument that aversive procedures per se are unethical because they involve pain or discomfort to clients or patients is totally without validity. Indeed, if the absence of pain were a necessary condition of treatment we all would have succumbed to one or another variety of infectious conditions from which we have been immunized by *painful* inoculations. . . . Obviously, the conscientious administration of an aversive procedure is hardly undertaken with the sole aim of inflicting pain on clients. It is undertaken with the goal of ameliorating a behavioral problem, and in this sense the pain involved is incidental."

And yet, abuses occur as they would with any developing technology. But abuses with aversive procedures are potentially more dangerous than abuses of other therapeutic techniques. In 1967 Cotter [38] reported administering several thousand electroconvulsive shock treatments (ECT) to all patients in a Vietnam hospital who refused to work. If ECT was not effective, patients were told they could not eat. In Iowa mentally ill prisoners received chemical aversion (apomorphine) for "not getting up, for giving cigarettes against orders, for talking, for swearing, or for lying" [85].

To prevent such abuses, state licensing boards and professional societies should oversee therapeutic practices, particularly as applied to nonvoluntary populations in institutions. Fortunately, some reasonable guidelines are emerging to assist these bodies. Sandler [133] states, *"Depending on circumstances, nonaversive techniques designed to counter undesirable behavior should be considered as the treatment of choice.* If aversive methods are invoked, when possible, nonphysical painful techniques should be attempted before resorting to painful stimuli. Thus, *with relatively mild, nonthreatening or nondangerous problem conditions, highly aversive techniques should rarely be employed. Conversely, given a serious condition in which an individual's biological or psychological integrity is in jeopardy, aversive techniques must be immediately considered."*

To this, Hersen [75] would add that informed consent must be obtained from the patient or his advocate, that the practitioner must be competent, and that clear measures of the problem behavior should be administered to document effectiveness or the lack of it. In fact, the state of Minnesota has recently adopted similar guidelines, including specified competencies for those who would apply this procedure (generally, a thorough knowledge of behavioral principles) for institutions administered by the Department of Public Welfare (Minnesota Rule DPW 39). These developments are welcome and should ensure the humane use of an invaluable set of therapeutic techniques to relieve human suffering.

References

1. Agras, W. S. Behavior therapy in the management of chronic schizophrenia. *American Journal of Psychiatry* 124:240, 1967.
2. Alexander, A. B., Chai, H., Creer, T. L., Miklich, D. R., Renne, C. M., and Cardoso, R. R. The elimination of chronic cough by response suppression shaping. *Journal of Behavior Therapy and Experimental Psychiatry* 4:75, 1973.
3. Ashem, B. The use of covert sensitization in the treatment of overeating. Paper presented at the Association for the Advancement of Behavior Therapy, Miami, 1970.
4. Ashem, B., and Donner, L. Covert sensitization with alcoholics: A controlled replication. *Behavior Research and Therapy* 6:7, 1968.
5. Azrin, N. H., and Wesolowski, D. M. Theft reversal: An overcorrection procedure for eliminating stealing by retarded persons. *Journal of Applied Behavior Analysis* 7:577, 1974.
6. Baer, D. M. A case for the selective reinforcement of punishment. In C. Neuringer and J. L. Michael (Eds.), *Behavior Modification in Clinical Psychology*. New York: Appleton-Century-Crofts, 1970.
7. Bancroft, J. Aversion Therapy of homosexuality. *British Journal of Psychiatry* 115:1417, 1969.
8. Bancroft, J. A comparative study of aversion and desensitization in the treatment of homosexuality. In L. E. Burns, and J. L. Worsley (Eds.), *Behavior Therapy in the 1970's*. Bristol: Wright, 1970.
9. Bandura, A. *Principles of Behavior Modification*. New York: Holt, Rinehart & Winston, 1969.
10. Bandura, A., and Walters, R. H. *Social Learning and Personality Development*. New York: Holt, Rinehart & Winston, 1963.
11. Barlow, D. H. Increasing heterosexual responsiveness in the treatment of sexual deviation: A review of the clinical and experimental evidence. *Behavior Therapy* 4:655, 1973.
12. Barlow, D. H. The treatment of sexual deviation: Towards a comprehensive behavioral approach. In K. S. Calhoun, H. E. Adams, and K. M. Mitchell (Eds.), *Innovative Treatment Methods in Psychopathology*. New York: John Wiley, 1974.
13. Barlow, D. H., and Agras, W. S. Fading to increase heterosexual responsiveness in homosexuals. *Journal of Applied Behavior Analysis* 6:355, 1973.
14. Barlow, D. H., Agras, W. S., Leitenberg, H., Callahan, E. J., and Moore, R. C. The contribution of therapeutic instructions to covert sensitization. *Behavior Research and Therapy* 10:411, 1972.
15. Barlow, D. H., Leitenberg, H., and Agras, W. S. The experimental control of sexual deviation through manipulation of the noxious scene in covert sensitization. *Journal of Abnormal Psychology* 74:596, 1969.
16. Barlow, D. H., Reynolds, E. H., and Agras, W. S. Gender identity change in a transsexual. *Archives of General Psychiatry* 28:569, 1973.
17. Begelman, D. A. Ethical and legal issues of behavior modification. In M. Hersen, R. M. Eisler, and P. M. Miller (Eds.), *Progress in Behavior Modification*: Vol. 1. New York: Academic Press, 1975.
18. Bigelow, G., Liebson, I., and Griffiths, R. Alcoholic drinking: Suppression

by a brief time-out procedure. *Behavior Research and Therapy* 12:107, 1974.
19. Birk, L., Huddleston, W., Miller, E., and Cohler, B. Avoidance conditioning for homosexuality. *Archives of General Psychiatry* 25:314, 1971.
20. Blackly, P. H. An "electric needle" for aversive conditioning of the needle ritual. *International Journal of the Addictions* 6:327, 1971.
21. Blake, B. G. The application of behavior therapy to the treatment of alcoholism. *Behavior Research and Therapy* 3:75, 1965.
22. Blanchard, E. B., Libet, J. M., and Young, L. D. Apneic aversion and covert sensitization in the treatment of a hydrocarbon inhalation addiction. *Journal of Behavior Therapy and Experimental Psychiatry* 4:383, 1973.
23. Boren, J. J., and Coleman, A. D. Some experiments on reinforcement principles within a psychiatric ward for delinquent soldiers. *Journal of Applied Behavior Analysis* 3:29, 1970.
24. Boudin, H. M. Contingency contracting as a therapeutic tool in the deceleration of amphetamine use. *Behavior Therapy* 3:604, 1972.
25. Brady, J. P. A behavioral approach to the treatment of stuttering. *American Journal of Psychiatry* 125:155, 1968.
26. Brownell, K., and Barlow, D. H. The behavioral treatment of sexual deviation. In E. Foa, A. Goldstein, and J. Wolpe (Eds.), *Handbook of Behavioral Intervention*. New York: John Wiley & Sons. In press.
27. Brownell, K., and Barlow, D. H. Experimental analysis in the treatment of multiple sexual deviations. Paper presented to the American Psychological Association, Washington, D.C., 1976.
28. Burchard, J. D., and Barrera, F. An analysis of timeout and response cost in a programmed environment. *Journal of Applied Behavior Analysis* 5:271, 1972.
29. Calhoun, K. S., and Matherne, P. The effects of varying schedules of time-out on aggressive behavior of a retarded girl. *Behavior Therapy and Experimental Psychiatry* 6:139, 1975.
30. Callahan, E. J., and Leitenberg, H. Aversion therapy for sexual deviation: Contingent shock and covert sensitization. *Journal of Abnormal Psychology* 81:60, 1972.
31. Canton-Dutari, A. Combined intervention for controlling unwanted homosexual behavior. *Archives of Sexual Behavior* 3:367, 1974.
32. Cautela, J. R. Treatment of compulsive behavior by covert sensitization. *Psychological Record* 16:33, 1966.
33. Cautela, J. R., and Baron, M. G. Multi-faceted behavior therapy of self-injurious behavior. *Journal of Behavior Therapy and Experimental Psychiatry* 4:124, 1973.
34. Chapman, R. F., Smith, J. W., and Layden, T. Elimination of cigarette smoking by punishment and self-management training. *Behavior Research and Therapy* 9:255, 1971.
35. Clancy, J., Vanderhood, E., and Campbell, P. Evaluation of an aversive technique as a treatment for alcoholism. *Quarterly Journal of Studies on Alcohol* 28:476, 1967.
36. Colson, C. E. Olfactory aversion therapy for homosexual behavior. *Journal of Behavior Therapy and Experimental Psychiatry* 3:185, 1972.
37. Corte, H. E., Wolf, M. M., and Locke, B. J. A comparison of procedures

for eliminating self-injurious behavior of retarded adolescents. *Journal of Applied Behavior Analysis* 4:201, 1971.
38. Cotter, L. H. Operant conditioning in a Vietnamese mental hospital. *American Journal of Psychiatry* 124:23, 1967.
39. Cunningham, C. E., and Linscheid, T. R. Elimination of chronic infant ruminating by electric shock. *Behavior Therapy* 7:231, 1976.
40. Danaher, B. G., Lichtenstein, E., and Sullivan, J. M. Comparative effects of rapid and normal smoking on heart rate and carboxyhemoglobin. *Journal of Consulting and Clinical Psychology* 44:556, 1976.
41. Davidson, A., and Denney, D. R. Covert sensitization and information in the reduction of nailbiting. *Behavior Therapy* 7:512, 1976.
42. Davidson, W. S. Studies of aversive conditioning for alcoholics: A critical review of theory and research methodology. *Psychological Bulletin* 31:571, 1974.
43. Davison, G. C. Elimination of a sadistic fantasy by a client-controlled counterconditioning technique: A case study. *Journal of Abnormal and Social Psychology* 73:84, 1968.
44. Davison, G. C. Homosexuality: The ethical challenge. *Journal of Consulting and Clinical Psychology* 44:157, 1976.
45. Davison, G. C., and Wilson, G. T. Attitudes of behavior therapists toward homosexuality. *Behavior Therapy* 4:686, 1973.
46. Dawley, H. H., Ellithorpe, D. B., and Tretola, R. Aversive smoking: Carboxyhemoglobin levels before and after rapid smoking. *Journal of Behavior Therapy and Experimental Psychiatry* 7:13, 1976.
47. Dericco, D. A., Brigham, T. A., and Garlington, W. K. Development and evaluation of treatment paradigms for the suppression of smoking behavior. *Journal of Applied Behavior Analysis*. In press.
48. Diament, C., and Wilson, G. T. An experimental investigation of covert sensitization in an analogue eating situation. *Behavior Therapy*. In press.
49. Elkins, R. L. Conditioned flavor aversions to familiar tap water in rats: An adjustment with implications for aversion therapy treatment of alcoholism and obesity. *Journal of Abnormal Psychology* 83:411, 1974.
50. Elkins, R. L. A note on aversion therapy for alcoholism. *Behavior Research and Therapy* 14:159, 1976.
51. Elliott, C. H., and Denney, D. R. Weight control through covert sensitization and false feedback. *Journal of Consulting and Clinical Psychology* 43:842, 1975.
52. Elliott, R., and Tighe, T. Breaking the cigarette habit: Effects of a technique involving threatened loss of money. *Psychological Record* 18:503, 1968.
53. Epstein, L. H., Doke, L. A., Sajwaj, T. E., Sorrell, S., and Rimmer, B. Generality and side effects of overcorrection. *Journal of Applied Behavior Analysis* 7:385, 1974.
54. Evans, D. R. An exploratory study into the treatment of exhibitionism by means of emotive imagery and aversive conditioning. *Canadian Psychologist* 8:162, 1967.
55. Farrar, C. H., Powell, B. J., and Martin, L. K. Punishment of alcohol consumption by apneic paralysis. *Behavior Research and Therapy* 6:13, 1968.
56. Feldman, M. P., and MacCulloch, M. J. The application of anticipatory

avoidance learning to the treatment of homosexuality. I. Theory, technique, and preliminary results. *Behavior Research and Therapy* 2:165, 1965.
57. Feldman, M. P., and MacCulloch, M. J. *Homosexual Behavior: Theory and Assessment*. Oxford: Pergamon Press, 1971.
58. Flanagan, B., Goldiamond, I., and Azrin, N. Operant stuttering: The control of stuttering behavior through response-contingent contingent consequences. *Journal of the Experimental Analysis of Behavior* 1:173, 1958.
59. Foreyt, J. P., and Hagan, R. L. Covert sensitization: Conditioning or suggestion? *Journal of Abnormal Psychology* 82:17, 1973.
60. Foreyt, J. P., and Kennedy, W. A. Treatment of overweight by aversion therapy. *Behavior Research and Therapy* 9:29, 1971.
61. Foxx, R. M., and Azrin, N. H. Restitution: A method of eliminating aggressive-disruptive behavior of retarded and brain damaged patients. *Behavior Research and Therapy* 10:15, 1972.
62. Foxx, R. M., and Azrin, N. H. The elimination of autistic self-stimulatory behavior by overcorrection. *Journal of Applied Behavior Analysis* 6:1, 1973.
63. Foxx, R. M., and Martin, E. D. Treatment of scavenging behavior (coprophagy and pica) by overcorrection. *Behavior Research and Therapy* 13, 153, 1975.
64. Franks, C. M., and Wilson, G. T. (Eds.) *Annual Review of Behavior Therapy: Theory and Practice*, Vol. 3. New York: Brunner-Mazel, 1975.
65. Freund, K. Some problems in the treatment of homosexuality. In H. J. Eysenck (Ed.), *Behavior Therapy and the Neuroses*. New York: Pergamon Press, 1960.
66. Garcia, J., Hankins, W. G., and Rusiniak, K. W. Behavioral regulation of the milieu interne in man and rat. *Science* 185:824, 1974.
67. Gelperin, A. Rapid food-aversion learning by a terrestrial mollusk. *Science* 189:567, 1975.
68. Guidry, L. S. Use of a covert punishing contingency in compulsive stealing. *Behavior Therapy and Experimental Psychiatry* 6:169, 1975.
69. Hallam, R. S., and Rachman, S. Current status of aversion therapy. In M. Hersen, R. M. Eisler, and P. M. Miller (Eds.), *Progress in Behavior Modification*, Vol. 2. New York: Academic Press, 1976.
70. Hallam, R. S., Rachman, S., and Falkowski, W. Subjective, attitudinal, and physiological effects of electrical aversion therapy. *Behavior Research and Therapy* 10:1, 1972.
71. Harris, S. L., and Romanczyk, R. G. Treating self-injurious behavior of a retarded child by overcorrection. *Behavior Therapy* 7:235, 1976.
72. Hauser, R. Rapid smoking as a technique of behavior modification: Caution in selection of subjects. *Journal of Consulting and Clinical Psychology* 42:625, 1974.
73. Hayes, S. C., Brownell, K., and Barlow, D. H. The use of self-administered covert sensitization in the treatment of exhibitionism and sadism. Paper presented at the American Psychological Association, Washington, D.C. 1976.
74. Haynes, S. M., and Geddy, P. Suppression of psychotic hallucinations through time-out. *Behavior Therapy* 4:123, 1973.
75. Hersen, M. Aversive techniques. In A. S. Bellack and M. Hersen (Eds.), *Behavior Modification: An Introductory Textbook*. Baltimore: Williams and

Wilkins. In press.
76. Hsu, J. J. Electroconditioning therapy of alcoholics: A preliminary report. *Quarterly Journal of Studies on Alcohol* 26:449, 1965.
77. Hunt, G. M., and Azrin, N. H. A community-reinforcement approach to alcoholism. *Behavior Research and Therapy* 11:91, 1973.
78. Hunt, W. A., and Matarazzo, T. D. Three years later: Recent developments in the experimental modification of smoking. *Journal of Abnormal Psychology* 81:107, 1973.
79. Janda, L. H., and Rimm, D. C. Covert sensitization in the treatment of obesity. *Journal of Abnormal Psychology* 80:37, 1972.
80. Kantorovich, N. V. An attempt of curing alcoholism by associated reflexes. *Novoye v Refleksologii i Fiziologii Nervnoy Sistemy* 3:436, 1929.
81. Kazdin, A. E. Response cost: The removal of conditioned reinforcers for therapeutic change. *Behavior Therapy* 3:533, 1972.
82. Kazdin, A. E. *Behavior Modification in Applied Settings*. Illinois: Dorsey Press, 1975.
83. Kellam, A. M. Shop lifting treated by aversion to a film. *Behavior Research and Therapy* 7:125, 1969.
84. Kendell, R. E., and Staton, M. C. The fate of untreated alcoholics. *Quarterly Journal of Studies on Alcohol* 26:685, 1965.
85. *Knecht* v. *Gillman*. 488 F.2d 1136, 1139 (8th Cir. 1973).
86. Koenig, K. P., and Masters, J. Experimental treatment of habitual smoking. *Behavior Research and Therapy* 3:235, 1965.
87. Kohlenberg, R. J. The punishment of persistent vomiting: A case study. *Journal of Applied Behavior Analysis* 3:241, 1970.
88. Kushner, M., and Sandler, J. Aversion therapy and the concept of punishment. *Behavior Research and Therapy* 4:179, 1966.
89. Lang, P. J., and Melamed, B. G. Case report: Avoidance conditioning therapy of an infant with chronic ruminative vomiting. *Journal of Abnormal Psychology* 74:1, 1969.
90. Lawson, D. M., and May, R. B. Three procedures for the extinction of smoking behavior. *The Psychological Record* 20:151, 1970.
91. Lemere, F., and Voegtlin, W. L. An evaluation of the aversion treatment of alcoholism. *Quarterly Journal of Studies on Alcohol* 2:199, 1950.
92. Lemere, F., Voegtlin, W. L., Broz, W. R., O'Hollaren, P., and Tupper, W. E. Conditioned reflex treatment of chronic alcoholism: VII. Technic. *Diseases of the Nervous System* 3:243, 1942.
93. Lesser, E. Behavior therapy with a narcotics user: A case report. *Behavior Research and Therapy* 5:251, 1967.
94. Liberman, R. Aversive conditioning of drug addicts: A pilot study. *Behavior Research and Therapy* 6:229, 1968.
95. Lichtenstein, E. How to quit smoking. *Psychology Today* 4:42, 1971.
96. Lichtenstein, E., Harris, D. E., Birchler, G. R., Wahl, J. M., and Schmahl, D. P. Comparison of rapid smoking, warm, smoky air, and attention placebo in the modification of smoking behavior. *Journal of Consulting and Clinical Psychology* 40:92, 1973.
97. Liversedge, L. A., and Sylvester, J. D. Conditioning techniques in treatment of writer's cramp. *Lancet* 1:1147, 1955.

98. Lovaas, O. I., and Simmons, J. O. Manipulation of self-destruction in three retarded children. *Journal of Applied Behavior Analysis* 2:143, 1969.
99. Lublin, I., and Joslyn, L. Aversive conditioning of cigarette addiction. Paper read at the annual meeting of the American Psychological Association, San Francisco, 1968.
100. MacCulloch, M. J., Feldman, M. P., Oxford, J. F., and MacCulloch, M. L. Anticipatory avoidance learning in the treatment of alcoholism: A record of therapeutic failure. *Behavior Research and Therapy* 4:187, 1966.
101. Maletzky, B. M. "Assisted" covert sensitization: A preliminary report. *Behavior Therapy* 6:117, 1973.
102. Mann, R. A. The behavior-therapeutic use of contingency contracting to control an adult behavior problem: Weight control. *Journal of Applied Behavior Analysis* 5:99, 1972.
103. Mann, R. A. The use of contingency contracting to facilitate durability of behavior change: Weight loss maintenance. *Addictive Behaviors* 1:245, 1976.
104. Marks, I. M., and Gelder, M. G. Transvestism and fetishism: Clinical and psychological changes during faradic aversion. *British Journal of Psychiatry* 113:711, 1967.
105. Marks, I. M., Gelder, M., and Bancroft, J. Sexual deviants two years after electric aversion. *British Journal of Psychiatry* 117:173, 1970.
106. Marks, I. M., Rachman, S., and Gelder, M. G. Methods for assessment of aversion therapy in fetishism with masochism. *Behavior Research and Therapy* 3:253, 1965.
107. Marshall, W. L. A combined treatment approach to the reduction of multiple fetish-related behaviors. *Journal of Consulting and Clinical Psychology* 42:613, 1974.
108. Mastellone, M. Aversion therapy: A new use for the old rubber band. *Journal of Behavior Therapy and Experimental Psychiatry* 5:311, 1974.
109. McConaghy, N. Subjective and penile plethysmograph responses following aversion-relief and apomorphine aversion therapy for homosexual impulses. *British Journal of Psychiatry* 115:723, 1969.
110. McConaghy, N. Penile response conditioning and its relationship to aversion therapy in homosexuals. *Behavior Therapy* 1:213, 1970.
111. McConaghy, N. Aversive and positive conditioning treatments of homosexuality. *Behavior Research and Therapy* 13:309, 1975.
112. McConaghy, N., and Barr, R. F. Classical, avoidance, and backward conditioning treatments of homosexuality. *British Journal of Psychiatry* 122:151, 1973.
113. McFall, R. M., and Hammen, C. L. Motivation, structure, and self-monitoring: Role of nonspecific factors in smokng reduction. *Journal of Consulting and Clinical Psychology* 36:80, 1971.
114. Merbaum, M. The modification of self-destructive behavior by a mother-therapist using aversive stimulation. *Behavior Therapy* 4:442, 1973.
115. Meyer, V., and Crisp, A. H. Aversion therapy in two cases of obesity. *Behavior Research and Therapy* 2:143, 1964.
116. Meyer, V., and Mair, J. M. M. A new technique to control stammering: A preliminary report. *Behavior Research and Therapy* 1:251, 1963.
117. Miller, E. C., Dvorak, A., and Turner, D. W. A method of creating aver-

sion to alcohol by reflex conditioning in a group setting. *Quarterly Journal of Studies on Alcohol* 21:424, 1960.
118. Miller, M. M. Treatment of chronic alcoholism by hypnotic aversion. *Journal of the American Medical Association* 171:1491, 1959.
119. Miller, P. M. A behavioral intervention program for chronic public drunkenness offenders. *Archives of General Psychiatry* 32:915, 1975.
120. Miller, P. M., and Barlow, D. H. Behavioral approaches to the treatment of alcoholism. *Journal of Nervous and Mental Disease* 157:10, 1973.
121. Miller, P. M., and Hersen, M. Quantitative changes in alcohol consumption as a function of electrical aversive conditioning. *Journal of Clinical Psychology* 28:590, 1972.
122. Miller, P. M., Hersen, M., Eisler, R. M., and Hemphill, D. P. Electrical aversion therapy with alcoholics: An analogue study. *Behavior Research and Therapy* 11:491, 1973.
123. Ober, D. C. Modification of smoking behavior. *Journal of Consulting and Clinical Psychology* 32:543, 1963.
124. Oliver, S. D., West, R. C., and Sloane, H. N. Some effects on human behavior of aversive events. *Behavior Therapy* 5:481, 1974.
125. Polakow, R. L. Covert sensitization treatment of a probationed barbiturate addict. *Behavior Therapy and Experimental Psychiatry* 6:53, 1975.
126. Rachman, S., and Teasdale, J. *Aversion Therapy and Behavior Disorders: An Analysis*. Coral Gables: University of Miami Press, 1969.
127. Raymond, M. J. The treatment of addiction by aversion conditioning with apomorphine. *Behavior Research and Therapy* 1:21, 1964.
128. Risley, T. R. The effects and side-effects of punishing the autistic behaviors of a deviant child. *Journal of Applied Behavior Analysis* 1:21, 1968.
129. Rooth, F. G., and Marks, I. M. Persistent exhibitionism: Short term response to aversion, self-regulation and relaxation treatments. *Archives of Sexual Behavior* 3:227, 1974.
130. Russell, M. A. H., Armstrong, E., and Patel, U. A. Temporal contiguity in electrical aversion therapy for cigarette smoking. *Behavior Research and Therapy* 14:103, 1976.
131. Sajwaj, T. E., and Hedges, D. Functions of parental attention in an oppositional retarded boy. Paper submitted to the American Psychological Association, Washington, D.C., 1971.
132. Sajwaj, T. E., Libet, J., and Agras, S. Lemon-juice therapy: The control of life-threatening rumination in a six-month-old infant. *Journal of Applied Behavior Analysis* 7:557, 1974.
133. Sandler, J. Aversion methods. In F. H. Kanfer and A. P. Goldstein (Eds.), *Helping People Change*. New York: Pergamon Press, 1975.
134. Schachter, S. Obesity and eating. *Science* 161:751, 1968.
135. Schmahl, D. P., Lichtenstein, E., and Harris, D. E. Successful treatment of habitual smokers with warm smoky air and rapid smoking. *Journal of Consulting and Clinical Psychology* 38:105, 1972.
136. Scholander, T. Treatment of an unusual case of compulsive behavior by aversive stimulation. *Behavior Therapy* 3:390, 1972.
137. Seligman, M. E. P. On the generality of the laws of learning. *Psychological Review* 77:406, 1970.

138. Serber, M. Shame aversion therapy. *Journal of Behavior Therapy and Experimental Psychiatry* 1:213, 1970.
139. Sobell, M. B., and Sobell, L. C. Alcoholics treated by individualized behavior therapy: One year treatment outcome. *Behavior Research and Therapy* 11:599, 1973.
140. Sobell, M. B., and Sobell, L. C. Individualized behavior therapy for alcoholics. *Behavior Therapy* 4:49, 1973.
141. Steffy, R. A., Meichenbaum, D., and Best, J. A. Aversive and cognitive factors in the modification of smoking behavior. *Behavior Research and Therapy* 8:115, 1969.
142. Stevenson, J., and Jones, I. H. Behavior therapy technique for exhibitionism: A preliminary report. *Archives of General Psychiatry* 27:839, 1972.
143. Tanner, B. Shock intensity and fear of shock in the modification of homosexual behavior in males by avoidance learning. *Behavior Research and Therapy* 11:213, 1973.
144. Tanner, B. A comparison of automated aversive conditioning and a waiting list control in the modification of homosexual behavior in males. *Behavior Therapy* 5:29, 1974.
145. Tate, B. G. Case study: Control of chronic self-injurious behavior by conditioned procedures. *Behavior Therapy* 3:72, 1972.
146. Tate, B. G., and Baroff, G. S. Aversive control of self-injurious behavior in a psychotic boy. *Behavior Research and Therapy* 4:281, 1966.
147. Thomason, I. G., and Rathod, N. H. Aversion therapy for heroin dependence. *Lancet* 2:381, 1968.
148. Toister, R. P., Condron, C. J., Worley, J., and Arthur, D. Faradic therapy of chronic vomiting in infancy: A case study. *Behavior Therapy and Experimental Psychiatry* 6:55, 1975.
149. Tursky, B. Factors that can affect the use of electric shock in behavior therapy. *Behaviorial Engineering* 2:61, 1975.
150. Turksy, B., Watson, P. D., and O'Connell, D. N. A concentric shock electrode for pain stimulation. *Psychophysiology* 1:296, 1965.
151. Tyler, J., and Brown, G. The use of swift, brief isolation as a control device for delinquents. *Behavior Research and Therapy* 5:1, 1967.
152. Voegtlin, W. L., Lemere, G., Broz, W. R., and O'Hollaren, P. Conditioned reflex therapy of alcoholic addiction: Follow-up report of 1042 cases. *American Journal of Medical Science* 203:525, 1942.
153. Wagner, M. K., and Braff, R. A. Comparing behavior modification approaches to habit decrement—smoking. *Journal of Consulting and Clinical Psychology* 34:258, 1970.
154. Whitman, T. L. Modification of chronic smoking behavior: A comparison of three approaches. *Behavior Research Therapy* 7:257, 1969.
155. Wickramasekera, I. Aversive behavior rehearsal for sexual exhibitionism. *Behavior Therapy* 7:167, 1976.
156. Wiens, A. N., Montague, J. R., Manaugh, T. S., and English, C. J. Pharmacologic aversive counterconditioning to alcohol in a private hospital: One year follow up. *Journal of Studies on Alcohol*. In press.
157. Wilde, G. J. S. Behavior therapy for addicted cigarette smokers. A preliminary investigation. *Behavior Research and Therapy* 2:107, 1964.

158. Wilson, G. T., and Davison, G. C. Aversion techniques in behavior therapy: Some theoretical and metatheoretical considerations. *Journal of Consulting and Clinical Psychology* 33:327, 1969.
159. Wilson G. T., and Davison, G. C. Behavior therapy and homosexuality: A critical perspective. *Behavior Therapy* 5:16, 1974.
160. Wilson, G. T., Leaf, R. C., and Nathan, P. E. The aversive control of excessive alcohol consumption by chronic alcoholics in the laboratory setting. *Journal of Applied Behavior Analysis* 8:13, 1975.
161. Wilson, G. T., and Tracey, D. A. An experimental analysis of aversive imagery versus electrical aversive conditioning in the treatment of chronic alcoholics. *Behavior Research and Therapy* 14:41, 1976.
162. Wincze, J. P., and Bachman, J. The effects of contingent and noncontingent electrical shock punishment on self-injurious and associated behaviors. Paper presented at the annual meeting of the Association for Advancement of Behavior Therapy, San Francisco, 1975.
163. Winkler, R. C. Management of chronic psychiatric patients by a token reinforcement system. *Journal of Applied Behavior Analysis* 3:47, 1970.
164. Wisocki, P. A. The successful treatment of a heroin addict by covert conditioning techniques. *Journal of Behavior Therapy and Experimental Psychiatry* 4:55, 1972.
165. Wolf, M. M., Risley, T., and Mees, H. Application of operant conditioning procedures to the behavior problems of an autistic child. *Behavior Research and Therapy* 1:305, 1964.
166. Wolpe, J. Conditioned inhibition of craving in drug addiction. *Behavior Research and Therapy* 2:285, 1965.
167. Yates, A. J. The application of learning theory to the treatment of tics. *Journal of Abnormal and Social Psychology* 56:175, 1958.
168. Zvonikov, M. A. A modification of the technique of conducting conditioned reflex apomorphine and suggestive therapy of alcoholism. *Zhurnal Nevropatologii i Psikhiatrii* 68:596, 1968.

6. Relaxation Training and Related Techniques

C. Barr Taylor

Editor's Introduction

Relaxation training, once firmly linked to the procedure of systematic desensitization, has come into its own of late as a treatment for psychophysiologic disorders such as essential hypertension. Although the procedure and related techniques such as meditation or hypnosis have been used for many years, this research area is new, and the findings are as yet more tentative than for some of the areas already reviewed.

The technique is simple to teach, and a typical procedure is outlined on pages 136–138. No advantage has been demonstrated for one method of relaxation training over another, although for both tension headaches and insomnia the combination of electromyographic feedback and relaxation training may be more beneficial than either procedure used alone. In most conditions, the simplest training procedure seems to produce as much benefit as the more complex. Four to eight hours' training, with practice at home for 20 minutes daily, suffices to produce maximum effects. Intriguingly, it is not clear which components of training are either necessary or sufficient, although regular practice seems to be important. This should remind us that long-term efficacy depends upon adherence to practicing the technique, just as the efficacy of much medical care depends upon adherence to the medical regimen.

The mechanism of effect is also obscure. Sitting still produces physiologic effects similar to those of relaxation, while one can feel relaxed in the midst of exercise. Whether there is a physiologic response specific to relaxation is not known, although rather broad-gauge effects on the cardiovascular and musculoskeletal systems occur, perhaps arguing for a centrally mediated, trophotropic, hypometabolic state. Whether being relaxed is a muscle state or mental quietude or whether it is induced by pleasant fantasy is equally mystifying. Nonetheless, we must assume that some form of muscle quietude combined with a narrowing of attention and perhaps focusing on a particular physiological response are all involved in producing the therapeutic effects associated with relaxation training [38].

The most striking series of studies has begun to define the usefulness of relaxation training in the treatment of essential hypertension, as described on pages 151–153. It seems clear that immediate benefit is conferred, a benefit that adds to the effect of medication and that is larger in individuals with higher blood pressures [38]. Moreover, the effect does not seem to be attributable to nonspecific or placebo factors. However, patients must be cautioned not to stop taking their medication unless prescribed by their physician, and occasional deleterious side effects of relaxation training do occur (see page 149). Importantly, it has yet to be demonstrated that relaxation training leads to further reduction of morbidity and mortality for hypertensives. This is not surprising, since more evidence of long-term therapeutic effect is needed before embarking on the large-scale clinical trial necessary to investigate morbidity and mortality.

Less certain, but definitely promising, are the effects of relaxation training in tension headache (page 154), insomnia (page 157), and perhaps asthma. Nonetheless, this is an exciting new area that is rapidly developing and that promises to facilitate our understanding of stress and enhance the treatment of at least some of the psychosomatic disorders.

W. S. A.

Relaxation training, defined here as a procedure aimed at achieving muscle and mental relaxation, entered behavior therapy with the advent of systematic desensitization. Wolpe [82] argued that "if a response inhibitory to anxiety can be made to occur in the presence of anxiety-evoking stimuli, it will weaken the connection between the stimuli and the anxiety responses," a principle he referred to as counterconditioning. Although Wolpe described a number of procedures supposedly inhibitory to anxiety, relaxation training became the most popular. However, as behavior therapists began to tease out the effective subcomponents of desensitization, it became clear that subjects could achieve behavior changes in relationship to fear-arousing situations without the aid of relaxation [1, 47]. On the other hand, relaxation appeared to be useful in a variety of conditions. Thus, in this chapter a typical relaxation procedure will be described, the physiologic basis of relaxation and related procedures will be reviewed, and the clinical uses of relaxation will be evaluated.

Relaxation Training
Relaxation instructions involve several components. The patient assumes a passive, relaxed position in a quiet environment while alternately contracting and relaxing muscles, breathing regularly and deeply, and associating the breathing and relaxing with a state of mental calmness or

repetitive phrases such as "Relax" or "Let go," or both. Patients are asked to practice for 20 to 30 minutes once or twice a day, either by themselves or while listening to a tape. Many therapists ask patients to relax when they feel tense during the day. For instance, patients may squeeze their hand and hold their breath, releasing both hand tension and breath while thinking "Relax" or "Let go."

A typical set of muscle relaxation instructions (adapted from Marquis [46] and Taylor, Nelson, Farquhar, and Agras [77] begins by having the patient assume a relaxed, passive position in a comfortable setting, remove glasses, loosen clothing, place both feet on the floor, and uncross limbs, so as to exert no effort to maintain posture. The usual instructions might then continue:

(1) "Now that you are comfortable, close your eyes and keep them closed for the remainder of the procedure. I am going to teach you to relax verydeeply. To do this, I will ask you to concentrate on, and relax, one group of muscles at a time. We will start with your hands. Begin by making a tight fist. Pay attention to how these muscles feel when they are tense—study the tension in these muscles." After some 10 or 15 seconds, the instructor continues. "Now relax. Release all tension in these muscles. Let all the tension go. Keep on letting go until the muscles seem completely relaxed. Even now, when these muscles seem completely relaxed, see if you can relax them more; let those muscles relax completely."

Using the same basic instructions, other muscle groups are relaxed systematically, usually beginning with the forearms. (Special instructions for a muscle group are added in parentheses.)

(2) Upper portion of face. (a) Eyebrows. ("Pull your eyebrows together and hold that tension, study it, and then relax. Tighten your eyebrows again and then let half of the tension go, then half of that, then the remaining tension.") (b) Muscles around the eyes; eye muscles. ("Roll your eyes around in a big circle, noting the little shifts in tension as they move from one position to another. Now, move your eyes to the right and bounce your eyes farther to the right a few times, building up tension; then let them relax as though you were staring blankly forward.") These instructions are then repeated for the left. ("Now visualize a familiar object—for example, the Washington Monument—and note the little shifts in tension as you study this object. Begin at the top of the monument and go down the side, noting little shifts in muscle tension as you do.")

(3) Lower portion of face. (a) (The patient is instructed to wrinkle his nose, smile, and pucker.) (b) Muscles of tongue and swallowing ("Move your tongue to the right against your cheek; study that tension and then let it go." Repeat for left, up, down, and forward. Swallow and study the muscles that relax as you swallow.") (c) Muscles of the vocal cords. ("When I instruct you, I want you to say the letters of the alphabet out loud, at a rate of one letter per second. Note the changes in the muscles of your vocal cords as I instruct you to say the letters more softly, then only to yourself, and, finally, only to think them. OK, begin.")

(4) Muscles of the neck. ("Imagine your neck muscles so relaxed that a gentle breeze could blow your neck back and forth. Now, let these muscles relax and move your head gently back and forth, noting any tension in these muscles.")

(5) Muscles of the back. (Warn patients not to tense these muscles too severely.)

(6) Muscles of the stomach.

(7) Muscles of the lower extremity.

Following the muscle tension and relaxation, patients are asked to breathe deeply and slowly and to note that at the "top of their breath," as they begin exhaling, their lungs seem to relax on their own. As they breathe deeply and slowly, they are asked to imagine a peaceful place or situation of their own choosing, such as lying on a beach by the ocean, floating in clouds, or sitting in a pleasant mountain meadow. At the same time they are asked to tell themselves to "let go" or "relax" when they reach the "top of their breath." Subjects practice this deep regular breathing paired with pleasant thoughts for several minutes and are then told, "Now, keeping your eyes closed, follow my instructions once more. Simultaneously, tense your hands, arms, forearms, shoulders, face, neck, back, abdomen, and lower legs. Hold this tension! Take a deep breath. Hold it. Now, let your muscles relax and let your breath go." Subjects experience a very relaxed feeling when they follow these instructions, which can usually be omitted once they learn the technique. Finally, subjects are told to continue breathing deeply and regularly and to identify any remaining tension in their muscles. "Once you identify any tension, let those muscles relax."

Subjects are usually asked to listen to a taped version of these instructions once or twice a day until they are able to feel very relaxed. A week later progress is reviewed, questions are answered, and subjects are asked to relax briefly. The instructor may then introduce the notion of relaxing during times of particular stress during the day by saying to the patient, "Gently squeeze your right hand, and then take a deep breath. Release your hand and breath together and tell yourself to 'relax' or 'let go.' " Most subjects can learn to relax on cue in a few weeks and to achieve deep relaxation when they listen to tape-recorded instructions and eventually on their own.

Relaxed patients show physical signs such as forehead wrinkles smoothing out, the jaw falling slightly open, the head falling forward against the chest, and breathing becoming regular and slow. The instructor can pick up a patient's arm and shake it gently to check for any residual muscle tension in order to determine if the patient is relaxed. Patients should also report feeling relaxed and calm after practicing the exercise. On a scale of 0–100, where 100 is the most tense they can imagine and 0 the most relaxed, patients report a score between 5 and 10 after learning and practicing these procedures. Other investigators [63] use physiologic criteria such as muscle tension or cardiovascular changes as end points in teaching a subject to relax, but these are arbitrary.

Related Training Procedures
Several adjunctive techniques to teach relaxation have been developed, although the usefulness of one over another rests as much on personal preference as upon data.

TAPE-RECORDED INSTRUCTION. The need for an in vivo session for relaxation training is uncertain. Davidson and Hiebert [23] found that subjects given taped instruction reported decreases in anxiety to a stressor film equal to the decreases experienced by subjects given live instructions. However, in clinical practice subjects often report that they feel more relaxed when listening to live instructions than to taped ones. The relaxation procedure rapidly becomes monotonous to teach, and many therapists probably prefer to use a tape recording for this reason.

METHOHEXITONE (BREVITAL). Friedman [31] and Brady [13] first reported the facilitative effects of intravenous methohexitone in subjects who had difficulty relaxing using the standard training procedures. While Friedman and Brady used the procedure to achieve relaxation in subjects undergoing systematic desensitization, methohexitone may be useful in helping subjects achieve relaxation for other purposes. Brady [13] reported favorable results with 40 patients using methohexitone infusion preceded by four minutes of instruction in relaxation. He reports that none of his patients found the procedure "physiologically unpleasant and only one failed to achieve a state of deep muscular relaxation and emotional calm." However, Lader and Mathews [41] found no significant difference between physiologic measures of three treatments—relaxation, a saline solution of 0.30 milligrams per kilogram (mg/kg), or 9–45 mg/kg methohexitone injected over 30 seconds—except that the Brevital group showed significant tachycardia. This pharmacologic effect was to be expected at the doses used and was the opposite of the effect to be anticipated if the subjects were relaxing.

BIOFEEDBACK-INDUCED RELAXATION. Several authors have discussed an apparatus that facilitates relaxation by providing EMG feedback [17]. A typical procedure is as follows: Assuming a relaxed position, subjects are connected to a polygraph. They hear a tone with a frequency proportional to the EMG activity in the relevant muscle group. As they learn to relax the muscle, the gain of the feedback system is increased, thus requiring the subject to have a lower EMG to hear the tone. The authors who developed the procedure found that subjects reported significant subjective relaxation as they learned EMG activity. However, EMG does not necessarily correlate with subjective anxiety [42, 49], and EMG changes induced by biofeedback in one muscle group do not necessarily generalize to other muscle groups (see page 141).

OTHER TRAINING PROCEDURES. Many other ingenious techniques have been used to facilitate or maintain relaxation. Brady [12] has developed a metronome device that facilitates ongoing relaxation during the day by having subjects think "Relax" or "Let go" when they hear the metronome beat. Other investigators have used cued relaxation procedures for a variety of problems [64, 66, 67, 71].

Theoretic Basis
Jacobson [39], who popularized the muscle relaxation technique in modern times with his progressive relaxation procedure, believed that peripheral

muscle input directly affected the central nervous system and, that when this input was reduced, tension "in the brain" would cease. This explanation is incompatible with current physiologic data on the effect of relaxation on the central nervous system. For instance, subjects who have been completely curarized and have no peripheral muscle activity report subjective anxiety [22]. More generally, subjects who reduce EMG activity do not necessarily report subjective reduction in anxiety or mental calmness [42, 49].

Another hypothesis, first introduced by Gellhorn [32] and since popularized by Benson, Beary, and Carol [8] is that relaxation affects autonomic balance, decreasing ergotropic (posterior hypothalamic) activity while increasing trophotropic (anterior hypothalamic) dominance. Trophotropic dominance is assumed to inhibit the sympathetic arousal system. Benson suggests that relaxation is one of many procedures that elicit the "relaxation response." Others such as autogenic training, hypnosis, some forms of meditation, and perhaps even biofeedback share with relaxation training a passive attitude—subjects are directly or implicitly encouraged to allow distracting thoughts or images to "pass"; there is a decrease in muscle tonus; a quiet environment is provided; and a mental device is used—a word or sound repeated as a constant stimulus. As evidence for the hypothesis that the "relaxation response" elicits a trophotropic response, Benson notes that studies of hypnosis, autogenic training, and transcendental meditation have been demonstrated to lower oxygen consumption, respiration, and heart rate, while alpha activity and skin resistance increase—all responses compatible with inhibited sympathetic activity.

The trophotropic hypothesis deserves further study, and perhaps a general relaxation response will be demonstrated in the future. A fourth hypothesis has been presented by Lader and Wing [43], who view the primary effect of relaxation as decreasing central nervous system arousal. Evidence from Brenner [15] supports this notion, although Conner [20] found contradictory results. The method by which relaxation affects autonomic activity remains to be demonstrated.

The Physiology of Relaxation
Studies of the physiology of relaxation are frustrated by several factors. First, in the absence of a direct measure of mental calmness or mental relaxation, self-report of relaxation can be correlated with behavioral and

physiologic data, but there is no way of knowing if a subject is *really* relaxed. Second, and compounding the problem of relying on self-report, the subcomponents of the relaxation procedure induce physiologic changes. For instance, simply sitting quietly induces similar changes in skin conductance even without relaxation instructions. Again, merely breathing regularly and deeply induces a series of complex physiologic changes akin to, but probably independent of, relaxation [65].

Most commonly, skin conductance and fluctuation, electromyogram, heart rate, and respiration are used to determine the physiologic effects of relaxation. In Table 1 changes in these measures are noted for five different studies of relaxation, where continuous physiologic monitoring occurred. In four studies, heart rate decreased significantly; in one there was no change. EMG decreased in two studies, and showed no change in another. In three studies respiration rate decreased; skin conductance level decreased in four studies but increased in one. While the results are inconclusive, short or prolonged periods of relaxation seem to lead to decreases in skin conductance, respiration, and heart rate. However, when the physiologic effects of these relaxation procedures are compared with merely sitting quietly listening to music or other controls, the results are more uncertain. Table 2 lists studies comparing a relaxation procedure with a control one. Paul [60] compared a relaxation procedure with hypnosis and a control. He measured forehead EMG, heart rate, and respiration, all of which significantly decreased compared with subjects told to relax. Skin conductance did not change significantly. Grossberg [35], however, comparing relaxation with a similar control (simple instructions to rest and listen to music) found no differences between the groups on forehead and forearm EMG, skin conductance, and heart rate. Grossberg's procedure has been criticized because he used a taped relaxation instruction, while Paul used in vivo relaxation instructions.

Mathews and Gelder [49] compared a relaxation group (six weekly sessions lasting one hour—modeled after Jacobson) with a control group who met for a similar period and were provided with reassurance and advice but no relaxation training. No significant differences for self-reported or clinical anxiety occurred for either group; both groups showed a decrease in extensor EMG and extensor skin conductance. In a subsequent phase of this study, the relaxation group showed a lower level of EMG activity, lower frequency of skin conductance fluctuations, and a

Table 1. Effects of various relaxation techniques on some physiologic variables

Study	Procedure	No. Subjects	Physiologic Measure				
			EMG (forehead)	Heart Rate	RR	SC	(level)
Paul [60]	Brief relaxation training	20	D (forearm) (measured during relaxation)	D	D	D	
Mathews and Gelder [49]	Brief relaxation training	7	D	D	D	D	
Conner [20]	Brief relaxation training	84	—	D	—	D	
Pollack and Zeiner [61]	Bensonian relaxation	10	—	D	D	D	
Delman and Johnson [26]	Progressive muscle relaxation	10	No change	No change	—	Increase	

KEY: D = decrease; RR = respiratory rate; SC = skin conductance.

Table 2. Comparison of various relaxation techniques with controls

Study	Procedure	No. Subjects	EMG (forearm)	(frontalis)	Heart Rate	RR	SC (level)
Paul [60]	Brief relaxation training versus control ("Relax as best you can.")	20	C		C	C	B
Grossberg [33]	Brief relaxation tape versus simple instructions to relax listening to music	30 30	B B	B B	B B		B B
Mathews and Gelder [49]	Relaxation training (after Wolpe) measured during relaxation instructions versus measured during control instructions	7		B	B	B	C
Conner [20]	Brief relaxation training (after Lang); time estimation control tape—listening to music	84			B B		B B
Pollack and Zeiner [61]	Bensonian-type relaxation versus self-relaxation, sitting quietly	10 10		B A	B B		B B

A = control showed greater effect than relaxation; B = no difference between control and relaxation; C = relaxation showed greater effect than control.

greater decrease in skin conductance level compared with the controls. EMG changes did not correlate with self-ratings of relaxation, although respiration rate did. The most consistent correlation occurred between self-report measures and skin conductance fluctuation.

Conner [20] found that brief relaxation training was no more effective than music in lowering heart rate and skin conductance, although these subjects showed less skin conductance and heart rate response to aversive tone or threat of "thermal stimulation." Two recent reports confuse the picture further. Delman and Johnson [26] compared a biofeedback control with progressive muscle relaxation and a self-relaxation control. Frontalis EMG dropped sharply for the biofeedback group, with controls remaining at initial levels and relaxation subjects maintaining higher readings. Tonic heart rate results paralleled those for EMG—large decreases for the group biofeedback and smallest decrease for the relaxation group. Curiously, relaxation for all subjects was accompanied by relative peripheral vasoconstriction and skin conductance increases. Pollack and Zeiner [61] compared a relaxation group with a group told to relax without being given specific training, and a group of persons sitting quietly with their eyes closed. The only measure that discriminated between groups was heart rate, the sitting group showing the largest drop.

These contradictory findings suggest that, while relaxation produces some general physiologic changes, such as decrease in EMG, heart rate, respiratory rate, and perhaps skin conductance and fluctuation, these changes may not vary significantly from control groups simply told to relax or sit quietly. Furthermore, a general relaxation state and specific mechanisms of action have yet to be demonstrated. Mathews [50] has stated the point clearly: "It seems reasonable to suggest that several specific procedures may have the effect of reducing autonomic and muscular activity, but whether effects are observed, and in which measure (e.g., heart rate, respiratory rate, etc.), depends on details of the procedure and timing used, the length of training, and the nature of the comparison control process."

Relaxation Compared with Similar Procedures
The similarities of relaxation to hypnosis, autogenic training, and some types of meditation and biofeedback were noted previously. In this section, I shall review studies that have compared the impact of relaxation upon

autonomic responses with that of other procedures. Other studies, in which several procedures have been tried in order to compare their effect on an independent variable such as blood pressure, will be reviewed later.

Hypnosis
Litvak [44] notes that relaxation instructions bear many similarities to hypnotic induction techniques, including direct suggestions to relax, therapeutic subject expectation that obeying the instructions will lead to relaxation, actual relaxation training, and the use of imagination and autogenic suggestion. On the other hand, relaxation procedures attempt to leave control with the subject and to minimize the use of suggestion. In light of the similarities between these procedures, we would expect similar physiologic effects. In fact, Paul [60] found that forehead EMG, heart rate, respiration rate, and skin resistance decreased significantly more with mental relaxation than with hypnosis. However, Paul's results have been criticized for failure to use an adequate hypnosis procedure. His results differ, for instance, from those reported by Barber and Hahn [6], who found no differences between hypnosis and relaxation and whose hypnosis groups showed significantly greater effects than Paul's. Walrath and Hamilton [78] measured autonomic correlates of meditation and hypnosis and added a control group, whose members were told to "reduce autonomic function, relax as much as possible, ignore or render neutral all external stimuli and let thoughts come as they may." This sounds like relaxation without the muscular components. All procedures significantly affected heart rate, skin resistance, and respiration rate.

Mather and Degun [48] found no significant change in heart rate when comparing hypnosis and relaxation, although they found that subjects carried out more suggestions under hypnosis. The impression from these and other studies reviewed earlier is that relaxation induced by hypnotic suggestion is similar to that induced through muscle exercises.

Biofeedback
Biofeedback has been used in two ways to produce relaxation. Some authors [17, 79] have used biofeedback techniques to reduce EMG potentials in particular muscles in order to induce general relaxation. Others have used alpha feedback to induce relaxation. In direct comparison with relaxation training, relaxation facilitated or induced by EMG does not ap-

pear to be particularly superior. For instance, Coursey and Frankel [21] compared EMG feedback, instructions to relax, and self-relaxation. They found that all groups reported similar decreases in subjective anxiety. This result is not surprising, since EMG does not necessarily correlate with subjective anxiety [49]. As noted earlier, subjects with no muscle tonus (e.g., curarized) still report anxiety [22], and EMG changes induced by biofeedback in one muscle group do not necessarily generalize to other muscle groups [4]. Brenner [15] has suggested that the main effect of biofeedback is to facilitate or induce a generalized relaxation state, which occurs more as a result of the setting and instructions given than of any specific relaxation technique.

Alpha biofeedback has also been studied as a technique to induce relaxation. In a report of a series of studies, Lynch, Paskewitz, and Orne [45] report that alpha changes are mostly artifacts of the experimental situation and the subject's natural alpha density. Grynol and Jamieson [36] found that patients given false alpha feedback reported as much relaxation and decrease in anxiety as those given real alpha feedback.

Autogenic Training
Autogenic training, a technique popularized by Schultz and Luthe [68], involves a series of instructions to help patients gain control over autonomic functions. During the first two stages of training, patients assume a relaxed, passive position and repeat monotonous or repetitive instructions. However, Jus and Jus [40] argue that only the first two stages of autogenic training are similar to relaxation. They note that the subsequent instructions are directed at achieving control over autonomic functions, which necessitates attending to such functions. Unfortunately, comparative data for autogenic training and relaxation are too scanty to differentiate between the procedures or to demonstrate the advantages of one over another. In comparative studies where other independent variables are used besides peripheral physiologic responses, the results are contradictory or the procedures seem to have similar effects [11, 25, 56]. Several of these studies will be reviewed later.

Meditation
There are many types of meditation procedures, of which transcendental meditation is probably the most closely related to relaxation. Walrath and

Hamilton [78] compared meditation, hypnosis, and relaxation, finding significant but similar changes in heart rate and respiratory rate and fluctuations in galvanic skin responses for all three groups. He concluded that relaxation was as effective as transcendental meditation. The similarities and differences between meditation procedures and their specific usefulness require much further research; however, the transcendental meditation culture, with its frequent meetings and group support to continue meditation, offers a method for subjects to continue practicing a relaxation technique, if, in fact, it is important that subjects do continue.

Which Components of Relaxation are Necessary?
Jacobson's progressive relaxation, which involved weeks or months of practice, has been reduced to several hours or even minutes in most programs today, and the therapist has been replaced to some extent by taped instructions. Unfortunately, there is only inferential information about which technique or which aspect of a particular program is necessary. While more research is needed to elicit the active components of the relaxation technique, we have some data on the importance of some of these components.

Instructional Set
As noted in previous chapters (see pages 20-23) many experiments have demonstrated the importance of instructions and therapeutic expectancy to treatment outcome. By inference, the instructional set given patients asked to relax is important to the treatment outcome.

A Quiet Environment, Passive Attitude
While it seems easiest to learn to relax in a quiet environment, it has not been demonstrated to be necessary. In fact, many relaxation programs encourage patients to learn to relax even in a noisy environment. Acquiring the skill may require a different situation from practicing it.

Muscle Relaxation
Muscle relaxation is also unnecessary to learn to relax. For instance, Driscoll [27] recently noted that actively exercising subjects report subjective relaxation, and Hilgard [37] has observed that subjects can be hypnotized while pedaling a bicycle. Similarly, relaxation has not been demonstrated

to be necessary in systematic desensitization [1, 47]. However, as in systematic desensitization, muscle relaxation may provide a technique that suggests or promotes mental relaxation and facilitates subjects' spending a certain amount of time in one place. It also provides an exercise associated with mental relaxation that subjects can carry out on their own. In addition, it helps subjects learn to identify muscle tension as an indicator of tension. Finally, it provides a simple procedure for teaching mental relaxation.

Deep, Regular Breathing
The importance of deep, regular breathing has not been carefully tested. Deep, regular breathing, facilitates several interacting physiologic processes that may by themselves produce relaxation. The deep breathing may serve the same purposes with relaxation procedures as the muscle relaxation.

Pleasant Thoughts or Images
Rachman [62] has suggested that mental relaxation is the most important aspect of relaxation. The importance of this variable has yet to be teased out.

Frequency of Practice
Most therapists recommend that subjects practice relaxation once or twice per day, but, again, there is little evidence that this is necessary. The regular practice component was varied systematically in a study by Brady [12] using a single-case design. Relaxation training was found to decrease diastolic blood pressure over a measurement only baseline. When subjects stopped practicing in the next phase, blood pressure increased. Thus, we may conclude that regular practice contributed to the maintenance of the treatment effect, but the optimal practice schedule remains to be determined.

Using Relaxation in Stressful Situations
Many authors recommend that subjects practice relaxation when they feel tense during the day. The importance of this in reducing stress is uncertain. Practitioners of meditation achieve effects on independent measures (e.g., blood pressure) without incorporating the practice into their daily lives except during scheduled times.

Complications and Side Effects

Relaxation appears to be a remarkably safe technique; however, a few complications and side effects have been reported. Individuals can strain muscles by overly tightening them. Muscles at mechanical disadvantage (such as feet and back muscles) are at greatest risk. Similarly, individuals may experience pain when muscle groups protecting an injured or irritated part of the musculoskeletal system relax. One subject, who suffered a paresis in his throat muscles as a result of a war injury, reported extremely painful spasm in these muscles when he practiced relaxation. Mental side effects of relaxation have also been reported. Some patients report unpleasant and even anxiety-provoking thoughts or images when they undergo relaxation. Benson, Beary, and Carol [8] noted that several cases of acute psychosis have been reported with subjects who practice transcendental meditation; presumably, since the techniques are related, the same risk should be present with relaxation.

Noncompliance with medical regimens may occur with some subjects. Because relaxation is becoming widely used for many medical problems where medications are of clear benefit, the following case is presented to forewarn therapists to exercise caution in their instructions to patients. A 64-year-old woman was referred from a medical clinic for participation in a hypertension-relaxation project and was randomly assigned to the relaxation group. After missing two scheduled appointments, she appeared, was taught relaxation and given a tape recorder and relaxation tape, and instructed to return in one week. She was told to continue her medication treatment at the medical clinic and that the relaxation was an adjunct to her medical treatment. The patient did not return to the relaxation program (although her therapist wrote her two letters). She appeared in an emergency room six weeks later in a hypertensive crisis (blood pressure greater than 220/150) and claimed that she had stopped her hypertension medication because "my other doctor told me that relaxation would work better than medication and I didn't need to take it." Her high blood pressure was presumably related to her not taking medication. While this patient had a history of noncompliance with medical regimens, the relaxation program provided a ready excuse for her to stop her medications.

Uses of Relaxation

Until the past few years the main use of relaxation in behavior therapy was as part of the procedure of systematic desensitization (see Chapters 7 and 8). Now, however, relaxation has been applied to many clinical problems as a separate technique. Predictably, the most common use has been with problems thought to be related to anxiety and stress—problems usually classified as psychosomatic. Jacobson [39] originally developed the technique for similar problems, but the notion that relaxation is useful in such conditions considerably precedes him [5]. Relaxation has been used for its many nonspecific therapeutic effects, such as increasing visual imagery.

While relaxation has been applied to many clinical problems and appears useful in some, the results of these studies must be interpreted with caution, since many suffer from the methodologic problems that have long plagued psychosomatic research, such as the use of single-case and anecdotal reports, inadequate controls, poor design, and no follow-up. An adequate between-group experimental design should include an experimental group receiving a clearly specified treatment; a no-treatment group; and a group receiving pseudotreatment designed to control for nonspecific therapeutic effects. In addition, several therapists should each treat the same number of patients in each group to control for therapist bias and unequal experience. Finally, the response of interest should be carefully defined and objectively measurable, and adequate follow-up should be provided.

Data on the effect of placebos on hypertension emphasize the importance of adequate experimental design. The systolic blood pressure response of an individual given a milk injection by an enthusiastic investigator who believed that milk was a powerful antihypertensive is shown in Figure 6. As can be seen, the patient's blood pressure dropped dramatically following this inert treatment and remained significantly below baseline for the rest of the time blood pressure was recorded. To examine the effect of placebos more closely, data from a number of controlled hypertension studies in which placebos were used are pooled in Figure 7. As can be seen, the placebo effects reached a peak at around seven weeks and seemed to disappear by 14 weeks, suggesting that placebo effects are powerful and relatively long-lasting. Unfortunately, many of the clinical uses of relaxation have been for problems analogous to blood pressure, conditions in which "placebo" or nonspecific effects are well known to occur. Because of these nonspecific effects, anecdotal and inadequately designed trials of relaxation training must be viewed with caution.

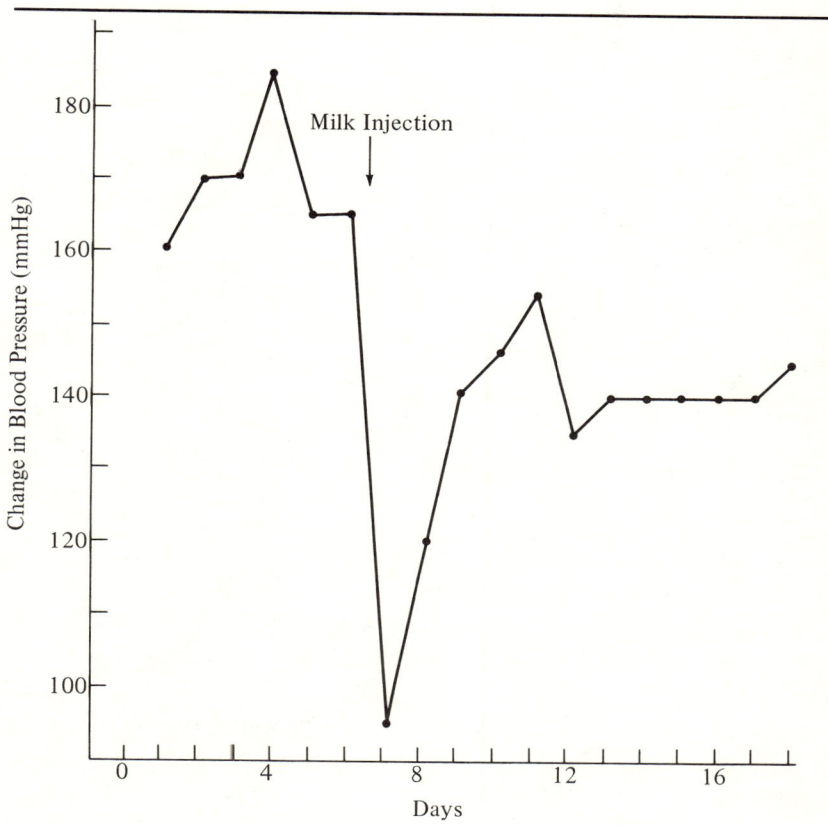

Figure 6. *The effect of a placebo (milk) injection on the blood pressure of a hypertensive patient. Both the dramatic initial effect and the extended effect lasting several days should be noted.*

Blood Pressure

Jacobson [39] was the first to suggest that progressive relaxation would reduce high blood pressure, and recently several others have confirmed his views (see reference [38] for a detailed review of this area). Benson, Rosner, Marzetta, and Klemchuk [10] trained 14 pharmacologically treated hypertensive patients in a relaxation procedure. Systolic blood pressure fell an

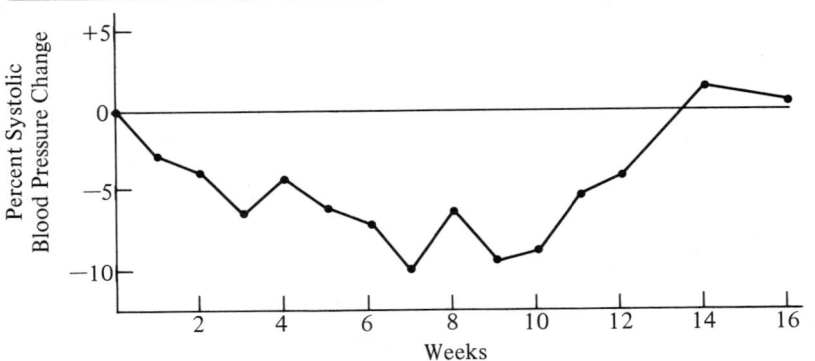

Figure 7. *The time course of the placebo effect upon blood pressure. These data, taken from a series of placebo studies, illustrate the relatively prolonged effect of various kinds of placebo medication.*

average of 11 mmHg (p < 0.01) from baseline recording, while diastolic blood pressure fell an average of 5 mmHg (p < 0.05). Unfortunately, no control group was used and no follow-up data were reported. In a randomized design Deabler, Fidel, Dillenkoffer, and Elder [25] used relaxation and hypnosis to reduce the blood pressure of nine subjects receiving hypertensive medication and of six subjects on no drugs. Over a nine-session treatment period, systolic blood pressure fell by 8 to 12 percent in the no-drug group, with hypnosis leading to a further reduction of blood pressure of about 5 percent. Both results were significantly better than the no-treatment control.

In the most impressive series of studies to date, Patel [57–59] reported that relaxation-like procedures may have long-term effects. In the first study, 20 patients with hypertension were trained in yoga and in EMG and GSR biofeedback during weekly half-hour sessions over two months. During treatment, antihypertensive medications were stopped in five patients and reduced in another seven by 33 to 60 percent. The mean blood pressure for the treated group was reduced from 121 mmHg to 101 mmHg, despite a 41 percent decrease in drug requirements. The study was flawed by having no controls or follow-up, and the experimenter managed both medication changes and the behavioral treatment. However, in a later study

Patel [58] followed up the same patients on a monthly basis and added a nonrandomly selected control group for comparison. The treatment group showed a statistically significant reduction in blood pressure and antihypertensive medication for the 12-month period as compared with the controls. To improve further on the design, Patel and North [59] randomly assigned subjects to either a yoga and EMG biofeedback group or to a placebo group told to sit quietly in the therapist's office. Seventeen subjects were treated in each group, using a crossover design in which the control group received treatment during the second phase of the experiment. In the first phase, systolic blood pressure was reduced by a mean of 26 mmHg for the treated subjects compared with 9 mmHg for the controls, and diastolic pressure was reduced by 15 mmHg for the treated subjects compared with 4 mmHg for the controls. The control group was then treated and achieved blood pressure drops comparable to those of the initially treated group.

Taylor, Nelson, Farquhar, and Agras [77] compared relaxation therapy, nonspecific therapy (in which subjects spent an equal amount of time with the therapist and were given general instructions as to how to deal with stress in their lives), and medical treatment only with essential hypertensives, all of whom were receiving medical treatment. The relaxation therapy group showed a 10 percent change in systolic blood pressure between the beginning and the end of treatment, a change that diminished slightly at six-month follow-up. The nonspecific therapy group showed only a 2 percent change in systolic blood pressure at the end of treatment but improved to 3 percent six months later. The medical treatment-only group showed no significant change at the end of treatment but dropped to nearly five percent six months later. There was a significant difference between the systolic blood pressure of the relaxation group and that of the nonspecific therapy group at the end of treatment and at six-month follow-up. There was also a significant difference in systolic blood pressure between the relaxation and medical treatment-only groups at the end of treatment. However, this significant difference was lost at six months. The conclusion from this study and from those of Patel is that although nonspecific therapy adds little to the medical management of essential hypertension, telling patients to relax confers a small additional benefit, and teaching relaxation techniques confers a larger and apparently clinically significant benefit. Maintenance techniques similar to those outlined by Patel appear to be necessary to achieve longer-term effects.

Other Cardiovascular Problems
Relaxation is now being applied to other cardiovascular problems in which stress may play a role. Benson, Alexander, and Feldman [7], working on the assumption that premature ventricular contractions are increased by stress, found that a relaxation technique reduced their frequency.

Headache
The effects of relaxation on tension headache have been examined in several studies. Since prolonged tension in the neck muscles appears to produce some of the pain of tension headaches, relaxation of these muscles would, presumably, alleviate headaches. Clinicians have often injected small doses of local anesthetic into painful muscles, with the idea of breaking the pattern of muscle spasm. Budzynski, Stoyva, and Adler [16] were among the first to apply EMG feedback-induced relaxation to relieve tension headaches. Five subjects were trained in the procedure for four weeks to two months, and significant pretest to posttest differences were found. Wickramasekera [80] also used EMG feedback training in five patients with tension headaches. His design involved three weeks of baseline, followed by three weeks of false feedback, followed by two weeks of real feedback. All subjects reported a decrease in both the intensity and the frequency of headaches during the contingent feedback phase, but not during the false feedback or baseline phase. Finally, in a randomized trial involving 35 subjects exposed to various combinations of relaxation training and EMG biofeedback [19], relaxation training was found to reduce headache frequency more effectively than either biofeedback or a no-treatment control. However, for headache severity a combination of EMG feedback and relaxation training was the most effective. Despite the lack of a behavioral or physiologic measure of headache, it seems reasonable to conclude that relaxation training used in combination with EMG feedback is an effective treatment for tension headache.

However, the effect of relaxation on migraine headaches is less certain. These headaches are caused by cerebral, meningeal, and extracranial arterial vasoconstriction followed by dilatation and distention of cranial vessels, especially the external carotid artery. The persistent dilation is followed by a phase of muscle contraction with pain. Wolff [81] observed that migraines worsen when subjects take time off from their usual pressures. In light of the proposed etiology of migraine headaches and of the general unimpressive effects of relaxation on the pain caused by tension headaches, one might wonder if relaxation would be of any benefit in this condition. Benson, Klemchuk, and Graham [9] studied 17 patients who regularly elicited the relaxation response through the practice of transcendental meditation. They stated that the technique had limited usefulness in the treatment of severe migraine headaches, but, in fact, six of the 17 subjects reported improvement.

Asthma
As stress may play a role in increasing the incidence and severity of asthmatic attacks [70], relaxation would appear to be useful. Furthermore, subjects experiencing asthmatic attacks report increased anxiety that may, in turn, lead to increased breathing difficulties. In an early study, Moore [54] treated 12 asthmatics with systematic desensitization, relaxation, and direct suggestion. All groups improved, although only the desensitization group showed an increase in peak expiratory flow rate, a function of airway resistance that is increased in asthmatics. Davis, Saunders, Creer, and Chai [24] compared preairway and postairway resistance in asthmatic children treated with relaxation training, with and without biofeedback assistance, with preairway and postairway resistance in children given reading material and told to relax. Nonsevere asthmatics trained in either relaxation technique showed a significant reduction in airway resistance immediately after treatment but not one week later. Relaxation training combined with biofeedback produced greater changes than did relaxation alone.

Similarly, Alexander [3] found that relaxation-trained subjects showed a significant improvement in peak expiratory flow rate when they were practicing relaxation as compared with when they merely sat quietly. Thus, relaxation may be a useful adjunctive treatment with some asthmatics.

Stress and Anxiety
The psychologic literature is not clear on the meaning of stress or in differentiating between stress and anxiety. In fact, such terms as *stress, anxiety, emotional distress, extreme environmental conditions, frustration,* and *tension arousal* are often used interchangeably. Unfortunately, lacking a clear measure of stress, we must rely on behavioral, psychological, and biochemical data that suggest that an organism is undergoing the kinds of changes that we associate with stress. We have already reviewed several

pathophysiologic conditions thought to be related to stress (hypertension, irregular cardiac rhythms, and asthma) and have suggested that relaxation is a useful adjunct to the medical treatment of these conditions. Another approach to determine the impact of relaxation on stress is to compare the reaction to supposedly stressful stimuli of subjects practicing or trained in relaxation with that of subjects not skilled in relaxation. Davidson and Hiebert [23] showed a stressful film to a group of subjects trained in relaxation, a group given relaxation instructions only, and a control group given no instructions on relaxation. All groups reported decreased anxiety when they were repeatedly exposed to the stress film, but only the relaxation group and the relaxation instruction group showed change in skin conductance, the sole physiologic measure used.

When we turn to a more commonly encountered stress, relaxation training was found to be more effective than hypnosis or a control for reducing stress in a dental situation for subjects with high baseline skin conductance [51]. The opposite was true for subjects with a medium basal skin conductance, and there was no difference between treatments for low skin conductance levels. Similarly, Conner [20] found that subjects trained in brief relaxation showed less physiologic response to an anxiety-evoking stimulus than did control subjects. Finally, Aiken and Henrichs [2] used systematic relaxation with a group of pre-open heart surgery patients. The relaxation group had fewer "psychiatric problems" than a no-treatment control group, but the groups were not matched for operation duration—a variable that may account for the difference.

Another approach is to measure the biochemical changes accompanying exposure to stress. In a recent study, Stone and Deleo [75] found that subjects trained in relaxation showed a significant reduction in dopamine beta hydroxylase compared with a control group and their own baseline measurement. Dopamine beta hydroxylase may provide a direct index of sympathetic nervous activity, which is thought to be increased in stressful situations. Unfortunately, the usefulness of dopamine beta hydroxylase as an index of sympathetic nervous activity is controversial, but this study may point the way to further work in this important area.

While anecdotal reports abound on the usefulness of relaxation on "pervasive" or general anxiety (e.g., [18, 30, 39]), no controlled studies have been undertaken in this area. This is surprising when one considers the frequent use of relaxation by many therapists to treat anxiety.

Insomnia

Based on the notion that anxiety is related to insomnia, relaxation has been used to treat both sleep-onset insomnia and frequent awakening. There are many anecdotal case studies attesting to the efficiency of this procedure with insomnia (e.g., [33, 39, 63]), but there are few controlled trials. (For a review of recent behavioral treatments for insomnia see reference [53].)

In one controlled trial, progressive relaxation, hypnotic relaxation, self-relaxation, and a no-treatment control were compared [11]. Subjective measures of sleep indicated that all three treatment conditions were significantly more effective than the control conditions, but the differences between the three conditions were small. Other authors have compared relaxation alone with systematic desensitization [11, 14] and have found both treatments equally effective and superior to a no-treatment control. Again, Nicassio and Bootzin [55] found that progressive relaxation was as effective as autogenic training for treating insomnia and that both were better than controls. Thus, relaxation seems to be a useful approach to insomnia.

Other Problems

Relaxation has been used for muscle tension; thus, Gessel and Alderman [34] used relaxation to reduce the pain secondary to dysfunction of the temporal-mandibular joint. They noted that subjects who were depressed and tense improved most. Relaxation training has also been used with some success to treat tics and muscle spasms; its use with tension headaches was noted previously. In addition, the technique has been reported to be useful for other medical problems, including gastric acid secretion and motility [73], phantom limb pain [52], dysmenorrhea [76], and urinary retention [66].

Finally, relaxation is used in many programs for various nonspecific purposes. Thus, it has been reported to decrease anger [56], to help with ongoing psychotherapy [72], as a general coping skill [69], to increase visual imagery [29], and as an alternative response (e.g., relaxing instead of smoking or drinking [74]).

Overview

Although relaxation achieved popularity in behavior therapy as a component of systematic desensitization, it has since been used by itself for a number of conditions in which increased autonomic activity appears to play a part in the pathophysiology. *Specific* physiologic effects of relaxation have not been demonstrated, although relaxation, like the related procedures of hypnosis, autogenic training, and meditation, may lead to a generally relaxed state, with effects on the autonomic nervous system. Consistent with its use for such conditions, relaxation leads to peripheral physiologic changes suggestive of decreased autonomic activity. However, these changes can also be produced by sitting quietly and other control procedures and may not reflect a central or specific relaxation state. While relaxation shares features with other procedures such as hypnosis, meditation, biofeedback, and autogenic training, and while it has been taught by tape recording and facilitated by drugs, biofeedback, and metronomes, no advantage for the uses we have described have been demonstrated for one of these over another. Furthermore, relaxation is a relatively safe procedure, although some side effects have been reported.

Several carefully controlled trials suggest that relaxation may be useful as an adjunct to medical treatment in a number of pathophysiologic conditions. The most carefully controlled and impressive studies have been done with blood pressure, although anecdotes and less carefully controlled studies suggest usefulness as an adjunct to medical treatment for asthma, tension headaches, and insomnia. Less clear evidence suggests that relaxation may be useful in reducing stress or anxiety. How much relaxation, what kind, and for what other pathophysiologic problems will have to await further exploration.

References

1. Agras, W. S., Leitenberg, H., Barlow, D. H., Curtis, N., Edwards, J., and Wright, D. Relaxation in systematic desensitization. *Archives of General Psychiatry* 25:511, 1971.
2. Aiken, L. H., and Henrichs, T. F. Systematic relaxation as a nursing intervention technique with open heart surgery patients. *Nursing Research* 20:212, 1971.
3. Alexander, A. B. Systematic relaxation and flow rates in asthmatic children: Relationship to emotional precipitants and anxiety. *Journal of Psychosomatic Research* 16:405, 1972.
4. Alexander, A. B., and Hanson, D. B. Experimental test of assumptions related to the use of EMG biofeedback as a general relaxation training technique. *Proceedings of the Biofeedback Society*, Annual Meeting, p. 41, 1974.
5. Bagchi, B. K. Mental hygiene and the Hindu doctrine of relaxation. *Mental*

Hygiene 20:424, 1936.
6. Barber, T. X., and Hahn, K. W. Hypnotic induction and "relaxation." *Archives of General Psychiatry* 8:295, 1963.
7. Benson, H., Alexander, S., and Feldman, C. C. Decreasing PVC's through use of the relaxation response in patients with stable ischemic heart disease. *Lancet* ii:308, 1975.
8. Benson, H., Beary, J. F., and Carol, M. P. The relaxation response. *Psychiatry* 37:37, 1974.
9. Benson, H., Klemchuk, H. P., and Graham, J. R. The usefulness of the relaxation response in the treatment of headache. *Headache* 14:49, 1974.
10. Benson, H., Rosner, B. A., Marzetta, B. R., and Klemchuk, H. M. Decreased blood pressure in pharmacologically treated hypertensive patients who regularly elicited the relaxation response. *Lancet* i:289, 1974.
11. Borkovec, T. D., and Fowles, D. C. Controlled investigation of the effects of progressive and hypnotic relaxation on insomnia. *Journal of Abnormal Psychology* 82:153, 1973.
12. Brady, J. P. Metronome-conditioned relaxation: a new behavioral procedure. *British Journal of Psychiatry* 122:729, 1973.
13. Brady, J. P. Comments on methohexitone-aided systematic desensitization. *Behavior Research and Therapy* 5:259, 1967.
14. Brady, J. P., Luborsky, L., and Kron, R. E. Blood pressure reduction in patients with essential hypertension through metronome-conditioned relaxation: a preliminary report. *Behavior Therapy* 5:203, 1974.
15. Brenner, J. Factors influencing the specificity of voluntary cardiovascular control. In L. Dicara (Ed.), *Limbic and Autonomic Nervous Systems Research*. New York: Plenum Press, 1974.
16. Budzynski, T. H., Stoyva, J., and Adler, C. Feedback induced muscle relaxation: application to tension headache. *Journal of Behavior Therapy and Experimental Psychiatry* 1:205, 1970.
17. Budzynski, T. H., and Stoyva, J. M. An instrument for producing deep muscle relaxation by means of analogy information feedback, *Journal of Applied Behavior Analysis* 2:231, 1969.
18. Cautela, J. A behavioral therapy approach to pervasive anxiety. *Behavior Research Therapy* 4:99, 1966.
19. Chesney, M. A., and Shelton, J. L. A comparison of muscle relaxation and electromyogram biofeedback treatment for muscle contraction headache. *Journal of Behavior Therapy and Experimental Psychiatry* 7:221, 1976.
20. Conner, W. H. Effects of brief relaxation training on autonomic responses to anxiety evoking stimuli. *Psychophysiology* 11:591, 1974.
21. Coursey, R. B., and Frankel, B. L. EMG feedback as a relaxation technique. *Proceedings of the Biofeedback Research Society*, Annual Meeting, p. 43, 1974.
22. Davidson, G. C. Anxiety under total curarization: Implication for the role of muscular relaxation in the desensitization of neurotic fears. *Journal of Nervous and Mental Disease* 143:443, 1966.
23. Davidson, P. O., and Hiebert, S. F. Relaxation training, relaxation instructions and repeated exposure to a stressor film. *Journal of Abnormal Psychology* 78:154, 1971.
24. Davis, M. H., Saunders, D. R., Creer, T. L., and Chai, H. Relaxation train-

ing facilitated by biofeedback apparatus as a supplement treatment in bronchial asthma. *Journal of Psychosomatic Research* 17:121, 1973.
25. Deabler, H. K., Fidel, E., Dillenkoffer, R. I., and Elder, S. T. The use of relaxation and hypnosis in lowering high blood pressure. *American Journal of Clinical Hypnosis* 16:75, 1973.
26. Delman, R. P., and Johnson, H. J. Biofeedback and progressive muscle relaxation: a comparison of psychophysiological effects. *Psychophysiology* 13:181 (abstract), 1976.
27. Driscoll, R. Anxiety reduction using physical exertion and positive images. *Psychological Record* 26:87, 1976.
28. Edelman, R. I. Effects of progressive relaxation on autonomic process. *Journal of Clinical Psychology* 26:421, 1970.
29. Foulkes, D., and Fleisher, S. Mental activity in relaxed wakefulness. *Journal of Abnormal Psychology* 84:66, 1975.
30. French, A. P., and Tupin, J. P. Therapeutic application of a simple relaxation method. *American Journal of Psychiatry* 28:282, 1974.
31. Friedman, D. A new technique for the systematic desensitization of phobic symptoms. *Behavior Research Therapy* 4:139, 1966.
32. Gellhorn, E. *Principles of Autonomic-somatic Integrations*. Minneapolis: University of Minneapolis Press, 1967.
33. Gershman, L., and Clouser, R. A. Treatment of insomnia with relaxation and desensitization in a group setting by an automated apparatus. *Journal of Behavior Therapy and Experimental Psychiatry* 5:31, 1974.
34. Gessel, A. H., and Alderman, M. M. Management of myofascial pain dysfunction syndrome of the temporal-mandibular joint by tension control training. *Psychosomatics* 12:302, 1971.
35. Grossberg, J. M. The physiological effectiveness of brief training in differential muscle relaxation. *Technical Report No. 9*. La Jolla, Calif.: Western Behavioral Science, Inc., 1966.
36. Grynol, E., and Jamieson, J. Alpha feedback and relaxation: a cautionary note. *Perceptual and Motor Skills* 40:53, 1975.
37. Hilgard, E. Personal communication, 1976.
38. Jacob, R. G., Kraemer, H. C., and Agras, W. S. Relaxation therapy in the treatment of hypertension: A review. *Archives of General Psychiatry*. In press.
39. Jacobson, E. *Progressive Relaxation*. Chicago: University of Chicago Press, 1938.
40. Jus, A., and Jus, K. Some remarks on "passive" concentration and the autogenic shift. In: L. Chertok (Ed.), *Psychophysiological Mechanism of Hypnosis*. Berlin: Springer-Verlag, 1969.
41. Lader, M. H., Mathews, A. M. Comparison of methods of relaxation using physiological measures. *Behavior Research Therapy* 8:331, 1970.
42. Lader, M. H., and Mathews, A. M. Electromyographic studies of tension. *Journal of Psychosomatic Research* 15:479, 1971.
43. Lader, M. H., and Wing, L. *Physiological Measures: Sedative Drugs and Morbid Anxiety*. New York: Oxford University Press, 1966.
44. Litvak, S. B. Hypnosis and the desensitization behavior therapies. *Psychological Report* 27:787, 1970.
45. Lynch, J. J., Paskewitz, E. A., and Orne, M. T. Some factors in the feed-

back control of human alpha rhythm. *Psychological Medicine* 36:399, 1974.
46. Marquis, J. Relaxation tape and instructional manual. Distributed by Self-Management School, Los Altos, California, 1974.
47. Marshall, W., Strawbridge, H., and Keltner, A. The role of mental relaxation in experimental desensitization. *Behavior Research Therapy* 10:355, 1972.
48. Mather, M. D., and Degun, G. S. A comparative study of hypnosis and relaxation. *British Journal of Medical Psychology* 48:55, 1975.
49. Mathews, A. M., and Gelder, M. G. Psychophysiological investigations of brief relaxation training. *Journal of Psychosomatic Research* 13:1, 1967.
50. Mathews, A. M. Psychophysiological approaches to the investigation of desensitization and related procedures. *Psychological Bulletin* 76:73, 1971.
51. McAmmond, D. M., Davidson, P. O., and Kovitz, D. M. A comparison of the effects of relaxation training on stress reactions in a dental situation. *American Journal of Clinical Hypnosis*, 13:233, 1971.
52. McKechnie, R. J. Relief from phantom limb pain by relaxation exercises. *Journal of Behavior Therapy and Experimental Psychiatry* 6:263, 1975.
53. Montgomery, I., Perkin, G., and Wise, D. A review of behavioral treatments for insomnia. *Journal of Behavior Therapy and Experimental Psychiatry* 6:93, 1975.
54. Moore, N. Behavior therapy in bronchial asthma: A controlled study. *Journal of Psychosomatic Research* 9:257, 1965.
55. Nicassio, P., and Bootzin, R. A comparison of progressive relaxation and autogenic training as treatment for insomnia. *Journal of Abnormal Psychology* 83:253, 1974.
56. O'Donnel, C. R., and Worell, L. Motor and cognitive relaxation in the desensitization of anger. *Behavior Research Therapy* 11:473, 1973.
57. Patel, C. H. Yoga and biofeedback in the management of hypertension. *Lancet* ii:1053, 1973.
58. Patel, C. H. Twelve month follow up of yoga and biofeedback in the management of hypertension. *Lancet* i:62, 1975.
59. Patel, C. H., and North, W. R. Randomized controlled trial of yoga and biofeedback in management of hypertension. *Lancet* ii:93, 1975.
60. Paul, G. L. Physiological effects of relaxation training and hypnotic suggestion. *Journal of Abnormal Psychology* 74:425, 1969.
61. Pollack, M. H., and Zeiner, A. R. Physiological correlates of Bensonian relaxation training with controls for relaxation and sitting. *Psychophysiology* 13:181 (abstract), 1976.
62. Rachman, S. The role of muscular relaxation in desensitization therapy. *Behavior Research Therapy* 6:159, 1968.
63. Raskin, M., Johnson, G., and Rondestvedt, J. W. Chronic anxiety treated by feedback-induced muscle relaxation. *Archives of General Psychiatry* 28:263, 1973.
64. Reeves, J. L., and Mealiea, W. L. Biofeedback-assisted cue-controlled relaxation for the treatment of flight phobias. *Journal of Behavior Therapy and Experimental Psychiatry* 6:105, 1975.
65. Richards, W. D. Circulatory effects of hyperventilation and hypoventilation. In P. Dow (Ed.), *Handbook of Physiology*, Sec. 2: Circulation, Vol. II. Washington, D.C.: American Physiological Society, 1970.

66. Roy, I., and Murphy, J. Metronome conditioned relaxation and urinary retention. *Canadian Psychiatric Association Journal* 20:139, 1975.
67. Russell, R. K., and Sipich, J. F. Treatment of test anxiety by cue-controlled relaxation. *Behavior Therapy* 5:673, 1974.
68. Schultz, J. H., and Luthe, W. *Autogenic Training*. New York: Grune and Stratton, Inc., 1959.
69. Sherman, A. R. Two-year follow-up training in relaxation as a behavioral self-management skill. *Behavior Therapy* 6:149, 1975.
70. Siegal, S. Current trends in bronchial asthma. *New York Journal of Medicine* 67:621 and 67:1057, 1967.
71. Sirota, A. P., and Mahoney, M. J. Relaxation on cue: the self-regulation of asthma. *Journal of Behavior Therapy and Experimental Psychiatry* 5:65, 1974.
72. Snaith, R. P. A method of psychotherapy based on relaxation techniques. *British Journal of Psychiatry* 92:473, 1974.
73. Stacher, G., Berner, P., Naske, R., Schuster, P., Bauer, P., Starker, H., and Schulze, D. Effect of hypnotic suggestion of relaxation on basal and metrazole-induced gastric acid secretion. *Gastroenterology* 68:656, 1975.
74. Steffen, J. J. Electromyographically induced relaxation in the treatment of chronic alcohol abuse. *Journal of Consulting and Clinical Psychology* 43:275, 1975.
75. Stone, R. A., and Deleo, J. Psychotherapeutic control of hypertension. *New England Journal of Medicine* 294:80, 1976.
76. Tasto, D. L., and Chesney, M. A. Muscle relaxation treatment for primary deponemorhea. *Behavior Therapy* 5:668, 1974.
77. Taylor, C. B., Nelson, E., Farquhar, J., and Agras, W. S. The effects of relaxation on high blood pressure. *Archives of General Psychiatry*. In press.
78. Walrath, L. C., and Hamilton, D. W. Autonomic correlates of meditation and hypnosis. *American Journal of Clinical Hypnosis* 17:190, 1975.
79. Wickramasekera, I. Electromyographic feedback training and tension headache: preliminary observation. *American Journal of Clinical Hypnosis* 15:83, 1972.
80. Wickramasekera, I. Heart rate feedback and the management of cardiac neurosis. *Journal of Abnormal Psychology* 83:758, 1974.
81. Wolff, H. G. *Headache and Other Pains* (Second Edition). New York: Oxford University Press, 1958.
82. Wolpe, J. *Psychotherapy by Reciprocal Inhibition*. Stanford: Stanford University Press, 1958.

7. Exposure Treatments: Conceptual Issues
Isaac Marks

Editor's Introduction

In the next two chapters, approaches to the treatment of behavior problems such as phobia and obsessive-compulsive disorders that might—as noted in Chapter 3—be hypothesized to be maintained by negative reinforcement will be discussed. This area of research owes its recent momentum to the introduction of systematic desensitization by Wolpe. In his original animal experiment, Wolpe [160] produced "neurotic" behavior in cats by applying strong electric shocks. Feeding the cats in a series of situations that gradually approximated the one in which the animal had been punished led to the disappearance of maladaptive behavior. In the application of this demonstration to humans, Wolpe took a great conceptual leap and equated imaginary exposure with real exposure, and relaxation with feeding. While desensitization has been shown to be more effective than nontreatment or verbal psychotherapy in controlled-outcome studies (see page 204), recent work suggests that the variable involved in overcoming avoidance behavior is neither the pairing of relaxation with imagined fear-evoking scenes nor the graduated approach, but exposure to the actual feared situation. This theme is the main thrust of the next two chapters.

Exposure may be gradual and largely imagined, as in desensitization, or as rapid as possible and in the real-life situation, as in flooding. Related techniques include shaping (reinforced practice), paradoxical intention, and response prevention. Paradoxical intention (page 192) is derived from existential therapy but effectively exposes patients to their feared situation by asking them to try deliberately to bring on the feared consequences of their behavior instead of avoiding situations. Thus, the agoraphobic with a fear that she will faint if she walks alone is told to try to faint. She finds that she cannot and is enabled to confront her phobic situation. Response prevention was introduced by Meyer (pages 218–231). In this procedure, the compulsive patient is prevented from carrying out rituals, thus ensuring exposure to the feared situation that has hitherto been avoided by ritualistic behavior.

The basic mechanisms underlying many of these procedures as well as their efficacy have been investigated in animals (pages 168–172), in analogue populations (pages 174–188), and, as described in Chapter 8, in the clinic. Marks's conclusion is that exposure to the feared situation in reality is the basic mechanism shared by all successful therapies, be they those used in the past, as described on pages 188–193, or behavior therapies such as desensitization, shaping, implosion, and flooding—with or without modeling (see pages 204–213). In Marks's terminology, the patient should be exposed to all aspects of the (fear-) evoking stimulus (ES) until the evoked responses (ER), be they avoidance behavior, autonomic arousal, or worrying thoughts, are completely overcome.

This conclusion, that the best therapy consists of changing behavior in the environment in which it occurs, echoes the theme of earlier chapters, where it is demonstrated that a therapeutic environment is one in which the patient is motivated to practice adaptive behaviors and drop maladaptive behaviors. The token economy ward and the classroom are environments of this type, while the family is another example of an environment in which therapy can be arranged. Techniques such as role playing and modeling that allow the acquisition of skills within an interpersonal relationship may also work in part by exposure to feared social situations and are described in the section on assertive training in Chapter 9.

W. S. A.

Exposure treatments are the most common behavioral approach to adult neuroses such as phobia and obsessive-compulsive disorders. Such treatments share the common element of contact with stimuli that evoke discomfort (the evoking stimuli: ES) until the discomfort subsides. The procedures can be ordered along a continuum of approach to those situations that evoke the patient's distress. At one end is *flooding*, in which the approach is rapid and prolonged, and the patient usually evinces substantial emotion. Although in flooding there is some grading of approach, this gradient is steeper than in desensitization, in which exposure is slow, graded, brief, and largely imaginal, with minimum tension and with a contrasting experience such as relaxation. Commonly, the approach is somewhere between these extremes, and the choice of terms such as flooding or desensitization becomes rather arbitrary. The label *exposure* is less confusing, especially if it specifies the following: the duration of exposure; whether the gradient of approach was steep or gradual; whether exposure was to live stimuli or to filmed or fantasied ones; whether the patient was exposed to the ES individually or with others in a group; what instructions were given about self-exposure between treatment sessions; and whether

Table 3. Varieties of approach to the ES (exposure treatment)

Therapist-assisted exposure/self-exposure homework

Fantasy/film/live/ ± interval between fantasy and live exposure
  ± behavior rehearsal
  tape-recorded/live therapist
Slow (desensitization)/fast (flooding)
  start at top/bottom of hierarchy
  order high–low/low–high
Individual/group—cohesive/noncohesive unstructured
  ± home program of self-exposure
Cues: — supplied/controlled by patient/therapist
  imposed externally by therapist or abreacted spontaneously by patient
  Content: phobic stimulus ± approach/phobia-irrelevant threat/
         "psychodynamic"
  Style: coping/mastery/helplessness
  Affect: anxiety (catharsis)/anger/relaxation/meditation/humor
± therapeutic expectancy
± stress immunization, coping, anxiety management
± modeling in fantasy/film/live
± reward

Duration: short/long of exposure within/over total sessions; spaced/massed of intervals within/between sessions

Endpoint of:
  session — Is it best to end on good note?
  treatment — How far over hump must patient go for improvement to stabilize?

---

the patient saw a model undergoing similar exposure first. Table 3 summarizes the main forms of approach and therefore of exposure treatment and provides a framework for understanding the complex terminology that has burgeoned in the literature.

Terminology

Exposure treatments are usually *therapist-assisted*, in which case the patient ventures into the phobic situation (fantasied or real ES) in the presence of a therapist. However, between sessions patients are commonly instructed to continue going into phobic situations by themselves, and this is termed *self-exposure homework*. Systematic homework of this kind might be a crucial therapeutic ingredient. If research confirms this, treatment programs or packages (see Chapter 9) might be devised to be largely self-administered or family-administered and so economical of therapist time.

Exposure in real life, otherwise called exposure in vivo, or practice of such treatment can occur in many ways. In what was termed *counterphobic treatment* [142], a therapist suddenly thrust a live snake into the hands of snake-fearful subjects, who had to hold them for two six-minute periods. In a more graded approach, called *prolonged exposure*, a phobic patient rapidly came into continuous contact with the real phobic object for several hours [151]. When this occurred with several patients together, it was termed *group exposure in vivo* [55, 57] or *group confrontation* [162]. *Flooding in vivo* denotes rapid real-life exposure, with deliberate maximization of the patient's anxiety during exposure. Rapid, prolonged flooding is sometimes described as a form of *massed practice*, which refers to repeated practicing of any behavior without much rest between trials. Exposure in vivo without avoidance has been termed *arugamama* in Japanese descriptions of Morita therapy [75]. Maneuvers for patients to exaggerate their fears deliberately have been termed *paradoxical intention* [43].

Graded exposure in vivo has been called *participation, participant modelling*, and *contact desensitization* [5, 84, 85, 105, 117]. Here the subject watches a model being exposed to the real phobic situation and then is exposed himself. Graded exposure without modeling has been called *practical retraining* or *practice* [1, 27, 78]. When patients carry out exposure in vivo themselves, this has been called *self-observation* [37] or *exposure homework* [93]. Graded exposure in vivo accompanied by contingent reward is termed *shaping, reinforced practice,* or *successive approximation* [1, 41, 79]. Exposure in vivo has also been timed to coincide with coping techniques, such as *respiratory relief*, or running [111, 125]. In *aversion relief*, shocks are associated with termination of a brief period of exposure to a phobic slide or object [137].

Deconditioning describes the reduction of anxiety in hospitalized soldiers who had been subjected to repeated air raids [124]. The soldiers were moved in stages from the more protected ground floor to the first and then the second floor of the hospital. Saul and Leuser [129] and McLaughlin and Miller [88] called a similar approach in soldiers with combat anxiety *desensitization*. Patients saw graded war films or heard air raid noises, while modifying the sound level with their own volume controls.

Exposure in Fantasy. Imaginal approaches are equally varied. *Implosion* refers to continuous, prolonged exposure in fantasy, usually with much anxiety [138]. An alternative term is *flooding in fantasy* or *flooding in imagination*. *High-intensity stimulation* denotes implosion in man and flooding in animals [30, 113]. *Reactive inhibition* is the term used for the process of presentations of imaginal phobic stimuli from a hierarchy for 30 seconds at a time with the instruction that subjects attend to the sensations accompanying anxiety [24]. Similar procedures have been called *catharsis* [101], *programmed fantasy* [26], and *graduated extinction* [53]. In *prolonged exposure in fantasy* [35] phobic scenes from a hierarchy were imagined for up to eight minutes at a time, with instructions to experience feelings naturally. Repeated exposure to phobic slides has been called *cognitive desensitization* [145].

Counterconditioning, reciprocal inhibition, or *systematic desensitization* usually implies intermittent imagining of phobic scenes with a contrasting experience, such as relaxation or assertion [160]. In *metronome-conditioned relaxation*, relaxation is associated with a metronome [22]. When the contrasting experience to the phobic scene is a rewarding scene, this is called *covert reinforcement* [21], and when the contrasting experience is a pleasant vibration, this has been called *emotional training* [114].

With *induced anxiety* [3, 106, 136] patients are relaxed under hypnosis and encouraged to experience anxiety and other affects to the full, meanwhile associating these with past events. The process continues until the emotion subsides or, if time does not permit this, is terminated by suggestions to relax. This method seems to be a special form of catharsis or abreaction. Related approaches include *guided fantasy, imagining* or *daydreaming* [161], *initiated symbol projection,* and *release therapy* in children [82]. In *implosive expressive therapy* [131] the patient not only talks about his fantasies but also acts them out in a controlled setting. In the *acoustic mirror* technique, patients listen to audiotapes of their own behavior while the therapist stimulates self-awareness and appropriate responses, the exposure to unpleasant self-knowledge being graded [128].

Stress inoculation, stress immunization, cognitive modification and *cognitive insight,* and *anxiety management training* are forms of coping training or the learning of stoicism, either directly in the phobic situation or with another stressful experience [100, 144]. Similar mechanisms appear at work in *cognitive restructuring* and *self-instruction*.

Animal Work Relevant to Exposure
Experiments on Extinction of Avoidance
The reduction of clinical anxiety and avoidance behavior by exposure has interesting parallels in animals. Extinction of fear in animals is commonly said to depend upon repeated exposure of the animal to the aversive conditioned stimulus (CS complex) in the absence of the noxious unconditioned stimulus (US). Fear is extinguished more slowly when it is stronger or when it began with an intense and painful stimulus. Various methods of exposing animals to the frightening CS have been used. One technique (desensitization) is to start with weak stimuli that elicit only minimal fear and gradually to increase their strength. Alternatively, one might "flood" the animals by exposure to the total situation until the fear subsides. In a typical active avoidance extinction procedure, the CS is presented (e.g., a tone) without being followed by the US (e.g., shock) and the animal is allowed to escape. Escape usually occurs before the animal can discover that no shock would occur if it simply did nothing. Under these conditions, avoidance responses are hard to extinguish. Similarly, once established, human phobias and obsessions tend to continue unchanged for many years without treatment. However, when experimenters exposed animals for prolonged periods to the CS, faster extinction occurred.

Several forms of animal exposure have been called flooding. This denotes confrontation with stimuli that the subjects have been conditioned to escape or avoid or that evoke freezing or other signs of fear. Other terms to describe this procedure are *forced exposure, forced reality testing* [11], environmental press [95], response prevention [11], or *detainment* [157]. In animal experiments, the subjects are forced physically to confront the feared situation, while in patients such exposure is voluntary, although encouragement and social pressure by the therapist constitute indirect restraint.

Flooding in the form of response prevention extinguished rat avoidance in shuttleboxes [19, 31, 116, 147] and in other apparatus [11]. Baum's extensive studies in the rat suggest human parallels and deserve detailed description [12-17]. Figure 8 shows a schematic representation of Baum's experiments, in which avoidance-responding (jumping) was acquired (A), maintained (B and C), and extinguished (D). Rats were placed on the grid floor of a cage (the to-be-conditioned stimulus—CS); a few seconds later they recieved a shock (unconditioned stimulus—US) through the floor

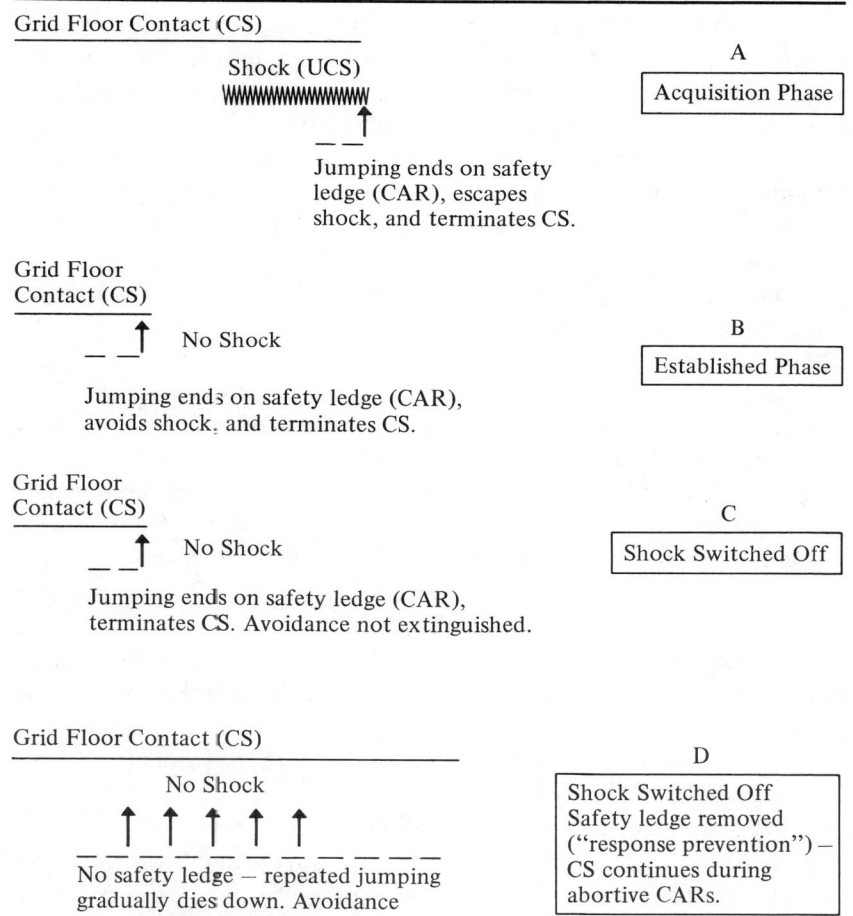

Figure 8. *Schematic representation of Baum's experiments, in which avoidance responding (jumping) was acquired (A), maintained (B and C), and extinguished (D).*

unless they jumped to a ledge halfway up the side of the cage (conditioned avoidance response—CAR). They quickly learned to jump to the safety ledge before the shocks were delivered (B). When the shock was turned off, they continued to jump automatically to the ledge each time they were placed on the grid floor (C). If the safety ledge was now removed, the rat when placed on the grid initially attempted strenuously to jump to a nonexistent shelf. These jumps rapidly diminished, after which the rat remained placidly on the floor (D). In Baum's experiments the CS was contact with the grid floor and, because the ledge was not available, the complete avoidance response was not possible. However, it could be argued that the rat's initial jumps in the cage were abortive avoidance responses that were not prevented, and that the active therapeutic ingredient was not response prevention but, rather, forced contact with the grid floor (exposure to the CS) in the absence of shock.

Longer durations of response prevention hastened extinction [10]. In rats trained to avoid low levels of shock, one minute of response prevention had no effect, but periods of three or five minutes were effective. Thirty minutes' response prevention (or exposure to CS) was necessary to extinguish avoidance learned in relation to strong shock, where random shocks had preceded avoidance training [135]. Massing of trials by shortening the intertrial intervals facilitated extinction [15, 109]. In clinical work with phobias and obsessions, exposure to the ES is followed by decreased avoidance and discomfort. This is comparable to the extinction of avoidance in rats by exposure to the CS. In man, as in rats, a longer exposure is better for the reduction of phobias [91, 139] and of compulsive rituals [112].

Extinction was also quicker if fearful rats were in the company of non-fearful rats [10, 147], or if response prevention was accompanied by opportunities to see other rats undergoing the same procedure [147]. However, observational learning alone was less predictably effective than response prevention alone, which was highly effective. These findings remind us that company reduces the fear of agoraphobics, though it does not lead to extinction, and that exposure of agoraphobics to the ES in groups produces slightly better results than does individual exposure. Extinction in Baum's rats was also facilitated by forcing them to move around and explore the cage, and thus to come into more intimate contact with the CS; this was done by direct handling, or by using a loud buzzer, which increased exploratory activity. Conversely, confinement hindered extinction—a finding that could be construed as preventing the rat from exposure to many facets of the CS that constituted the grid floor. These findings accord with clinical experience—that it is important to bring phobic and obsessive patients into contact with as many facets of the ES complex as possible.

Other findings in animals have no clinical counterparts. The efficacy of flooding was greater if accompanied by positive intracranial stimulation to the right lateral hypothalamus [51]. With repeated reacquisition and extinction, avoidance responses became steadily weaker, so that by the fifth extinction, performance was at the same level as after flooding [14].

Several workers found that continuing the CS (e.g., the buzzer) after the avoidance response had been executed helped to facilitate extinction of avoidance in rats, whether or not the CS was intermittent or continuous [132]. The longer the CS continued after the jump, the more rapidly rats ceased to avoid the CS [33, 69]. However, more important than continuing the CS beyond the moment of the avoidance response was exposure to the CS without the US for a few seconds after the avoidance response had been made [19, 33]. In several experiments the addition of a positive stimulus such as eating (an analogue of desensitization) failed to hasten extinction [31, 32, 34]. Delprato concluded that the therapeutic effectiveness of his techniques in rats was primarily a matter of exposure without the shock and that "counterconditioning" was unimportant. The same applies clinically; "counterconditioning" is not particularly helpful during exposure to the phobic stimulus [1, 18, 91], but repeated, prolonged exposure to the ES reliably produces lasting reduction of avoidance and fear in most human phobias and obsessions.

Shortcomings of Animal Models

One problem in extrapolating the results of animal conditioning experiments to patients is the difference in time span over which the events occur. Many animal experiments produce acquisition of avoidance, treatment, and extinction testing on the same day [11], although a few do so over several days. Most investigations study only one sequence of acquisition and extinction in a given animal species; few so far have examined repeated acquisition and extinction. Rules that govern avoidance behavior may well differ when acquisition and extinction occur in one sequence or in repeated sequences, as opposed to when the events take place over one day, many days, weeks, or longer [2, 14]. By the time patients come for treatment their phobias and obsessions have often been present for years, running a fluctuating course, with repeated partial reacquisition and reextinction. Generalizable rules would also be easier to deduce from animal experiments that included more species and more stimulus-response systems. It is dangerous to overgeneralize when most experiments are based on a narrow range of stimuli and responses in one species—the rat.

From Conditioning to the Clinic: The ES-ER Paradigm
Conditioning terms derived from laboratory experiments can confuse clinicians. A crucial difficulty is definition of the conditioned and unconditioned stimuli in human pathology. There is usually no history of a clearly traumatic onset to human phobias and obsessions, and we cannot assume that they have been "conditioned," only that they have been acquired. It is unnecessary for clinicians to make an untestable assumption that phobias and obsessions are a CS, with a consequent fruitless search for an unknowable US. Instead, we might talk not of the CS but simply descriptively of the ES, the *evoking stimulus* that elicits the ER phobias and obsessions. These terms make no assumptions about the antecedents of psychopathology.

This simpler analysis of phobias and obsessions has a major advantage for the clinician: it indicates at once the therapeutic strategy required, namely, continued exposure of the patient to the ES until the ER subsides. In an agoraphobic this may be a complex ES, such as being alone in public places, crowds, elevators, or stores. The ES evokes the ER, which is a cluster of behaviors such as avoidance and its autonomic concomitants. In an obsessive, the ES could be the sight or even thought of dirt, disarray, or uncertainty, which evokes compulsive washing, tidying, or checking. The therapist's task is to seek out all components of the ES that evoke any ER, so that exposure of the patient to the ES can be contrived and continued until the ER no longer occurs. Thus, an agoraphobic is persuaded to go for long periods into crowded stores; the compulsive tidier and checker is asked to untidy his possessions and deliberately to refrain from checking rituals. In both animals and humans, exposure to the ES usually leads to reduction of avoidance and fear. With continued exposure patients eventually learn that discomfort will gradually subside whether or not they escape from the ES. Avoidance is therefore unnecessary for discomfort to be reduced and gradually drops out.

The ES-ER paradigm has the advantage of focusing on crucial questions about mechanisms of improvement. We need to specify what the differences are between traumatic or sensitizing exposure and therapeutic exposure. The differences are likely to be multivariate. They may lie in duration of exposure to the ES, or in the length of time between exposure trials. They may lie in attenuation of the ES during exposure because of distraction, or in the changed meaning of the ES when patients define the situation as therapeutic instead of noxious. The type of ER emitted on contact with the ES may also be relevant, as may biochemical parameters.

Exposure in Volunteers with Fears
Numerous studies involve analogue research with volunteers who happen to have a fear for which they would not normally seek aid. The intensity of fear in these studies varies widely. Some researchers select only the most handicapped from a large screened population, while others take almost all comers, most of whom have trivial fear. The greater the demands in facing a standard frightening task, the fewer who will refuse and thus be called phobic [20, 103]. Until recently most analogue experiments concerned snake fears, but the epidemic of snake phobia in American students is now being replaced by widespread shyness, judging from recent studies teaching assertiveness.

Limitations of Analogue Studies
Analogue research usually involves psychology students, in most cases women, who appear to be the new "white rats" of clinical psychology. Such individuals represent but a small section of the general population, since they are intelligent, middle-class, and usually white. Moreover, volunteers from such a limited background, who are not sufficiently distressed by a fear to seek treatment until sought out by a keen experimenter, differ in important respects from psychiatric patients with severe phobias or obsessions [91]. Although patients with specific phobias often resemble volunteers with fears, those with complex agoraphobic and obsessive-compulsive syndromes differ greatly. Not only are their phobias likely to be more intense and extensive, but commonly associated problems such as pervasive anxiety and disruptive social relationships complicate treatment. In some patients their presenting psychopathology is the least of their difficulties. A phobia or obsession can simply be a respectable admission ticket for treatment of another problem, such as frigidity, loneliness, or depression. Even patients with specific phobias may present for treatment

because they happen to be depressed rather than because of their longstanding phobia. The differences between patient and volunteer populations outweigh the overlap so much that analogue results cannot be assumed to apply automatically to patients. However, such studies do form a bridge between animal studies and clinical studies and have led to the testing of an abundance of relevant hypotheses.

A recurrent weakness of most analogue studies is a failure to measure sufficient aspects of fear behavior, reliance usually being placed exclusively on behavioral avoidance tests at one point in time. Such tests in an experimental situation are often a poor guide to performance in more natural situations [57]. Moreover, few studies provide a reasonable follow-up. Ephemeral effects are of little interest to clinicians, whose interest is in stable change. In volunteer studies, often but a few minutes or at most a few weeks elapse before final testing, whereas reasonable stability of changes can be judged only after a minimum follow-up of six months, at which time measures of several modalities of fear behvior are needed.

Results in Volunteers
The majority of controlled studies of exposure have been in fantasy, while a few have been carried out in vivo without additional factors such as modeling, praise, or relaxation. However, all the in vivo exposure studies [49, 86, 133, 142] were effective in reducing fearful behavior, with a mean duration of 29 minutes' exposure. A good description of exposure in vivo was given by Curtis, Nesse, Buxton, Wright, and Lippman [28], who treated 12 volunteers with specific phobias, mainly of animals. Several strategies were used to facilitate exposure, including *navigation*—guidance from the therapist; *command*—firm, sustained pressure to enter the phobic situation; *seduction*—persuasion into the situation; *cheerleading*—enthusiastic praise for progress; and *mothering*—considerate concern while this is going on. Eleven of the investigators' 12 phobics were much improved after exposure in vivo for a mean of 2.9 hours and they sustained this improvement at one-year follow-up.

Further "response induction aids" to exposure in vivo were described by Bandura, Jeffrey, and Wright [6] during their treatment of snake-phobic volunteers. These workers found it helpful to have the experimenter touch the snake together with the clients, to grade the severity and timing of approach, to wear gloves while touching the snake, and to start with a baby snake first. Treatment was completed in a mean of 81 minutes, needing only 41 minutes for three-quarters of the clients. Patients were followed up for only one week after treatment. Subjects with few response-induction aids made slow progress, but progres was rapid when the therapist used an array of performance-induction aids.

A novel question was examined by Curtis, Buxton, Lippman, Nesse, and Wright [29], who carried out rapid exposure in vivo during the circadian phase of minimal cortisol secretion. In seven animal-phobic volunteers (six female), they found that although in vivo exposure for one hour produced much subjective anxiety and attempted avoidance of the phobic object, there was no increase in cortisol secretion during treatment. This lack of cortisol response to anxiety was the more striking in that these patients had shown increased cortisol secretion in response to the novelty of the experimental situation just before exposure, indicating that the endocrine system was still capable of responding, although not to anxiety. Intriguing questions arise as to whether treatment might be more potent during certain endocrine phases than others.

DURATION OF EXPOSURE. On average, effective exposure in fantasy was longer than in unsuccessful studies, with a total duration of 173 versus 70 minutes and session lengths of 54 versus 33 minutes, but with comparable duration of phobic scenes within sessions [91]. Most experiments without significant effects utilized tape-recorded instructions, while few successful studies did so. An interactional model might explain these findings. The duration of exposure necessary to reduce fear might be increased with treatment in fantasy rather than in real life, by tape recorder rather than by a therapist, and by intermittent exposure rather than continuous exposure. The shortest effective duration would then be associated with a combination of continuous exposure in real life conducted by a therapist who modeled the approach to the feared situation and praised the patient for achieved progress.

Apart from the rough guide that longer seems better, the optimum duration of exposure still requires much study. In animal experiments [11, 119, 120] longer durations of exposure to the CS hasten extinction of fear. The same applies to man. Duration of exposure can refer to particular stimulus presentations, to the total exposure time during any one session, or to exposure over the whole course of treatment. Equally important might be the intervals between stimuli or between sessions. It is also relevant whether "longer" or "shorter" refers to seconds, minutes, hours, days, weeks, or months. Furthermore, there may be interactions between duration and intensity of fear during exposure. We may conclude, however, that in volunteer experiments, significant fear reduction is more likely to occur with longer sessions and with longer total duration of exposure across sessions, while duration of scenes within sessions seems less important.

SPACING OF SESSIONS. In volunteer studies this has not seemed important for outcome [56, 94]. Nevertheless, it might be important under certain conditions. If exposure homework in the natural setting is therapeutic and treatment sessions act mainly by facilitating "homework" exposure, then spacing sessions to allow opportunities for patients to practice self-exposure and coping skills between sessions may be crucial for lasting improvement to occur. It might also be important for facilitating necessary interaction with family members in their role as cotherapists [93].

WITHIN-SESSION EXPOSURE DURATION. In snake-fearful schoolgirls, exposure to a live snake for 15 minutes was followed by less increase in subsequent approach to the snake than after no exposure or after exposure for 30 or 45 minutes [206]. In another study of female students who were afraid of snakes, those exposed to a snake for 15 minutes showed less approach to the snake 30 minutes later than did those who had been exposed for 0 or 45 minutes [141]. Similarly, in snake-fearful students, one session of continuous exposure to a snake for 30 minutes led to more subsequent approach than did three 10-minute sequences of exposure with five-minute rests in between [49].

In spider-fearful students, Mathews and Shaw [97] found that six successive eight-minute sequences of audiotaped exposure stories separated by four-minute sequences of neutral material were better than a 48-minute identical sequence of exposure stories, but only when the students' arousal level was low.

In patients, two controlled studies are now available concerning duration of exposure in vivo. Thus, in agoraphobics, two hours of continuous exposure in vivo produced significantly greater improvement within, and between, sessions than did four half-hour sessions on the same afternoon, separated by half-hours of neutral activity [139]. A similar experiment in obsessive-compulsive ritualizers yielded similar findings [112].

Turning to shorter periods of exposure within sessions in snake-fearful students, exposure scenes in fantasy lasting 30 seconds produced more improvement than did those lasting 12 or 3 seconds, both at posttest and at one-month follow-up [123]. Sue [143] found that 30-second scenes produced more fear reduction than did 5-second scenes, whether or not the students were relaxed. Similarly, in mixed agoraphobic patients and insect-phobic volunteers, Watts [153–155] found 30-second scenes to be significantly better than 5-second scenes for high-hierarchy items, both during treatment and some days afterward. Scenes lasting 45 seconds were only slightly better than 15-second ones. In the same population, Watts found that *interstimulus intervals* of 40 seconds produced more desensitization of high-hierarchy items than did 15 seconds, but the longer interstimulus interval did not affect long-term decrement over a week. Strong items thus desensitized faster if long imaginal presentations were used with longer interstimulus intervals. Briefly, in patients, hours of exposure seem preferable to minutes, and half a minute of exposure to a few seconds.

STIMULUS TERMINATION. It is unclear whether progress during exposure treatment is faster if the patient or the therapist controls the presentation of the phobic stimulus. In snake-fearful students, progress occurred at the same rate whether or not subjects controlled the presentation of phobic images [104]. During in vivo exposure with modeling, improvement in snake-fearful children was the same whether the children performed each step after an experimenter model or whether they remained still while the experimenter approached with a snake in her hands [105]. During in vivo exposure of snake-fearful subjects, the addition of self-directed exposure subsequently increased approach, but self-directed subjects also had longer exposure, which confounded outcome [7].

Perception of control, however, affects arousal during exposure [59]. In a single-session experiment, snake-fearful students developed tachycardia while drawing a snake nearer toward themselves. However, when they decided to stop, their heart rate declined, even though at that point the snake was closer to them than when the tachycardia had developed.

A related problem is whether there is an optimum point at which to terminate a given session. Is it best to end on a good note? Again, in snake-fearful students, terminating the session when arousal decreased on all of three criteria (heart rate variability, subjective anxiety, and observed anxiety) produced no more improvement than termination when arousal decreased on only one criterion, for example, heart rate variability alone, or subjective anxiety alone [45]. Clear guidelines are thus not yet available for the clinician about optimum criteria for the termination of sessions.

GRADUAL VERSUS SUDDEN EXPOSURE. Little work has examined this issue while keeping other conditions constant. The evidence available indicates that fantasy exposure is as good when it starts at the top of the fear hierarchy and works down as is the reverse. A few workers found an advantage for a rapid approach; thus, Cohen and Dean [25] observed that subjects desensitized along a progressive, graded hierarchy required significantly more trials than those desensitized to items at the top of the hierarchy. In two single-session experiments, evidence supported the value of a faster approach. Eberle, Rehm, and McBurney [36] found that habituation was greatest for the most frightening slides in the series, while Hastings and Walker [59] found that fearful subjects terminated their approach to a snake significantly later in the sequence when approaching fast (over a couple of minutes) than when approaching slowly (up to eight minutes). Although clinical impression suggests that a faster, more prolonged approach to the most handicapping situation that the patient allows will yield the quickest durable results, experimental testing of this idea remains to be done.

FANTASY VERSUS LIVE EXPOSURE. Although many workers have indirectly compared fantasy exposure with live exposure, conclusions are usually difficult to draw because of confounding influences, such as the duration and gradient of exposure, or accompanying relaxation, praise, or modeling. Two analogue studies compared live exposure with fantasy exposure without these confounding variables. LoPiccolo [86] demonstrated that two sessions of graded exposure in vivo produced marked improvement in snake-fearful volunteers. Relaxation training did not add to the efficacy of graded exposure in vivo, which was significantly more effective than systematic desensitization in fantasy on subjective, behavioral, and physiologic measures.

In 54 female students with swimming fears [133], one of six treatments was given in a 2 × 3 factorial design. The factors were desensitization in fantasy ± live exposure; pretreatment discussion of fear of swimming and its treatment ± live exposure; and neither desensitization nor pretreatment discussion ± live exposure. In vivo exposure consisted of graded water activities in a swimming pool, done with a minimum of tension in a total of three weekly sessions. Follow-up was after a two-week swimming course that followed the end of treatment. Repeated live exposure produced the best results for performance anxiety, questionnaire reports, and overall improvement, and this gain was still evident at two weeks' follow-up. Those who were desensitized only in fantasy showed little transfer of improvement to the real situation. Furthermore, desensitization in fantasy required seven hours' treatment, whereas live exposure required only one hour.

Further comparison of in vivo exposure with fantasy exposure was made in a third analogue study [5], in which 48 snake-fearful adult volunteers were subjected to live modeling with exposure in vivo (subjects watched models engaging in gradually bolder interactions with the snake in real life and were then themselves brought into gradual physical contact with the snake). This procedure yielded significantly better results than did symbolic modeling (subjects watched a film of models engaging in gradually bolder interactions with the same snake, were taught to relax throughout the procedure, and controlled the rate of presentation of the film sequence). The authors interpreted the outcome as demonstrating the effect of modeling. However, it argues more powerfully for the role of in vivo exposure, since of the two groups that had modeling, the one that also had live exposure did much better.

There have been four comparisons of in vivo exposure with fantasy exposure in patients. A pilot study [152] showed significantly better results immediately after treatment in agoraphobics who had been treated with in vivo exposure than in those who received fantasy exposure. Follow-up was not possible because of the crossover design employed. Similarly, in agoraphobic patients, Emmelkamp and Wessels [39] found exposure in vivo to be superior to fantasy exposure at the end of treatment. Improvement continued to one-month follow-up, especially in fantasy exposure patients, at which time the significant difference was no longer present. In obsessive-compulsive patients Rabavilas, Boulougouris, and Stefanis [112] once more found exposure in vivo to be superior to exposure in fantasy in a crossover design.

An exception, in which no difference was found between imaginal exposure and in vivo exposure, is the study in agoraphobics reported by Mathews [96] and by Johnston, Lancashire, Mathews, Munby, Shaw, and Gelder [65], described in detail in Chapter 8 (page 210). However, homework-exposure in vivo might have eliminated differences between the two conditions. This study excepted, the results support the indirect evidence from volunteers and patients that real-life exposure is one of the most powerful therapeutic factors so far identified. A further relevant issue is whether preceding fantasy treatment can potentiate subsequent exposure in vivo. Data in agoraphobics do not support this idea [39, 98], although in obsessive-compulsives, Rabavilas, Boulougouris, and Stefanis [112] reported that 80 minutes of exposure in fantasy potentiated improvement from subsequent exposure in vivo of similar duration.

IMAGERY DURING EXPOSURE. Patients' imagery during treatment can be suggested entirely by the therapist, as in systematic desensitization, or evoked by patients themselves. The latter is a guided fantasy technique, where the therapist only steers with a few prompts when the patient dries up or gets off the required theme. Which of these two methods is used may make little difference, but comparisons are lacking.

During treatment, unpleasant imagery that the subject cannot control sometimes develops [8]. When strong affects accompany past memories during treatment, patients can be encouraged to live through them until the affect is dissipated and then to continue with the exposure process to the live situation. It is not surprising that treatment that emphasizes contact with stimuli hitherto avoided should sometimes produce cognitive avoidance or resurrect old memories of earlier contact with the stimuli. Such associations were reported in two patients who abreacted affect during their recall, which was followed by impressive therapeutic advance [130]. Boulougouris and Bassiakos [23] reported organic "memories" when an obsessive-compulsive patient with a phobia of venereal disease was taken to a VD hospital. He began coughing and remembered being in a tuberculosis hospital near a syphilitic patient years before. In the case of a height-phobic woman treated by the author, being taken to the top of a high building during exposure in vivo brought back an unpleasant memory of the onset of her phobia, when she saw a fireman falling to his death from a great height. Turning to recollections evoked by pleasant stimuli, a patient who carried a vibrator in his hand to use while in the phobic situation remembered his fantasies of omnipotence as a boy of 12 years with a toy pistol in his hand on the beach [114].

RELAXATION. Since the topic of relaxation has been covered in detail in Chapter 6, only a brief review will be made here. There is little evidence that autonomic responses decrease or habituate more effectively at the low levels of arousal induced by relaxation instructions than at normal arousal levels. Data so far confirm Mathews' [96] conclusion that "no direct evidence has been found for one of the central postulates of reciprocal inhibition theory that relaxation reduces or prevents the autonomic anxiety responses associated with phobic imagery." Nor is there much evidence that relaxation affects outcome by the end of treatment and follow-up. Of 20 controlled studies on the subject published from 1969 onward, 17 found no lasting value in trained muscular relaxation being added to exposure to the phobic stimulus, whether in fantasy, in vivo, or in the course of counseling techniques [91, 132]. Two studies employed psychophysiologic measures to determine whether relaxation had occurred. In a report about rat-fearful students [149] Waters, McDonald, and Koresko maintain that during rat slide presentation [149], desensitization subjects showed less skin conductance, though not lower heart rate activity, than did nonrelaxation controls. Yet both groups improved similarly in avoidance, GSR, and heart rate. Arousal during treatment was thus not associated with better outcome. The same was found in phobic patients by Benjamin, Marks, and Huson [18].

As regards relaxation without exposure, several controlled studies in obsessive-compulsive patients have found this to have no significant effect on outcome, though exposure in vivo with response prevention, but no relaxation, did reduce rituals significantly [121]. In children fearful of going to the dentist, relaxation without exposure had no therapeutic effect, whereas imaginal exposure led to some improvement [115]. One controlled analogue study did find that relaxation without exposure reduced anxiety as much as systematic desensitization. This was "cue-controlled relaxation" of test-anxious students [126], but follow-up was only one week after the final session, so no data are available about durable effects.

The overwhelming controlled evidence is that, to achieve lasting fear reduction, systematic training in muscular relaxation is redundant and time-wasting. Therapeutic time is better spent on straightforward exposure to the phobic stimulus, using any strategies that help the subject to remain in its presence and attend to it. More needs to be known about the effects on fear reduction of simple instructional sets (as opposed to systematic training) to relax or tense up during exposure, and of relaxation-like procedures such as autogenic training and meditation. Since most phobic and obsessive-compulsive patients obtain lasting benefit from 3 to 15 sessions of exposure treatment, such adjuvants would be clinically useful only if they produced extra fear reduction without prolonging treatment.

ANXIETY AROUSAL DURING EXPOSURE. Several workers have reported that while muscle-tensing or arousing instructions can increase anxiety and autonomic responses at rest and during exposure to phobic stimuli, the effect on outcome is variable. In agoraphobic patients who were exposed in vivo while the therapist either raised their anxiety deliberately or simply emphasized the importance of contact without avoidance, both groups improved comparably [55], even though they reported different amounts of anxiety during treatment. In other agoraphobics treated by group exposure in vivo, reduction of discomfort to exposure by a small dose of diazepam did not enhance outcome [55]. Thus, there is no clear evidence that anxiety provocation per se is helpful during exposure, either in fantasy or in vivo. Anxiety may be an unfortunate by-product of exposure rather than a facilitator of change. Moreover, the amount of anxiety experienced during treatment by exposure does not correlate with outcome [47, 92, 98].

Such findings apparently contradict observations of anxiety reduction after abreaction of anxiety, anger, or other unpleasant affects [90, 150]. The size and duration of abreaction effects remain to be worked out, but the exposure paradigm must accommodate observations that fear can be reduced after experience of intense emotion not obviously related to the phobic or compulsive stimuli. One could argue that improvement after experiencing unpleasant affects results from exposure to generally unpleasant affects, which provides a coping experience. However, if eventually pleasant ecstatic experiences turn out to be as therapeutic as unpleasant ones, the exposure hypothesis would be negated. But that experiment remains to be done. For practical purposes, exposure treatments work well when emphasis is on contact with the ES until the ERs subside, and concentration on anxiety evocation seems unnecessary, though more work in this area is required.

MODELING. In anxiety reduction studies, modeling nearly always involves the client observing a model entering the feared situation, which implies previous exposure. The influences of modeling and of exposure are thus confounded. Bandura, Grusec, and Menlove [4] studied dog-phobic children who either saw a peer model approach a dog or passively observed the dog without approach or a model. The modeling children who improved most thus had both modeling and interactional exposure, while the non-modeling subjects had neither, again confounding two variables.

Another typical confounding of duration of interactional exposure with modeling variables is found in an experiment in which children who were afraid of swimming were taught to swim by watching a model swim for eight minutes, by 10 minutes of real-life tuition in swimming, or by both modeling and participation. The combined group did best but received 18 minutes of interactional exposure, compared with 8 and 10 minutes for the first two groups [83].

Where the exposure time has been controlled, modeling usually adds little. As an example, nonassertive students improved significantly in social behavior after behavior rehearsal without modeling, while adding video-taped modeling did not enhance outcome [87]. In obsessive-compulsive patients, modeling of relaxation after the therapist did not reduce rituals, whereas watching a therapist expose herself to contaminating situations had a significant effect; modeling with live participation (exposure) conferred the greatest benefits, as is usual in experiments in this area [121]. That modeling without exposure is not helpful is further emphasized by results from Emmelkamp and Emmelkamp-Benner [38] that watching a filmed model discussing treatment, without actual exposure, was not therapeutic.

Experiments by Kazdin [70, 71] throw further light on this issue. His subjects had snake fears or social inhibitions and were treated by fantasied scenes. All his experiments included a "no-model" scene control in which, despite the label, subjects imagined a model in the background not interacting with the phobic stimulus (the snake or the social situation; e.g., the snake was merely present somewhere, sticking its head out of the cage). In contrast, the modeling conditions depicted interaction of models with the relevant ES. Modeling conditions did better than the "no-model" scene controls, who did not improve over 30 minutes of treatment, a time that is less than in most successful studies of exposure in fantasy. The results of Kazdin's work argue not for the effect of pure modeling but for that of *interactional* rather than static exposure. Scene-only subjects, in fact, watched a model who simply stood near the ES but did not interact with it, whereas modeling groups visualized interaction. This suggests that the operative ingredient might be interaction with the phobic stimulus, with or without modeling.

That interactional exposure is crucial is supported by further results from Kazdin [72]. He employed snake-fearful students and studied two factors, the role of coping versus mastery models and, of special relevance here, fantasies of the client herself compared with fantasies of the model coping with the snake. Images of the client coping with a snake were as good as those of a model doing the same, supporting the idea that what is important is not so much the model as what is done with the phobic stimulus (i.e., exposure).

In other experiments in nonassertive volunteers [74] scenes of four models being assertive produced better results than did those of one model until four-months follow-up. It is obvious that four models produce a greater variety of interactional exposure experiences, experiences that could be obtained as well without a model. Similarly, in a second experiment on timid volunteers [73], a modeling condition was said to yield better results than a no-modeling one until three-month follow-up. However, here modeling was confounded with role rehearsal, which includes a form of interactional exposure.

In brief, the value of pure modeling for fear reduction is not yet proved as an addition to interactional exposure. In practice, however, little time is lost by the therapist demonstrating how to approach the ES, provided the patient does it in real life afterward. The role of pure modeling would be of practical importance if research eventually showed that self-exposure homework was as good as therapist-assisted exposure. In that case, self-exposure homework might become the most economical treatment, and modeling would be time-consuming to arrange unless done by the family: the latter would be worthwhile only if modeled interactional exposure were clearly better than interactional exposure alone.

REINFORCEMENT. Praise of therapeutic progress is a natural part of most therapies. With phobic and obsessive-compulsive problems this involves praising the subject's approach to the ES, so that reward is invariably compounded with exposure. The question is whether *systematic* reward enhances outcome. For this, a contrast is needed between identical exposure with and without systematic reward. The available evidence does not suggest a large contribution from systematic reinforcement added to exposure, though common sense points to the desirability of encouraging clients' efforts as much as possible.

FEEDBACK. Information as to progress seems a useful adjunct to exposure. Successful completion of a task such as fear reduction requires accurate monitoring of one's progress, and to that extent feedback can be construed as an aid to self-control. As noted in Chapter 2 (page 28) the findings of Leitenberg, Agras, Thompson, and Wright [77] and of Leitenberg, Agras, Edwards, Thomson, and Wincze [80] suggest that augmented performance feedback facilitates progress, especially in the initial phases of therapy. Such feedback may be an important component of systematic desensitization; thus, Watts [156] found that three phobic patients showed greater decrease in anxiety when they had to report discomfort levels after every presentation of an image during desensitization than when they reported discomfort only after every alternative image. As Rutner [127] put it: "What else does systematic desensitization do for the patient other than present a phobic object in a gradually increasing anxiety hierarchy and give feedback about behavior whenever the therapist proceeds up the hierarchy?" In a sense, patients supply their own feedback through self-report. Feedback of autonomic behavior such as heart rate has not been found clinically useful in phobic patients, in that although they significantly decrease heart rate during exposure in vivo, the effect does not generalize to enhancing the rate of decrement of subjective anxiety, skin conductance, or respiratory rate—at least not in the short term [107, 108].

THERAPEUTIC INSTRUCTIONS AND EXPECTANCY. Conflicting findings on this issue might partly reflect the variability across experiments in the timing and frequency of expectancy manipulations, and the differing ways in which those manipulations might have been perceived by experimental subjects. It may make a difference whether the manipulation of therapeutic instructions occurs just once before treatment, at every session, or more frequently. Moreover, expectancies do not depend only on what the therapist says; for example, perception of the procedure itself can influence expectations. Furthermore, expectations concerning treatment can change in both subjects and therapists between the start and the end of treatment and thus reflect efficacy as well as determine it. Other variables also decide whether expectancy has an effect, including the potency of treatment, the criteria of outcome, the type of problem being treated, and its severity.

In phobic patients, neither Stern and Marks [139] nor Gelder, Bancroft, Gath, Johnston, Mathews, and Shaw [47] found significant correlations between outcome and *patients'* expectation of improvement at the start of treatment. Johnston, Lancashire, Mathews, Munby, Shaw, and Gelder [65], on the other hand, found that agoraphobic patients' expectancy about target problems did correlate with final outcome. Conflicting findings were reported by Emmelkamp-Benner [38], whose significant correlation between agoraphobic patients' expectancy and outcome contrasted with an earlier experiment where there was no relationship [39]. Similarly, comparing a treatment rationale with an experimental rationale, the treatment set slightly enhanced outcome in snake-fearful students [40] but made other students less willing to undergo desensitization (see also Chapter 2, page 20). *Therapists'* as well as patients' expectancies might also play a role, though results negating this were noted in the treatment of school-phobic children [9] and in adult phobic patients [150].

In reviewing this topic, Rosen [122] cited Vodde and Gilner [148] with approval that "any contingency which provides an incentive for the subject to remain in the presence of the fear-arousing stimulus, and to attend to it, will facilitate extinction of the avoidance response to that stimulus, in the absence of real aversive consequences." It does seem obvious that the more a patient cooperates in a difficult treatment the better the outcome might be, and that greater efforts to cooperate will be made if they are expected to bear tangible fruit.

SELF-REGULATION. Whether subjects will expose themselves to distressing stimuli until they become used to them may depend, as noted in Chapter 2, upon coping self-regulatory processes that are only dimly understood. In enhancing approach to feared situations, the process amounts to teaching stoicism. Some elements in self-regulation processes were explored by Kanfer [66] and his colleagues, who measured stress tolerance by the length of time students held a hand in iced water. Stress tolerance increased if subjects were committed to an explicit written contract rather than to an oral agreement conveying the same content [67]. After an interpolated experience, students who believed they had failed to meet contract conditions tolerated iced water longer than those who believed the experimenter had failed to fulfill the contract. Further enhancement of stress tolerance came from anticipation of reward for fulfillment of their contract. Commitment to carrying out the test was diminished when the iced water was visible before the experiment and when there was a high chance of being selected to carry out the task. Stress tolerance thus depended in part upon demand and other characteristics of the situation and on the subject's commitment to further action.

Practice in thinking about other things while one's hand is in iced water helps to increase pain tolerance; for example, students trained in the use of controlling thoughts and scenes about having a drink with a friend or planning and having a party were subsequently able to prolong the time they kept their hands in iced water, as were students who viewed travel slides, especially if they advanced the slides themselves. Focusing on sensations of relaxation helped less. Ordinary suggestions that discomfort would decrease were not successful. Systematic generation of alternative thoughts beforehand were better than simple distraction between trials [52]. Similarly, children instructed to say aloud the aversive consequences of a forbidden act, such as turning around to look at a toy display, or told to repeat the rewards from not looking, were able to inhibit this action longer than children who were simply told not to look. The content of the verbalization was critical, since children who were instructed to repeat task-irrelevant statements did not differ from controls not instructed to verbalize [58].

Control can be enhanced when subjects have an instrumental response that they perceive as terminating an aversive stimulus, such as noise [50] or shock [46]. In male students undergoing a half-hour shock-avoidance procedure, the provision of optional control over rest periods reduced systolic blood pressure relative to yoked subjects, who had comparable rest periods imposed on them [60]. Attribution alone, however, is less useful. Snake-fearful students improved equally after desensitization whether their relaxation was perceived as being self-induced or drug-induced [158]. Similarly, therapeutic changes in agoraphobic patients were comparable whether they attributed these to drugs or to exposure treatment [64].

More accurate expectations and knowledge about dealing with an impending stress can increase self-control and diminish the damage. In gastroscopy patients [81], it was found that those who were instructed the night before about which sensations to expect during gastroscopy (e.g., gagging, full stomach) or how to cooperate (e.g., when to breathe through their mouths and when to swallow) developed less subsequent gagging and tachycardia than did patients who received no information the night before the gastroscopy. Thus, response to stress can be more controlled and less disturbing when people know what stress to expect and are advised how to deal with it.

Relaxation during traditional desensitization can be construed as an exercise in self-control [134], as can *cue-controlled relaxation* without exposure [125] and *covert reinforcement*, in which an imagined reward is used instead of relaxation [21, 159]. In subjects with test anxiety, Wisocki [159] found covert reinforcement to be significantly better on self-report than a no-treatment control.

Elements of self-management are also present in *rational-emotive therapy*, during which the irrational basis of fears is discussed, more rational behavior is described, and subjects rehearse how to deal better with future situations [68, 146]. Clients can be taught to utilize anxiety responses as cues to bring coping responses into play, for example, to imagine alternative scenes. This is reminiscent of thought-stopping techniques and of covert sensitization.

A major hindrance to advance in this area of self-control is our lack of operationally defined criteria of "coping responses." Negative self-statements might be just as therapeutic as positive ones, since patients who are asked during flooding or paradoxical intention to get as frightened as possible usually improve at least as much as those who relax. If experimental data eventually confirm that negative self-statements also help subjects to cope, what then is a noncoping response? Conceptual clarity is badly needed if further advances are to be made.

Past Applications of Exposure

Justice cannot be done to this subject simply by examining formal experiments of recent years. Despite their ingenuity, such studies have so far covered but a tiny segment of a rich area. A glimpse at allied techniques used in the past in different uncontrolled contexts is essential for perspective before we can consider clinical experimental work in Chapter 8.

Studies by Jersild and Holmes

Parents have long taught their children to overcome fear by various forms of confrontation. Jersild and Holmes in 1935 [63] interviewed parents about the methods they used to reduce fear in their children. One technique was compelling the child to participate in the phobic situation by force or by ridicule. Though Jersild and Holmes commented that "such tactics seldom succeeded," several examples of successful application of exposure were presented; for example, "parents compelled the child to go alone into a dark bedroom; according to the parents' report, the child in the end completely overcame his fear of the dark room." In another case, a father repeatedly brought his child back to an enclosure in which there were horses that the child feared; after many such visits (in the company of his father) the child grew interested in the horses and appeared to lose his fear. As a contribution to other fear-reducing techniques, this kind of exposure was successful in 50 percent of cases. It was noted that ridicule or invidious comparisons never helped a child.

Jersild and Holmes [63] maintained that the most useful methods were those that increased the child's skills and competence in dealing with the feared situation. "By 'skills' and 'competence' were included all activities and techniques designed to bring the child into *direct active contact with* or *participation in* the situation that he feared or any feature of the thing that is feared with a view to helping the child, with such experience, to be able to cope with the situation and thus overcome his fear." An attractive stimulus was primarily useful not as a means of changing associative connotations of the feared event but as an auxiliary means of luring the child into activities that would increase his knowledge and competence in dealing with the feared situation.

Also dealing with children, Jacobsen [62] reviewed methods that helped children with school phobias to return to school and concluded that one of the most important aspects of treatment was to get such children back into the school setting quickly, in spite of their fearful protestations. She stressed the importance of firmness in this regard. If need be, the mother might accompany the child for a while.

Senoi Dream Interpretation

Intriguing reports suggest that exposure procedures have been an aspect of child rearing in some cultures [140]. In 1935, Stewart [1969] studied the Senoi—a small, isolated tribe of jungle folk living in the remote rain forest of the central range of the Malay Peninsula. His report is fragmentary and anecdotal and idealizes this tribe; however, it is so thought-provoking as to deserve detailed summary, despite its paucity of hard fact. The Senoi tribe appeared to have unusually little violent crime or intercommunal strife, and this was attributed to their methods of child rearing and healing. These centered around particular kinds of dream interpretation that were a feature of child education and common knowledge among adult Senoi. The average adult Senoi practiced interpretation of his family's and associates' dreams as a regular feature of education and daily social intercourse. Breakfast in the Senoi house was like a dream clinic, with the father and elder brothers listening to and analyzing the dreams of all the children. At the end of the family clinic, the male population gathered in the council, at which the dreams of the elder children and all the men in the community were reported, discussed, and analyzed.

Much of the Senoi dream interpretation emphasized exposure practices. An example is the handling of dreams that provoked anxiety or terror.

When a Senoi child reports a falling dream, an adult answers with enthusiasm, "That is a wonderful dream, one of the best dreams a man can have. Where did you fall to, and what did you discover?" He makes the same comment when the child reports a climbing, traveling, flying, or soaring dream. The child at first answers, as he would in our society, that it did not seem so wonderful, and that he was so frightened that he awoke before he had fallen anywhere.

"That was a mistake," answers the adult authority. "Everything you do in a dream has a purpose beyond your understanding while you are asleep. You must relax and enjoy yourself when you fall in a dream. Falling is the quickest way to get in contact with the powers of the spirit world, the powers laid open to you through your dreams. Soon, when you have a falling dream, you will remember what I am saying, and as you do you will feel that you are traveling to the source of the power which has caused you to fall. The falling spirits love you. They are attracting you to their land, and you have but to relax and remain asleep in order to come to grips with them. When you meet them you may be frightened of their terrific power, but go on. When you think you are dying in a dream, you are only receiving the powers of the other world, your own spiritual power which has been turned against you and which now wishes to become one with you if you will accept it."

Over a period of time, with this type of social interaction, praise, or criticism, imperatives, and advice, the dream that started out with fear of falling changed into the joy of flying.

The Senoi also believed and taught that the dreamer—the "I" of the dream—should always advance and attack in the teeth of danger, calling on the dream images of his fellows if necessary, but fighting by himself until they arrived. Dream characters were bad only as long as one was afraid and retreated from them and would continue to seem bad and fearful as long as one refused to come to grips with them.

Use with Adults

In adults many workers of divergent theoretic hues have made sporadic use of exposure or related methods. Freud [44] himself stressed the importance of exposure to the phobic situation in real life for improvement to occur: "One can hardly ever master a phobia if one waits till the patient lets the analysis influence him to give it up . . . one succeeds only when one can induce them through the influence of the analysis to . . . go about alone and struggle with the anxiety while they make the attempt." Ferenczi [42], one of Freud's most notable pupils, illustrated the use of this principle in a young woman with severe stage fright, who had shown little improvement in previous analysis. He asked the patient to sing a song. After several hours' encouragement she was able to move from a halting voice to singing clearly and then was asked to get up and sing expressively like her sister. The patient enjoyed these performances, and Ferenczi noted that improvement was followed by the evocation of many childhood memories.

Yet another psychoanalytic account of exposure stressed that agoraphobics must reenter the phobic situation repeatedly until the anxiety dissipates. This was accomplished by using a gradual approach, with the therapist sometimes accompanying the patient, or the patient being armed if need be with sedative pills, or a certificate of safe conduct. Writings on learning describe similar maneuvers; for example, Guthrie [54] cited how a girl overcame her car phobia by being driven for hours through the streets of Washington, her anxiety during treatment having reached a great peak.

Malleson [89] described treatment in which "the patient is helped to break the phobic cycle by having him make a deliberate effort to feel and to experience fully his fear without trying to escape from it." The patient was an Indian student with examination panic 48 hours before an examination. He had already failed a previous examination because of a similar attack of panic. "He was made to sit up in bed, and try to feel his fear. He was asked to tell of the awful consequences that he felt would follow his failure—derision from his colleagues in India, disappointment from his family, financial loss. . . . At first, as he followed the instructions, his sobbings increased. But soon his trembling ceased. As the effort needed to maintain a vivid imagination increased, the emotion he could summon began to ebb. Within half an hour he was calm." He was instructed to experience his fears repeatedly. "Every time he felt a little wave of spontaneous alarm he was not to push it aside, but was to enhance it, to try to experience it . . . more vividly." The patient was intelligent and assiduous, practiced his exercises methodically, and became almost unable to feel frightened. He passed his examinations without difficulty.

Writers have also claimed an existential basis for techniques such as paradoxical intention that include exposure methods. Frankl [43] asked his patients to cease fleeing from, or fighting, symptoms and instead to bring them on deliberately, or even to exaggerate them. Gerz [48] illustrated the use of paradoxical intention in a man afraid that he might die of a heart attack: "When I asked the patient in my office to 'try as hard as possible' to make his heart beat fast and die of a heart attack 'right on the spot,' he laughed and replied 'Doc, I'm trying hard but I can't do it.' Following Frankl's technique I instructed him to 'go ahead and try to die from a heart attack' each time his anticipatory anxiety troubled him. As the patient started laughing about his neurotic symptoms, humour helped him to put distance between himself and his neurosis. The patient . . . (was) instructed to die at least three times a day of a heart attack, and instead of trying hard to go to sleep, try hard to remain awake. . . . In the moment he started laughing at his symptoms and when he became willing to produce them (paradoxically) intentionally, he changed his attitude toward his symptoms. . . . With this change in attitude, he . . . interrupted the vicious cycle and strangled the feedback mechanism."

The rationale and method of paradoxical intention bear certain resemblances to rapid exposure. As the rationale for use of such an approach, Malleson [89] suggested that "fear or panic is always integrally bound up with the wish to escape. So long as that wish persists, reciprocally the fear persists." This suggestion is reminiscent of John Hunter's rationale for his treatment of impotence in the eighteenth century; as long as a patient was afraid of failing with his mistress, he failed miserably. As soon as he was told not to engage in intercourse, his potency returned [61].

Oriental and Other Psychotherapies
Exposure and self-regulatory approaches share some elements with traditional forms of meditation. Research into this has hardly dawned, so it is premature to judge which similarities are trivial and which important. Describing the stages of training in Zen Buddhist meditation, Maupin [99] wrote: "There is an initial phase in which concentration, difficult at first, eventually becomes more successful. Relaxation and a kind of pleasant 'self-immersion' begin to follow. At this point internal distractions, often of an anxiety-arousing kind, come to the fore . . . the only way to render this disturbance inoperative is 'to look at it equably and at last grow weary of looking.' "

Morita psychotherapy practiced in Japan uses similar methods. In patients with severe anxiety and fear of death, Kora [75] noted that "the patient will always entertain a premonitory fear that the seizure (of anxiety) might attack him any moment and his sphere of activity is usually very much limited because of this anxiety . . . he should be told that it is important not to upset the regular pace of his life, by accepting such fear as it is calmly and passively. When he does not have the fit, the patient should be made to go out all by himself even if he has an anticipatory fear or is suffering from anxiety. He should ride the bus or the streetcar if that is necessary and should attempt to enlarge his sphere of activity in any way possible. If he takes advantage of his disease and leads a life like that of a patient by capitalizing on his condition, he will never be cured." Similarly, in the treatment of intrusive thoughts, "the only solution is to accept the desultory thoughts as something inevitable and to keep on reading without repelling them but tolerating them as they are. If this state of self-resignation is achieved, there will no longer be any antagonistic ideas."

Overview
While a more detailed overview will be presented at the conclusion of the next chapter, it seems worthwhile to recapitulate the main conclusions that can be reached after reviewing the burgeoning number of animal and ana-

logue research studies on fear reduction. First and central to an understanding of the most effective clinical approaches to phobia and compulsive behavior is the notion that exposure to all the fear-evoking stimuli is essential to the reduction of avoidance behavior and autonomic arousal. The majority of the evidence reviewed so far supports this notion. Thus, other therapeutic procedures are effective insofar as they lead to such exposure. For some procedures, such as relaxation training, there is surprisingly little support for efficacy, while other procedures, such as therapeutic instructions, reinforcement, feedback, and observation of others, seem to increase the probability of successful exposure.

The main thrust of research, then, is to define the various parameters of exposure, such as trial length, intertrial interval, rapid versus gradual exposure, and so on. A body of research results is slowly accumulating which has led to an increasing number of pertinent clinical studies. These will be described in the next chapter.

References

1. Agras, W. S., Leitenberg, H., and Barlow, D. H.   Social reinforcement in the modification of agoraphobia. *Archives of General Psychiatry* 19:423, 1968.
2. Akiyama, M.   Effects of extinction techniques on avoidance response. *Bulletin of Faculty of Education*, Hiroshima University, 17:173, 1968.
3. Ascough, J. C.   Quantitative differences in patients responding to induced anxiety: A reply to Noonan. *Psychotherapy: Theory, Research and Practice* 9:22, 1972.
4. Bandura, A., Grusec, J. E., and Menlove, F. L.   Vicarious extinction of avoidance behaviour. *Journal of Personality and Social Psychology* 5:16, 1967.
5. Bandura, A., Blanchard, E. B., and Ritter, B.   Relative efficacy of desensitization and modeling approaches for inducing behavioural, affective and attitudinal changes. *Journal of Personality and Social Psychology* 13:173, 1969.
6. Bandura, A., Jeffrey, R. W., and Wright, C. L.   Efficacy of participant modeling as a function of response induction aids. *Journal of Abnormal Psychology* 83:56, 1974.
7. Bandura, A., Jeffrey, R. W., and Gajdoz, E.   Generalizing change through participant modeling with self directed mastery. *Behavior Research and Therapy* 13:141, 1975.
8. Barrett, C. L.   "Runaway imagery" in systematic desensitization therapy and implosive therapy. *Psychotherapy: Theory, Research and Practice* 7:238, 1968.
9. Barrett, C. L.   One year follow-up of study using behaviour therapy, psychotherapy and waiting list control with phobic children. Paper presented at the Meeting of the Society for Psychotherapy Research, Nashville, June 1972.

10. Baum, M. Extinction of an avoidance response following response prevention: Some parametric investigations. *Canadian Journal of Psychology* 23:1, 1969.
11. Baum, M. Extinction of avoidance responding through response prevention (flooding). *Psychological Bulletin* 74:276, 1970.
12. Baum, M. Avoidance training in both alcohol and non drug states increases the resistance to extinction of an avoidance response in rats. *Psychopharmacologia* 18:87, 1971.
13. Baum, M. Flooding (response prevention) in rats: The effects of immediate vs. delayed flooding and of changed illumination conditions during flooding. *Canadian Journal of Psychology* 26:190, 1972a.
14. Baum, M. Repeated acquisition and extinction of avoidance in rats using flooding (response prevention). *Learning and Motivation* 3:272, 1972b.
15. Baum, M. Extinction of avoidance behaviour: Comparison of various flooding procedures in rats. *Bulletin of the Psychonomic Society* 1:22, 1973a.
16. Baum, M. Extinction of avoidance in rats: The effects of chlorpromazine and methylphenidate administered in conjunction with flooding (response prevention). *Behavior Research and Therapy* 11:165, 1973b.
17. Baum, M. Instrumental learning. In M. P. Feldman and A. Broadhurst (Eds.), *Theoretical and Experimental Bases of the Behaviour Therapist.* New York: John Wiley, 1976.
18. Benjamin, S., Marks, I. M., and Huson, J. Active muscular relaxation in desensitization of phobic patients. *Psychological Medicine* 2:381, 1972.
19. Berman, J. S., and Katzev, R. D. Factors involved in the rapid elimination of avoidance behaviour. *Behavior Research and Therapy* 10:247, 1972.
20. Bernstein, D. A., and Nietzel, M. T. Behavioural avoidance tests: The effects of demand characteristics and repeated measures on two types of subjects. *Behavior Therapy* 5:183, 1976.
21. Blanchard, E. B., and Draper, D. O. Treatment of a rodent phobia by covert reinforcement: A single subject experiment. *Behavior Therapy* 4:559, 1973.
22. Brady, J. P. Metronome-conditioned relaxation: A new behavioural procedure. *British Journal of Psychiatry* 122:729, 1973.
23. Boulougouris, J. C., and Bassiakos, L. Prolonged flooding in obsessive-compulsive neurosis. *Behavior Research and Therapy* 11:227, 1973.
24. Calef, R. A., and MacLean, G. D. A comparison of reciprocal inhibition and reactive inhibition therapies in the treatment of speech anxiety. *Behavior Therapy* 1:51, 1970.
25. Cohen, R., and Dean, S. J. Group desensitization of test anxiety. *Proceedings of the Seventy-sixth Annual Convention of the American Psychological Association* 3:615, 1968.
26. Crowder, J. E., and Thornton, D. W. Effects of systematic desensitization, programmed fantasy and bibliotherapy on a specific fear. *Behavior Research and Therapy* 8:35, 1970.
27. Crowe, M. J., Marks, I. M., Agras, W. S., and Leitenberg, H. Time-limited desensitization, implosion and shaping for phobic patients: A crossover study. *Behavior Research and Therapy* 10:319, 1972.
28. Curtis, G., Nesse, R., Buxton, M., Wright, J., and Lippman, D. Flooding

in vivo as research tool of treatment method for phobias. A preliminary report. *Comprehensive Psychiatry* 17:153, 1976a.
29. Curtis, G., Buxton, M., Lippman, D., Nesse, R., and Wright, J. Flooding during the Circadian phase of minimal cortisol secretion. Unpublished paper, 1976b.
30. de Moor, W. Systematic desensitization versus prolonged high intensity stimulation (flooding). *Journal of Behavior Therapy and Experimental Psychiatry* 1:45, 1970.
31. Delprato, D. J. An animal analogue to systematic desensitization and elimination of avoidance. *Behavior Research and Therapy* 11:49, 1973a.
32. Delprato, D. J. Exposure to the aversive stimulus in an animal analogue to systematic desensitization. *Behavior Research and Therapy* 11:187, 1973b.
33. Delprato, D. J. Post-response exposure to warning signal in avoidance extinction. *Animal Learning and Behavior*, 1974.
34. Delprato, D. J., and Jackson, D. E. Counterconditioning and exposure only in the treatment of specific (conditioned suppression). *Behavior Research and Therapy* 11:453, 1974.
35. D'Zurilla, T. J., Wilson, G. T., and Nelson, R. A preliminary study of effectiveness of graduated prolonged exposure in the treatment of irrational fear. *Behavior Therapy* 4:672, 1973.
36. Eberle, T. M., Rehm, L. P., and McBurney, D. H. Fear decrement to anxiety hierarchy items effects of stimulus intensity. *Behavior Research and Therapy* 13:255, 1975.
37. Emmelkamp, P. M. G. Effects of expectancy or systematic desensitization and flooding. *European Journal of Behavior Analysis and Modification*, 1:1, 1975.
38. Emmelkamp, P. M. G., and Emmelkamp-Benner, A. Effects of historically portrayed modeling and group treatment on self-observation: A comparison with agoraphobics. *Behavior Research and Therapy* 13:135, 1975.
39. Emmelkamp, P. M. G., and Wessels, H. Flooding in imagination v. flooding in vivo. A comparison with agoraphobics. *Behavior Research and Therapy* 13:7, 1975.
40. Emmelkamp, P. M. G., and Straatman, H. A psychoanalytic reinterpretation of the effectiveness of systematic desensitization: Fact or fiction? *Behavior Research and Therapy*, 1976.
41. Everaerd, W. T., Rijken, H. M., and Emmelkamp, P. M. G. A comparison of "flooding" and successive approximation in the treatment of agoraphobia. *Behavior Research and Therapy* 11:105, 1973.
42. Ferenczi, S. *Further Contributions to the Theory and Technique of Psychoanalysis*. London: Hogarth Press, 1926, Chapter XVI.
43. Frankl, V. E. Paradoxical intention: A logotherapeutic technique. *American Journal of Psychotherapy* 14:520, 1960.
44. Freud, S. Turnings in the Ways of Psychoanalytic Therapy. In James Strachey, ed., *Collected Papers*, Vol. 2. London: Hogarth Press and Institute of Psychoanalysis, 1919, p. 399.
45. Gauthier, J., and Marshall, W. L. Optimal criteria for determining exposure duration to phobic stimulus in flooding therapy. Unpublished paper, 1977.
46. Geer, J. H., Davison, G. C., and Gatchel, R. I. Reduction of stress in

humans through non-veridical perceived control of aversive stimulation. *Journal of Personality and Social Psychology* 16:731, 1970.
47. Gelder, M. G., Bancroft, J. H. J., Gath, D. H., Johnston, D. W., Mathews, A. M., and Shaw, P. M. Specific and non-specific factors in behavior therapy. *British Journal of Psychiatry* 123:445, 1973.
48. Gerz, H. O. The treatment of the phobic and the obsessive-compulsive patient using paradoxical intention. *Journal of Neuropsychiatry* 3:375, 1962.
49. Girodo, M., and Henry, D. R. Cognitive, physiological and behavioural components of anxiety in flooding. *Canadian Journal of Behavioral Science*, 8:224, 1976.
50. Glass, D., and Singer, J. E. *Stress and Adaptation: Experimental Studies of Behaviour Effects of Exposure to Aversive Events*. New York: Academic Press, 1972.
51. Gordon, A., and Baum, M. Increased efficacy of flooding (response prevention) in rats through intracranial stimulation. *Journal of Comparative and Physiological Psychology* 75:68, 1971.
52. Grimm, L., and Kanfer, F. H. Tolerance of aversive stimulation. 1977. In press.
53. Guilani, B. The role of competing response and manner of presentation of the aversive stimulus in modification of avoidance behavior. Unpublished doctoral dissertation, University of California, 1972.
54. Guthrie, E. R. *The Psychology of Human Learning*. New York: Harper, 1955.
55. Hafner, J., and Marks, I. M. Exposure in vivo of agoraphobics. Contributions of diazepam, group exposure and anxiety evocation. *Psychological Medicine* 6:71, 1976.
56. Hall, R. A., and Hinkle, J. E. Vicarious desensitization of test anxiety. *Behavior Research and Therapy* 10:407, 1972.
57. Hand, I., Lamontagne, Y., and Marks, I. M. Group exposure (flooding) in vivo for agoraphobics. *British Journal of Psychiatry*, 124:588, 1974.
58. Hartig, M., and Kanfer, F. H. The role of verbal self-instructions in children's resistance to temptation. *Journal of Personality and Social Psychology* 25:259, 1973.
59. Hastings, J. E., and Walker, M. J. The effects of level of fear and rate of approach on cardiac rate and avoidance of a phobic stimulus. *Behavior Therapy* 6:445, 1975.
60. Hokanson, J., DeGord, D., Forest, M., and Britain, T. Availability of avoidance behaviors in modulating vascular stress responses. *Journal of Personality and Social Psychology* 19:60, 1971.
61. Hunter, J. Treatise on Venereal Disease (1786). In R. Hunter and J. MacAlpine (Eds.), *Three Hundred Years of British Psychiatry*. London: Oxford University Press, 1963.
62. Jacobsen, V. Influential factors in the outcome of treatment of school phobia. *Smith College Study on Social Work* 18:181, 1948.
63. Jersild, A. T., and Holmes, F. G. Methods of overcoming children's fears. *Journal of Psychology* 1:75, 1935.
64. Johnston, D., and Gath, D. Arousal levels and attribution effects in diazepam assisted flooding. *British Journal of Psychiatry* 122:463, 1973.

65. Johnston, D., Lancashire, M., Mathews, A. M., Munby, M., Shaw, P. M., and Gelder, M. G.   Imaginal flooding and exposure to real phobic situations: Changes during treatment. *British Journal of Psychiatry* 129:372, 1976.
66. Kanfer, F. H., and Seidner, M. L.   Self-control: Factors enhancing tolerance of noxious stimulation. *Journal of Personality and Social Psychology* 25:381, 1973.
67. Kanfer, F. H., Cox, L. E., Griner, J. M., and Karoly, P.   Contracts, demand characteristics, and self-control. *Journal of Personality and Social Psychology* 30:605, 1974.
68. Karst, T. O., and Trexler, L. D.   An initial study using fixed-role and rational emotive therapy in treating public speaking anxiety. *Journal of Consulting and Clinical Psychology* 34:360, 1970.
69. Katzev, R.   Extinguishing avoidance responses as a function of delayed warning signal termination. *Journal of Experimental Psychology* 75:339, 1967.
70. Kazdin, A. E.   Covert modeling and the reduction of avoidance behavior. *Journal of Abnormal Psychology* 81:87, 1973.
71. Kazdin, A. E.   Effects of covert modeling and model reinforcement on assertive behavior. *Journal of Abnormal Psychology* 83:240, 1974.
72. Kazdin, A. E.   Covert modeling, model similarity, and reduction of avoidance behavior. *Behavior Therapy* 5:325, 1974a.
73. Kazdin, A. E.   The effect of model identity and fear-relevant similarity on covert modeling. *Behavior Therapy* 5:624, 1974b.
74. Kazdin, A. E.   Effects of covert-modeling and model reinforcement on assertive behavior. *Journal of Abnormal Psychology* 83:240, 1974c.
75. Kora, T.   A method of instruction in psychotherapy. *Jikeikai Medical Journal* 15:316, 1968.
76. Lang, P. J.   *Acquisition of heart rate control.* In D. J. Levis (Ed.), *Learning Approaches to Therapeutic Behavior Change.* Chicago: Aldine, 1970.
77. Leitenberg, H., Agras, W. S., Thompson, L. E., and Wright, D. E.   Feedback in behavior modification: An experimental analysis in two phobic cases. *Journal of Applied Behavior Analysis* 1:131, 1968.
78. Leitenberg, H., Agras, S., Edwards, J. A., Thomson, L. E., and Wincze, J. P.   Practice as a psychotherapeutic variable: An experimental analysis within single cases. *Journal of Psychiatric Research* 7:215, 1970.
79. Leitenberg, H., and Callahan, E. J.   Reinforced practice and reduction of different kinds of fears in adults and children. *Behavior Research and Therapy* 11:19, 1973.
80. Leitenberg, H., Agras, W. S., Allen, R., Butz, R., and Edwards, J.   Feedback and therapist praise during treatment of phobia. *Journal of Consulting and Clinical Psychology* 43:396, 1975.
81. Leventhal, H.   The emotions: A basic problem for social psychology. Unpublished manuscript, University of Wisconsin, 1973.
82. Levy, D. M.   Trends in therapy: III Release therapy. *American Journal of Orthopsychiatry* 9:713, 1939.
83. Lewis, S.   A comparison of behavior therapy techniques in the reduction of fearful avoidance behavior. *Behavior Therapy* 5:648, 1974.
84. Lick, J. R., and Bootzin, R. R.   Expectancy, demand characteristics, and contact desensitization in behavior change. *Behavior Therapy* 1:176, 1970.
85. Litvak, S. B.   A comparison of two brief group behavior therapy techniques

on the reduction of avoidance behavior. *Psychological Record* 19:329, 1970.
86. LoPiccolo, J. Effective components of systematic desensitization. Unpublished doctoral dissertation, Yale University, 1969.
87. McFall, R. M., and Twentyman, C. T. Four experiments on the relative contributions of rehearsal, modeling, and coaching to assertion training. *Journal of Abnormal Psychology* 81:199, 1973.
88. McLaughlin, F. L., and Miller, W. M. Employment of air-raid noises in Psychotherapy. *British Medical Journal* 2:158, 1941.
89. Malleson, N. Panic and phobia: Possible method of treatment. *Lancet* 1:225, 1959.
90. Marks, I. M. *Patterns of Meaning in Psychiatric Patients: Semantic Differential Responses in Obsessivers and Psychopaths.* Maudsley Monograph No. 13. Oxford University Press, 1965.
91. Marks, I. M. Behavioural treatments of phobic and obsessive-compulsive disorders: A critical appraisal. In M. Hersen, R. M. Eisler, and P. M. Miller (Eds.), *Progress in Behavior Modification.* New York: Vol. 1. Academic Press, 1975.
92. Marks, I. M., Boulougouris, J., and Marset, P. Flooding versus desensitization in phobic disorders. *British Journal of Psychiatry* 119:353, 1971a.
93. Marks, I. M., Connolly, J., Hallam, R. S., and Philpott, R. *Nursing in Behavioural Psychotherapy.* Paperback book in Research Series of Royal College of Nursing, Henrietta Square, London, WIM OAB.
94. Marshitz, M. H., Almarza, M. T., Barra, E., and Medina, A. M. Massed and spaced practice in systematic desensitization of test anxiety. Paper presented at the Third Annual Conference of the European Association of Behavior Therapy. Amsterdam, July, 1973.
95. Masserman, J. H. *Behavior and Neurosis.* Chicago: University of Chicago Press, 1943.
96. Mathews, A. M. Psychophysiological approaches to the investigation of desensitization and allied procedures. *Psychological Bulletin* 76:73, 1971.
97. Mathews, A. M., and Shaw, P. M. Continuous exposure and emotional arousal in flooding. *Behavior Research and Therapy* 11:587, 1973.
98. Mathews, A. M., Johnstone, D. W., Lancashire, M., Munby, M., Shaw, P. M. and Gelder, M. G. Imaginal flooding and exposure to real phobic situations: Treatment outcome with agoraphobic patients. *British Journal of Psychiatry* 129:362, 1976.
99. Maupin, E. W. Zen Buddhism: A psychological review. *Journal of Consulting Psychology* 26:362, 1962.
100. Meichenbaum, D. H. Cognitive factors in behavior modification: Modifying what clients say to themselves. Paper presented at the meeting of the Association for Advancement of Behavior Therapy, Washington, D.C., September 1971a.
101. Melamed, B. G. The habituation of psychophysiological response to tones, and to filmed fear stimuli under varying conditions of instructional set. Unpublished doctoral dissertation, University of Wisconsin, 1969.
102. Miller, B. V., and Levis, D. J. The effects of varying short visual exposure times to a phobic test stimulus on subsequent avoidance behavior. *Behavior Research and Therapy* 9:17, 1971.
103. Miller, B. V., and Bernstein, D. A. Instructional demand in a behavioral

avoidance test for claustrophobic fears. *Journal of Abnormal Psychology* 80:206, 1972.
104. Miller, H. R., and Nawas, M. M.   Control of aversive stimulus termination in systematic desensitization. *Behavior Research and Therapy* 8:57, 1970.
105. Murphy, C. M., and Bootzin, R. R.   Active and passive participation in the contact desensitization of snake fear in children. *Behavior Therapy* 4:203, 1973.
106. Noonan, J. R., and Lewis, P. M.   Reverse psychology psychotherapy techniques. A review and evaluation. Paper presented at the meeting of the Southeastern Psychological Association, Louisville, April, 1970.
107. Nunes, J., and Marks, I. M.   Feedback of true heart rate during exposure in vivo. *Archives of General Psychiatry* 32:933, 1975.
108. Nunes, J., and Marks, I. M.   Feedback of true heart rate during exposure in vivo: Partial replication with methodological improvement. *Archives of General Psychiatry*, 1977. In press.
109. Oler, I., and Baum, M.   Facilitated extinction of an avoidance response through shortening of the inter-trial interval. *Psychological Science* 11:323, 1968.
110. Orwin, A.   Augmented respiratory relief. *British Journal of Psychiatry* 122: 171, 1973.
111. Orwin, A., Leboeuf, A., Dovey, J., and James, S.   A comparative trial of exposure and respiratory relief therapies. *Behavior Research and Therapy* 13:205, 1975.
112. Rabavilas, A. D., Boulougouris, J. C., and Stefanis, C.   Duration of flooding sessions in the treatment of obsessive-compulsive patients. *Behavior Research and Therapy*, 1976. In press.
113. Rachman, S.   Treatment by prolonged exposure to high intensity stimulation. *Behavior Research and Therapy* 7:295, 1969.
114. Ramsay, R. W.   Emotional training on extension of desensitization. *Behavioral Engineering*, 1974.
115. Rezin, V. A., and Mathews, A. M.   Imaginal exposure with dental phobics. Paper presented to the British Association of Behavior Therapy Annual Meeting, Exeter, July, 1976.
116. Reynierse, J. H., and Wiff, L. I.   Effects of temporal placement of response prevention of avoidance on extinction of avoidance in rats. *Behavior Research and Therapy* 11:119, 1973.
117. Rimm, D. C., and Mahoney, M. J.   The application of reinforcement and participant modeling procedures in the treatment of snake-phobic behavior. *Behavior Research and Therapy* 7:369, 1969.
118. Ritter, B.   The group desensitization of children's snake phobias using vicarious and contact desensitization procedures. *Behavior Research and Therapy* 6:1, 1968.
119. Rohrbaugh, M., and Riccio, D. C.   Paradoxical enhancement of learned fear. *Journal of Abnormal Psychology* 75:210, 1970.
120. Rohrbaugh, M., Riccio, D. C., and Arthur, A.   Paradoxical enhancement of conditioned suppression. *Behavior Research and Therapy* 10:125, 1972.
121. Roper, G.   Leonhard's individual therapy and its relation to behaviour therapy. *Behavior Research and Therapy* 14:239, 1976.
122. Rosen, G. M.   Subjects' initial therapeutic experiences and awareness of

therapeutic goals in systematic desensitization. A Review. *Behavior Therapy* 7:14, 1976.
123. Ross, S. M., and Proctor, S. Frequency and duration of hierarchy item exposure in a systematic desensitization analogue. *Behavior Research and Therapy* 11:303, 1973.
124. Rudolf, G. Deconditioning and time therapy. *Journal of Mental Science* 107:1097, 1961.
125. Russell, R. K., and Mathews, C. O. Cue-controlled relaxation in in vivo desensitization of a snake phobia. *Journal of Behavioral Therapy and Experimental Psychiatry* 6:49, 1974.
126. Russell, R. K., Miller, D. E., and June, L. N. Group cue-controlled relaxation in the treatment of test anxiety. *Behavior Therapy* 5:572, 1975.
127. Rutner, I. T. The effects of feedback and instructions on phobic behavior. *Behavior Therapy* 4:338, 1973.
128. Sanford, E. F. The acoustic mirror technique – psychodynamic and behavioristic approaches are psychotherapeutically compatible and complementary. Paper presented to the Fifth World Congress of Psychiatry, Mexico, p. 514, 1965.
129. Saul L., Rome, H., and Leuser, E. Desensitization of combat fatigue patients. *American Journal of Psychiatry* 102:476, 1946.
130. Segraves, R. T., and Smith, R. C. Treatment of four neurotic outpatients by concurrent psychotherapy and behaviour therapy. Paper presented to the Annual Meeting of the American Psychiatric Association, Anaheim, May, 1975.
131. Serber, M., Goldstein, A., Piaget, G., and Kort, F. The use of implosive-expressive therapy in anxiety reaction. In R. D. Rubin and C. M. Franks (Eds.), *Advances in Behavior Therapy, 1968.* New York: Academic Press, 1969.
132. Sherman, A. R. Response-contingent CS termination in the extinction of avoidance learning. *Behavior Research and Therapy* 8:227, 1970.
133. Sherman, A. R. Real life exposure as a primary therapeutic factor in desensitization treatment of fear. *Journal of Abnormal Psychology* 79:19, 1972.
134. Sherman, A. R., and Plummer, I. L. Training in relaxation as a behavioral self-management skill: an exploratory investigation. *Behavior Therapy* 4:543, 1973.
135. Siegeltuch, M., and Baum, M. Extinction of well established avoidance responses through response prevention (flooding). *Behavior Research and Therapy* 9:103, 1971.
136. Sipprelle, C. N. Induced Anxiety. *Psychotherapy: Theory, Research and Practice* 4:36, 1967.
137. Solyom, L., Heseltine, G. F. D., McClure, D. J., Ledwidge, B., and Kenny, F. Comparative study of aversion relief and systematic desensitization in the treatment of phobias. *British Journal of Psychiatry* 119:299, 1971.
138. Stampfl, T. G. Implosive therapy: The theory, the subhuman analogue, the strategy and the technique: Part I, The theory. In S. G. Armitage (Ed.), *Behavior Modification Techniques in the Treatment of Emotional Disorders.* Battle Creek, Mich.: VA Publication, pp. 22–37. 1967.
139. Stern, R. S., and Marks, I. M. A comparison of brief and prolonged flood-

ing in agoraphobics. *Archives of General Psychiatry* 28:210, 1973a.
140. Stewart, K.   Dream theory in Malaya. In C. Tart (Ed.), *Altered States of Consciousness*. New York: John Wiley, 1969.
141. Stone, N. M., and Borkovec, T. D.   The paradoxical effect of brief CS exposure on analogue phobic subjects. *Behavior Research and Therapy* 13:51, 1975.
142. Strahley, D. F.   Systematic desensitization and counterphobic treatment of an irrational fear of snakes. Unpublished doctoral dissertation. University of Tennessee, 1965.
143. Sue, D.   The effect of duration of exposure on systematic desensitization and extinction. *Behavior Research and Therapy* 15:55, 1975.
144. Suinn, R. M., and Richardson, F.   Anxiety management training: a nonspecific behavior therapy program for anxiety control. *Behavior Therapy* 2:498, 1971.
145. Sushinsky, L. W., and Bootzin, R. R.   Cognitive desensitization as a model of systematic desensitization. *Behavior Research and Therapy* 8:29, 1970.
146. Trexler, L. D., and Karst, T. O.   Rational-emotive therapy, placebo, and no treatment effects on public-speaking anxiety. *Journal of Abnormal Psychology* 79:60, 1972.
147. Uno, T., Greer, S. E., and Coates, L.   Observational facilitation of response prevention. *Behavior Research and Therapy* 11:207, 1973.
148. Vodde, T. W., and Gilner, F. H.   The effects of exposure to fear stimuli on fear reduction. *Behavior Research and Therapy* 9:169, 1971.
149. Waters, W. F., McDonald, D. G., and Koresko, R. L.   Psychophysiological responses during analogue desensitization and nonrelaxation control procedures. *Behavior Research and Therapy* 10:381, 1972.
150. Watson, J. P., and Marks, I. M.   Relevant vs. irrelevant flooding in the treatment of phobias. *Behavior Therapy* 2:275, 1971.
151. Watson, J. P., Gaind, R., and Marks, I. M.   Prolonged exposure: a rapid treatment for phobias. *British Medical Journal* 1:13, 1971.
152. Watson, J. P., Mullett, G. E., and Pillay, H.   The effects of prolonged exposure to phobic situations upon agoraphobic patients treated in groups. *Behavior Research and Therapy* 11:531, 1973.
153. Watts, F. N.   Desensitization as an habituation phenomenon: I. Stimulus intensity as determinant of the effects of stimulus lengths. *Behavior Research and Therapy* 9:209, 1971.
154. Watts, F. N.   Desensitization as an habituation phenomenon: II. Studies of interstimulus interval length. *Psychological Reports* 33:715, 1973.
155. Watts, F. N.   The control of spontaneous recovery of anxiety in imaginal desensitization. *Behavior Research and Therapy* 12:57, 1974.
156. Watts, F. N.   Self-report of anxiety in imaginal desensitization. *British Journal of Social and Clinical Psychology*, 15:211, 1976.
157. Weinberger, N. M.   Effect of detainment on extinction of avoidance responses. *Journal of Comparative Physiological Psychology* 60:135, 1965.
158. Wilson, G. T., and Thomas, M. G. W.   Self- versus drug-produced relaxation and the effects of instructional set in standardized desensitization. *Behavior Research and Therapy* 11:279, 1973.

159. Wisocki, P. A. Treatment of obsessive-compulsive behavior by covert sensitization and covert reinforcement: a case report. *Journal of Behavioral Therapy and Experimental Psychiatry* 1:233, 1970.
160. Wolpe, J. *Psychotherapy by Reciprocal Inhibition.* Stanford: Stanford University Press, 1958.
161. Wolpin, M. Guided imagining to reduce avoidance behaviour. *Psychotherapy: Theory, Research and Practice* 6:122, 1969.
162. Zane, M. Fighting fear by group confrontation. *World News*, pp. 76–80, Feb. 1972.

8. Exposure Treatments: Clinical Applications

Isaac Marks

During the past few years an impressive array of controlled clinical studies have appeared on phobic and obsessive-compulsive patients, a body of work more directly relevant to clinicians than are analogue studies on volunteers or on animals. This work will be reviewed according to each clinical syndrome, after which general principles will be outlined.

Application to Phobia
Exposure in Fantasy: Desensitization (in Fantasy)
This has been shown to produce significant improvement in phobic patients in at least 10 controlled studies since 1970, and also improvement of a general psychiatric population in one study but not in another [53]. Improvement after desensitization was found in one study to be maintained up to four years after treatment, although 15 percent of patients who were followed up required further treatment for depressive episodes, during which phobias were temporarily aggravated [51]. Other studies on phobic patients have found that desensitization in fantasy produces equally good outcome with and without muscular relaxation [1, 3, 25, 89], and it may be concluded that muscular relaxation training is redundant during desensitization fantasy. Moreover, taped desensitization had comparable effects to that given by live therapists [18].

In the early 1970s, much interest centered on the relative merits of desensitization versus flooding in fantasy. Short-term advantages for flooding in fantasy were reported when flooding was combined with administration of thiopental [32], and Marks, Boulougouris, and Marset [56] found an advantage for flooding in fantasy without drugs. However, no significant difference between desensitization and flooding in fantasy was found in other studies [12, 23, 87]. It is possible that the superiority of flooding over desensitization obtained by Marks and his colleagues [56] and by Gelder, Bancroft, Gath, Johnston, Mathews, and Shaw [23] might be attributable to manipulation of exposure conditions in vivo rather than to the difference between the two fantasy treatments.

One question about the mechanism of improvement with implosion or flooding in fantasy was whether fear imagery needed to be relevant to the patient's phobia. A controlled study compared frightening phobia-relevant imagery (excluding psychodynamic material) with irrelevant fear imagery concerning scenes such as being caught by a tiger, being burned to death, and drowning [95]. At the end of treatment, relevant and irrelevant fear imagery produced similar therapeutic effects, though there were several pointers that they might be operating through different mechanisms. Thus, relevant fear cues seemed to protect patients from anxiety during subsequent irrelevant fear sessions, but the reverse did not apply. Furthermore, the more anxious patients became during imagery at initial assessment, the more likely they were to improve with relevant fear, and the less likely with irrelevant fear. Finally, outcome to relevant fear did not correlate with anxiety experienced during treatment, whereas outcome to irrelevant fear was better in those patients who showed more anxiety during treatment sessions. It was suggested, therefore, that abreaction might be an operative element in irrelevant fear but not in relevant flooding in fantasy.

Exposure in Vivo
The value of prolonged live exposure was suggested by uncontrolled studies [96, 97] in 10 patients with specific phobias, who improved after treatment for an average of six hours each, spread over two to three afternoons. A subsequent controlled study [92] using a Latin square crossover design found that duration of exposure in fantasy made little difference, although the fantasy had been given by tape recorder, which might have accounted for its lack of effect. Two continuous hours of in vivo exposure of the agoraphobics yielded significantly greater reduction of phobias than did four interrupted half-hours separated by 30-minute rest periods.

A logical therapeutic development was to use prolonged exposure in vivo in groups to save time and possibly enhance potency through social cohesion and observational learning. In the first study of this point, Hand, Lamontagne, and Marks [29] treated 25 chronic agoraphobics in groups of four to five patients each in two balanced conditions with high and low social cohesion. Over one week each patient had three four-hour sessions of group exposure in vivo. There was one session per day lasting four continuous hours, interrupted at midday for a half-hour lunch break. Instructions for anxiety management (coping) were the same for all patients during both treatment and follow-up. During exposure in vivo, patients were trained to deal with anxiety by accepting that it would occur, attending to the cues that denoted its presence, rating the signs without exaggeration, watching how long it took for anxiety to subside, and attending to events to master the situation. The aim was not so much to extinguish anxiety as to manage it so that it did not govern the patient's actions. The actual method of regulation was not crucial.

Group panic did not appear during any treatment sessions. However, several patients had horror reactions or depression during the nights or the free day between treatment sessions. These reactions were remedied by immediate reexposure and motivating group discussion. Although humor is rare during individual exposure during in vivo sessions, joking was common during group exposure in vivo, especially with cohesive groups. Outcome for all groups was at least as good as from previous trials with individual patients. Patients from cohesive and noncohesive groups improved similarly on phobic scales three days after treatment, but at follow-up three to six months later patients from cohesive groups had improved further; there were also fewer dropouts from cohesive groups than from noncohesive ones. All the patients improved significantly in work, leisure, and social adjustment, despite several exacerbations of preexisting marital and personality problems.

Another value of group exposure was its unplanned contribution to social skills and assertive training. This presumabably resulted from the rehearsal of social behavior that occurred naturally during group treatment. Several patients became used to contacting strangers when anxious in the phobic situation and obtained relief by talking to them about their anxiety.

A second study also found group exposure to be effective in the treatment of agoraphobics [27]. Fifty-seven chronic agoraphobic patients were assigned at random to group exposure or individual exposure in vivo for comparable lengths of time. Group treatment was along the lines of Hand, Lamontagne, and Marks [29], but with moderate social cohesion. Treatment included a total of 12 hours of exposure in vivo, in groups of four to seven patients, spread over four days in a two-week period. Three hours of exposure in vivo was given on each treatment day. Forty-one patients completed group exposure, which was divided into exposure with use of diazepam and a placebo condition. Twelve patients completed individual exposure. Individual exposure was of the same duration but began in the presence of the therapist rather than the group; half the patients had high anxiety induced by the therapist without reassurance, while half had low anxiety with reassurance.

Improvement as a result of group exposure was comparable to that obtained by Hand and his colleagues and was maintained for six months. However, improvement did not increase during this time, thus resembling the outcome in the noncohesive groups studied by Hand, Lamontagne, and Marks. There was a consistent trend for individually treated patients to improve slightly *less* than group-treated patients. However, this difference was significant only on nonphobic measures such as general anxiety, leisure activities, and the number of visits to hospital requested by patients during follow-up. Therapists, however, found that exposure sessions were easier to conduct in moderately cohesive groups than with individual patients.

Other workers have also found significant improvement from group exposure in vivo of agoraphobics [98]. Much less benefit was obtained from taped group exposure in fantasy. Some improvement was lost during five months' follow-up. A fourth study also found group exposure for agoraphobics to be valuable. These workers tried to replicate the highly group-cohesive condition of Hand, Lamontagne, and Marks [29], using comparable conditions of treatment and measurement, although the amount of group cohesion in fact turned out to be midway between the high and low cohesive groups of Hand and his colleagues. Three groups of five, five, and eight patients had three five-hour treatment sessions over one week. The immediate effects were similar to those of previous studies. As with patients from Hafner and Marks's moderately cohesive groups, improvement was maintained at six-month follow-up, but did not actually increase during that time. The question arises: Does cohesion need to be especially high, as in the highly cohesive groups of Hand and his colleagues, for improvement to increase over follow-up, perhaps by patients maintaining contact with, and encouraging, one another to carry out self-exposure? If this is so, such high group cohesion may not be easy to engineer.

In contrast to the preceding four studies of group exposure in vivo, different group meetings were studied in agoraphobics by Emmelkamp and Emmelkamp-Benner [16]. Their group meetings, however, consisted of discussion of exposure homework and of therapy sessions, but there was no actual group exposure in vivo. Thirty-one agoraphobic patients, mainly female, completed treatment, with two factors being varied—with and without group meetings, and with and without seeing a videofilm depicting "ex-clients" relating their experiences with the same treatment; that is, graded self-exposure in vivo. The models in the videotapes were not seen actually carrying out exposure in vivo; moreover, the film lasted 23 minutes and was seen only once, just before the first treatment session. Treatment was over four nine-minute-long sessions with follow-up to one month. The exposure sessions were given individually and consisted of graded in vivo exercises, with instructions to turn back if the patient became too anxious, and then to try again. Similar instructions were given for the patients to try self-exposure homework between sessions.

One viewing of the model on videofilm did not increase the treatment effect. This is consistent with the idea that watching a model is not fear-reducing unless it involves actual approach to the discomforting situation. The group meetings made no difference to the outcome at the end of one-month follow-up. Patients' expectancy of improvement at the start of treatment correlated significantly though weakly with the posttreatment score.

Finally, Butollo and Mittaelstadt [9] have performed a controlled comparison of group exposure with individual exposure in vivo using specific phobics, not agoraphobics, and volunteers as well as patients. A further difference is that the clients within groups had different phobias from one another, while the preceding studies were homogeneous with respect to agoraphobia. These workers treated 30 outpatients in 11 sessions over four months, and clients from the groups of five or six met monthly after treatment to discuss progress. Individually treated subjects actually did slightly better than group-treated clients up to two-month follow-up, but they had had rather more in vivo exposure than group-treated subjects because group treatment included some nonexposure discussion.

The saving of therapist time gives a clear advantage to group exposure over individual exposure in vivo, even though the results are comparable. The five studies of group exposure in vivo agree on the clinical usefulness of this approach. Whether high social cohesion enhances the process is a matter for further study.

Home-based Treatment
No systematic comparison has yet been made of treatments for agoraphobics at home rather than in the clinic. In one uncontrolled report of home-based treatment [61], 12 married women living with husbands who agreed to cooperate were treated. Patients and spouses were given a detailed manual emphasizing the selection of target behaviors, the importance of regular graded self-exposure in vivo, the appropriate use of tranquilizers, and the management of panic. Each couple was visited at home by the therapist three times in the first week, twice weekly during the next two

weeks, and once in the fourth week. Only in the first week did the therapist assist exposure. Other sessions were spent on the progress of patient and spouse in the self-exposure homework program, as recorded in a detailed diary kept by the patient. Patients improved to the same extent during this program as in previous studies. The total time spent by the therapist with the patient and spouse amounted to nine hours, and travel time to and from the home took another eight hours, making a mean of 17 hours' treatment—less therapist time than in previous studies, but comparable to the time spent by nurse-therapists treating agoraphobics in hospital-based programs [59]. Patients' improvement actually increased during six months' follow-up, especially in their use of automobiles, but not in the time they spent out alone on foot. This study is uncontrolled and leaves unanswered the role of the spouse, of the instruction manual, and of practice in the home situation. Nevertheless, it raises the question; Might not self-exposure homework be an economical form of treatment for agoraphobics?

Most of the controlled studies of Emmelkamp and co-workers employed home-based treatment, although they did not examine this particular issue [13, 15, 19]. In their first study, improvement was small [15]. Sixteen agoraphobics, mostly patients, were assigned at random to repeated practice of in vivo exposure, either without praise (self-observation) or with praise for progress (shaping, successive approximation). Practice consisted of clients' being encouraged to go out for increasingly long periods, to leave the situation if they felt tense, to write the time down in a book, and then to try again. Subjects had six 90-minute sessions twice weekly of each condition in a balanced crossover design. Both treatments improved patients significantly and equally, but gains were small.

In a later study, Everaerd, Rijken, and Emmelkamp [19] used home-based treatment with 14 chronic agoraphobic volunteers (not patients) from a phobic club. They compared practice in vivo with praise (shaping) with 45 minutes of fantasy exposure to phobia-relevant cues, followed by in vivo practice without praise. There were six 90-minute sessions, given twice weekly, of each condition in balanced order. Again, both treatment groups improved significantly and equally until three-month follow-up.

From both these home-based studies we can conclude that repeated brief self-exposure in vivo can be therapeutic and that systematic reward does not add significantly to this effect. In another home-based study in agoraphobics, Emmelkamp and Wessels [17] compared flooding in imagination with flooding in vivo separately and together. Each condition involved four 90-minute sessions of treatment given three times weekly by experienced psychologists. Patients had either (1) *prolonged exposure in vivo* without anxiety reducers such as an umbrella, bicycle, or sunglasses or (2) *exposure in fantasy* with a live therapist (not tape-recorded), with psychodynamic cues being excluded, or (3) *combined flooding in fantasy* for 45 minutes followed immediately by exposure in vivo for 45 minutes. After the first four sessions, improvement in the three conditions differed significantly. Most benefit occurred from the prolonged exposure in vivo condition, the next best from the combined fantasy and in vivo condition, and the least from the pure fantasy condition. Thereafter, all patients had eight 90-minute sessions of graded self-exposure in vivo ("self-observation"), as in previous experiments, being accompanied by therapists in the first two of these sessions. After this additional in vivo practice (self-observation) further significant improvement occurred to one-month follow-up. Patients' expectation of change at the start of treatment did not correlate significantly with outcome at the end of treatment.

In Vivo Exposure versus Fantasy Exposure
Two days after the end of treatment, Emmelkamp and Wessels [17] found a clear advantage for prolonged exposure in vivo rather than in fantasy. However, all patients subsequently had graded in vivo exposure, so this contrast could not be examined in their later experimental and follow-up phases. Similarly, Stern and Marks [92] found taped fantasy exposure had no effect when measured immediately after treatment, although prolonged in vivo exposure had a significant effect when measured three days later. However, effects were confounded by differing times of outcome measure, and the crossover design precluded conclusions about long-term effects during follow-up. Furthermore, taped fantasy exposure might be less effective than that given by a live therapist. In a similar comparison, again in agoraphobics, Watson, Mullett, and Pillay [98] also found that group exposure in vivo was significantly superior to taped group exposure in fantasy. However, outcome was measured immediately after treatment, and the crossover design again precluded conclusions about long-term effects.

In another comparison of imaginal exposure with in vivo exposure [62], agoraphobic women were randomly assigned to three therapists for treatment in weekly sessions in one of three conditions: eight sessions of 90 minutes of imaginal exposure followed by eight sessions of in vivo exposure; or 16 sessions of 45 minutes' imaginal exposure followed by 45 minutes of in vivo exposure; or 16 sessions of 90 minutes' exposure in vivo. Sessions were given once weekly. Patients were instructed to practice agreed phobic items at home before the next treatment appointment and to record these in the form of daily diaries, which were discussed at the start of each treatment visit. Agoraphobic patients went out on average once daily.

No significant difference was found between the imaginal conditions and in vivo exposure ones on clinical scales after either eight or 16 sessions, or at follow-up at one, three, and six months. As in the study by Emmelkamp and Wessels, preceding exposure in fantasy did not potentiate exposure in vivo immediately afterward. Self-rated anxiety was nearly twice as high during imaginal exposure as during in vivo treatment. There was no increase in "calmness" ratings immediately after imaginal exposure, despite long-term improvement. Patient outcome correlated significantly with patients' initial emotional stability and with their initial expectations of improvement.

The apparent contradiction of results from this study with those of Emmelkamp and Wessels [17] might be explained by two points, one of which was suggested by Emmelkamp [14], namely, that the hierarchy items used by Mathews and his colleagues [62] were more graded, whereas Emmelkamp and Wessels used top anxiety items for both in vivo and fantasy exposure. Emmelkamp thought his own steeper gradient of exposure in vivo might be more effective than the more gradual approach he ascribed to Mathews and co-workers. The second difference between the two studies might be even more important. Strong instructions by Mathews and his colleagues that patients should practice self-exposure between sessions and record this in daily diary form might have obscured differences resulting from the weekly sessions of therapist-assisted exposure. In the experiment by Emmelkamp and Wessels, no homework instructions were given, and treatment was more frequent—three times a week rather than once weekly—which left less time between sessions for an effect to develop from uninstructed self-exposure. However, this does raise the possibility that an important aspect in treatment is self-exposure and that all therapist-assisted strategies, such as desensitization or flooding in fantasy, or prolonged exposure in vivo, are simply elaborate maneuvers toward persuading the patient to expose himself to the ES.

Biofeedback during Exposure in Vivo

Little controlled work has appeared on this topic in patients. The main point was well expressed to the author in the course of true feedback of heart rate to a specific phobic patient during exposure in vivo. When praised because her true heart rate slowed after prolonged exposure, she simply retorted, "Yes, I know my heart is beating more slowly, but that does not help me—it's what I feel up in my head that is important." The question is how much true biofeedback can promote therapeutic advance. Both physiology and behavior can be easier to influence than subjective feelings. During rapid exposure in vivo of specific phobic patients, Nunes and Marks [70] found that pulse rates were significantly reduced over half-hour exposure periods containing visual feedback of true pulse rate, with instructions to lower it, compared with half-hour control exposure periods without such feedback. However, enhanced decline in heart rate did not affect the rate of decline in subjective anxiety during the two-hour session.

A second study [71] was undertaken as a partial replication to clarify three issues raised by the first study: (1) Did the provision of feedback have an effect beyond that of the simple instruction to reduce heart rate while looking at an oscilloscope screen? (2) Would training in reduction of heart rate with the aid of feedback facilitate the effect during subsequent exposure treatment? (3) Would this effect spread to an additional dimension? The second experiment thus made the following changes: (a) Epochs of instructions to reduce heart rate without feedback were added. (b) An hour's training with feedback was added before treatment. (c) The effect on respiratory rate and skin conductance as well as on heart rate and subjective anxiety was measured.

As in the first experiment, 10 specific phobic patients, all women, were treated by exposure in vivo during a mean of two sessions in a balanced design. Patients improved as expected, and short-term results replicated those of the first study, in that self-control of heart rate with the aid of biofeedback significantly reduced heart rate during treatment, but this did not hasten reduction of subjective anxiety, nor of respiratory rate or skin conductance responses. An hour's pretreatment training in self-control of heart rate with the aid of biofeedback did not enhance the effect. Mere instructions to lower heart rate without feedback also significantly lowered the rate during treatment, but the addition of heart rate feedback to instructions further and significantly augmented the decline.

These studies emphasize the point that, with few exceptions, biofeedback has so far been of more theoretic than clinical value [4, 68]. Phobias and other problems, for example, obsessions, can be regarded as consisting of several response systems coupled imperfectly together, and improvement in only one of these, the autonomic response system, need not transfer to other systems as well. That improvement in subjective feelings lags behind improvement in approach and heart rate in phobias is well known [97], and these results are in line with such work. Similar cognitive lag, behind reduction in GSR responses, was noted in snake-phobic volunteers [86].

Distinct Phobias and Allied Syndromes

Although similar principles of exposure apply to the treatment of most anxiety syndromes, certain phobias and allied problems have special features that merit separate consideration.

Sexual Fears

Sexual fears are an excellent case in point. One crucial feature of the Masters and Johnson approach is anxiety reduction through graded exposure to the real sexual situation. Another major component is skills training. Management of the interaction between the couple presents such distinctive requirements as to lie outside the scope of this chapter (see ref. [54] for a detailed review of this area). Several controlled studies have found training programs in sexual skills—including the behavioral components of Masters and Johnson such as graded exposure—to be significantly superior to other forms of treatment [2, 19].

Urination Phobias

These can assume two forms, either *inability to urinate* in toilets outside the home, or *excessive frequency* of urination, leading to a need to be near a toilet at all times. The latter problem can be associated with urges to defecate as well.

One partially successful approach to two patients with inability to urinate, was to conduct sessions after they had consumed excessive fluids, in which they were asked to remain in a hospital toilet (the phobic situation) until they had managed to urinate at least a few drops. Initially, this took up to two hours. Once urination was possible, the phobic situation was made progressively more difficult by having people stand outside the lavatory door. Exercises were also prescribed in toilets outside the hospital. Patients became able to void urine increasingly completely in successive sessions, and improvement generalized and remained to one-year follow-up, despite residual difficulties. A similar technique was employed successfully by Glasgow [26] after desensitization had failed. The patient remained well at four-month follow-up.

The foregoing studies employed the principle of prolonged exposure in vivo to the inhibiting situation—being in a public toilet—until at least some urination occurred. A modification was described by Wilson [99] in a man who was unable to urinate or defecate in toilets outside his home. Desensitization in fantasy produced no real-life improvement. The subject was then asked to urinate in "safe" conditions alone, but just at the moment when urination became inevitable, to imagine someone walking in. He then had to fade in the scene progressively earlier, and after two weeks he was able to imagine himself urinating next to another man, after which he was required to do this in real life. Although urination improved, he remained unable to defecate in a public toilet.

Behavioral treatment of urinary frequency has rarely been reported in the literature. In 1956 Jones described treatment of a young woman who gave up her career as a stage dancer because of urinary frequency [35]. During treatment a manometer was inserted into her bladder, and she was trained to associate the urge to micturate with the pressure shown on the manometer scale. Next, unknown to the patient, lower readings were shown on the manometer than actually resulted from fluid being introduced into the bladder. Ability to tolerate increased fluid in the bladder gradually improved, urinary frequency disappeared, and the patient was well at 15-month follow-up.

In a recent, simpler approach [72] a 24-year-old male student with excessive frequency of urination for seven years was treated by asking him to refrain from urinating for progressively longer periods during a daily fixed 12-hour period, while allowing him to urinate freely during the remaining 12 hours. Over 31 weeks, urinary frequency gradually declined to normal during both the fixed and free periods. Improvement continued to three-year follow-up.

Similarly, the author has successfully treated patients with urinary frequency simply by asking them to refrain from urinating for progressively longer periods of time, while carefully charting the time periods.

Blood and Injury Phobias

Although fainting at the sight of blood is part of our folklore, only recently has it been observed that fainting in phobics occurs significantly more during exposure to blood or injury phobia situations, or both, than during exposure to other phobic stimuli [10, 11, 20]. This fainting is associated with bradycardia. In contrast, exposure to other phobic situations produces tachycardia, which eventually subsides to normal levels during exposure in vivo [54, 57, 60]. Bradycardia to blood or injury stimuli can take several minutes to develop and may not occur when the stimulus is visible for only a few seconds. As an example, subjects who saw slides of surgery for only 10 seconds developed no bradycardia [73].

The time sequence of changes in heart rate was documented by Cohn, Kron, and Brady [10]. They showed blood or injury slides, or both, to a 28-year-old man who, since the age of four years, had often fainted on seeing injuries. Looking at control slides had no effect on his heart rate or subjective discomfort. Blood or injury slides, or both, were shown for 1, 5, 15, 30, 60, and 120 seconds; after 60 seconds' exposure the heart rate dropped to 47, and after 75 seconds to 30 beats per minute. This was followed by three minutes of asystole and fainting. On recovery, heart rate increased and rebounded to 100.

Whatever the contributions of phylogenesis and learning to the association of fainting and slow heart rate with blood or injury situations, or both, the stimulus-specific phobic response can still be extinguished by graded exposure in vivo, heart rate rising to normal after treatment [28, 46, 56]. An important procedural caution during exposure in vivo of people with blood or injury phobias, or both, is to have the patient *lying down* while seeing phobic stimuli, so that when the heart rate slows the chances of fainting are minimized and blood supply to the brain is maximized. Nevertheless, fainting can occur even in the prone position if there is asystole.

Dental Phobia

Although commonly associated with fears of blood, injury, and hospitals, fear of dental procedures often occurs on its own, and may be a problem in about 5 percent of adults [22, 38]. Avoidance of dentists commonly leads to serious dental caries. Refusal to have dental treatment when it is indicated, as occurs sometimes in the army, has led soldiers to being court-martialed, or to refusal to do army service [5]. Dental fears can be very dependent on cues in the dentist's surgery. One young woman fainted every time a session began in the chair as long as her dentist wore a white coat; when once he wore a business suit instead, she did not faint, although she fainted again at the next session, which was conducted by the dentist in a white coat. Thereafter, the dentist wore a sports shirt during her treatment, and the fainting stopped. The patient then disclosed nightmares concerning a childhood tonsillectomy and memories of the white uniforms of doctors and nurses [5].

Dental fears present special problems in treatment because it is not easy to arrange graded exposure in vivo, though this can be arranged with sympathetic dentists. Borland recommended that dentists' attitudes to dental fear should be to regard it as part of the problems they are called upon to deal with, rather than an annoying obstacle that stands in the way of their proper function. It can be helpful to let patients have some control over the procedure. Borland [5] installed a push button on the armrest of his dental chair, connected so as to allow the patient to stop the dental engine by pressing the button. Nearly every patient pressed the button once or twice during the first few minutes of drilling but hardly ever used it thereafter to interrupt treatment. However, prearranged hand signals to stop drilling seemed just as useful.

Suitable education might well reduce dental fears in the population. Previous play experiences in a dental surgery can reduce subsequent fear and avoidance of dentists. Melamed, Weinstein, Hawes, and Katin-Borland [63] and Melamed, Hawes, Helby, and Glick [64] showed young children a videofilm of a peer model coping with anxiety during dental procedures just before they themselves had similar dental restoration. The model received praise from the dentist for cooperation and was given a trinket at the end of the session. The children then underwent dental procedures and showed significantly less disruptive behavior and anxiety with the dentist than did control children who simply drew pictures or saw a video of a similar young child in scenes not connected with dentistry.

Flying Phobias

An obvious complication in treating passengers with flying phobias is the difficulty of arranging systematic exposure in vivo. Several clubs have come into existence to encourage flight-phobic people to charter airplanes in which they can fly together as part of a treatment regimen. So far, such clubs have not endured long, perhaps because of the difficulty in arranging the necessary transactions. Others have resorted to forms of fantasy exposure.

Solyom, Shugar, Bryntmick, and Solyom [89] reported treatment of 40 airplane phobics in one of four conditions: (1) Desensitized patients had sessions in fantasy and viewings of flight films. (2) Aversion relief subjects wrote their own phobic narrative, which was taped, and then had aversion relief shocks while they were listening to this narrative, and then while they watched flight films. (3) "Habituation" subjects had the same experience as aversion relief patients, but without shocks. (4) "Group psychotherapy" patients discussed air travel fears and other experiences. They then met a pilot and discussed air travel at an airport, and subsequently had a 15-minute practice flight as a group with the therapist. Results showed that the first three groups improved significantly but did not differ significantly from one another or from the patients in the "group psychotherapy" conditions. They indicate that widely varying forms of exposure produce relief of flying fears.

Depression

A common complication of phobias and obsessions [36, 50, 51], depression can retard progress with exposure techniques. It is usually treated with tricyclic drugs. When drugs fail, the question arises: Can exposure help depression—is it the main problem, or a complication of other problems? The treatment paradigm to be described assumes that grief reactions and other forms of depression are maintained by avoidance of painful feelings about a lost loved person, or of other unpleasant topics (see also Chapter 3, pages 45–47).

A few anecdotal reports of fantasy flooding of depression are encouraging [8, 79, 80]. In one study [8], two patients with chronic hypochondriasis and depression were treated with nine sessions of exposure in fantasy for an hour given twice weekly. Psychodynamic cues were not used. Improvement in both patients continued to 18-month follow-up, the second patient improving despite feeling no anxiety during treatment.

Ramsay [80] described a 40-year-old woman whose daughter died 2½ years earlier, subsequent to which the patient had sleeplessness, with early waking, irritability, and loss of weight that did not respond to extensive treatment. Treatment involved five sessions of exposure in fantasy, totaling nine hours. They dealt with the patient's imagining loss of her daughter, handling her belongings, and visiting places reminding her of their relationship. At 10-month follow-up the patient was much improved, had put on weight, had lost most of the bereavement pain, was working full-time, and had joined several clubs, including one for young children.

This approach to depression is still experimental and poses many theoretic questions concerning the nature of improvement after any form of exposure and abreaction. During treatment of depression by exposure in fantasy, emotional reactions during sessions tend to subside progressively with each session, but, as we saw above, improvement can occur without any emotional experience. This is congruous with observations that the amount of anxiety experienced by phobics during exposure does not correlate with outcome.

Obsessive-Compulsive Disorders
Compulsive Rituals
Modern treatment of compulsive rituals by exposure in vivo with response prevention was foreshadowed long ago by Janet's [33] observation that certain institutional practices limited the opportunity to engage in rituals, with corresponding improvements. Janet observed 14 "accidental" cures of obsessive-compulsive neurosis during military service and described one patient who, when his term of service was over, took refuge in a seminary, "in order to have chiefs and to be subject to discipline once more." Many cases remained well in convents. Firm spouses, too, could be beneficial. One husband was able to check his wife's crises of overscrupulousness for four years. Similarly, Lewis [43] described severe obsessions that disappeared during war service but returned afterward, and Leonhard [40, 82] described methods for treating phobics and obsessive-compulsives that were very smiilar to current forms of exposure in vivo with modeling.

When one turns to the more recent literature, systematic attempts at desensitization *in fantasy* have usually been unsuccessful [21, 55], although occasional improvement has been reported [47, 100]. Forms of exposure *in vivo* have been far more encouraging, as numerous uncontrolled reports [37, 85] first attested [7, 24, 49, 78, 81, 88]. The largest uncontrolled series is of 10 patients treated by Meyer and colleagues [41, 65-67]. In his first report, Meyer called the treatment modification of expectations. Compulsive rituals were interrupted while patients were brought into contact with situations that triggered those rituals. Treatment involved 24-hour supervision by nurses to prevent the patient from ritualizing. To stop this, the patient was engaged in other activities, discussion, cajoling, and, rarely, mild physical restraint (with his agreement). When total prevention of rituals had been achieved, continuous supervision was continued for one to four weeks, during which the patient was gradually exposed to situations that previously evoked rituals (e.g., dust, lavatories) and was again prevented from carrying these out. Supervision was then gradually decreased until finally the patient remained totally unsupervised but was occasionally observed. At two-year follow-up, of the original 10 patients six were much improved, two were somewhat improved, and two remained unchanged.

In a later report comparing the effects of daily response prevention for 24 hours and for one hour, similar results were obtained at 18-month follow-up, with no advantage for continuous supervision. At follow-up all 13 patients were improved, 11 a great deal.

CONTROLLED TRIALS. The first of these studies was carried out by Rachman, Hodgson, and Marks [31, 52, 76, 77], who treated 20 patients with chronic obsessive-compulsive rituals evoked by identifiable environmental stimuli. Again, exposure in vivo was helpful, even though this time response prevention was purely self-imposed, not supervised. There were five comparison conditions, including relaxation, and four exposure in vivo conditions, the latter comprising five patients each. In all five conditions, treatment took 15 sessions over three weeks with the subjects as inpatients, sessions lasting 50 minutes. First, 10 patients had (1) relaxation without modeling, followed by random assignment to (2) exposure in vivo at the top of the hierarchy without modeling, or (3) exposure in vivo from the bottom of the hierarchy with modeling. When these patients had finished, five more had relaxation followed by (4) exposure in vivo at the top with modeling. Up to this point 15 patients had had three weeks of relaxation followed by three weeks in one of three exposure conditions. To control for this invariant order, a final five patients were added, who (5) had three weeks of exposure in vivo at the top with modeling, but without the preceding relaxation phase.

Patients were admitted for one week of baseline measurements and then six weeks' treatment, the first three weeks being with relaxation and the second three weeks with exposure. Patients in condition (5) had only three weeks' treatment with exposure. After the six-week experimental period (three weeks in condition [5]) patients were followed up, and treatment was continued when necessary. Overall, patients had a mean of 23 sessions of in vivo exposure.

The relaxation control sessions began with general inquiries about patients' health and mood. Patients were then given tape-recorded relaxation instructions followed by a request to think about an obsessive worry during the final 10 minutes of each session. Exposure in vivo involved prolonged contact of the patient in real life with those stimuli that occasioned discomfort or rituals, for example, wearing unwashed clothing, touching sticky food, or looking at objects resting out of place on a desk. Response prevention involved asking patients to desist from rituals for increasing periods of time, with or without therapist supervision. Modeling refers to the therapist's demonstrating the required behavior to patients before asking them to follow suit.

As an example of exposure from the top of the hierarchy without modeling in a patient who feared contamination by animals, during the first session she was encouraged to touch items from the top of her hierarchy (i.e., a hamster and a dog). The hamster was then set free to run around on her bed, towel, clothes, and personal belongings. It was placed in her handbag for a few minutes and on her hair. This almost total "contamination" of her environment was accomplished during the first session and was repeated daily. Several times throughout treatment she was encouraged to stroke the dog and to "contaminate" her clothes, hair, and face.

During exposure from the bottom of the hierarchy with modeling, the patient was encouraged gradually to enter each of the situations that evoked avoidance, and rituals were introduced, commencing with the least upsetting and graduating to the increasingly disturbing ones. Each step was first demonstrated by a calm and reassuring therapist, and the patient then "shadowed" the therapist's actions. This was repeated until the patient completed the sequence without assistance. As an example, in a patient with fear of contamination from hospitals, the first session began with the lowest item of the hierarchy. The therapist repeatedly touched a bandage on his own clothes, hair, and face; the patient was then asked to imitate his actions. During three weeks of inpatient treatment all items in the hierarchy were dealt with the same way; for example, toward the top of the hierarchy the patient wanted the therapist to walk up to the hospital entrance and touch an ambulance. She then copied the therapist's actions.

An example of rapid exposure from the top of the hierarchy with modeling is given in some detail to illustrate the treatment. One patient had obsessive fears that she might pass on a disease to her loved ones, to babies, or to old people. Treatment consisted of touching dreaded sources of "contamination" and then touching babies, touching chairs and tables in the geriatric ward, touching visiting relatives, and also sending daily "contaminated" letters to her parents. The patient was "contaminated" by the therapist's taking her to visit local hospitals, by touching a bottle of tetanus serum without washing afterward, which was very distressing for her, and by being taken to a town where she had once met a man who had just recovered from hepatitis.

Treatment progressed well, although some stages provoked anxiety, tears, and obsessive thoughts about the well-being of her parents and boyfriend. Toward the end of treatment (one month) the head nurse accompanied her to her parents' home, 200 miles away, and made sure that both parents and house were "contaminated" by the patient. There were 29 treatment sessions in all, four of which were at home.

Results showed that the 15 patients who had first received three weeks of relaxation treatment did not improve after relaxation on any measures of obsessive-compulsive phenomena, even though relaxation produced significant improvement in self-rated depression, anxiety, and depersonalization. Patients enjoyed relaxation, but it did their compulsions no good. In contrast, treatment by exposure in vivo improved compulsions significantly more than did relaxation. The five patients who had exposure without preceding relaxation improved as much as the 15 whose exposure followed relaxation. Modeling did not significantly enhance the effect of exposure.

Patients' ability to reduce rituals between sessions during the first few days of treatment was usually a good prognostic index. For those who could not resist rituals to some extent between treatment sessions, extensive nursing supervision was not of great help, in that determined patients found ways of evading supervision.

Improvement was maintained over 24-month follow-up. Of the 20 patients, 14 responded very well, one moderately well, and five only slightly or not at all. Although exposure in vivo was effective in reducing compulsive rituals, both clinically and on objective tests, some improved patients still experienced problems in resisting rituals and dealing with obsessive thoughts. However, six patients were symptom-free. The stability of improvement after treatment was gratifying. All eight patients who had been much improved after three weeks of treatment by exposure remained so at two-year follow-up, as did all 12 patients who had been much improved at six-month follow-up. Improvement never began after relaxation treatment but only after exposure treatment, in all but one patient, who improved without treatment at six-month follow-up.

Three of the much improved cases required booster sessions after discharge. Patients needed to be instructed that any tendency toward relapse should be reported early so that this could be dealt with. One patient who remained improved at two-year follow-up still had periods during which her rituals and depression returned to some extent. On such occasions she was given booster treatment at home and further encouragement, and she responded well to the session.

A case illustration might clarify the extent of improvement experienced by patients who were almost symptom-free but still had occasional difficulties. One woman always avoided areas in and around London and the nearby town of Basingstoke, where she had felt contaminated. Before treatment, the mere mention of Basingstoke had evoked washing rituals, and a visit to that town could not be contemplated. Before treatment she had washed her hands at least 50 times each day and had used seven giant packets of soapflakes and many bars of soap each week. She had moved house five times in the three years before admission, in order to escape contamination, and had thrown away much "contaminated" clothing (especially boots), even though she could ill afford to replace them. To prevent contamination she had to clean the whole house every day, including curtains, carpets, floors, and shelves.

Treatment involved the complete "contamination" of her hospital environment and of her husband and child when they visited. Some sessions were devoted to shopping expeditions in areas that she avoided;

most of these evoked intense anxiety and occasional tearful outbursts. A trip to Basingstoke, undertaken with her permission, resulted in total "contamination," severe depression, and a threat to discharge herself. Her depression lifted after 24 hours. Throughout treatment she managed to resist excessive washing, even though she was not supervised. She was simply told that performance of her rituals would interfere with treatment.

At the end of treatment and again at six-month follow-up there was no evidence of excessive washing and cleaning rituals, but she still had some thoughts about contamination. She traveled to Basingstoke a few months after treatment, and, although she felt contaminated for eight hours afterward, she managed to resist the urge to wash. Similar feelings occurred from time to time but were always resisted. One week after the six-month follow-up she became depressed and referred herself to the Emergency Clinic. There had been no return of her washing rituals and after talking to the emergency-room physician she felt better. At two-year follow-up she was going out to work every day and was no longer crippled by obsessive thoughts or compulsive rituals. She was not as socially skilled as she would like to be and occasionally felt contaminated. However, she believed that she would never resume her washing rituals.

This patient's experience is similar to that of seven patients in the much improved group. She managed to resist the recurrence of time-consuming and frustrating rituals, even though she experienced occasional feelings of contamination and depression. During the two-year follow-up, if anything there was evidence of further improvement rather than deterioration.

The five patients who failed treatment did so for various reasons. Two would not allow complete "contamination" of their homes, and a third could not have more than one domiciliary visit because she lived too far from hospital. A fourth would check the position and identity of particular objects some 200 times daily. These checks were eliminated during treatment sessions but could not be controlled between sessions; for example, he was observed to look repeatedly through a window at a deck chair about five yards away, explaining that he was trying to make sure it was a deck chair and not a piece of cloth. Such checks were often unobservable and therefore unstoppable.

The fifth failure is important theoretically, because the patient was completely cooperative in treatment in the hospital and at home. However, although she could resist rituals in the hospital, improvement did not generalize to her home when the therapist was not there. Tape-recorded instructions at home did not help. A month of supervision by a relative at home had no long-term effect, nor did further treatment during a second admission to hospital. A sixth patient failed to improve during exposure treatment but subsequently claimed to do so at follow-up six and 24 months later. Between treatment sessions she would decontaminate her belongings by washing and by "magical" wipes with a damp cloth.

Active Ingredients of Treatment
Relaxation treatment was not followed by improvement in compulsive rituals, while in vivo exposure was equally effective whether or not it was preceded by relaxation (control) treatment. Improvement in compulsions began only after one of the four variants of exposure in vivo, testifying to the crucial role of exposure. There was no significant difference between those patients who were exposed rapidly and those exposed slowly with modeling [31]. Similarly, a controlled study by Rabavilas, Boulougouris, and Stefanis [74] in 12 compulsive ritualizers employed a Latin square design to compare long and short exposure in fantasy and in vivo. The design was similar to that employed by Stern and Marks in agoraphobics, but this time balancing the order of fantasy versus in vivo exposure. Neither 80 continuous minutes nor eight 10-minute sequences of short fantasy exposure produced much improvement. However, 80 minutes of exposure in vivo was significantly better given in one continuous bout than in four separate periods of 20 minutes on the same day. This finding is similar to that of Stern and Marks [93] in agoraphobics, that two hours of continuous exposure in vivo was better than four half-hours with intervals in between.

The same conclusions concerning the effect of in vivo response prevention can be drawn from a series of controlled simple case studies reported by Mills, Agras, Barlow, Baugh, and Mills [69]. Response prevention produced improvement, while strong suggestion within a placebo treatment produced only short-term benefit. Longer, rather than shorter, response prevention was again found to be better. In addition, after compulsions had been removed, further exposure to "contaminating" situations was necessary in most cases to reduce remaining anxiety and avoidance behavior.

In fact, the role of response prevention per se is not yet known and may be important only insofar as it prolongs the period of exposure to the fear-evoking stimuli. This point was examined in a small-scale pilot experiment on short-term effects by Lipsedge [45]. Patients were allowed to wash for as long as they wished but were continually contaminated throughout the washing procedure. These patients showed the same improvement over one week as did other patients who were contaminated but not allowed to wash. The design did not permit conclusions about long-term effects but suggests that response prevention per se may not be a necessary adjuvant to exposure.

The addition of modeling to in vivo exposure did not significantly enhance results [77]. In this context, modeling can be defined as *observation of a therapist carrying out a therapeutic maneuver*. That it is the particular maneuver being demonstrated which is important, rather than the act of observation itself, was shown in a controlled study [83] of 10 chronic obsessive-compulsive ritualizers, who were assigned at random to one of two conditions of inpatient treatment over six weeks, divided into two three-week blocks of 15 sessions. In the first block, patients had one of two conditions. The first condition was modeling of relaxation, during which the therapist modeled relaxation exercises *without* exposure to the contaminating or ritual-evoking situations but asked the patients to carry out similar relaxation exercises. Patients in this condition hardly changed their rituals; merely observing the therapist carrying out a "therapeutic" exercise was not helpful.

The contrasting condition in the first three-week block was passive modeling of exposure; that is, patients passively observed the therapist engaging in anticompulsive behavior, such as deliberately contaminating herself or making things untidy. Compulsions of patients in this passive exposure condition improved significantly more than in the passive relaxation condition, even though modeling was present equally in both conditions.

After the first three weeks, all 10 patients crossed over to three weeks of participant modeling of exposure, in which the patient was required to engage in compulsive behavior in the way the therapist had demonstrated. Patients were also given instructions for self-imposed response prevention between treatment sessions. These instructions had not been given in the first three weeks, which confounded interpretation of the finding that participant modeling of exposure was significantly superior to both modeling or relaxation and to passive modeling of exposure. The greatest improvement in rituals was obtained with participant modeling of exposure together with instructions for self-imposed response prevention between sessions; this was significantly better than passive modeling of exposure without instructions for response prevention, which in turn was significantly greater than passive modeling of relaxation without exposure. Patients maintained their improvement to the last follow-up available, six months after treatment.

Exposure with response prevention, with and without modeling, was also examined by Heyse [30] in 24 patients with compulsive rituals. After treatment the two groups improved similarly, although overall results were not as encouraging as in the previous series reported. Though a significant effect of pure modeling could not be demonstrated, patients' reports about its value conflicted. Some claimed benefit from modeling, whereas others were emphatic that it did not help. One man kept an image of the therapist with the trash can lid balanced on his head as a coping response that he thought reduced his avoidance of "dirty" objects and situations. In contrast, another patient stated, "I *know* other people don't have trouble with this. Therefore watching it does not help at all." It is still unclear in which patients modeling is of particular benefit.

PATIENT MOTIVATION AND THE TREATMENT SETTING. Since patients need to participate actively in treatment, therapy cannot be thrust upon them against their wishes. Treatment should not be offered immediately, but patients should be given a chance to think about, understand, and agree beforehand to the prerequisites for treatment. These include therapist-assisted exposure in vivo and self-exposure homework between sessions, the various treatment settings (e.g., hospital and home), and family involvement as required. Rapid exposure is now used where possible, the rate of exposure being governed by the patient, who is told about the importance of prolonged exposure to threatening situations. It is probable that the faster one can proceed with a patient's permission, the better. Such permission is crucial, and one cannot push patients beyond a certain point. Calm, gentle, yet firm persuasion is helpful, but where the patient resists strongly little can be done.

Patients are told that exposure treatment is an approach that requires the development of self-coping skills after discharge. They will not be cured but, rather, improved. Despite a tendency for rituals to recur, patients are reassured that they will learn to nip these in the bud by any exposure-confrontation approach. Explicit advice about regular homework may be needed for many months after discharge.

It is obvious that treatment requires a good working relationship between patient and therapist, and a sense of humor helps patients over difficult situations. Patients often comment that they can follow the therapist's instructions to touch contaminated material although they could not perform the same action when asked to do so by spouses before treatment, and cannot do so even during treatment. Nevertheless, relatives can be successfully trained to act as co-therapists. The essential ingredient for treatment may be a willingness for the patient to accept and follow instructions from an informed person, whoever this may be. Patients need to understand their responsibility for treatment, which includes homework between sessions. Failure to carry out homework is probably a poor prognostic sign. Occasionally, it is useful to have patients sign written contracts, in which they agree in advance to undertake specified aspects of treatment.

An *inpatient* phase of treatment is indicated where rituals are extensive. Other patients can be treated on an outpatient basis. Where rituals are triggered by home cues, which is true for most patients, treatment needs to be carried into the home setting. Where families assist rituals, patients need to agree to the therapist's teaching relatives how to withhold reassurance, how to refrain from helping patients with their rituals, and how to encourage patients while not hounding them. Contracts can be exchanged between patients and other family members, in which they agree to reward one another for various behaviors, including reduction of rituals. Family counseling may be indicated for nonobsessive family problems where these are present.

To facilitate family involvement in treatment, the author runs a family group for some patients. Patients joined the group after the experimental phase of Marks, Rachman, and Hodgson [58] was completed and, for patients outside the trial, toward the end of intensive treatment. Up to seven patients and their key relatives meet together with a therapist in a group of about 16 people. The family group meets every four to six weeks, sessions lasting two hours. The group is open-ended, and patients who overcome their rituals eventually leave, while new patients and their relatives join at intervals.

During meetings families discuss and share common problems that the compulsions create for patients and their relatives, and ways to deal with these. As an example, patients who seek repeated reassurance from their spouses about contamination are requested to ask for this from the spouse in the presence of the group. The spouse is then taught to reply, "Hospital instructions are that I don't answer you." After several role rehearsals on these lines, the spouses became able to resist giving reassurance at home. Other patients rehearse their contamination exercises in the group with the aid of other members. A warm, mutually supportive, and helpful atmosphere is generated in the group, which is oriented toward solving problems. Families seem to find it helpful, and relatives are facilitated in their role as co-therapists. This kind of family group seems to have potential as an adjuvant to, but not a replacement for, treatment of individual patients. Moreover, it contains multiple therapeutic ingredients, some of which may turn out to be redundant on systematic enquiry.

Patients who live a long way from hospital are especially difficult if they require domiciliary treatment, because of the traveling time involved. Other professionals who live in the patient's area may be enlisted to act as co-therapists. Sometimes this works well, but at other times the co-therapists know little about treatment and find it difficult to conduct, even if they have seen it briefly in operation in a hospital. In a nonexperimental case, a clergyman was enlisted briefly as co-therapist for a patient who worried about contamination from semen following masturbation at home, but who, on religious grounds, refused to masturbate in hospital to produce such contamination. When the clergyman gave religious sanction to such masturbation, the patient complied and improved. On another occasion, however, a second patient simply ignored the clergyman's comments.

When relatives are uncooperative, it may be desirable for young patients to leave home to avoid recurrence of rituals. A limitation in a few patients is the absence of suitable halfway houses, where the patients can try out their wings after discharge from hospital and before returning home or to an independent existence. Very few hospitals or day centers have personnel trained in the requisite treatment methods, who can fade out treatments in a structured environment as the patient slowly acquires confidence. Such facilities might prevent some failures in the transfer of improvement from hospital to community.

REPRESENTATIVENESS OF EXPERIMENTAL SAMPLES. The patient samples in the Maudsley series [45, 58, 83] had an unusual female preponderance, and problems had to be amenable to evaluation on a live avoidance test. Only ruminators were excluded on the latter count. Several patients were excluded because their problem was too mild to warrant inpatient treatment, but the sample was otherwise representative of severe obsessive-compulsive ritualizers in psychiatric hospitals. Of 125 patients seen in the author's unit between 1970 and 1974, 82 were treated for their obsessions, 25 as outpatients, and the rest as inpatients. Twenty-five of these 82 had antidepressant treatment during some stage of antiobsessive treatment. Eleven more patients had purely antidepressant treatment. Twenty-seven patients were offered, but refused, treatment for obsessions, and five were rejected as unsuitable for treatment. Thus, most of the obsessive-compulsives referred were accepted for treatment, and only one-fifth refused treatment. Of those who were offered treatment for their compulsions, as opposed to their depression, one-quarter refused treatment. Of those who began active treatment for their obsessions, only five dropped out before an adequate trial of treatment had been given. Figures indicate that most patients accept the conditions of treatment and few drop out after starting it.

None of the 20 patients of Marks, Rachman, and Hodgson [58] dropped out during the six-week trial period after initial assessment. One patient refused domiciliary treatment after discharge. The infrequency of drop-outs might reflect the commitment that was expected from patients for admission. They were told they had a reasonable chance of improving with treatment, but it would not be easy and would require considerable effort from themselves; for example, at appropriate stages they would have to agree to touch contaminated materials in hospital and later on at home. They would also have to agree to relatives' involvement as necessary. Several patients in various series were asked to sign written contracts agreeing to specified details of treatment, both in hospital and at home. By itself, commitment to treatment does not produce improvement, but it helps patients to comply in swallowing the pill of exposure in vivo that leads to change.

COST-EFFECTIVENESS. Limitations of time and staff make it necessary to decide at an early stage whether treatment of a given patient is practicable. As long as patients show signs of improvement with treatment, it seems worth continuing, provided extrapolation of the curve of improvement suggests that treatment need not go on for years before worthwhile gains accrue in the patient's life. With most patients, fortunately, such gains are obtained within one to two months of exposure treatment. It is helpful to keep a careful budget of time expended in treatment that can be compared with the gains made, so that at periodic review clinical decisions can be made about whether to continue toward attainment of the goal set, or to cut one's losses at a particular stage.

The therapeutic efforts required to improve rituals vary greatly [52]. Sometimes, when the principles of exposure in vivo with response prevention are explained to the relatives of patients, they apply these successfully without the need for further treatment by a therapist [58]. Rarely, compulsive rituals disappear after one or two afternoons of exposure, with response prevention by a therapist. More commonly, several weeks of concerted effort by therapist and patient are required for significant improvement. In a few cases, many months of work are needed. Treatment at home or as an inpatient is not always essential, and occasionally, rapid results can be obtained by simple outpatient advice.

In brief, there is now good evidence from several series of patients in three independent centers that improvement in compulsive rituals is maintained up to the third year of follow-up [6, 58, 74]. Although many compulsive patients respond gratifyingly to exposure and response prevention, with or without modeling, there are occasional dramatic failures for reasons that are obscure. Some patients may not respond while they are depressed. In these cases, tricyclic drugs can be helpful. Although depression is usually associated with some increase in the obsessive-compulsive features, this has not always been found to be true. Marks, Rachman, and Hodgson [58] found that five patients out of 20 showed the same fluctuating depression during follow-up that they had had before treatment. This responded to tricyclic drugs, while the improvement in rituals was maintained. For Marks and his colleagues, as a whole, although compulsive rituals declined sharply until the end of follow-up, the overall level of depression remained unchanged. The same finding was noted by Boulougouris [6].

DIRECT VERSUS INDIRECT TREATMENT OF COMPULSIONS. Sometimes, exposure approaches make no impact on compulsive rituals, yet subsequent different tactics result in rapid amelioration. No rules can be given as to when to use a direct or an oblique approach, but two detailed case histories to illustrate this are given by Marks [53, pages 132–133]. In the first, after the failure of exposure in fantasy and in vivo, the modeling of maternal behavior for a young woman led to a reduction in compulsive picking of scabs on her 18-month-old son's face and body. In the second, reported by Stern and Marks [93], after the failure of exposure in fantasy and in vivo, conjoint contract marital therapy led to rapid reduction in rituals and improvement in the marital relationship. Although this couple separated one year after treatment ended, the rituals remained in abeyance.

Compulsive Slowness: Time and Motion Treatment
These cases present special problems in treatment [75]. The lives of such patients and their families can be crippled because the patient may take several hours to get dressed or undressed, have a bath, or cross the road. Treatment can be carried out by prompting and pacing the patient in more rapid sequences of behavior, with modeling of these when necessary. The patient is prompted to carry out the necessary actions, is paced while he carries them out, and is given targets of time to complete each action. The targets are steadily whittled away toward a normal baseline. A kitchen timer helps them to do this on their own. Results with this approach can be encouraging in some patients, while in others it is so time-consuming that it is not practicable. Management of an unusual case was reported by Lindley, Marks, Philpott, and Snowden [44]. The patient presented at age 18 years with a history of childhood autism and more recent compulsive rituals and slowness. He was given extensive treatment by exposure in vivo with modeling, response prevention, prompting, pacing, and tricyclic drugs. During follow-up over three years, many of the rituals remained improved, but the other problems persisted, and the patient did not maintain regular employment.

Obsessive Thoughts without Rituals
Several procedures have been used for these, including some exposure to

the undesired thoughts. One such procedure is thought-stopping [39, 90, 101]. Here, the patient is relaxed and is asked to think of his obsessive thought. The therapist shouts "Stop!" and makes a sudden noise at the same time. The patient is then taught to shout "Stop!" in order to dispel the thought, then to whisper, and eventually to employ a subvocal command. Instead of saying "Stop!" to these obsessive thoughts, patients can stop them by shocking themselves from a portable shock box. As another alternative, they can wear an elastic band on their wrist and snap it to disrupt the thoughts [48].

An interesting description of thought-stopping a century ago comes from Lewis [42, 84], the extract (below) from his work also illustrating the changing nature of what are considered to be undesirable thoughts. The patient concerned was a man with thoughts of nude women and intercourse. He was instructed: "Fix it in your mind that a sensual idea is dangerous and harmful; the instant one comes it will startle you. By an effort you change the subject immediately. . . . If there is a moment's doubt spring up and engage in some active exercise of the body. Each effort will be easier, until after a week or two you will have, in this particular, complete control of your thoughts." Lewis also instructed his patient on the use of a cue card that listed alternative topics to think about. Thus, the patient was to stop his sensual thoughts by fixing the threat of danger in his mind. He was then to engage in a competing activity involving either an alternative topic or physical exercise.

Two months later the patient wrote a letter to his doctor: "I found it difficult to control my thoughts at first, but as you advised, I soon fixed the thought of danger in my mind, so that when a lascivious fancy appeared, it startled me, and immediately I took out of my pocket the card you suggested, on which I had written ten words, each suggesting a subject in which I am interested. Looking over this card, I had no difficulty in changing the subject at once. . . . I can now meet my lady friend and converse with her with real pleasure. My thoughts are not more lecherous and unclean than they would be in the presence of sisters." Touching as this last sentence rings a century later, it makes one wonder how our moral codes will seem to our successors. The treatment described by Lewis involves several components—persuading the patient to expose himself to the "dangerous" ideas; then learning to think about, or do, something else; and external prompts to help this process. These methods all interrupt undesirable behavior repeatedly, and this might be the operative mechanism.

It could be argued that thought-stopping is a form of exposure to obsessive thoughts in repeated brief sequences, rather like desensitization in fantasy. Whether the relaxation or the aversive component that often accompanies thought-stopping is, in fact, essential is debatable. Thought-stopping could also be construed as a form of self-regulation and coping that patients learn to employ in controlling their thoughts. In a controlled trial [91], four patients improved as much by learning to stop neutral thoughts as by stopping obsessive ones. This argues for the acquisition of a coping set rather than specific extinction of the obsessive ideas. A subsequent series of six patients treated in the author's unit by thought-stopping yielded variable results, as was the case with five ruminators treated by Emmelkamp [14]. The value of thought-stopping is thus unpredictable and uncertain.

Thought-stopping procedures all aim to interrupt undesirable thoughts repeatedly. This, by itself, could be the operative mechanism. An argument against this idea, however, is that sometimes the opposite technique of prolonged exposure in fantasy also helps patients. A variant of exposure in fantasy could be called satiation. Here, patients are asked to write out a long, detailed description of troublesome thoughts every day.

Exposure in fantasy was also described anecdotally during Morita therapy in a nun aged 45 years who had suffered for two years from visionary "obsessions" of snakes [94]. The patient was instructed to observe the visions directly and patiently, even if jumping with fear: "Never close your eyes, never cover them with a cloth, never try to avoid the fear by other means, and never try to distract your feeling of suffering or fear." She was asked to observe the detailed appearance of the visions and behavior of the snake. She was not allowed to complain to her attendants about the visions, and the attendants were given strict orders to ignore her complaints. The visions disappeared, as did accompanying vertigo, and the patient was well at 22-year follow-up. The procedure was called self-realization therapy. Components of prolonged exposure and of inattention to complaints may have helped.

None of the treatments of obsessive thoughts, be they exposure in fantasy, thought-stopping, or any of their variants, is as predictably effective as exposure in vivo treatment for compulsive rituals.

Overview
Exposure denotes a range of procedures in which the patient is exposed to the various situations evoking distress until such situations can be tolerated. Good controlled evidence is available from independent centers that exposure in vivo effectively relieves diverse forms of phobia, including those where free-floating anxiety is present, and that it is the treatment of choice for most compulsive rituals. Improvement has been maintained over the two- to four-year follow-ups available. Exposure in vivo programs need to be tailored to meet the special problems involved in treating certain conditions—for example, blood or injury phobias, or both, where fainting is a common complication; and sexual and social phobias, where interpersonal situations require distinctive management. Training programs for sexual skills and social skills include a central component of exposure in vivo, and there is increasing controlled evidence to support their value. Exposure approaches might also be useful in other conditions, such as certain forms of depression and obsessive ruminations, and in the treatment of obsessive slowness by "time and motion" treatment. But further research is required in these conditions.

Patients need to understand what is required of them in exposure treatment. Prior commitment is necessary to the details of treatment that will be carried out in various settings, and that in obsessive-compulsive ritualizers often includes the home and involvement of affected relatives as co-therapists, be they spouses or others. Commitment must include completion of self-exposure homework between sessions, in order to learn how to expose oneself to the stimuli that evoke discomfort. This may be the key ingredient to relief of these problems. If further research confirms this to be so, then treatment regimens might be devised that will be even more economical of therapists' time than at present, perhaps with the aid of do-it-yourself manuals and lay instruction groups.

Meanwhile, with therapist-assisted exposure most phobics and obsessive-compulsives can be helped in 3 to 25 sessions. Time-budgeting of therapist expenditure matched against the curve of patient improvement enables one to tell when therapeutic efforts are producing worthwhile results. When patients do not respond because of lack of cooperation or, more rarely, for unknown reasons, further waste of time can be avoided by terminating treatment that is having no visible effect. Nurse-therapists can make an important contribution, and group exposure yields significant savings of therapists' time. Self-help groups so far have had limited value in this area, and a viable social structure remains to be worked out for them to become workable instruments of therapeutic change, rather than of simple support.

The principles of clinical practice are being increasingly worked out directly in controlled studies of patients, with analogue studies in volunteers and in animals becoming of less direct relevance. Findings from these three different populations can enhance our understanding of basic conceptual issues. Analogue studies usually involve volunteer students, who are unrepresentative of the general population and who differ from patient populations in being less phobic and having fewer other problems that complicate management. Animal-fear experiments tend to be over too short a time base compared with that involved in clinical syndromes, and more work is needed on repeated reacquisition and reextinction of avoidance. Conditioning language can confuse clinicians. Instead, a simple ES-ER strategy allows clinicians to plan treatment; that is, search for the ES, those stimuli which evoke the ERs, the discomfort, and avoidance behavior, and persuade the patient to remain in contact with them until the ERs die down.

Exposure to the ES can occur slowly or rapidly, with or without relaxation, anxiety evocation, modeling, shock, or other procedures. The most efficient form of exposure so far seems to be prolonged exposure in vivo, although, rarely, a few patients do not respond even to this. When exposure in vivo is not feasible, fantasy methods may be helpful in the form of guided fantasy or rehearsal of exposure situations.

Longer in vivo sessions appear more potent than shorter ones, although the optimum duration is unknown. Less than 15 minutes seems too short, but a period of one to two hours is useful. Duration alone may be a less satisfactory criterion than that of terminating the session only after the patient's distress has ceased, but research is lacking on this point. Some short durations of exposure might actually increase fear. Interstimulus intervals need more study. The duration of exposure necessary to reduce fear might be increased when treatment is in fantasy rather than in real life, by tape recorder rather than by a therapist, and intermittent rather than continuous.

Arousal level during exposure does not seem crucial for improvement, which proceeds at a similar rate whether patients are relaxed, neutral, or anxious during exposure. Controlled work shows both relaxation and deliberate anxiety evocation to be redundant, time-wasting, and unnecessary for the treatment of phobias and obsessions. Systematic reward also has not been found especially helpful, though it assists motivation. Pure modeling, that is, the act of observing a therapist carrying out a therapeutic action, is not therapeutic. Experiments in this area so far have confounded modeling with exposure. A few patients find it helpful to watch the therapist approaching the ES first. No data are yet available on the optimum speed of approach during exposure in vivo. It is also not known whether patients' motivation is essential purely to make treatment practicable, or whether motivation directly enhances habituation to the ES.

Exposure appears to be especially effective when it is *interactional*, with the patient actively approaching and grappling with the ES in some way. However, while it is easy enough to define "interactional" with respect to exposure to a crowd or a train, it is more moot for exposure to heights. Perhaps the key issue is stimulus variation to promote habituation to all aspects of the ES. Definition of interactional versus static exposure poses problems related to those in defining coping. That experience of irrelevant fear and of stress immunization can be helpful suggests that extinction is not necessarily specific to the ES alone but can be part of a more general process of learning to cope with noxious situations. However, better operational definitions of coping as opposed to noncoping responses and of interactional as opposed to passive exposure are needed for further advances.

The concepts of exposure and coping do not account for at least three awkward facts. First, some phobics and obsessives seem to improve with "antidepressant" drugs without actual exposure treatment—perhaps such drugs affect habituation mechanisms. Second, interpersonal therapy occasionally leads to dramatic resolution of anxiety syndromes, apparently without exposure. Finally, and most important, it is unknown why exposure to stressful stimuli sometimes sensitizes and at other times habituates subjects.

The role of avoidance is still debatable, as is that of response prevention during treatment. Response prevention (blocking of avoidance) may act simply by prolonging contact with the ES and so allowing greater opportunity for habituation. The contribution of abreaction to outcome may be that of a minor factor that helps under special conditions. Biofeedback of physiologic responses has so far been of dubious value; while it can reduce heart rate during exposure in vivo, this has not led to more rapid reduction of subjective anxiety, skin conductance, or respiratory rate in the short term.

Despite the many conceptual puzzles, exposure treatment can usually produce worthwhile and lasting benefit in cooperative phobics and obsessives, even when they have chronic, severe, and extensive handicaps. New findings are appearing regularly. Much work is currently in progress, from which further advances can be expected in this thriving area.

References
1. Agras, W. S., Leitenberg, H., Barlow, D. H., Curtis, N., Edwards, J., and Wright, D. The role of relaxation in systematic desensitization. *Archives of General Psychiatry* 25:511, 1971.
2. Bancroft, J. H. J. Issues in sex therapy. In J. C. Boulougouris and A. Rabivilas (Eds.), *Studies in Phobic and Obsessive-Compulsive Disorders*. Oxford: Pergamon. In press.
3. Benjamin, S., Marks, I. M., and Huson, J. Active muscular relaxation in desensitization of phobic patients. *Psychological Medicine* 2:381, 1972.
4. Blanchard, E. B., and Young, L. D. Clinical applications of biofeedback training. *Archives of General Psychiatry* 30:573, 1974.
5. Borland, L. R. Odontophobia – inordinate fear of dental treatment. *Dental Clinics of North America* Nos. 683–695, 1962.
6. Boulougouris, J. C. Variables Affecting the Behaviour of Obsessive-Compulsive Patients Treated by Flooding. In J. C. Boulougouris and A. Rabivilas (Eds.), *Studies in Phobic and Obsessive-Compulsive Disorders*. Oxford: Pergamon. In press.
7. Boulougouris, J. C., and Bassiakos, L. Prolonged flooding in obsessive-compulsive neurosis. *Behavior Research and Therapy* 11:227, 1973.
8. Boulougouris, J. C., and Tsahtsiris, F. Flooding in depression. Paper presented at the Third Annual Conference of the European Association of Behaviour Therapy, Amsterdam, July 1973.
9. Butollo, W., and Mittaelstadt, J. Systematic combination of treatment components for severe phobic disorders. In J. C. Boulougouris and A. Rabivilas (Eds.), *Studies in Phobic and Obsessive-Compulsive Disorders*. Oxford: Pergamon. In press.
10. Cohn, C. K., Kron, R. E., and Brady, J. P. A case of blood-illness-injury phobia treated behaviorally. *Journal of Nervous and Mental Disease* 162:65, 1976.
11. Connolly, J., Hallam, R. S., and Marks, I. M. Selective association of fainting with blood-injury phobias. *Behavior Therapy* 7:8, 1976.
12. Crowe, M. J., Marks, I. M., Agras, W. S., and Leitenberg, H. Time-limited desensitization, implosion and shaping for phobic patients: A crossover study. *Behavior Research and Therapy* 10:319, 1972.
13. Emmelkamp, P. M. G. Self-observation vs. flooding in the treatment of agoraphobia. *Behavior Research and Therapy* 12:229, 1974.
14. Emmelkamp, P. M. G. Phobias: Theoretical and clinical considerations.

Paper presented at the European Association of Behavior Therapy meeting, Spetsae, Greece, September, 1976. In J. C. Boulougouris and A. Rabavilas (Eds.), *Studies in Phobic and Obsessive-Compulsive Disorders.* Oxford: Pergamon. In press.

15. Emmelkamp, P. M. G., and Ultee, K. A. A comparison of "successive approximation" and "self-observation" in the treatment of agoraphobia. *Behavior Therapy* 5:606, 1974.
16. Emmelkamp, P. M. G., and Emmelkamp-Benner, A. Effects of historically portrayed modeling and group treatment on self-observation: A comparison with agoraphobics. *Behavior Research and Therapy* 13:135, 1975.
17. Emmelkamp, P. M. G., and Wessels, H. Flooding in imagination vs. flooding in vivo. A comparison with agoraphobics. *Behavior Research and Therapy* 13:7, 1975.
18. Evans, P. D., and Kellam, A. M. P. Semi-automated desensitization: A controlled clinical trial. *Behavior Research and Therapy* 11:641, 1973.
19. Everaerd, W. T., Rijken, H. M., and Emmelkamp, P. M. G. A comparison of "flooding" and successive approximation in the treatment of agoraphobia. *Behavior Research and Therapy* 11:105, 1973.
20. Fryrear, J. L., and Werner, S. Treatment of a phobia by use of a videotaped modeling procedure. *Behavior Therapy* 1:391, 1976.
21. Furst, J. B., and Cooper, A. Failure of systematic desensitization in two cases of obsessive-compulsive neurosis marked by fears of insecticide. *Behavior Research and Therapy* 8:203, 1970.
22. Gale, E. N., and Ayer, W. A. Treatment of dental phobias. *Journal of the American Dental Association* 78:1304, 1969.
23. Gelder, M. G., Bancroft, J. H. J., Gath, D. H., Johnston, D. W., Mathews, A. M., and Shaw, P. M. Specific and non-specific factors in behavior therapy. *British Journal of Psychiatry* 123:445, 1973.
24. Gentry, W. D. In vivo desensitization of an obsessive breast cancer fear. *Journal of Behavior Therapy and Experimental Psychiatry* 1:315, 1970.
25. Gillan, P., and Rachman, S. An experimental investigation of behavior therapy in phobic patients. *British Journal of Psychiatry* 124:392, 1974.
26. Glasgow, R. E. In vivo prolonged exposure in the treatment of urinary retention. *Behavior Therapy* 6:701, 1975.
27. Hafner, J., and Marks, I. M. Exposure in vivo of agoraphobics. Contributions of diazepam, group exposure and anxiety evocation. *Psychological Medicine* 6:71, 1976.
28. Hand, I. Film shown at the European Association of Behavior Therapy meeting, Spetsae, Greece, September, 1976 (Columbia Broadcast Company).
29. Hand, I., Lamontagne, Y., and Marks, I. M. Group exposure (flooding) in vivo for agoraphobics. *British Journal of Psychiatry* 124:588, 1974.
30. Heyse, H. Response prevention and modeling in the treatment of obsessive-compulsive neurosis. Paper presented at the Second Annual Conference of the European Association of Behavior Therapy, Wexford, Eire, September, 1972.
31. Hodgson, R., Rachman, S., and Marks, I. M. The treatment of obsessive-compulsive neurosis: Follow-up and further findings. *Behavior Research and Therapy* 10:181, 1972.

32. Husein, M. Z. Desensitization and flooding (implosion) in treatment of phobias. *American Journal of Psychiatry* 127:1509, 1971.
33. Janet, P. *Psychological Healing,* Vol. II. New York: Macmillan, 1925.
34. Johnston, D., Lancashire, M., Mathews, A. M., Munby, M., Shaw, P. M., and Gelder, M. G. Imaginal flooding and exposure to real phobic situations: Changes during treatment. *British Journal of Psychiatry* 129:372, 1976.
35. Jones, H. G. The application of conditioning and learning techniques to the treatment cf a psychiatric patient. *Journal of Abnormal and Social Psychology* 52:414, 1956.
36. Kendell, R. E., and Discipio, W. J. Obsessional symptoms and obsessional personality traits in patients with depressive illnesses. *Psychological Medicine* 1:65, 1970.
37. Kenny, R. T., Solyom, L., and Solyom, C. Faradic disruption of obsessive ideation in the treatment of obsessive neurosis. *Behavior Therapy* 4:448, 1973.
38. Kleinknecht, R. A., Klepac, R. K., and Alexander, L. D. Origin and characteristics of fear of dentistry. *Journal of the American Dental Association* 86:842, 1973.
39. Kumar, K., and Wilkinson, J. C. M. Thought-stopping: A useful treatment in phobias of 'internal stimuli'. *British Journal of Psychiatry* 119:305, 1971.
40. Leonhard, K. *Individual therapie der Neurosen.* Jena: Gustav Fischer Verlag, 1973.
41. Levy, R., and Meyer, V. Ritual prevention in obsessional patients. *Proceedings of the Royal Society of Medicine* 64:1115, 1971.
42. Lewis, D. *Chastity: Or Our Secret Sins.* Philadelphia: George MacLean & Sons, Ltd., 1875.
43. Lewis, A. J. Problems of obsessional illness. *Proceedings of the Royal Society of Medicine* 29:325, 1936.
44. Lindley, P., Marks, I. M., Philpott, R., and Snowden, J. Treatment of obsessive-compulsive neurosis with history of childhood autism. *British Journal of Psychiatry,* 1977.
45. Lipsedge, M. S. Therapeutic approaches to compulsive neurosis. Unpublished M.Phil. dissertation. University of London, 1974.
46. Lloyd, G. G., and Deakin, H. G. Phobias complicating treatment of uterine carcinoma. *British Medical Journal,* IV, Oct.-Dec., 440, 1975.
47. McGlynn, F. D., and Linder, L. H. The clinical application of analogue desensitization: A case study. *Behavior Therapy* 2:385, 1971.
48. Mahoney, M. J. The self-management of covert behavior: A case study. *Behavior Therapy* 2:575, 1971.
49. Marks, I. M. *Patterns of Learning in Psychiatric Patients: Semantic Differential Responses in Obsessives and Psychopaths.* Maudsley Monograph No. 13, Oxford: Oxford University Press, 1965.
50. Marks, I. M. *Fears and Phobias.* London: Academic Press, 1969.
51. Marks, I. M. Phobic disorders four years after treatment. A prospective follow-up *British Journal of Psychiatry* 118:683, 1971.
52. Marks, I. M. New approaches to the treatment of obsessive-compulsive disorders. *Journal of Nervous and Mental Disease* 156:420, 1973.
53. Marks, I. M. Behavioural treatments of phobic and obsessive-compulsive

disorders: A critical appraisal. In M. Hersen, R. M. Eisler, and P. M. Miller (Eds.), *Progress in Behavior Modification.* Vol. 2. New York: Academic Press, 1975.
54. Marks, I. M.   Management of sexual disorders. In H. Leitenberg (Ed.), *Handbook of Behavior Modification and Behavior Therapy.* London: Prentice-Hall, 1976.
55. Marks, I. M., Crowe, M., Drewe, E., Young, J., and Dewhurst, W.   Obsessive-compulsive neurosis in identical twins. *British Journal of Psychiatry* 115:991, 1969.
56. Marks, I. M., Boulougouris, J., and Marset, P.   Flooding vs. desensitization in phobic disorders. *British Journal of Psychiatry* 119:353, 1971a.
57. Marks, I. M., and Huson, J.   Physiological aspects of neutral and phobic imagery: Further findings. *British Journal of Psychiatry* 122:567, 1973.
58. Marks, I. M., Rachman, S., and Hodgson, R.   Treatment of chronic obsessive compulsive neurosis by in vivo exposure. *British Journal of Psychiatry* 13:271, 1975.
59. Marks, I. M., Connolly, J., Hallam, R. S., and Philpott, R.   *Nursing in Behavioral Psychotherapy.* Paperback book in Research Series of Royal College of Nursing, Henrietta Square, London, WIM OAB (1976).
60. Mathews, A. M.   Psychophysiological approaches to the investigation of desensitization and allied procedures. *Psychological Bulletin* 76:73, 1971.
61. Mathews, A. M., Teasdale, J., Munby, M., Johnston, D., and Shaw, P.   A home-based treatment programme for agoraphobics. Unpublished paper, 1977.
62. Mathews, A. M., Johnston, D. W., Lancashire, M., Munby, M., Shaw, P. M., and Gelder, M. G.   Imaginal flooding and exposure to real phobic situations: Treatment outcome with agoraphobic patients. *British Journal of Psychiatry* 129:362, 1976.
63. Melamed, B. G., Weinstein, D., Hawes, R., and Katin-Borland, M.   Reduction of fear related dental management problems with use of filmed modeling. *Journal of the American Dental Association* 90:822, 1975a.
64. Melamed, B. G., Hawes, R. R., Heiby, E., and Glick, J.   Use of filmed modeling to reduce uncooperative behavior in children during dental treatment. *Journal of Dental Research*, 54:797, 1975b.
65. Meyer, V.   Modification of expectations in cases with obsessional rituals. *Behavior Research and Therapy* 4:273, 1966.
66. Meyer, V., and Levy, R.   Treatment of obsessive-compulsive neurosis. *Proceedings of the Royal Society of Medicine* 64:1117, 1971.
67. Meyer, V., and Levy, R.   Behavioural treatment of a homosexual with compulsive rituals. *British Journal of Medical Psychology* 43:63, 1970.
68. Miller, N.   The role of learning in physiological response to stress. In G. Serban (Ed.), *The Psychopathology of Human Adaption.* New York: Plenum Press, 1975.
69. Mills, H. L., Agras, W. S., Barlow, D. H., Baugh, J. R., and Mills, J. R.   The treatment of compulsive rituals by response prevention: A sequential analysis of treatment variables. *Archives of General Psychiatry* 28:529, 1973.
70. Nunes, J. S., and Marks, I. M.   Feedback of true heart rate during exposure in vivo. *Archives of General Psychiatry* 32:933, 1975.

71. Nunes, J. S., and Marks, I. M. Feedback of true heart rate during exposure in vivo: Partial replication with methodological improvement. *Archives of General Psychiatry* 33:1346, 1976.
72. Poole, A. D., and Yates, A. J. The modification of excessive frequency of urination: A case study. *Behavior Therapy* 6:78, 1975.
73. Prigatano, C. P., and Johnston, H. J. Autonomic nervous system changes associated with a spider phobic reaction. *Journal of Abnormal Psychology* 83:169, 1974.
74. Rabavilas, A. D., Boulougouris, J. D., and Stefanis, C. Duration of flooding sessions in the treatment of obsessive-compulsive patients. *Behavior Research and Therapy.* In press.
75. Rachman, S. Primary obsessional slowness. *Behavior Research and Therapy* 12:9, 1974.
76. Rachman, S., Marks, I. M., and Hodgson, R. The treatment of obsessive-compulsive neuroses. *Behavior Research and Therapy* 9:237, 1971.
77. Rachman, S., Marks, I. M., and Hodgson, R. The treatment of obsessive-compulsive neurotics by modeling and flooding in vivo. *Behavior Research and Therapy* 11:463, 1973.
78. Rainey, C. A. An obsessive-compulsive neurosis treated by flooding in vivo. *Journal of Behavior Therapy and Experimental Psychiatry* 3:117, 1972.
79. Ramsay, R. W. Behavior therapy and bereavement. Paper presented at the meeting of the European Association of Behavior Therapy, Wexford, Eire, September, 1972.
80. Ramsay, R. W. Grief. Film presented to the European Association of Behavior Therapy meeting, Spetsae, Greece, September, 1976 (Columbia Broadcast Company).
81. Ramsay, R. W., and Sikkel, R. J. Behaviour therapy and obsessive-compulsive neurosis. Paper presented at the meeting of the European Association of Behavior Therapy and Modification, Munich, July, 1971.
82. Roper, G. Leonhard's individual therapy and its relation to behaviour therapy. *Behavior Research and Therapy* 14:239, 1976.
83. Roper, G., Rachman, S., and Marks, I. M. Passive and participant modeling in exposure treatment of obsessive-compulsive neurotics. *Behavior Research and Therapy* 13:271, 1975.
84. Rosen, G. M., and Orenstein, J. A historical note on thought-stopping. *Journal of Consulting and Clinical Psychology* 44:1016, 1976.
85. Rubin, R. D., and Merbaum, M. Self-imposed punishment versus desensitization. In R. D. Rubin, H. Fensterheim, A. A. Lazarus, and C. M. Franks (Eds.), *Advances in Behavior Therapy, 1969.* New York: Academic Press, 1971.
86. Shapiro, D., Schwartz, G. E., Schnidman, S. R., Nelson, S., and Silverman, S. Operant control of fear-related electrodermal responses in snake-phobic subjects. Paper presented at the Eleventh Annual Meeting of the Society for Psychophysiological Research, Clayton, Missouri, October, 1971.
87. Shaw, P. Three behaviour therapies in the treatment of social phobia. Paper presented to the Annual Meeting of the British Association of Behavior Therapy, Exeter, July, 1976.
88. Solyom, L., Garze-Perez, J., Ledwidge, B. L., and Solyom, C. Paradoxical

intention in the treatment of obsessive thoughts: A pilot study. *Comprehensive Psychiatry* 13:291, 1972a.
89. Solyom, L., Shugar, R., Bryntwick, S., and Solyom, C.   Treatment of fear of flying. *American Journal of Psychiatry* 4:423, 1973.
90. Stern, R. S.   Treatment of a case of obsessional neurosis using thought-stopping technique. *British Journal of Psychiatry* 117:441, 1970.
91. Stern, R. S., Lipsedge, M. S., and Marks, I. M.   Thought stopping of neutral and obsessive thoughts: A controlled trial. *Behavior Research and Therapy* 11:659, 1973.
92. Stern, R. S., and Marks, I. M.   A comparison of brief and prolonged flooding in agoraphobics. *Archives of General Psychiatry* 28:210, 1973a.
93. Stern, R. S., and Marks, I. M.   Contract therapy in obsessive-compulsive neurosis with marital discord. *British Journal of Psychiatry* 123:681, 1973b.
94. Usa, G., and Usa, I.   A case of a nun who suffered from visionary obsessions of snakes treated by Morita therapy. *Psychologia* 1:226, 1958.
95. Watson, J. P., and Marks, I. M.   Relevant vs. irrelevant flooding in the treatment of phobias. *Behavior Therapy* 2:275, 1971.
96. Watson, J. P., Gaind, R., and Marks, I. M.   Prolonged exposure: A rapid treatment for phobias. *British Medical Journal* 1:13, 1971.
97. Watson, J. P., Gaind, R., and Marks, I. M.   Physiological habituation to continuous phobic stimulation. *Behavior Research and Therapy* 10:269, 1972.
98. Watson, J. P., Mullett, G. E., and Pillay, H.   The effects of prolonged exposure to phobic situations upon agoraphobic patients treated in groups. *Behavior Research and Therapy* 11:531, 1973.
99. Wilson, G. T.   Innovations in the modification of phobic behaviors in two clinical cases. *Behavior Therapy* 4:426, 1973.
100. Wisocki, P. A.   Treatment of obsessive-compulsive behavior by covert sensitization and covert reinforcement: A case report. *Journal of Behavior Therapy and Experimental Psychiatry* 1:233, 1970.
101. Yamagami, T.   The treatment of an obsession by thought-stopping. *Journal of Behavior Therapy and Experimental Psychiatry* 2:233, 1971.

9. Therapeutic Packages: Tools for Change

James M. Ferguson and Gary R. Birchler

Editor's Introduction

One of the recurrent themes of this book has been that many of the so-called mental disorders may be more usefully defined as a set of discrete, observable behavior problems. The goal of behavior therapy is to remove such problems directly, either in real life or within an artificial situation structured to aid in eliminating them. In the case of behavioral deficits, therapy is designed to build a new repertoire in small, progressive steps. The behavior disorder to be treated is specified, as is the therapeutic approach to be used. This specificity of approach, combined with what is known about effective behavior change procedures, leads naturally to the creation of a set of treatments sufficiently specific to be listed with their therapeutic indications (see Therapeutic Index, pages 293-301). The need to administer repeatedly the same or similar series of specific treatment procedures for some of the more prevalent behavioral disorders—for example, overweight—leads naturally to the formation of therapeutic packages.

The advantages of such packaged therapies lies in their ease of transmission, the relative uniformity of results obtainable by therapists with varying backgrounds, and their wide applicability, often at reduced cost. One of the disadvantages is that some efficacy may be lost, since problems may not be defined as uniquely as they deserve.

Treatment for three specific behavior problems—enuresis, overweight, and unassertiveness—are discussed in detail in this chapter. Each of the three areas is at a somewhat different stage of development, and none is entirely satisfactory. In the case of toilet training (pages 248-255), the component skills needed by the child and the means to teach them have been carefully outlined by Azrin and Foxx [6, 7], with excellent therapeutic results. Moreover, other workers have been able to replicate the results with only a little loss of efficacy when parents become the therapists. Yet there has been no controlled-outcome study comparing treatment with no treatment, and no study of the relative effectiveness of different approaches to treating enuresis; for example, the bell and pad method compared with Azrin's skill training or "dry bed" approach—important steps in the evaluation of therapeutic packages.

In the case of overweight (pages 255-268), the ingredients of the usual treatment approach are well defined, and a body of research is beginning to suggest that the obese and nonobese do show differences in eating behavior, confirming at least some of the theoretic underpinnings of this particular treatment approach. Moreover, many of the subcomponents of the package described have been shown to be effective in producing weight loss, at least in the short term. However, it is not clear which components of treatment are essential and which are superfluous, and overall the results of treatment are quite modest. Finally, it is not clear whether a purely dietary approach might not be just as effective as the more complex behavior change package described.

For assertiveness training, the definition of the behavior to be changed is less clear than in the case of the previous treatment packages, and it is possible that, in the future, specific therapeutic packages for rather more narrowly defined aspects of assertiveness will emerge.

The development of well-specified, easily transmissible therapies for well-defined behavior problems is in sharp contrast to the usual style of psychotherapeutic practice and evaluation. In the recent study of Sloane, Staples, Cristol, Yorkston, and Whipple [81], for example, outpatients treated with behavior therapy and psychodynamic psychotherapy were compared with each other and with a waiting list control group in a randomized study. Broad-gauge nonbehavioral measures of outcome were used, and the experienced therapists were allowed to treat their patients as they saw fit. Given the lack of precise measurement and therapies that were not always very different, it is not surprising that behavior therapy and psychotherapy were found to be about equally effective, with perhaps an edge for behavior therapy, particularly for patients with more severe problems.

In my view, the future of therapeutic research will increasingly be devoted to assessing the efficacy of well-defined therapeutic packages in precisely defined and measured behavior disorders. The one method for all disorders—the broad-gauge therapy—is rapidly giving way to the use of a variety of procedures for different kinds of behavior problems. Combined with experiments aimed mainly at assessing outcome will be a larger number of therapeutic studies exploring the process of behavior change, together with the outcome of change induced by subcomponents of various therapeutic packages. Only in this way will the effectiveness of therapy be improved and new interventions introduced.

Finally, as Ferguson and Birchler point out in the following chapter, *the entire nature of therapeutic services could, and should, change. An educational model would seem a far more satisfactory means to provide service for the majority of behavior problems short of the psychoses, rather than perpetuating treatment services that essentially view behavioral disturbance as illness and stigmatize by way of diagnosis. Patients become students, therapists become teachers, and therapy becomes education—to the benefit of all.*

W. S. A.

In a recent book, Goldstein [38] suggests that the main thrust of mental health care systems has been in the wrong direction, or at best severely limited by social class and structure of the therapeutic delivery system.

> We are urging ... increased utilization of treatment approaches which are less a function of our own life styles and professional preferences, and more responsive to the needs, life styles, and environmental realities of the lower class patient. One such approach appears to be what we have termed Structured Learning Therapy, in which explicit focus can be placed upon skills training—*via* the use of modeling, role playing, and social reinforcement—to enhance patient autonomy, assertiveness, internal control, role-taking ability, sense of mastery, social interaction skills, accuracy of affective perception and communication, tolerance for frustration and ambiguity, and a host of other useful behaviors in which he may be deficient.

This approach suggests that where there are skill deficits that lead to maladaptive behavior, an educational program can be developed to overcome the problem. The packaging of "disorder-specific" programs facilitates transmission of therapeutic tools to therapists, allows dissemination to paraprofessionals or nontherapists who may be interested in aiding their peers, and makes available self-help programs for patients with problems that may not require therapist intervention. In each case the agent of change is provided with instructional material, step-by-step programmatic exercises, evaluative materials, instruments for feedback, and suggested rewards for successful performance.

Basic Assumptions in Behavioral Packaging

The author of a therapeutic package is torn between the desire to individualize treatment and the wish to be sufficiently general to allow a wide range of individuals manifesting the target symptom to be treated by the package. In the preparation of behavioral treatment packages several assumptions are made:

1. The treatment steps necessary for a successful therapeutic intervention can be adequately described and organized in a way that allows transmission from researcher to practitioner.
2. The efficacy of the packaged therapy is unrelated to the presence of the originating researcher or therapist.
3. The educational preparation of the recipient therapist can be specified; for example, packages to be implemented by doctoral-level therapists, schoolteachers, friends, parents, or the individual himself.
4. The educational approach can be independent of a trained "psychotherapist."
5. The diagnostic criteria for the disorder to be treated are commonly accepted.
6. The disorder to be treated is fairly homogeneous.
7. The skill deficit or maladaptive learning problem defined in a functional behavioral analysis (diagnosis) can be corrected by an educational approach.
8. The package of instructional material will be sufficiently broad to help multiple individuals with the same behavioral problem and sufficiently specific to retain therapeutic effectiveness.
9. The redundancy and nonspecificity inherent in packaging will not be sufficiently aversive for clients to cause the program to fail or clients to leave the program.
10. Many subsets of therapeutic interventions can be presented to clients with a complex disorder—for example, obesity—with a combined therapeutic benefit.
11. A combination of techniques will retain their effectiveness when presented together or sequentially to clients.
12. Packaged programs can be defined with time limits, for example, a five-, 10-, or 20-week program, and the rate of learning of most clients will allow assimilation of the program material within those time limits.
13. Package-induced changes will persist over time, and learned behaviors will be maintained by environmental contingencies.
14. Methodology for evaluating therapeutic packges can be specified and built into programs for ongoing evaluation of efficacy.

Elements Included in Behavioral Packages

Each behavioral program begins with a statement of the problem the package is designed to treat and usually includes information describing the historical development of the program. Thus, Stuart and Davis [87], in outlining their program for the treatment of overweight, spend several chapters discussing concepts of obesity, consequences of the disorder, and the outcome of previous attempts to treat the disorder. After the informational stage for therapists has been set, a behavioral description of the disorder and a method of diagnosis are usually presented. Program applications, outcome data, and a discussion of the program limitations are also usually included in the package introduction.

In an attempt to obtain population homogeneity, increase motivation, and eliminate individuals who will probably not respond to therapy, client selection criteria are usually specified. Selection criteria may be in terms of characteristics present, for example, individuals more than 20 percent above life insurance normal weight; in terms of characteristics absent, for example, lack of eye contact during conversation; and in terms of program exclusions, for example, individuals who are psychotic, undergoing severe marital discord, or mentally retarded.

In all therapeutic packages, a detailed description of the therapy is essential. This includes a discussion of the therapist or the change agent characteristics, with emphasis on communication skills; the therapy setting, for example, a quiet room with chairs for each participant; the materials needed in the therapy setting, for example, paper, pencils, and visual aids; the therapist's preparation for the course and for each session; and an adequate description of the therapy process, which will often be a sequenced program of therapeutic procedures aimed at both the antecedents and the consequences of behavior and often incorporating self-control procedures, as described in Chapter 2, pages 22-26. Often, a description of anticipated problems in therapy, suggested ways to combat "standard excuses" for not following therapeutic instructions, and hints for handling any impediments that may arise during the administration of the program are provided to help the less experienced therapist.

In any behavior change program, outcome measures are of vital importance. Each program contains a section on how to identify, quantify, and record data, and on how to use goal-setting and feedback of information about change in therapy, as well as instructions for program modification contingent upon ongoing data received from clients. Moreover, instruction in behavioral analysis and problem solving provides a significant tool for use by the client both during behavioral programs and subsequent to their formal termination. By teaching clients to track their own behaviors, to analyze the components of their behavior problems, to plan treatment strategies that include elements of monitoring, feedback, and goal setting, and to reward themselves, an element of autonomy is built into the programs that allows clients to become their own "therapists."

Many types of behavioral programs have been developed, each of which incorporates most of the above points. To illustrate the concept of therapeutic packaging, we have chosen to discuss in detail three types of packages. The first facilitates acquisition of a simple skill: toilet training. The second is a more complex habit change program: the treatment of overweight. The third is a complex social behavior change program: assertiveness training.

Research in the area of program development is difficult. For a simple skill acquisition program, replication is possible and has been carried out. The effective dissemination of toilet training materials from the researcher to trained "toilet trainers" to parents has been demonstrated. In the case of obesity, programs vary widely in their content, target populations, and mode of application. Although a series of habit change interventions directed at the same target symptom, obesity, would appear to have enough commonality to facilitate cross-program comparison, such is not the case. By way of additional contrast, in the social change program, assertiveness training, there is no consistent definition of assertiveness; and there are a lack of consensus in defining the basic target behaviors, a widely disparate series of techniques for intervention, many different subject populations, very few instruments to measure change, efficacy, or generalization effects, and very little outcome data or program replication.

A Skill-Specific Behavioral Package: Toilet Training

Urinary continence is a behavior of some concern to all parents in our society. Although the custom of toilet training varies from culture to culture, with some primitive societies delaying the acquisition of continence until the age of five or six years, the general consensus in our society is the sooner the better. For example, one survey [46] found the average

age for instituting toilet training in London, England, was 4.6 months. According to O'Leary and Wilson [71], the medical opinion on when to toilet-train children has varied from the United States Children's Bureau publication *Infant Care* in 1914, which advised bowel training by the third month without scolding or punishing the child, to a revision in 1921, when parents were told to begin toilet training by the end of the first month and finish by the end of the first year, to an updating in 1942, when parents were told to train infants at eight months, and finally to a revision in 1951, with training set between one year and 1½ years.

Spock [83] suggested that less attention be paid to toilet training, and in *Baby and Child Care* he outlines a permissive approach, with two general criteria for training readiness: biologic (the child should be 18 months to three years of age and able to go at least two hours between urinations), and behavioral (the child does not refuse to urinate in the toilet and makes premonitory signals prior to urination that alert the mother or other adult to his needs). For rapid toilet training, he suggests a noncontingent fixed schedule of toileting two hours after each episode of urination, at which time the child is to be placed on the toilet and instructed to urinate. "If you wait to put him on [the toilet] until he's been dry for 2 hours, you won't be going at his training too suddenly because you will find him dry only every few days at first. Gradually as the weeks pass, you will find him more dry more regularly."

For parents who prefer to go slow on training, he suggests that "most children are quite ready and willing the last part of the second year to begin to try to cooperate with a mother's wishes if she expresses them in an agreeable and encouraging manner and if she takes into account her child's readiness. To put it the other way around, it's unnecessary and sometimes confusing to a child if the mother is so afraid of interfering that she tries to keep it a secret that she wishes him to become trained" [84].

With this setting of permissiveness born of frustration, a lack of success of early training, and statements from the medical profession that forcing a child to comply might result in psychological damage, it is understandable that Dr. Spock's method generally prevails. The parent was left in a dilemma between the fear of being punitive, and harming his child, and the fear that if he did not pay enough attention to toilet training, the untrained child would be harmed in other ways.

It is against this background that Azrin and Foxx [6, 32, 34] developed a behavioral program to toilet-train children. Although it was initially designed to aid the toilet training of the retarded, they found that it worked well for normal children [7]. To facilitate toilet training, they analyzed the behaviors necessary to accomplish the act of toileting. These included awareness of need for toileting, approach to toilet behaviors, the ability to undress, to urinate in the toilet or potty, to empty the potty, and to wipe and re-dress themselves. The general method for establishing each of these toileting behaviors was to provide a learning experience that maximized factors important to learning the toileting skill, and then fade reinforcement for the individual factors once the overall skill had been acquired.

After an introduction for trainers or parents that includes a discussion of criteria for trainability (age; physical readiness, including bladder control; and instructional readiness) they provide a list of suggested pretraining experiences—for example, having the child watch other individuals urinate—and a list of items needed for the training experience, such as reinforcers in the form of both sweet and salty small snack items and a variety of desirable beverages, a potty chair, and a wetting doll to serve as a model for demonstrating correct toileting. They suggest the child wear loose, cloth training pants, and that after training the child not be allowed to wear diapers, since these may be a cue for pretoilet-training elimination behaviors and they are difficult for a child to remove should he want to toilet himself.

Foxx and Azrin list 16 components of their behavioral package:

1. *A distraction-free environment:*
   All toys and distracting objects in the training room are removed and the subject's presence in the room is used solely for the purpose of toilet training.
2. *Reinforced practice of dressing skills:*
   The child is taught to undress appropriately, to pull down pants and sit on the potty, and to re-dress after toileting.
3. *Reinforced practice for approaching the toilet:*
   The child is taught to come to the toilet from various locations in the house and is rewarded for approaching the toilet when the urge to urinate occurs.
4. *Detailed and continuing instruction for each act required in toileting:*
   The child is repeatedly instructed in all aspects of the learning procedure and the reinforcement contingencies. The "teacher" manually

guides the child through the acts of toileting, including helping pull down his pants, sit on the toilet, and re-dress until the child is able to do this alone. Each autonomous step toward completing this behavioral sequence is rewarded.

5. *Learning by imitation:*
The child is given a wetting rubber doll, which is filled with water. The child practices correct toileting with the doll by repeatedly engaging it in conversation, having it drink, taking it to the toilet, taking down its panties, squeezing it and allowing the "urine" to fall into the potty, reinforcing it with bits of potato chips and praise, and finally pulling up its pants.

6. *Increased trial frequency:*
The child is hydrated by giving him soft drinks, juices, and milk at the rate of approximately two cups per hour to increase the frequency of urination.

7. *A multiple reinforcement system:*
The child receives tangible reinforcements in the form of candy, potato chips, and soon, in addition to praise, hugging, and kisses, the use of reinforcing images, such as "What would Santa Claus think?" "Wouldn't your grandmother be happy if she knew?" for each successful step toward correct toileting.

8. *Immediate detection of correct toileting:*
The parent watches the child on the toilet to detect the sound of urination or has the child urinate in a mechanical potty that signals when urine falls into it.

9. *Immediate reinforcement for correct toileting:*
As soon as there is an indication of a correct toileting response, the parent rewards the child with candy, potato chips, praise, hugs, and kisses.

10. *Continued reinforcement for having dry pants:*
Every five minutes the trainer inspects the child's pants and has the child touch his own pants. If the pants are dry, he reinforces the child, preferably with a liquid to hydrate him further and increase the number of toileting trials.

11. *Gradual elimination of the need for toileting cues:*
As the child learns approach behaviors and begins to receive the contingent reward for approach on urge to urinate, the necessity for prompts is lessened, and the reinforcement for approach behavior *per se* is faded.

12. *Immediate detection of accidents:*

The teacher watches the child and his pants for any behavior or dampness that might indicate that he is urinating or defecating.

13. *Positive practice after accidents:*
    After accidents, the child receives verbal reprimand for the accident, positive practice in the form of required approach to the toilet, and further instruction to facilitate proper toilet approach behavior.
14. *Negative reinforcement for accidents:*
    The child is instructed to change his wet pants for dry pants, and social contact is eliminated for five minutes (time-out from positive reinforcement) to insure that the child is not reinforced for incorrect toileting.
15. *Gradual reduction of the need for immediate reinforcement:*
    After several hours of training, the amount of instruction is decreased, reinforcement for the initiation behaviors is faded, and prompting is carried out on an intermittent decreasing schedule.
16. *Posttraining attention to cleanliness:*
    Teachers are instructed to inspect the child's pants before each meal, snack, and nap, and at bedtime and to praise the child for having dry pants. If an accident has occurred, the parent is to reprimand the child, make him change his pants, and have him practice going to the toilet. The attention to the child's performance is continued for several days following training and then gradually faded.

In the training package developed for normal children, Azrin and Foxx developed an empiric behavioral screening test to ascertain the potential trainee's physiologic and intellectual readiness to undergo toilet training. The children are asked to point to their nose, eyes, mouth, and hair, to sit down, to stand up, to walk with their mother to another room, to look at their mother, to imitate their mother at a simple task, and to bring their mother a toy. Children who can follow these commands are considered ready for toilet training.

In Foxx and Azrin's initial study [33], 43 normal children were referred to the program for toilet training. Of these, nine could not satisfy the test for behavioral readiness. The mean age for the remaining 34 (22 boys, 12 girls) was 25 months, with a range of 20 to 36 months. Virtually all the parents mentioned prior difficulties in toilet training their children. The criterion for successful training was spontaneous toileting by the child without prompts. Training of these children was accomplished rapidly by an experienced toilet trainer in an average of 3.9 hours, with a range of half an hour to 14 hours. Children aged 26 to 36 months were trained in an average of five hours. Bowel and bladder training were accomplished concurrently, with no need for a differential training procedure. One-third of the children spontaneously stopped wetting the bed after training. Four months after their training, the degree of maintenance of toileting behaviors was virtually 100 percent (see Figure 9). Although Foxx and Azrin's experimental data and previous work with retarded children appeared to be extremely successful in the hands of trained therapists, Kimmel [50] expressed reservation about the utility of the therapeutic package for parents and questioned whether or not they would be able to follow the instructions outlined in it.

In one of the few independent investigations of the efficacy of a published behavioral program, Butler [13] presented the Foxx and Azrin program to parents, who in turn used it with their own children. He recruited 38 children and their parents from an Air Force base, and held three group classes for the parents, in which he discussed the following material: (1) the behavioral assessment of the pretraining activities needed for toilet training—for example, the physiologic and behavioral development of the child; (2) the actual procedures in the Azrin and Foxx book; and (3) a review of the first two class sessions and the behavioral package. In the final session he had parents set a specific date for toilet training after a three-week baseline count of the number of toileting accidents per day for each child. The experimenters contacted each parent from the training group daily by telephone for a program report. Only half the subjects were available for the entire series of follow-up interviews (2½ months). Butler's data do not represent a replication of the Foxx and Azrin studies. He had no contact with the children, he did not observe how the actual training was administered, and he had no direct observation of efficacy. His study was an evaluation of self-reported efficacy of the behavioral program.

Although the experiment relied solely on lectures and written material to transmit the behavioral method to parents, the results appear comparable to those reported by Foxx and Azrin (see Figure 9). The average length of time taken for toileting was 4.5 hours, with a range of 1.25 to 10 hours. Boys appeared to be more rapid in skill acquisition than girls, and those aged 25 months or more acquired toileting skills more rapidly than did

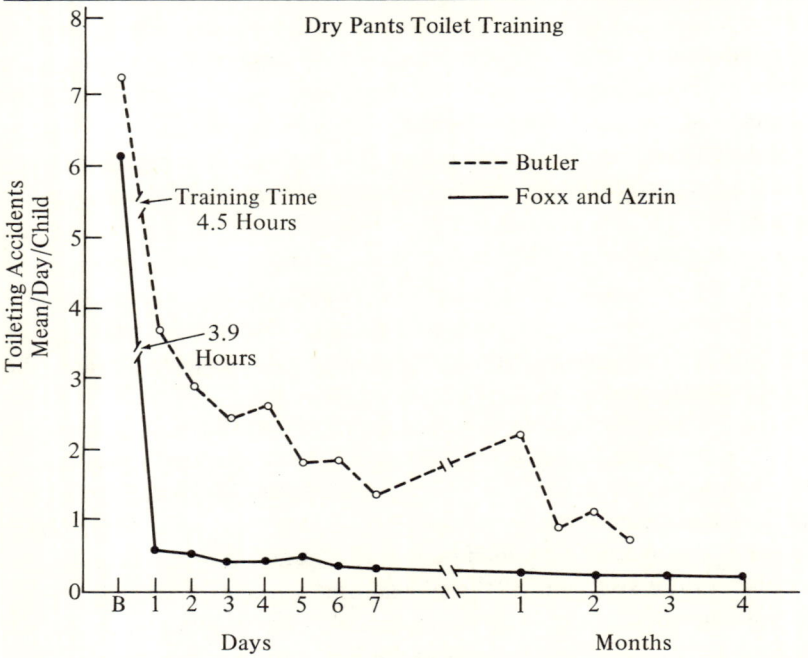

Figure 9. Data from Foxx, R. M., and Azrin, N. H. [33] and Butler, J. F. [13] showing the rate of decrease of toileting accidents (bowel and bladder combined) before and after Dry Pants Toilet Training. Only half of the children were available for the 1- to 2½-month follow-up data collection in the Butler experiment. The average training time for each program is indicated on the graph.

those under 25 months. Butler found a 20 percent generalization to bedtime and a reduction of bowel accidents that paralleled the trained urinary continence. Although the maintenance period was slightly less than that of Foxx and Azrin, the learned behavioral skill appeared to persist over time. The higher number of toileting accidents per day during maintenance may be attributable to a 50 percent reduction of sample size after the fourteenth day of the training, with a differential retention of poor toileters.

In this example of a packaged program of behavioral instructions, we see its effectiveness demonstrated both in an institutional research setting and in a home setting with trained therapists. Moreover, it is an effective tool in the home environment, with relatively untrained parents acting as trainers or "therapists."

A Behavioral Habit Change Program: The Treatment of Obesity

In contrast to toilet training, where the therapeutic goal is easily specified, the behavioral steps to reach the goal are explicitly stated, and the outcome criteria are well defined, the behavioral treatments for habit disorders are significantly more complex. Although obesity appears to be a well-defined disorder with clear treatment goals, the behavioral programs to achieve these goals are not well developed. Treatment programs are to a large extent based on postulated behavioral defects in the obese that may or may not exist [60] and on experimental evidence that is less than firmly established [96]. The wide variety of treatment techniques that have been used range from Fowler's simple, unidimensional treatment of shaving down the number of bites consumed per day [32] to Mahoney's complex cognitive, dietary, exercise, stimulus control, and reinforcement program [62]. All behavioral obesity treatment programs rely on a complex set of interactions between client and therapist and use outcome measures that are remote from the target behaviors. The most common dependent variable is, of course, weight change rather than eating behavior change.

Obesity is a physical symptom of major concern to physicians and health care personnel in this country. The Department of Health, Education and Welfare [18] estimates that between 40 and 80 million Americans are obese, and this excess weight is associated with an increased incidence in the morbidity and mortality from many major diseases [92]. In addition to its medical implications, excess weight often interferes with social functioning, athletic prowess, sexual performance, and occupational choice. Developing a successful treatment program for this disorder is, therefore, of some priority.

Obesity is a multidetermined disorder. There are hereditary predispositions for somatotype [62], endocrine influences on body shape, and physiologic determinants of body size that are established in utero [75] and in childhood [14] and that lead to an increase in the number of body fat cells. In addition, there are marked social and environmental influences that persist within families across generations (for a complete review, see ref.

[88]). Most obese clients, however, have no clear determinants for their obesity other than a presumed excess of caloric intake over caloric expenditure.

Treatments for obesity have traditionally been regarded as ineffective. Balanced low-caloric diets, 500-calorie semistarvation diets, "fad" high-fat or high-carbohydrate diets, starvation, various drugs (amphetamines, human chorionic gonadotrophin, diguanides, and thyroid analogues), hypnosis, and psychotherapy all lead to weight loss in some patients. In almost all cases this is followed by an equal or greater weight gain [73]. The state of the art was put concisely by Stunkard and McLaren-Hume in 1959: "Most obese persons will not enter treatment, of those who do enter treatment, most will not lose weight, [and] of those who do lose weight, most will regain it" [90].

Obesity can be defined operationally as a behavioral disorder. The obese individual eats in a way that results in excess retained caloric energy or body fat. Although this is a simplification of all the factors that lead to an individual's weight problem, it is a useful way to formulate the problem because it leads to a new therapeutic approach—changing eating behaviors rather than changing appetite or diet *per se*.

Current Programs
Several independent avenues of investigation have led to the current clinical behavioral weight control programs. Ferster, Nurnberger, and Levitt [28] were the first to suggest a learning approach to weight control. They postulated the existence of a difference in eating behavior between obese and thin individuals that resulted in the former consuming excess calories. To combat this difference, they developed a systematic behavior modification program to change abnormal eating behavior to normal eating behavior. This initial program was refined and elaborated by several groups of researchers over the following 15 years, with varying results. Another landmark experiment in the treatment of obesity was carried out in 1965 by London and Schreiber [58], who studied the effects of amphetamine appetite suppressants and placebo medication given in a supportive group therapy or individual treatment setting. They found a lower dropout rate and a greater weight loss for patients included in therapy groups regardless of drug or placebo medication treatment—suggesting that being in a group is a motivating experience. In a long series of experiments, Schacter [77]

and others appeared to demonstrate that obese individuals are more stimulus-bound and more under the influence of external environmental cues such as regularly appointed eating times, good taste, high visibility, and easy accessibility of food than are their thin counterparts. The obese appeared to respond to stimuli in their environment that they associated with eating or food by experiencing hunger or a drive to eat. Schacter reasoned that thin individuals eat in response to internal food cues, such as stomach contractions or hypoglycemia, and obese individuals experience hunger in response to learned external cues. To combat this difference in response to the environment, researchers have investigated a wide variety of stimulus control procedures. Stuart combined many of these techniques into a treatment program based on systematically changing the environmental stimuli that remind obese people to eat, along with attending to diet and exercise and developing alternative activities for eating responses. In 1967 he published the results of his treatment of 10 women for one year [86]. Two patients dropped out of treatment. Those remaining lost more than 25 pounds each, and four lost more than 40 pounds. This was a small, highly selected, but extremely successful group of patients and the first major success reported for the behavioral treatment of obesity. Since that report, many treatment programs have been developed, and the techniques available for use by therapists have been greatly expanded [25, 41, 42, 49, 55, 67, 72, 85, 95].

Figure 10 demonstrates the three primary behavioral approaches to weight control. Eating can be changed by altering preceding events, changing the behavior directly, or altering the consequences of the behaviors. For the purpose of discussion, the consequences, antecedents, and direct interventions are separated as though they were different types of therapy. In fact, elements of each enter into all phases of the therapist-client interactions concerning weight. The behavioral packages that have been developed to change eating behaviors vary considerably. All contain stimulus control exercises, self-monitoring, and instructions for reinforcement controlled either by the individual or by the therapist. An effort is usually made to increase the amount of environmental reinforcement available; at the same time the reinforcing value of food is negated with various stimulus control techniques by helping clients interact more successfully with those around them.

Three treatment areas are less consistently used in behavioral packages:

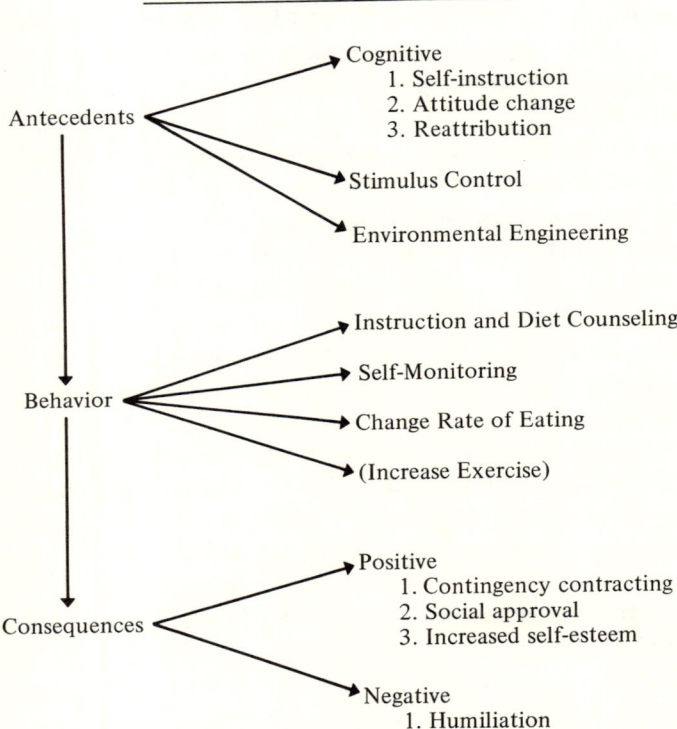

Figure 10. *The many strategies for controlling eating behaviors can be classified according to whether their primary focus is on the antecedents or the consequences of the behavior, or on the behavior itself. In practice, interventions affect all three categories to a greater or lesser extent. Exercise is included because of its importance in weight control programs.*

diet, exercise, and emotions. Stuart and Davis [87] presented a behavioral adaptation of a food exchange diet [93], in which the client is taught to shape down the number of calories consumed each day while maintaining a balanced diet. Ferguson [26] has clients increase their energy expenditure by shaping increased miles walked per day and minutes spent in physical activities, and Mahoney and Mahoney [62] devote considerable time to client "cognitive ecology" and changing their "emotional eating."

The behavioral package, *Learning to Eat* [26], is the most explicit attempt to package a behavioral weight control program in a step-by-step format designed to be used by anyone interested in leading a behavioral weight control group. It is a text divided into two parts, one for therapists and one for students. It begins with instructions for selecting a group leader, the style of leadership, the selection of patients, the size, setting, and type of meetings for the group, materials and records needed, and a description of suggested fees. It is written as a serial to be followed on a week-to-week basis or adapted to the specific needs of the particular needs of the therapist. Each lesson presents a psychological principle, an example, and appropriate homework. Discussion questions are included to aid the inexperienced therapist. The steps in the manual are:

Week 1: Introduction to behavioral control of weight—habit awareness. Clients are given an introductory lecture, which includes a summary of the behavioral principles they will learn over the next 15 weeks; they are told about the need for weekly feedback, about weight and food consumption, and about the values of intensive self-monitoring in the form of a daily food diary.

Week 2: Cue elimination—an introduction to stimulus control. Clients are requested to eat their meals at a designated appropriate place at home or at work; to change their habitual eating place at the table, to help break up long-standing social and physical eating cues at mealtime; to refrain from engaging in other activities while eating, for example, reading a newspaper; to remove food from all places in the house that are not appropriate storage areas; to avoid buying junk foods or to keep them out of sight, hidden, or in inaccessible places; and to reduce visual cues for eating in every possible way, for example, storing food in opaque containers, removing serving dishes from the table, and perhaps even taking the light bulb out of the refrigerator.

Week 3: Changing the act of eating—clients are instructed to put down their eating utensils between bites and to swallow their bites of food before they pick up more food.

Week 4: Behavioral chains and alternative activities—clients learn to identify antecedent behaviors that reliably lead to excess eating and to break the subsequent chain of behaviors by substituting an alternative activity, as outlined in Figure 11.

Substitute Activities

Pleasant Activities
1. *Singing – Washing Hair*
2. *Playing Piano – Biking*
3. *Sewing – Calling "Shut-ins"*

Necessary Activities
1. *Dusting*
2. *Vacuuming*
3. *Straighten House*

Situations when used
1. *Wanted Ice Cream – Delayed with Bath*
2. *Wanted Wheat Thins – Cleaned Up Yard*
3. *Wanted Snack – Went for Walk*
4. *Wanted Cookies – Did Dishes First*
5. *Saw Leftovers – Threw Them Out, Went for Bike Ride*
6. *Tempted By Cookies – Set Timer*
7. *Wanted Snack – Played Piano*

Behavior Chain

Identify the links in your eating response chain on the following diagram. Draw a line through the chain where it was interrupted. Add the link you substituted and the new chain of behaviors this substitution started.

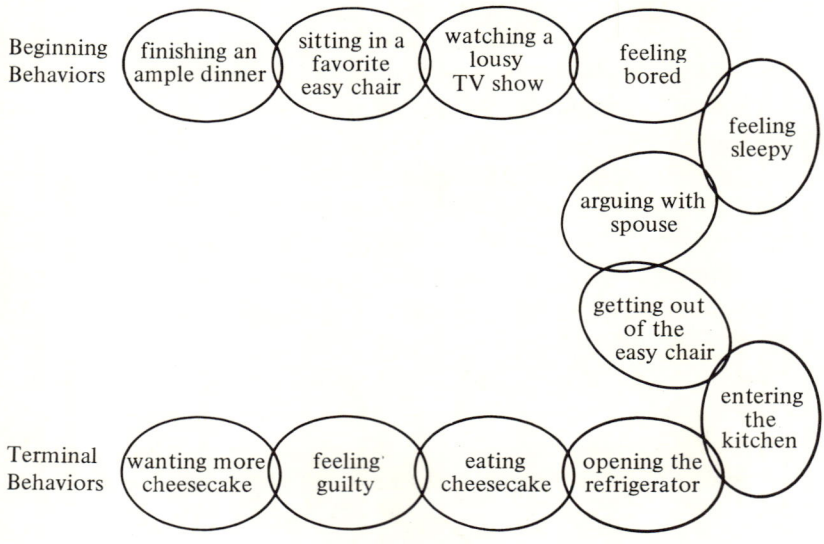

Week 5: Behavior analysis—progress and problem solving. Clients compare their food diaries for Week One and Week Four to measure their progress, identify a problem eating behavior, design a behavior change program including feedback and reinforcement, and commit themselves to implementing their program.

The fifth session is followed by five weeks' practice or maintenance training, when clients check in to be weighed each week but are given no additional instruction.

Week 11: Preplanning—clients are asked to write down their anticipated food intake before at least one meal per day, and to record intake after that meal, to correct their preplanning. They are also instructed to preplan food shopping with a shopping list that specifies the brand name and quantity of each item; they are also told to shop only after a meal.

Week 12: Cue elimination and energy use—food-related stimulus-narrowing techniques are presented, such as using smaller plates, leaving food on the plate at the end of a meal, taking smaller portions and going back for seconds only if still hungry at the end of a meal, throwing away food left on the plate immediately after a meal or storing it in an opaque container labeled with a specified preplanned use, asking for food rather than accepting it when it is passed at the table, and minimizing food contacts whenever possible. During this time, clients are asked to obtain an activity baseline by wearing a pedometer to record the number of miles walked each day, and to keep track of the number of minutes of exercise engaged in during the week.

Week 13: Energy use continued—clients are taught the value of energy expenditure in a weight control program and are asked to increase their energy use by doubling the number of miles walked each day, by purposely becoming less efficient in all their activities, for example, using the farthest bathroom at work or at home, and doubling the amount of physical exercise they engage in during the week.

Figure 11. *Clients are instructed to look at the chain of activities leading to habitual excess eating, to write down the links of the chain on a homework sheet, and to break the chain when possible. To facilitate chain-breaking, clients list alternative activities in advance and keep track of situations when these activities are used to avoid eating.*

Week 14: Snacks, cues, and holidays—the necessity for some knowledge about caloric content is presented in the context of coping with snacks and holiday feasts. Preplanning is combined with caloric prediction to plan for parties, meals outside the home, and holidays. A number of explicit hints are given to cope with hunger.

Week 15: Environmental support; family and friends—during the final group session, a discussion of the contents of the entire course is conducted for the families and illustrated with examples from the clients' experiences. The social environment—spouse, family, and friends—is presented as a new topic. An explicit discussion of the common ways in which a social environment can sabotage a weight loss program and of how supportive interactions can enhance the program is carried out with this group. Clients are specifically instructed to ask for support, praise, and feedback, and to thank people for helping them. It is suggested that everyone in the family must understand that the client is attempting a very difficult task and needs their help, and that only with continued family support can weight loss be maintained. The necessary help should range from a pat on the back at the right time to minimizing food topics in conversation and not rewarding each other with high-calorie foods.

Results

Most behavior modification programs for weight control report a rate of loss of 0.5 to 1.5 pounds per week. Because of differences in behavioral package composition, differences in populations treated (college students versus the obese medical referrals), differences in the motivation of the individuals treated (clinically obese versus obese psychology students), differences in treatment milieu (outpatient clinic versus day hospital treatment), different lengths of time patients are followed after treatment (no follow-up to two years), and differing needs of the individuals leading weight control groups (clinical treatment programs versus research programs involved with factor analysis or program development), it is difficult to compare programs. The most systematic studies of the variables involved in weight loss and maintanance have been from Stunkard's group at the University of Pennsylvania [49, 88, 89, 94]. This group reports a combination of group therapy and behavioral treatment that results in very significant weight losses. More than 50 percent of their patients lost more than 20 pounds and 80 percent of those patients either maintained their lower weight or lost more weight during the following two years.

For the *Learning to Eat* program, patients were both self-referred and physician-referred. As a prerequisite for entering the program, they were requested to fill out a detailed seven-page eating disorder questionnaire [2] and to participate in two interviews. During the first interview the questionnaire previously returned by mail was reviewed with the client, and the program was explained in detail. At the end of the interview, clients were given a week's supply of food diaries, asked to fill one out every day for a week, and asked to decide if they would like to take part in a program that required this type of rather dull, repetitive task for 20 weeks. In the second interview the client and spouse were interviewed together, and the spouse's aid was enlisted in the capacity of a "student" to whom the client could teach the program after each weekly lesson. Individuals were excluded from the program if they were severely depressed, psychotic, unable to follow directions, or experiencing severe marital discord. Therapy was carried out in groups of 8 to 13 individuals over a 20-week period by psychiatry residents, who expressed an interest in learning to conduct weight control groups. In addition to their extensive background in dealing with patients, these group leaders were trained in behavioral weight control techniques by being co-therapists in at least one group with an experienced behavior therapist before beginning their own group. In addition, they were closely supervised while they were leading the groups.

Initially, 62 clients were included in seven behavioral weight control groups. Four groups had 10 weeks of instruction and one follow-up session 10 weeks after their final session; the other three groups had five weeks of instruction alternating with five weeks of maintenance or practice for a total of 20 weeks. Eighty percent of the participants were women, whose average age was 37.5 years, with a range of 17 to 64 years. Clients' beginning weights ranged from 140 to 358 pounds, with an average of 218.8 pounds. Ninety-three percent of clients lost some weight, and 40 percent lost more than 10 pounds during the 10 weeks of instruction. The range of weight change recorded at the tenth treatment session varied between a maximum loss of 32.5 pounds and a gain of 7.5 pounds. The average weight loss for all group members was 9.7 pounds. There was no statistically significant difference on any change measure between the male and female clients or between individuals with adult- or childhood-onset obesity. The dropout rate for the program was 13 percent, and each of these left the program for idiosyncratic reasons. Only 53 percent of the patients were seen at a short follow-up of one to two months following the tenth session. At that time their average weight loss was 10.7 pounds, indicating an additional loss of 1.2 pounds after finishing the program. A difference in therapeutic results was seen between groups led by different leaders and between leaders with varying degrees of experience in the weight control program.

Figure 12 shows individual cumulative weight changes for one weight control group. The variability in outcome is typical of behavioral weight control programs. Although there are no predictors of who will be a successful client in this type of program, those who fail to respond to treatment by the fourth week continue to do poorly for the remainder of the program. On further investigation, many of these clients admit that they do not follow the instructions or that they use only the techniques they feel are most valuable or least onerous. The data in Figure 12 demonstrate several other apparent predictors of failure. Patient A was in the midst of a difficult marital situation when the group began, Patient B was a successful businessman who could not attend many of the group sessions, and Patient C had her weight loss interrupted by a five-week trip to Japan. The maintenance period for this group included Thanksgiving, Christmas, and New Year's Day. Despite some weight gain, many patients indicated amazement at their relative success in maintenance during these periods of traditional feasting.

To test the efficacy of a written program in the hands of nonbehavioral therapists, *Learning To Eat* was given to 19 dieticians who had no prior experience in behavior modification in the context of a college extension course for nutritionists. After two introductory lectures explaining the demography, sociology, and psychology of obesity, five class sessions were used to present material from the written program, both didactically in lectures and experientially by role-playing weight control group situations. At the beginning of the course, each dietician was asked to join with one or two of her class members and lead a behavioral weight control group based on the text. Clients were recruited from friends, fellow workers, and, in a few cases, clinical referrals. For most groups, only a small fee was charged, most of which was returned as a contingent refund for completing homework assignments.

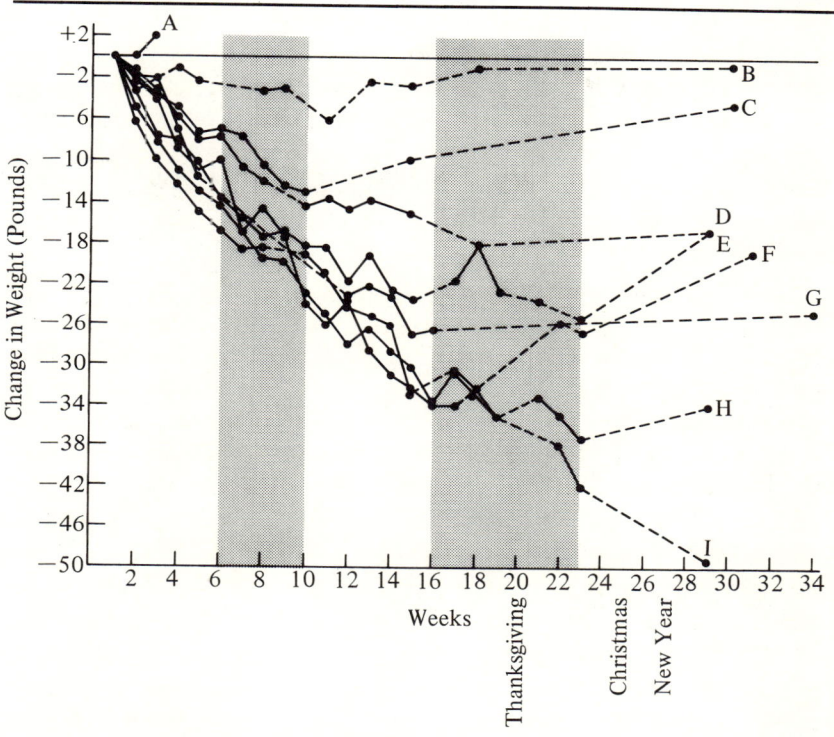

Figure 12. *Individual cumulative weight change for a behavioral weight group. The shaded areas represent periods of maintenance or practice. The solid lines represent periods of interrupted attendance.*

Figure 13 compares outcome data from the group led by the dieticians with those from groups led by psychiatric residents, who were somewhat more intensively trained in behavior modification techniques. As can be seen, the behavioral package appears to be successful when administered by dieticians with only brief classroom training in behavioral techniques. Figure 14 shows the comparative dropout rate for the two groups, which may bias the outcome results. The higher dropout rate for the dieticians may indicate a difference in client motivation between a clinical weight control program, where clients pay a significant fee for service, and a program for peers and fellow workers, where the clients do not pay a

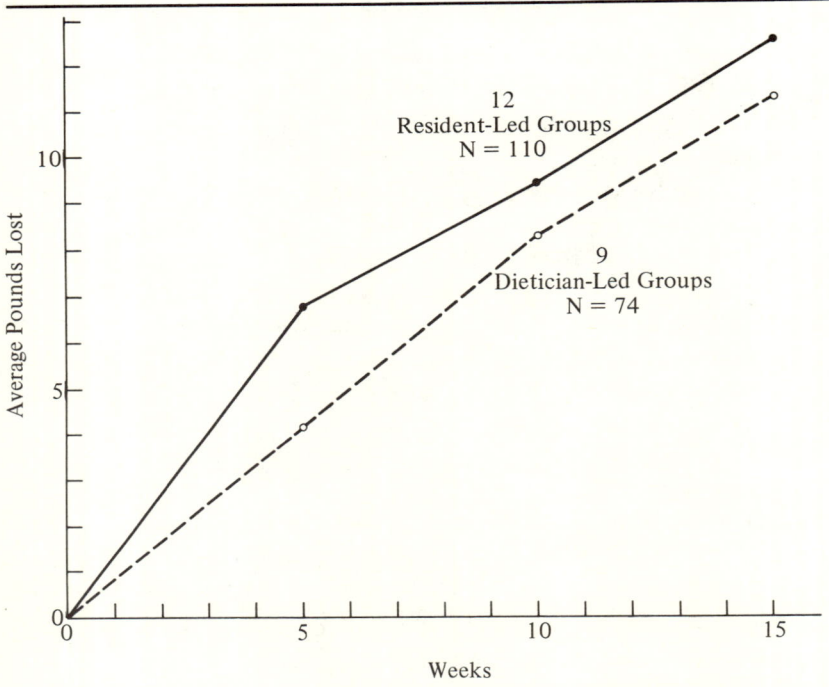

Figure 13. *Twenty-one behavioral weight control groups were taught the program in* Learning to Eat. *The first five weeks were classroom presentations, the second five weeks were a practice or maintenance training period, and the third five weeks were additional instruction. The solid line represents 12 resident-led groups, with a total of 110 clients; the broken line represents nine dietician-led groups, with a total of 74 clients.*

significant fee.

Although data from Levitz and Stunkard's [56] study of TOPS (Take Off Pounds) programs indicated a need for a fairly sophisticated behavior therapist to conduct a successful behavioral weight control program, there is some indication from our data that this need may not be as great as was formerly thought. Early experimental work from Hagen [41] indicated that bibliotherapy alone may be a successful approach to helping the obese. Despite a failure to replicate this study [27], there is clear evidence that the written word is effective, and additional research is needed to

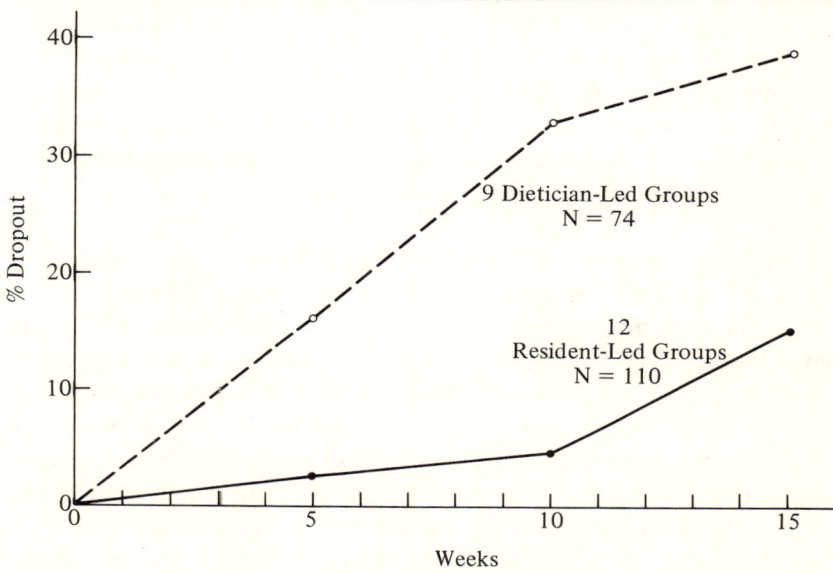

Figure 14. *The solid line represents the percentage of clients who did not remain in treatment in the psychiatric resident-led groups at Weeks 5, 10, and 15. The broken line represents the same data for the dietician-led groups.*

see to what degree dissemination of this type of material can be carried out without loss of therapeutic effectiveness.

The weight programs described in this section are "shotgun" attempts to deal with the problem of obesity. It must be remembered, however, that overweight individuals may not differ from their thin counterparts in any significant eating behaviors, that the behavioral changes claimed to result from behavioral intervention in this type of program may not actually occur, and that the behavior changes taught to individuals in weight control programs may not normalize their behavior—it may, rather, "abnormalize" their eating behaviors in a way that results in decreased caloric intake [1, 48, 59, 60]. Finally, obesity may have many nonlearned elements, for example, number of fat cells, genetically determined somatotype, ultradian rhythms, and hypothalamic hormones that cannot be changed by behavior modification techniques. Despite these theoretic flaws, the treatment appears to work modestly well and appears to be transmissible between therapists in the form of a written text. It remains for future research to show which of the specific treatment elements in what combination are most effective, to develop new parts for the therapeutic programs, and to decide what minimal levels of training are needed for individuals to administer the programs successfully.

A Complex Social Behavior Change Program: Assertiveness Training

Treatment packages for obesity concentrate largely on change of habit. The molecular behaviors include the way food is stored, the way food is put in the mouth, the way an individual exercises, and the use of discrete information feedback. By comparison, the field of assertiveness training is a quantum increase in complexity. Research has come from two directions—the enhancement of interpersonal and social behaviors in chronic mental health clinic populations—for example, improving eye contact, verbal interchange frequency, and other elementary social behaviors—and the development of techniques for use with college students, executives, and psychotherapists who are interested in aspects of "assertiveness," such as making direct statements, conquering anticipatory anxiety in social situations, and being more effective socially. Although programs differ in content and are advertised with titles that range from Personal Effectiveness to Self-Actualization, they share many common elements. This wide range of programmatic emphasis makes it somewhat difficult to interpret research data and to implement the behavioral packages.

In contemporary America, a large percentage of the population have only two modes of responding to stressful or frustrating social interactions: aggression or submission. Among the psychiatric population this percentage is increased, and a relative lack of alternative coping styles is often labeled pathologic. As much as 75 percent of the general psychiatric population appear to suffer from nonassertiveness [12, 24]. A lack of assertiveness, or inability to respond to social or stressful situations with other than aggressive or submissive behavior, is especially prominent in individuals classified as passive-aggressive or passive-dependent, those displaying inadequate or borderline personality disorders, the chronically dependent "mentally ill," and other individuals whose societal role is one of dependency.

Nonassertive behavior is one of the underpinnings of our Judeo-Christian ethic [79]. For example, the evangelist Matthew (5: 28) teaches us to "turn the other cheek" whenever we are attacked. As children we are selectively reinforced for being seen and not heard, for not talking back, and for being quiet in the classroom. As we approach adulthood we learn that institutions such as the armed services, large factories, and corporations tend to dispense reinforcement selectively to those who "do not make waves." Bandura [10] has suggested of the nonassertive: "Because of their behavioral deficits [they] may . . . receive insufficient reward to sustain what skills they already have, and are also periodically subjected to . . . punishment, rejection, ridicule and loss of income and other types of social and material rewards. This demoralized condition is frequently reflected in low levels of responsiveness, apathetic weak performances or generalized behavioral impoverishment."

The social learning interpretation of nonassertive or dependent behavior patterns leads to two alternative formulations to explain the development of these behavior patterns. The first type is primary inadequacy, caused by failure to learn appropriate interpersonal skills of an assertive nature in early life. These individuals have been selectively reinforced for nonassertive or aggressive responses during their early childhood and adolescence, with minimal parental or peer reinforcement or attention for appropriate assertion. The second type of nonassertive individual is typified by an institutionalized psychiatric patient, who has been selectively rewarded for passive behavior, being quiet, and being a good patient, with resulting extinction of normal interpersonal behaviors. Alberti and Emmons [3] differentiate between situational and general nonassertiveness and use this differentiation to explain why a few patients are able to assert themselves in some social situations but not in others. These individuals apparently have discriminative social stimuli for assertive, aggressive, or nonassertive behaviors rather than a lack of ability to respond appropriately.

The formulation of nonassertiveness has important treatment implications. To the extent that nonassertiveness relates to a behavioral deficit as opposed to a global trait, such as passive or aggressive personality, the missing skills can be identified, observed, and counted, and, presumably, their frequency can be modified. If an individual responds to certain situations with anxiety or an inability to be appropriately assertive despite an adequate repertoire of skills, these situations (the discriminative stimuli) can be specified and a behavioral treatment program implemented to correct the situation.

Unfortunately, "assertiveness" is not a unidimensional skill, and the wide variety of operational criteria used in assertiveness training underscores this complexity [4, 17, 47, 52, 80]. Table 4 summarizes how assertiveness differs from passivity and aggressiveness. Although individuals prone to aggression may be more likely to meet their needs than their passive counterparts, they may experience high levels of anxiety and guilt and are often nonassertive in social situations. They may also be hampered by an inability to express feelings appropriately, and eventually those feelings take an inappropriate or violent form. The consequences of either a passive or aggressive interpersonal style are usually the same. The individual appears insecure, is often without friends and social intimates, lacks self-confidence, tends to attribute problems in life to others, and has few meaningful relationships in which his own self-worth is, or can be, enhanced.

Therapeutic Approaches

In 1949, Salter in his book *Conditioned Reflex Therapy: The Direct Approach to the Reconstruction of Personality* [76] described his approach to the nonassertive individual, in which he instructed his patients how they should act and insisted on behavioral performance in his direct style. Ellis [22], Meichenbaum [68], and Thoresen and Mahoney [91] each attempt to restructure the client's cognitive set toward assertiveness by systematically teaching the ability to self-instruct the desired behaviors. Moreno's [70] psychodrama involved direct role playing of affect-laden scenes where assertiveness was appropriate. More recently, structured role playing in group therapy formats has been used by a number of investigators and clinicians to teach interpersonal effectiveness [3, 16, 51, 56].

The currently used intervention strategies in assertiveness training vary, depending on the program and client population. The types of interventions include teaching (1) nonverbal assertion skills; for example, maintaining eye contact; (2) verbal cognitive assertion skills; for example, analyzing irrational, self-defeating thoughts and cognitive restructuring; (3) a consideration of personal rights; for example, "I can say 'No' "; (4) protective skills, or "counter-manipulation"; for example, learning to agree with someone who is attacking you until his attack behaviors are extinguished; (5) individualized or standard assertive rehearsal situations; for example,

Table 4. How assertiveness differs from passivity and aggressiveness on behavioral dimensions

Passive Person	Assertive Person	Aggressive Person
Has rights violated; is taken advantage of	Protects own rights and respects the rights of others	Violates rights; takes advantage of others
Does not achieve goals	Achieves goals without hurting others	May achieve goals at expense of others
Feels frustrated, unhappy, hurt, and anxious	Feels good about self; has appropriate confidence in self	Defensive, belligerent; humiliates and depreciates others
Inhibited and withdrawn	Socially and emotionally expressive	Explosive; unpredictably hostile and angry
Allows others to choose for him	Chooses for self	Intrudes on others' choices

Adapted by James Teigen from *Your Perfect Right* [3].
From Liberman, King, DeRisi, and McCann [57].

taking an item back to the store for exchange; and (6) client self-assessment techniques; for example, use of self-rating scales. While most programs address these issues, each emphasizes a different aspect.

The program at Oxnard Mental Health Center [57] was developed primarily for a Day Treatment Center client population and staff, and later for clients and staff from associated outpatient clinics. The investigators concerned focus on the nonverbal aspects of assertiveness training (personal effectiveness) to help clients develop a full range of assertive and social skills. Their noncognitive approach was strongly influenced by the nature of their clients, by the early work of Serber [78], and by the extensive research of Hersen, Eisler, and Miller [19–21, 43, 44] and of Hersen, Eisler, Miller, Johnson, and Pinkston [45]. Through the use of active modeling, behavior rehearsal, coaching, prompting, positive social reinforcement, and shaping, trainers develop clients' use of eye contact, hand and head gestures, posture, facial expression, and voice volume, tone, frequency, fluency, and modulation. Once these skills are established, the client is helped with speech content and verbal expression.

Lange and Jakubowski [52], on the other hand, have developed an assertiveness training program biased in favor of cognitive and verbal skills and oriented primarily toward college students, trained professionals, and those seeking personal growth. They provide a detailed training program to help clients develop an assertive belief system and restucture their nonassertive cognitions. For example, they stress that assertion enhances life and improves interpersonal relationships, and that every person has the right, if not the responsibility, to express honest thoughts, feelings, and beliefs; for example, to agree passively to go on a trip with someone when you do not want to go, you know you will regret your decision, and yet you do not demonstrate your regret, violates your personal rights and the rights of the other person, who will have to live with your decision and your resentment. This type of decision is challenged as irrational thinking and nonassertive behavior. Attempts to restructure clients' cognitive processes by teaching them to challenge their mistaken ideas and remind themselves of desired coping and problem-solving behaviors have been well described, but the efficacy of such approaches is rather weakly supported by research data [23, 55, 61, 68].

A related cognitive method that may enhance therapeutic expectancies is a programmatic declaration of "personal rights"—for example, "You have the right to judge your own behavior, thoughts, and emotions, and to take the responsibility for their initiation and consequences upon yourself" [3]; and "You have the right to offer no reasons or excuses for justifying your behavior" [81]. Lange, Rimm, and Loxley [53] suggest that developing a belief system about personal rights prior to, and quite apart from, skill training or anxiety reduction is a primary goal for assertiveness training. They explain that many nonassertive individuals incur undesirable consequences either by violating the rights of others—for example, aggression—or by violating their own rights—for example, neglecting to engage in honest self-expression.

Training in "protective skills" or "counter-manipulation" is a technique designed to help individuals avoid the feelings of anger, fear, or guilt during social interchange and cope more effectively with manipulative behaviors directed toward them [82]. Flowers and Booraem [29] separate these techniques into the categories of "offensive," "defensive," and "not recommended," and point out that although "counter-manipulation" may be effective in foiling others, it is itself very manipulative. In practice, these techniques may anger or alienate persons on whom they are used and may result in realization of the irrational feared consequences of assertiveness.

Packaged assertiveness programs differ in the degree to which the program is individualized or offered in a "shotgun" fashion. In the former, clients work only on specific goals in relation to personal problems. In the latter, treatment is not tailored to the individual, but a "package" of general skills is taught, which is presumed to be of help to a greater number of people. All programs make use of some "stock scenes" as standard group exercises, "canned" homework assignments, and basic skills, which are practiced by all members. Some emphasize specification of clients' target behaviors at the beginning of the program [16, 56], while others rely more on standard exercises [3, 50], in which everyone participates for at least the first few group sessions. Goldstein, Gershaw, and Sprafkin [39] use standard modeling tapes in all their assertiveness training sessions but attempt to provide individualization through the homework assignments.

For Whom Is Assertiveness Training Indicated?

Several authors have addressed the issue of assessment in assertion training [11, 15, 48], and many written inventories have been developed to assess an individual's need for assertion training or deficiencies in assertiveness.

Although few of the test instruments have been well quantified or well validated, the Wolpe-Lazarus Assertiveness Questionnaire [97] and Alberti-Emmons's Assertiveness Inventory [5] appear to be helpful in identifying assertive and unassertive individuals. The College Self-Expression Scale [35], the Lawrence Assertive Inventory [54], the Rathus Assertiveness Schedule [74], and the Conflict Resolution Inventory [63], are more thoroughly researched and quantified but they are targeted for college students rather than a clinical population. The Adult Self-Expression Scale [37] and the Assertion Inventory [36] were developed for noncollege adults but they lack normative data and studies of their validity [52]. To date, no questionnaire provides an analysis of the specific elements of nonassertiveness or supplies the clinician with an indication of a client's specific needs. A clinical interview to obtain a history from prospective assertion trainees and to follow up responses on any of the assertion inventory items that are positive is necessary if the therapist is to make a careful analysis of the client's presenting problems.

Group Assertiveness Training versus Individual Assertiveness Training
Most assertiveness training manuals advocate a group training format. There are, however, three major indications for individual treatment: when a group is not available, when an individual's anxiety is so high as to be incapacitating in a group setting, and when the individual's particular problem is so specific that a group format would not be an efficient approach [15]. In the main, group training provides many advantages over the individual client format: (1) multiple models for illustrating assertive responses; (2) increased sources of feedback about appropriate or inappropriate assertive behavior during training sessions; (3) increased opportunity for the client to interact with, or practice, assertive skills with an appropriate "target" individual; (4) ample sources of positive social reinforcement, support, and encouragement; (5) an opportunity for vicarious learning by watching others role-play or rehearse assertive behaviors; and (6) an opportunity to serve not only as client but as coach, a process that may facilitate learning assertive behaviors [30, 31].

Groups usually consist of 6 to 12 individuals, and the optimum number is eight. Assertiveness training programs generally include 16 to 20 hours of instruction, with no single session longer than two hours and rarely more than two sessions per week. Clients are generally grouped according to the similarity and degree of their behavioral disturbance, but groups are heterogeneous with respect to age, social class, sex, and type of assertion problems. All the packaged programs recommend at least two instructors per group, preferably of opposite sexes for mixed-sex groups.

The Use of Information and Instruction

All assertiveness training programs emphasize the educational nature of their approach to clients. For example, many programs provide a variety of client introduction sheets, training notebooks, skill cards, and data collection sheets [16, 38, 57]. Lange and Jakubowski [52] emphasize "mini-lectures" on a variety of appropriate topics at the beginning of each session, and many programs recommend that clients read assertiveness books as homework, while some ask their clients to participate by reporting to the group on what they have read.

Behavior Change Techniques

Although assertiveness training programs are composed of a large number of complex behavioral (and cognitive) techniques and procedures, there is a fair degree of consistency in their application. At least eight basic procedures are common to most programs.

SPECIFYING THE TARGET BEHAVIOR. The client is helped to identify a specific "behavior" to be changed, for example, eye contact, saying "No," and so on. Often, this includes "setting the stage or scene" for practicing a more assertive behavior; for example, making eye contact with an interviewer when seeking a job, or saying "No" to someone who persists in asking for a donation at the front door.

THERAPEUTIC INSTRUCTION. Therapeutic instruction is employed throughout assertiveness training. Typically explicit instructions are given to the client or training group; for example, what to change, or how to change a particular response. Instruction often precedes and follows role modeling. When instruction is given during behavioral rehearsal it is referred to as *coaching*.

MODELING. An assertive pattern of behavior is often modeled for the client. The trainer, a co-participant, or an audiotaped [39] or videotaped [40] interaction or film [47] may be used for modeling.

BEHAVIOR REHEARSAL. The client is asked to role-play the target behavior(s) in a situation that simulates his social environment. Usually, the trainer or other group members play "significant others" in the scene. Rehearsal usually continues until the client shows little or no anxiety while carrying out the behavioral sequence, or in some cases until he has overlearned the response. Several behavior change techniques are included in this rather complex procedure—namely, instruction, overt and covert modeling, immediate feedback, positive reinforcement, shaping, overt and covert rehearsal, role reversal, coaching, prompting, and desensitization to imagined consequences.

FEEDBACK AND REINFORCEMENT. Postperformance feedback to the client is a standard part of training programs. Usually, this information is either positive social reinforcement—for example, "That was great the way you maintained eye contact"—or constructive criticism—for example, "It might help if you raise your voice volume just a little"—or a combination of the two—for example, "John, your facial expression was really much improved that time, in fact very good, but let's try it again using a little more expression with your hands, ok?" Feedback may be given verbally and nonverbally during rehearsal, using *prompting*, or immediately after the client's performance. Most trainers emphasize that feedback from trainers and group members should be positive. Similar feedback and reinforcement are used to assess homework assignments.

TRANSFER TRAINING. Goldstein, Gershaw, and Hunter [39] use the term "transfer training" to describe an active process for aiding the generalization of new behaviors to the client's natural environment. To facilitate generalization, the training experience simulates the client's real-life problems as closely as possible, and the client is instructed to behave assertively in his natural environment in ways that have a high probability of being reinforced. To accomplish this, homework assignments are often given in an increasingly difficult sequence; for example, the client might proceed from being asked to say "Good morning" to initiate a conversation with a stranger, to a more individualized assignment: "Tell your mother to stop giving you advice." The more difficult assignments are given only after the client has rehearsed the situation with little or no reported anxiety in the training situation, and when he is satisfied he will be able to carry it out successfully.

DATA COLLECTION. Clients are encouraged in some programs and required in others to keep a notebook or fill in data sheets that describe their daily social interactions. They may also be required to do interpersonal homework assignments. Data collection is useful for pinpointing situations in which clients are assertive or nonassertive and in facilitating transfer training.

SHAPING. Reinforcement of successive approximations to successful performance is used throughout most assertiveness training programs. At the beginning of a typical program, a client is reinforced for gradual improvements in interpersonal skills. Toward the end of the program reinforcement is dispensed for completed assertive behaviors. Hierarchic shaping patterns of behavior rehearsal can be used for complex behaviors (for example, "Practice eye contact," "Now practice eye contact and voice volume"); for introducing difficult target behaviors in a group setting; for arriving at increasingly difficult homework assignments; and for approaching situations and behaviors that are very anxiety-provoking or that require many social skills.

OTHER TECHNIQUES. Each program emphasizes a few "special" procedures. Cotler and Guerra [16] and Liberman, King, DeRisi, and McCann [57] actively help their clients to develop new behaviors by using *doubling* (trainer crouches next to trainee and momentarily takes over the role of the client in the scene), verbal and nonverbal *prompts* (brief interruptions by the coach to provide explicit instructions about what to say or do), and positive *ongoing feedback* (brief interruptions in the rehearsal to provide social praise, support, and a pat on the back). Cotler and Guerra [16] also teach their clients how to use the SUDS (Subjective Units of Discomfort Scale) technique for monitoring their anxiety level, and several programs provide *relaxation training* to help control anxiety. Lange and Jakubowski's program [52] outlines a *cognitive restructuring* technique for clients and recommends a number of exercises to help analyze and challenge irrational thoughts, to recognize faulty internal dialogues, to develop cognitive coping skills, and to develop self-assessment skills by self-questioning in problematic interpersonal situations. Prior to a modeling sequence and before in vivo behavior rehearsal, Alberti and Emmons [3] and Cotler and Guerra [16] use *covert rehearsal*, in which the client is asked to rehearse in fantasy how he would use the components of assertive behavior in a real-life situation. He is asked to report his SUDS level during the covert rehearsal as feedback for the trainers. Goldstein, Gershaw, and Sprafkin [39] use 60 prerecorded *audiotapes* as skill-training stimuli and assertion models. The tapes range from illustrations of "basic skills"—for example, starting a conversation, responding to praise—through "application skills" —for example, managing money, job seeking. After listening to the tapes, clients role-play the scenes they have listened to on tape. Since the clients play various roles while others are practicing their skills, experience in assertion-related behavior is provided by the experience. Only one experimental program reports extensive use of *videotaped* models of assertiveness skills [40].

A Therapeutic Package
The packaged programs range in complexity from Alberti and Emmons' basic primer guidebook [3] to comprehensive trainer handbooks complete with component-training programs [38, 57], although all lack outcome data or independent replication. The format for an assertiveness training "therapeutic package" is best seen in the program developed by Liberman, King, DeRisi, and McCann [57] for use in a day treatment center or an outpatient population. Their program, *Personal Effectiveness Training*, is offered as a complete four-component program for developing assertiveness and social skills. The components include the *Personal Effectiveness Basic Manual*, the brief *Client's Introduction* brochure, *Demonstration Film*, and *Program Guide*. The program guide is used in conjunction with the film and the basic manual to facilitate workshops of one to three days' duration. Sections in the guide parallel activities that are assigned in the basic manual and demonstrated on the film. A variety of instructions and thought-provoking questions are provided, which help the training group leader familiarize the counselor-trainees with the program. Personal-effectiveness training groups consist of 4 to 15 clients with two leaders. Except for a similar level of functional impairment—for example, outpatient populations versus day treatment center populations—the groups are heter-

ogeneous. The groups may be closed and time-limited or open, with new members and graduates reentering the group periodically.

The basic manual has five major sections:

1. *Information:*
   An explanation of what personal effectiveness is, for whom such training is intended, the role of the leader, and the basic training steps and procedures is given to the group. The training steps are: *identifying* problems in communicating or expressing feeling (the client is helped to specify the "where, when, how, what, and with whom" of the problem situation); *targeting* training goals, usually by developing new behaviors; *simulating* problem situations, using group members to role play or rehearse relevant scenes; *modifying* clients' expressive behavior by instruction, behavioral rehearsal, modeling, inserting and fading prompts, shaping, and so on; *providing feedback* from the group to the individual on his improved performance; and *assigning homework* to help transfer the behaviors rehearsed during role playing to real-life situations.
2. *Planning:*
   The entire assertiveness training group is involved in the planning phase, which lasts for the first 20 minutes of each session. Clients' homework is reviewed and reinforced, and a new "scene" or practice goal for that session is defined.
3. *Training:*
   In the training phase, most of the active behavioral procedures discussed earlier are used to develop new behaviors for clients. Initially, emphasis is placed on nonverbal expression, and only after these have been acquired are content skills developed—for example, conversation, protective skills, and making and refusing requests. At the end of each training session, clients are given a homework assignment that is standard or personalized to fit their needs. The basic manual includes many how-to-do-it exercises, questions, and illustrations.
4. *Evaluation:*
   The staff, and on occasion clients, review the immediately preceding training sessions. Feedback is given to one another, as are recommendations for improvement of staff or client performance.
5. *References:*
   This section contains an annotated bibliography of the assertiveness training literature.

Maintenance of Assertive Behaviors

Little attention has been paid to maintenance of assertive behaviors. Although trainers hope newly developed assertive behaviors will be maintained and reinforced by their positive consequences, they offer only a few suggestions to increase the probability of successful maintenance. These include sensitizing clients to the need to develop outside environmental supports for their new styles of interaction, and inviting assertive training graduates to return to new or ongoing groups for periodic "booster sessions," in order to share their experiences in previous training experiences with others and to sharpen their skills.

Outcome

With the proliferation of guides, manuals, training programs, and do-it-yourself books on assertiveness training, empiric validation of these therapies would seem important. Reviews of the available outcome data present a mixed, but optimistic, appraisal of the field. Assertiveness training with its specified procedures, paper-and-pencil tests for dependent variables, and a presumably observable outcome should be particularly amenable to empiric study [30]. However, as Hersen, Eisler, and Miller [43] point out: "Systematic research on the effects of assertive training has been difficult to conduct for several reasons. First, a diversity of treatment techniques has been used. Second, it is difficult to determine the specific behavior involved in 'being assertive' within various interpersonal settings. Third, it is difficult to find laboratory or analogue measures of assertive behavior that approximate real life situations."

Although there is considerable clinical and analogue evidence of an empiric nature suggesting that the procedures of modeling, behavioral rehearsal, social reinforcement, and therapeutic instruction are effective behavior change techniques, the area most vital to the client and most devoid of research is generalization of results outside the training or treatment setting. Although McFall and his colleagues [64–66] conducted a short-term experimental assertiveness program for college students and found there was generalization of skills to the natural environment, there are no published analogous findings for clinical populations, and no similar data are available for the published assertiveness packages. King, Liberman, and Roberts [51] conducted an outcome study of the Oxnard program with a clinical population of 30 clients from a psychiatric day treatment center.

They attended twice-weekly sessions for personal effectiveness training for four weeks. After role-playing scenes in the clinic, clients were told to repeat the scenes in "real life" as homework assignments. The outcome measures were (1) the number of homework assignments (out of 50) that clients *reported* having completed, and (2) the number of 50 subsequent homework assignments clients were *observed* to complete. Half the patients who carried out some of the first set of 50 assignments participated in the second 50 assignments. Patients reported completing 39 of 50, or 78 percent, of the first set of assignments, and they were observed to complete 40 of 50, or 80 percent, of the second set of assignments. While there are methodologic limitations to this study—for example, reliability of self-report for the first 50 assignments, and reactivity to accompanying observers during the second set, a lack of control groups for practice or training effects in both parts of the experiment, and lack of specified performance criteria for completing an assignment "effectively"—this study appears to support the hope for generalization of personal effectiveness training skills to clients' own environment.

Gutride, Goldstein, and Hunter [40] conducted two studies investigating the effect of their "structured learning therapy" (SLT) on two patterns of social interaction. Their first study used a $2 \times 2 \times 2$ design to assign 87 acute and chronic psychiatric inpatients to assertiveness training or no treatment. About half the patients also engaged in standard psychotherapy, and, as a control, about half did not. The structured learning therapy was administered by two trained undergraduates three times per week for four weeks. Videotaped models demonstrating social interactions (for example, initiating a conversation) were played for the patients, who then role-played the situation and were socially reinforced for their performance. The post-training dependent measures included observation of standardized and naturalistic social interactions. Results indicated that structured learning therapy, and not psychotherapy, yielded significant effects on four of seven social interaction measures in standard assessment situations—for example, smiling, responses to conversation, and so on—but no effect when naturalistic observation during mealtimes was used as a measure. Interaction effects were complicated but suggested a "mutual inhibition" of treatment effectiveness between assertive training and psychotherapy.

As a sequel to the first study, 106 psychiatric inpatients were assigned to one of five groups: (1) structured learning therapy (five weeks) and two week's training in the generalization setting (meal hall); (2) SLT (five weeks) and two additional weeks of SLT to control for the amount of training; (3) only five weeks of SLT; (4) companionship, attention-placebo control; and (5) no-treatment control. Modeling videotapes demonstrating ideal social behaviors at mealtime were presented to the three SLT groups. During standard (laboratory-observed role playing) and naturalistic observation periods (verbal and nonverbal social skills at mealtime), the three structured learning therapy groups did better than the control groups in interaction measures but were not significantly different from one another. The authors concluded that their therapy was effective and showed evidence of generalization. It is important to note that an important technique included in these two studies is not widely used in assertiveness training programs and is not available in marketed package programs: *videotaped modeling* stimuli and *videotape feedback*.

Programmatic Use of Packaged Behavior Therapies
With the development of therapeutic packages for behavioral change, a new format for "therapy" becomes possible. If an individual's problems can be defined in terms of a series of discrete behaviors, for which well-developed behavior change procedures are available, then services can be provided within an educational framework rather than a therapy framework. Thus, the Adult Development Program at the University of Washington, Seattle, has offered a series of behavior change classes for about six years. The goals of this program are to "foster clients' independence and provide them with maximal control over their lives" by providing a "school for behavioral change in a classroom format" [8]. The program proposes to help clients make any changes they desire. However, the only strategies offered are those that allow clients to be the direct change agent. Skills are taught directly, as either new ideas or new behaviors. Individuals are excluded from the program only if they are very disorganized, uncooperative, or suffering from organic brain disorders. All treatment is voluntary and without coercion from outside sources. Clients, or more properly students, determine their own goals and enter into a time-limited course of instruction. A brochure that includes a detailed description of each of the courses offered and a time schedule of classes is available. "Therapists" are introduced as teachers rather than as doctors, nurses, or social workers, and the student is instructed to consider the faculty as a

resource in the same way a student on a campus would be expected to use the instructors to enhance growth.

In an initial interview, students describe their problems and are helped to define them in terms of specific goals. If students cannot do this, then the first experience in the Adult Development Program is a "self-assessment class," where they learn how to define personal goals. Once the problems are defined and goals are set, students take a course or a "pathway" of several courses designed to help solve their problem. Each of the courses is a "packaged therapy" that makes use of teaching materials, planned laboratory experiences, and extensive homework assignments. Students leave the program when a course or pathway is finished. They may return for more course work but are requested to stay out of the program for at least four months between classes. The overall program was designed to offer a variety of services to a variety of persons. The curriculum for 1976 demonstrates the breadth of the program and is a model for the service that can be offered in this format.

Individual Courses

AGING AND RETIREMENT READINESS. Learn how to greet life with gusto in later years.

ASSERTIVENESS LABORATORY. Beginning, Intermediate, and Advanced: Choose new, more assertive behaviors and act them out over an extended period of time.

BEHAVIORAL REHEARSAL LABORATORY. Act out and practice new behaviors to help yourself be more at ease and feel more natural in social, business, and family situations.

CHANGING FOOD HABITS. Learn how to design a long-term eating plan for weight loss, gain, or staying the same that is tailored to your physical needs and life-style.

COMMUNICATION BETWEEN COUPLES. Learn how to disagree and negotiate with your partner without making each other feel miserable.

CRISIS INTERVENTION WORKSHOP. Learn how to cope with situations and feelings that you now believe are impossible to handle.

EFFECTIVE COMMUNICATION. Become aware of your communication style, and develop more effective and satisfying methods of interacting with others.

EFFECTIVE PARENTING. Learn the skills parents and children need to enjoy living together.

FIXED ROLE. Play a character role for an entire month to show yourself that you can change your behavior, make the change stick, and change the behavior of the people with whom you come into contact.

HUMAN RELATIONSHIPS LABORATORY. Understand your reactions to people and events by examining the sources of your feelings.

HUMAN SEXUALITY SEMINAR. Increase your knowledge of sexual behavior and learn how to be comfortable talking about sex.

HUMAN TERRITORIALITY SEMINAR. Learn that everyone has a need to control the major aspects of his life. Improve your bargaining skills, learn to resolve conflicts satisfactorily, and increase your self-confidence and enjoyment when you interact with other people.

INDIVIDUAL STUDY. Students have used Individual Study for work on a variety of projects, including overcoming insomnia; being more effective as a parent or spouse; mastering fears of snakes, elevators, or airplanes; and reducing the frequency of bothersome worries.

JOB INTERVIEW SKILLS. Become skillful at job interviews by learning and practicing how to make a good impression.

LEARNING TO BE MORTAL. Confront your own death and learn to live.

PERSONAL MANAGEMENT. Learn how to manage your time and activities to get better results.

PERSONAL MYTHS. Learn how to uncover and examine your self-image and how to change the way you act by changing the way you think and feel about yourself.

RELAXATION TRAINING. Learn how to relax.

SELF-ASSESSMENT. An introduction to the ADP and the techniques it teaches; an opportunity to define personal problems, to set goals, and to decide which of the ADP resources would be most helpful in reaching those goals.

SOCIAL GROWTH THROUGH DRAMA. Learn to use dramatic techniques to overcome self-consciousness so you can be outspoken, spontaneous and have fun.

TECHNIQUES OF MOOD AND BEHAVIOR CHANGE. A do-it-yourself kit of practical methods to alter and manage behavior.

SPECIAL SERVICES. This includes the art laboratory workshop; coffee shop, which is manned by volunteers; and crafts group.

Pathway Programs

MARITAL ENHANCEMENT PATHWAY. Remodel your marriage—the better to enjoy each other. The six classes in this pathway are: (1) Human Territoriality: Practical sessions in bargaining to resolve areas of conflict. (2) Assertiveness Training: Learn to recognize nonproductive fighting techniques, and learn one or more alternative methods of communication. (3) Precision Behavior Change: Partners learn specific techniques that they can apply in a mutually agreed upon fashion to bring about changes in each other and themselves. (4) Marital Myths: Learn to identify those ideas that you hold about yourself and your relationship that obstruct any possibility for change, and develop techniques for change. (5) Fixed Role: Couples act out the roles they design for themselves in Marital Myths Class to observe the potential for changing their marital relationship by altering personal behavior patterns. (6) Sensuality and Sexuality: Enhancing your ability to enjoy sexual relations in marriage.

OBESITY PATHWAY. A series of courses designed for the person who is seriously concerned about being obese. This pathway includes the following courses: (1) Changing Food Habits: Learn to design a long-term eating plan for weight loss, weight gain, or staying the same that is tailored to your physical needs and life-style. (2) Exercise Class: Learn how to develop a daily exercise routine. (3) Obesity Rap Group: Receive and offer support by sharing your ideas, problems, and goals with other pathway students. (4) Behavioral Aspects of Obesity: Master the eating habits that help you lose weight, keep it off, and help you resist growing fat again.

During the first five years experience with this program, Bakker and Armstrong [8, 9] feel they are providing a service to a population that might otherwise have been untreated. These are the less than wealthy, less than insight-oriented, less than educated population that normally would not be served by the psychiatric community. Several advantages over traditional therapies have emerged from this program. (1) Role differentiation allows staff members to subspecialize and master specific types of therapeutic intervention. This permits an efficient use of staff time, and maximum cross-consultation. (2) Neither an M.D. nor a Ph.D. degree is essential to be an effective mental health counselor in this system. (3) By avoiding diagnosis, and labeling the process of change as "education," some of the stigma of mental illness is avoided. (4) There are no criteria for cure in this system. Staff goals as well as patient goals are limited to attainable, demonstrable behavioral change. (5) Having clients select their own goals often increases motivation, as contrasted with prescribed psychotherapeutic programs. (6) The multiple-class structure allows a wide variety of learning experiences to be offered to individuals and allows the therapist/teacher/system to respond to the patient's variety of needs. (7) The modular format facilitates development of treatment and program packages and dissemination to mental health care professionals and other health-supporting professions.

Although the anecdotal report of success for the first 1500 patients passing through this program is encouraging, it will be several years before "hard" data are available and before an analysis of the impact upon patients, the general population of the area served, the health providers, and the mental health care delivery system in general can be completed.

Overview

The development of therapeutic packages for specific problems of living is a logical development in the field of behavior therapy. Procedures whose efficacy has been demonstrated, often in single-case controlled experiments, are assembled in a logical sequence so that they can be applied by therapists of widely varying backgrounds. The efficacy of such therapeutic programs must then be tested, first for replicability of effect in the hands of other therapists, and then to demonstrate greater effect than no treatment or greater effect than the standard therapeutic approach to such problems. For the three packages described, the effects of some of the elements have been separately tested, and replicability, in the hands of other therapists, has been ascertained. Controlled-outcome studies, however, have not been carried out. Other therapeutic packages exist—for example, relaxation training (see Chapter 6), or the Achievement Place model for the residential treatment of delinquents (see Chapter 4), and more will undoubtedly be developed.

This relatively new development may ultimately decrease the amount of training needed to produce effective counselors, and may facilitate the development of more uniformly effective mental health programs. Thus, the "therapist" of the future could provide a detailed behavioral evaluation and diagnosis and prescribe specific corrective therapeutic programs to ease an individual's pain or enhance the enjoyment of life. Through the use of therapeutic packaging, a cost-effective mental health care system with discrete, proved subparts could be developed.

For this type of educational therapy to be effective, additional assumptions must be met. The diagnosis must be adequate and appropriate; the therapeutic package or assemblage of subpackages must be sufficiently specific to be therapeutically effective, yet not so specific as to preclude its use for more than one individual. It must be a well-tested program, with demonstrated effectiveness in the hands of many therapists remote from the developer of the program. The therapist involved in the administration of the program must maintain sufficient flexibility and awareness of the client's condition to be able to modify the program if it is not successful, to question the initial diagnostic assumptions, and, if necessary, to abandon the therapeutic plan and construct a new one.

The potential use of package therapy is great. It opens the possibility of widespread dissemination of effective therapeutic materials, lessens the need for highly trained specialists to administer the materials, provides clear-cut outcome criteria for progress within a therapeutic program, and provides a true self-development potential for many individuals [91]. It provides tools for change.

References
1. Adams, N. The eating behavior of obese and nonobese women. Master's thesis, Stanford University, 1976.
2. Agras, W., Ferguson, J., Greaves, C., Qualls, B., Rand, C., Ruby, J., Stunkard, A., Taylor, C., Werne, J., and Wright, C. A clinical and research questionnaire for obese patients. In B. J. Williams, S. Martin, and J. P. Foreyt (Eds.), *Obesity: Behavioral Approaches to Dietary Management.* New York: Brunner-Mazel, Inc., 1976.
3. Alberti, R. E., and Emmons, M. L. *Your Perfect Right: A Guide to Assertive Behavior* (Second Edition). San Luis Obispo, Calif.: Impact Press, 1974.
4. *Ibid.*, p. 2.
5. *Ibid.*, p. 117.
6. Azrin, N. H., and Foxx, R. M. A rapid method of toilet training and the institutionalized retarded. *Journal of Applied Behavior Analysis* 4:89, 1973.
7. Azrin, N. H., and Foxx, R. M. *Toilet Training in Less Than a Day.* New York: Simon and Schuster, 1974.
8. Bakker, C. B., and Armstrong, H. E. An educational approach to the delivery of mental health services. Unpublished manuscript, Adult Development Program, University of Washington, Seattle, Washington, 1976.
9. Bakker, C. B., and Armstrong, H. E. The adult development program: Implementation of an educational approach to the delivery of mental health services. Unpublished manuscript, Adult Development Program, University of Washington, Seattle, Washington, 1976.
10. Bandura, A. A social learning interpretation of psychological dysfunctions. In P. London and D. Rosenhan (Eds.), *Foundations of Abnormal Psychology.* New York: Holt, Rinehart & Winston, 1968, p. 298.
11. Bodner, G. E. The role of assessment in assertion training. *The Counseling Psychologist* 5:90, 1975.
12. Brown, B. The multiple techniques of broad spectrum psychotherapy. In A. A. Lazarus (Ed.), *Clinical Behavior Therapy.* New York: Brunner-Mazel, 1972.
13. Butler, J. F. The toilet training success of parents after reading "Toilet Training in Less Than a Day." *Behavior Therapy* 7:185, 1976.
14. Charney, E., Goodman, H. C., McBride, M., Lyon, B., and Pratt, R. Childhood antecedents of adult obesity: Do chubby infants become obese adults? *New England Journal of Medicine* 295:6, 1976.
15. Cotler, S. B. Assertion training: A road leading where? *The Counseling Psychologist* 5:20, 1975.
16. Cotler, S. B., and Guerra, J. J. *Assertion Training: A Humanistic-Behavioral Guide to Self Dignity.* Champaign, Ill.: Research Press, 1976.

17. *Ibid.*, p. 3.
18. Department of Health, Education and Welfare. *Obesity and Health: A Source Book of Current Information for Professional Health Personnel.* Arlington, Va.: U.S. Public Health Service, 1966.
19. Eisler, R. M., Hersen, M., and Miller, P. M. Effects of modeling on components of assertive behavior. *Journal of Behavior Therapy and Experimental Psychiatry* 4:1, 1973.
20. Eisler, R. M., Miller, P. M., and Hersen, M. Components of assertive behavior. *Journal of Clinical Psychology* 29:295, 1973.
21. Eisler, R. M., Hersen, M., Miller, P. M., and Blanchard, E. B. Situational determinants of assertive behaviors. *Journal of Consulting and Clinical Psychology* 43:330, 1975.
22. Ellis, A. *Reason and Emotion in Psychotherapy.* New York: Lyle Stuart Press, 1962.
23. Ellis, A., and Harper, R. A. *A New Guide to Rational Living.* Englewood Cliffs, N.J.: Prentice-Hall, 1975.
24. Fensterheim, H. Assertive methods in marital problems. In B. Rubin, H. Fensterheim, and A. Henderson (Eds.), *Advances in Behavior Therapy.* New York: Academic Press, 1970.
25. Ferguson, J. A clinical program for the behavioral control of obesity. In B. J. Williams, S. Martin, and J. P. Foreyt (Eds.), *Obesity: Behavioral Approaches to Dietary Management.* New York: Brunner-Mazel, 1976.
26. Ferguson, J. *Learning to Eat: Behavior Modification for Weight Control* (Therapist and Student Manuals). Palo Alto, Calif.: Bull Publishing Co., 1975.
27. Fernan, W. The role of experimenter contact in behavioral bibliotherapy of obesity. Master's thesis, Pennsylvania State University, 1973.
28. Ferster, C. P. Nurnberger, J. I., and Levitt, E. B. The control of eating. *Journal of Mathematics* 1:87, 1962.
29. Flowers, J. V., and Booraem, C. D. Assertion training: The training of trainers. *The Counseling Psychologist* 5:29, 1975.
30. Flowers, J. V., Cooper, C. G., and Whiteley, J. M. Approaches to assertion training. *The Counseling Psychologist* 5:3, 1975.
31. Flowers, J. V., and Guerra, J. The use of client-coaching in assertion training with large groups. *Community Mental Health Journal* 10:414, 1974.
32. Fowler, R. S., Fordyce, W. E., Wade, V. D., and Masock, A. J. The mouthful diet: A behavioral approach to overeating. *Rehabilitation Psychology* 19:98, 1972.
33. Foxx, R. M., and Azrin, N. H. Dry pants: A rapid method of toilet-training children. *Behavior Research and Therapy* 11:435, 1973.
34. Foxx, R. M. and Azrin, N. H. *Toilet-Training the Retarded: A Rapid Program for Day and Night Time Independent Toileting.* Champaign, Ill.: Research Press, 1973.
35. Galassi, J. P., DeLo, J. S., Galassi, M. D., and Bastien, S. The college self-expression scale: A measure of assertiveness. *Behavior Therapy* 5:165, 1974.
36. Gambrill, E. D., and Richey, C. A. An assertion inventory for use in assessment and research. *Behavior Therapy* 6:550, 1975.
37. Gay, M. L., Hollandsworth, J. C., and Galassi, J. P. An assertiveness inventory for adults. *Journal of Counseling Psychology* 22:340, 1975.

38. Goldstein, A. P. *Structured Learning Therapy: Toward a Psychotherapy for the Poor*. New York: Academic Press, 1973, p. 69.
39. Goldstein, A. P., Gershaw, N. J., and Sprafkin, R. P. *Trainer's Manual for Structured Learning Therapy*. New York: Academic Press, 1974.
40. Gutride, M. E., Goldstein, A. P., and Hunter, G. F. The use of modeling and role playing to increase social interaction among asocial clinical patients. *Journal of Consulting and Clinical Psychology* 40:408, 1973.
41. Hagen, R. L. Group therapy versus bibliotherapy in weight reduction. *Behavior Therapy* 5:222, 1974.
42. Harris, M. B. Self-directed program for weight control: Pilot study. *Journal of Abnormal Psychology* 74:263, 1969.
43. Hersen, M., Eisler, R. M., and Miller, P. M. Development of assertive responses: Clinical, measurement, and research considerations. *Behavior Research and Therapy* 11:505, 1973.
44. Hersen, M., Eisler, R. M., and Miller, P. M. An experimental analysis of generalization in assertive training. *Behavior Research and Therapy* 12:295, 1974.
45. Hersen M., Eisler, R. M., Miller, P. M., Johnson, M. B., and Pinkston, S. G. Effects of practice, instructions, and modeling on components of assertive behavior. *Behavior Research and Therapy* 11:443, 1973.
46. Hindley, C. B., Follozat, A., Klackenberg, G., Nicolet-Meister, D., and Sand, E. A. Some differences in infant feeding and elimination training in five European longitudinal samples. *Journal of Child Psychology and Psychiatry* 6:179, 1965.
47. Jakubowski, P. A. Assertive behavior and clinical problems of women. In D. Carter and E. Rawlings (Eds.), *Psychotherapy for Women: Treatment toward Equality*. Springfield, Ill.: Charles Thomas. In press.
48. Jakubowski, P. A., and Lacks, P. B. Assessment procedures in assertion training. *The Counseling Psychologist* 5:84, 1975.
49. Jordan, H. A., and Levitz, L. S. A behavioral approach to the problem of obesity. *Obesity and Bariatric Medicine* 4:58, 1975.
50. Kimmel, H. D. Review of "Toilet Training in Less Than a Day: How to Do It," by Nathan H. Azrin and Richard M. Foxx. *Journal of Behavior Therapy and Experimental Psychiatry* 5:113, 1974.
51. King, L. W., Liberman, R. P., and Roberts, J. An evaluation of personal effectiveness training (assertion training): A behavioral group therapy. Unpublished manuscript, Oxnard Mental Health Center, Oxnard, Calif., 1975.
52. Lange, A. J., and Jakubowski, P. *Responsible Assertive Behavior: Cognitive/Behavioral Procedures for Trainers*. Champaign, Ill.: Research Press, 1976.
53. Lange, A. J., Rimm, D. C., and Loxley, J. Cognitive-behavioral assertion training procedures. *The Counseling Psychologist* 5:37, 1975.
54. Lawrence, E. S. The assessment and modification of assertive behavior. Ph.D. Dissertation, Arizona State University, 1970. *Dissertation Abstracts International* 31:396b, 1970. University Microfilms No. 70-11, 888.
55. Lazarus, A. A., and Fay, A. *I Can If I Want To*. New York: Morrow and Co., 1975.
56. Levitz, L. S., and Stunkard, A. J. A therapeutic coalition for obesity: Behavior modification and patient self-help. *American Journal of Psychiatry*

131:423, 1974.
57. Liberman, R. P., King, L. W., DeRisi, W. J., and McCann, M. *Personal Effectiveness: Guiding People to Assert Themselves and Improve Their Social Skills.* Champaign, Ill.: Research Press, 1976.
58. London, A. M., and Schreiber, E. D. A controlled study of the effects of group discussions and an anorexiant in outpatient treatment of obesity with attention to the psychological aspects of dieting. *Annals of Internal Medicine* 65:80, 1966.
59. Mahoney, M. J. The obese eating style: Bites, beliefs, and behavior modification. *Addictive Behaviors*, 1976. In press.
60. Mahoney, M. J. Fat fiction. *Behavior Therapy* 6:416, 1975.
61. Mahoney, M. J. *Cognition and Behavior Modification.* Cambridge, Mass.: Ballinger Publishing Co., 1974.
62. Mahoney, M. J., and Mahoney, K. *Permanent Weight Control: A Total Solution to the Dieter's Dilemma.* New York: W. W. Norton and Company, Inc., 1976.
63. Mayer, J. *Overweight: Causes, Cost, and Control.* Englewood Cliffs, N.J.: Prentice-Hall, 1968. Pp. 45–57.
64. McFall, R. M., and Lillesand, D. B. Behavioral rehearsal with modeling and coaching in assertion training. *Journal of Abnormal Psychology* 77:313, 1971.
65. McFall, R. M., and Marston, A. R. An experimental investigation of behavioral rehearsal in assertive training. *Journal of Abnormal Psychology* 76:295, 1970.
66. McFall, R. M., and Twentyman, C. T. Four experiments on the relative contributions of rehearsal, modeling, and coaching to assertion training. *Journal of Abnormal Psychology* 81:199, 1973.
67. McReynolds, W. T., and Paulson, B. K. Stimulus control as the behavioral basis of weight loss procedures. In B. J. Williams, S. Martin, and J. P. Foreyt (Eds.), *Obesity: Behavioral Approaches to Dietary Management.* New York: Brunner-Mazel, 1976.
68. Meichenbaum, D. H. Self-instructional methods (How to do it). In A. Goldstein and F. Kanfer (Eds.), *Helping People Change: Methods and Materials.* New York: Pergamon Press, 1975.
69. Meichenbaum, D. *Cognitive Behavior Modification.* Morristown, N.J.: University Programs Modular Studies, General Learning Corporation, 1974.
70. Moreno, Z. T. Psychodramatic rules, techniques, and adjunctive methods. *Group Psychotherapy* 18:73, 1965.
71. O'Leary, K. D., and Wilson, G. T. *Behavior Therapy: Application and Outcome.* Englewood Cliffs, N.J.: Prentice-Hall, Inc., 1975. Pp. 51–59.
72. Penick, S. B., Filion, R., Foxx, S., and Stunkard, A. J. Behavior modification in the treatment of obesity. *Psychosomatic Medicine* 33:49, 1971.
73. Penick, S. B., and Stunkard, A. J. The treatment of obesity. *Advances in Psychosomatic Medicine* 7:217, 1972.
74. Rathus, S. A. A 30-item schedule for assessing assertive behavior. *Behavior Therapy* 4:398, 1973.
75. Ravelli, G., Stein, Z. A., Susser, M. W. Obesity in young men after famine exposure in utero and early infancy. *New England Journal of Medicine* 295:

349, 1976.
76. Salter, A. *Conditioned Reflex Therapy: The Direct Approach to the Reconstruction of Personality*. New York: Capricorn Books, 1961.
77. Schacter, S. Some extraordinary facts about obese humans and rats. *American Psychologist* 26:129, 1971.
78. Serber, M. Teaching the nonverbal components of assertive training. *Journal of Behavior Therapy and Experimental Psychiatry* 3:1, 1972.
79. Shelton, J. L., and Ackerman, J. M. *Homework in Counseling and Psychotherapy*. Springfield, Ill.: Charles C. Thomas, 1974.
80. *Ibid.*, p. 22.
81. Sloane, R. B., Staples, F. R., Cristol, A. H., Yorkston, N. J., and Whipple, K. *Psychotherapy Versus Behavior Therapy*. Cambridge, Mass.: Harvard University Press, 1976.
82. Smith, M. J. *When I Say No, I Feel Guilty*. New York: Dial Press, 1975.
83. Spock, B. *Baby and Child Care*. New York: Hawthorne Books, Inc., 1968, p. 261.
84. *Ibid.*, p. 262.
85. Stuart, R. B. A three-dimensional program for the treatment of obesity. *Behavior Research and Therapy* 9:177, 1971.
86. Stuart, R. B. Behavioral control of overeating. *Behavior Research and Therapy* 5:357, 1967.
87. Stuart, R. B., and Davis, B. *Slim Chance in a Fat World: Behavioral Control of Obesity*. Champaign, Ill.: Research Press, 1972.
88. Stunkard, A. J. From explanation to action in psychosomatic medicine: The case of obesity. *Psychosomatic Medicine* 37:195, 1975.
89. Stunkard, A. J. New therapies for the eating disorders: Behavior modification of obesity and anorexia nervosa. *Archives of General Psychiatry* 26:391, 1972.
90. Stunkard, A. J., and McLaren-Hume, M. The results of treatment for obesity. *Archives of Internal Medicine* 103:79, 1959.
91. Thoresen, C. E., and Mahoney, M. J. *Behavioral Self-Control*. New York: Holt, Rinehart & Winston, 1974.
92. Thorn, G. W. Alterations in body weight. In E. Wintrobe (Ed.), *Harrison's Principles of Internal Medicine*. New York: McGraw-Hill, 1970.
93. Turner, D. *Handbook of Diet Therapy*. Chicago: University of Chicago Press, 1965. (See Chapter 8, "Modifications in Protein-Fat-Carbohydrate," prepared from the report of the Committee on Diabetic Diet Calculations, The American Dietetic Association, by Elizabeth K. Caso.)
94. Westlake, R. J., Levitz, L. S., and Stunkard, A. J. A day hospital program for treating obesity. *Hospital and Community Psychiatry* 25:609, 1974.
95. Wollersheim, J. P. The effectiveness of group therapy based upon learning principles in the treatment of overweight women. *Journal of Abnormal Psychology* 76:462, 1970.
96. Wooley, O. W., and Wooley, S. C. The experimental psychology of obesity. In T. Silverstone and J. Fincham (Eds.), *Obesity: Pathogenesis and Management*. Leonard, Lancaster, England: Medical and Technical Publishing Co., 1975.
97. Wolpe, J., and Lazarus, A. A. *Behavior Therapy Techniques*. New York: Pergamon Press, 1966.

Annotated Therapeutic Index

The following are behavior disorders that have been effectively managed with behavior therapy techniques. If more than one treatment has been found effective in dealing with a particular behavior disorder, the additional techniques have been listed. Page numbers refer to descriptions of a technique applied to the specific problem. Where there is no number, refer to the subject index (e.g., Systematic desensitization, Positive reinforcement) for a general discussion of the procedure. Cross-references apply to listings in the therapeutic index.

Agoraphobia
  Exposure by means of flooding or shaping, 8, 205
Alcoholism. *Note:* Interpersonal anxiety, family, and work problems also require attention
  Aversion therapy, 97
    Chemical aversion, 90, 97
    Covert sensitization (verbal aversion), 100
    Time-out, 101
Anorexia (in schizophrenic patients)
  Extinction, removal of attention for not eating, 52
Anorexia nervosa
  Shaping, reinforcement of eating behavior and feedback of improvement, usually combined with extinction for somatic complaints, 29
  Systematic desensitization, of anxiety themes associated with eating
Aphonia (hysterical)
  Aversion therapy, shock in an Avoidance paradigm
  Shaping, reinforcement of increasingly loud vocalization, 43
  Systematic desensitization, of anxiety themes associated with speaking
Assertive behavior (training in)
  Behavior rehearsal (role playing), includes feedback and shaping, often with modeling in a therapeutic package, 268
Astasia-abasia
  Shaping, of normal walking behavior, 48
Asthma
  Relaxation training, 103
  Systematic desensitization, with or without assertiveness training
Attention-seeking behaviors

Extinction, removal of social reinforcement for such behavior, 53, 55
Punishment, Time-out (with Positive reinforcement for appropriate behavior)

Autism (childhood)
Modeling, combined with positive reinforcement, 23
Shaping, of appropriate behavior
Shock, in avoidance training or punishment paradigm, combined with positive reinforcement, 114

Bedtime disturbances
Extinction, removal of social attention, 54

Blindness (hysterical)
Avoidance training or shaping using a light as signal to allow avoidance of shock or access to reinforcement, 48

Bowel retention
Operant conditioning, Shaping appropriate bowel behavior

Bruxism (teeth-gnashing)
Assertiveness training
Relaxation training

Cardiac arrythmia
Heart rate Biofeedback

Classroom behavior
Reinforcement and extinction, with or without a token economy, 48, 56, 78

Compulsive behavior
Flooding, exposure to fear-evoking stimuli in reality or in fantasy, with or without modeling, 220
Paradoxical intention, 192
Response prevention, prevention of the compulsive ritual, 218
Systematic desensitization, to anxiety themes maintaining the compulsive rituals

Deafness (hysterical)
Avoidance training, tone used as discriminative stimulus for avoidance response; that is, the patient can make use of sound to avoid a painful shock delivered 10 seconds after a tone

Delinquent behavior
- Aversion therapy, covert sensitization or shock (used most frequently with discrete behaviors, e.g., shoplifting), 119
- Token economy, or social reinforcement of academic, social, and work behaviors and punishment of inappropriate behavior by response cost or time-out, 75, 118

Delusions (in schizophrenia)
- Extinction, removal of social attention for delusional utterances, combined with positive reinforcement of appropriate speech content, 43, 52
- Reinforcement of nondelusional speech (often in a token economy), 43

Depression
- Extinction of depressive behaviors combined with reinforcement of prosocial, nondepressive behavior, 45

Disruptive behavior (in adults)
- Aversion therapy, time-out, shock, 118
- Extinction, 52

Disruptive behavior (in children)
- At home
  - Extinction, together with positive reinforcement of appropriate behavior, 50, 55
  - Punishment, for example, overcorrection response cost, time-out, slaps, combined with positive reinforcement of appropriate behavior, 118
- At school
  - Extinction, used with positive reinforcement of adaptive behavior with or without a token economy, 48, 56, 78
  - Punishment, time-out, or response cost, 93

Drug abuse
- Aversion therapy, 97
  - Apomorphine in a classic conditioning paradigm (*see* Alcoholism) may be combined with desensitization of social anxiety themes and assertiveness training
  - Shock (using portable shock apparatus) contingent on impulse to take drug, 100

Dysmenorrhea
- Systematic desensitization

Dyspareunia
   Systematic desensitization

Encopresis
   Shaping regular bowel habit
Enuresis
   Classical conditioning (most frequently, the bell and blanket technique)
   Toilet skills training package, 248

Frigidity
   Systematic desensitization

Gambling
   Aversion therapy, shock in a Punishment paradigm
Gilles de la Tourette's syndrome
   Negative practice. *See* Tics, Negative practice
   Reinforcement of incompatible behaviors
   Time-out contingent upon deviant behavior
Gross stress reaction (combat)
   Flooding in fantasy (implosion)
   Systematic desensitization of fear themes

Hallucination
   Time-out contingent on hallucinating, if the behavior can clearly be defined by observation
Headache
   EMG feedback, 154
   Relaxation training, 154
Hemiparesis (hysterical)
   Avoidance training (or escape)
Hiccoughing
   Aversion therapy, shock in a Punishment or Avoidance paradigm
Hyperactivity (in children)
   Extinction, with reinforcement for appropriate behavior
   Shaping attentive and other incompatible behaviors, using points or tokens

Hypertension (essential)
    Blood pressure Biofeedback
    Relaxation training, 151

Impotence
    Systematic desensitization of sexual anxiety-evoking themes
Insomnia
    Relaxation training, 157
    Systematic desensitization of anxiety themes
Isolate behavior (in children)
    Extinction with Positive reinforcement for appropriate behavior (social approach)

Mutism (elective)
    Shaping vocalization, 43

Nail-biting
    Negative practice. *See* Tics, Negative practice
Neurodermatitis
    Extinction, removing attention for scratching behavior, 53
    Punishment, shock contingent on scratching
Nightmare
    Systematic desensitization of anxiety themes of the nightmare

Obesity
    Aversion therapy
        Covert sensitization, 113
        Self-control treatment package (based largely on operant conditioning principles), 255
        Shock, in an Avoidance or Punishment paradigm
Obsessional thoughts
    Aversion therapy, shock in a punishment paradigm or thought-stopping, 231
    Systematic desensitization of phobic themes related to obsessional thoughts
Oppositional behavior (in children, *see* Disruptive behavior)

Paralysis (hysterical)
    Avoidance training, moves to avoid shock
    Shaping movement, 48
Pervasive anxiety (guilt feelings and feelings of devaluation)
    Systematic desensitization of relevant guilt and anxiety themes
Phobias
    Flooding (exposure to phobic situation in imagination and reality), 204
    Paradoxical intention
    Shaping, reinforced practice, 8
    Systematic desensitization
Premature ejaculation
    Systematic desensitization of sexual anxiety themes

Remedial education
    With low achievers
        Token economy
    With retarded children
        Modeling
        Shaping
Ruminative vomiting (in infants; *see* Vomiting)

Sadistic fantasy
    Aversion therapy
        Covert sensitization, 107
        Shock in a Punishment paradigm with positive Counterconditioning (masturbation) to appropriate stimuli
Schizophrenia
    Rehabilitation
    Token economy (*see also* Delusions, Hallucination, Hoarding behavior), 65
Scratching
    Extinction, 53
Screaming
    Extinction, 54
    Time-out
Self-care (training in)

    Modeling
    Self-reinforcement
    Shaping (token system)
Self-injury
    Extinction, removal of social reinforcement for the behavior, 53
    Punishment, using shock or time-out, 114
    Reinforcement of incompatible behaviors
Sexual behavior. *Note:* Assertiveness training, behavior rehearsal (role playing), and modeling are often used together with the aversive techniques to build socially appropriate behaviors, replacing the deviant behavior weakened or removed by aversion techniques
    Exhibitionism
        Assertiveness training
        Punishment, shock contingent on fantasy or behavior, 108
        Systematic desensitization
    Fetishism
        Aversion therapy, shock contingent on fantasy, or actual behavior, or both, 103
        Systematic desensitization of sexual anxiety themes
    Homosexuality
        Assertiveness training
        Avoidance training or classic conditioning, 105
        Covert sensitization, 107
        Fading, 19
        Systematic desensitization of heterosexual anxiety themes
    Masochism
        Aversion therapy, shock contingent on fantasies, 107
    Pedophilia
        Aversion therapy, shock contingent on fantasies of behavior and slides of erotic stimuli
        Covert sensitization
    Sadism
        Aversive therapy, verbal aversion, 107
Self-injurious behavior
    Extinction combined with reinforcement of incompatible behavior, 53
    Punishment, 114

Transvestism
    Aversion therapy, shock applied in a punishment paradigm both to cross-dressing and fantasies of the deviant behavior, 107

Smoking
  Aversion therapy
    Covert sensitization, 111
    Relaxation training
    Shock used in a punishment paradigm, 111
    Smoke used in a punishment paradigm, 112
    Systematic desensitization, to cues or anxiety themes associated with smoking

Social interaction
  Assertiveness training, 268
  Modeling
  Shaping, 38
  Token economy, 69

Speech (reinstatement or increase in rate)
  Shaping, 43
  Token economy

Spelling
  Positive reinforcement for correct spelling with extinction of incorrect attempts

Stealing. *See* Delinquent behavior

Stuttering
  Aversion therapy, using Avoidance training, in which patient avoids noise by talking more fluently
  Shaping, normal speech with or without a token economy

Tantrums
  Hair pulling
    Aversion therapy, noise or shock, time-out, 115
  Head-banging
    Aversion therapy, noise or shock, time-out, 115
  Screaming, or crying, or both
    Aversion therapy, Time-out
    Extinction, removal of social attention, 53, 54
  Self-injurious behavior (other than the preceding)
    Aversion therapy, shock, used in a punishment paradigm, 114

Reinforcement of incompatible behavior
Time-out
Sulking
Extinction
Tics
Aversion therapy, noise, used in a Punishment or Avoidance training paradigm
Negative practice. This technique, first described by Dunlap [2], has been used mainly in the treatment of tics. The procedure consists of encouraging the patient to reproduce the movement of the tic as exactly as possible and repeating this movement many times in sessions of half an hour to one hour. Repeated practice of this kind has been shown to lessen the frequency of both the voluntary and involuntary occurrence of tics, and several successful case reports have been published [1-3]
Torticollis
Aversion therapy, shock, in a passive avoidance paradigm
Shaping, normal head movements
Truancy
Shaping, in a token system with or without a punishment technique, such as response cost

Vaginismus
Systematic desensitization of sexual anxiety themes
Vocal nodules (resulting from continued hypertension of the laryngeal musculature)
Systematic desensitization
Vomiting
Aversion therapy, shock, time-out or other aversive stimulus, 116
Extinction, removal of attention for vomiting, 55

Withdrawal (social)
Shaping, reinforcement of social interaction, 38

References
1. Agras, W. S., and Marshall, C. The application of negative practice to spasmodic torticollis. *American Journal of Psychiatry* 122:579, 1965.
2. Dunlap, K. *Habits, Their Making and Unmaking.* New York: Liveright, 1932.
3. Yates, A. J. The application of learning theory to the treatment of tics. *Journal of Abnormal Social Psychology* 56:175, 1958.

Subject Index

Academic skills, 75
Achievement place, 76-78
Addictive behaviors. *See* Alcoholism; Cigarette smoking; Drugs, addiction
Aggressive behavior, 96, 268
Agoraphobia, 8-11, 21, 179, 205-208
Alcoholism, aversion therapy in, 97-103
  antabuse in, 103
  apomorphine therapy in, 97
  group therapy in, 98
  social factors in, 98
  succinycholine in, 99
  verbal aversion in, 100
Analogue experiments
  fear reduction, findings in, 174-188
    anxiety arousal, 182
    exposure duration, 176
    fantasy vs. live exposure, 188
    instructions, role of, 185
    reinforcement, role of, 184
    relaxation in, 181
  limitations of, 173-174
Anorexia
  nervosa, 29, 73
  in schizophrenia, 52
Antabuse, 103
Anxiety, 155
  abreaction, 182
  arousal, 182
  induced, 167
  relaxation training for, 156
  role in flooding, 204
  systematic desensitization for, 204
Apomorphine, 17, 97
Apotrepic therapy, 224
Arugamama, 166
Assertiveness training
  components of, 275-277
  group vs. individual therapy in, 274
  indications for, 273
  outcome of, 280
  phobia in, 206
  rationale for, 268-270
  therapeutic approaches in, 270-273
  therapeutic package for, 278-280
Astasia-abasia, 48, 73

Asthma, 155
Attention-seeking behavior, 74
Autistic children, 18-19, 114-119, 122
  stimulus control in, 18
Autogenic training, 140, 146, 157
Autonomic conditioning, 16, 26
Aversion relief, 98
Aversion therapy. *See also* Aversive stimuli
  clinical application, 86-120
    alcoholism in, 97-103
    cigarette smoking in, 110-113
    drug addiction in, 100, 102
    obesity in, 113
    ruminative vomiting in, 116
    sexual deviation in, 103-113
    socially disruptive behavior in, 118-120
  ethics of, 123-124
  generalization of, 120-121
  overview of, 120-123
  mechanism of action, 121-122
  paradigms for application of, 27, 86, 89-91
  permanence, 120-121
  side effects, 95-96
Aversive stimuli
  chemical, 90-91, 97-99, 104, 105, 107
  choice of, 94
  electrical (shock)
    alcoholism in, 99
    cigarette smoking in, 111
    electrodes for, 92
    exhibitionism in, 108
    homosexuality in, 105
    procedure, 91
    self-destructive behavior in, 115
  ethical considerations, 86, 117, 123
  lemon juice, 117
  noise, 94
  sensory modality, 95
  side effects of, 95-97
  smell, 93, 94
  smoke, 112
  social, 109
  types of, 86
  verbal, 92, 100, 107
Avoidance training, 90

Bed wetting, 243. *See also* Toilet training
Behavior modification
  definition of, 5
  history, 2-5
  relationship to psychoanalysis, 6-12
Behavior rehearsal, 276
Behavioral antecedents, 16-24
Behavioral consequences, 24-31
Behavioral contract, 261
Behavioral measurement
  agoraphobia in, 9
  fear in, 174
  mental disorders in, 243
  psychoanalysis in, 7
  social withdrawal in, 41
  token economy in, 64, 72
Behavioral objectives, 9, 39
Behavioral therapies. *See also specific type* (e.g., Apotrepic therapy; Aversion therapy; Covert sensitization; Desensitization; Flooding; Modeling; Paradoxical intention; Practice; Response prevention; Role playing; Shaping; and Behavior modification) *and specific disorder in Therapeutic Index*
  aims, 243
  definition of, 5
  development of, 2-5
  packages, 243-288
  social class in, 245
  specificity of, 243-245
  types, 6
  vs. psychoanalysis, 6-12, 244
Biofeedback
  alpha wave, 146
  asthma in, 155
  electromyographic, 30, 145, 150
  headache in, 154
  overview of, 30
  phobia in, 212
  relaxation training in, 145
Blood pressure. *See* Hypertension
Brevital, 138-139

Cigarette smoking, 110-113, 157

Classical conditioning. *See* Conditioning, classical
Classroom behavior, 48, 56, 78
Claustrophobia, 45
Compulsive behavior, treatment of, 218-233
  hand washing, 222-223
  modeling in, 225
  obsessive thoughts, 221-223
  relaxation in, 219-220, 224
  response prevention, 224
  rituals, 218-224
  slowness, 231
  thought stopping, 233
Communication skills, 283. *See also* Assertiveness training
Conditioning
  classical, 16-18, 89, 121
  operant, 5, 8-11, 18-20, 24-31, 36-42, 64. *See also* Extinction; Reinforcement; Token economy
Contingency management. *See* Conditioning, operant
Contract management, 261
Conversion reaction, 48, 73
Counterconditioning, 171. *See also* Reciprocal inhibition
Covert rehearsal, 278
Covert sensitization, 93, 100
Cross-dressing, 107

Delinquent behavior, 75-78, 118
Delusions
  speech, 43, 52
Depression
  aversion therapy in, 96
  behavioral theory of, 45
  flooding in, 217, 218
  phobia in, 173
  social attention in, 47
  treatment of
    neurotic, 45-47
    psychotic, 52
Dermatitis, 53
Desensitization, systematic
  analogue studies of, 173-188
  controlled clinical studies, 155, 157, 204
  efficacy of, 204

Desensitization, systematic—*Continued*
  hierarchy in, 211
  mechanism, 181
  procedure of, 167
  relaxation training in, 135–139
  theory of, 5, 135
Discriminative learning, 18
Disruptive behavior, 118–120
Dopamine beta hydroxylase, 156
Drugs
  addiction, 100, 102
  antabuse, 102
  apomorphine, 97
  emetine, 90
  methohexitone (Brevital), 138
  succinylcholine, 99
  sulfureted potash, 94

Eating behavior, 258. *See also* Anorexia nervosa; Obesity
Electroshock therapy, 124
Emetine, 90
Enuresis, 243–248. *See also* Toilet training
Ethics in aversive therapy, 123–124
Evoking stimulus, 171
Exercise, 261
Exhibitionism, 108–109
Expectancy, 11, 20, 147–150, 185, 226
Exposure
  biofeedback in, 212
  duration, 175–176
  group, 205–208
  home-based, 208–210
  imagery in, 180
  in fantasy, 167
  in vivo, 166, 205–213
  nurse therapists for, 209
  past applications of, 189–193
Extinction
  animal experiments, 168–171
  burst, 51
  combined with reinforcement, 54–57
  definition of, 26, 50
  procedure, 50
  therapeutic application, 52–54, 168

Fading, 19

Family
  problems, 11
  as therapists, 57, 208, 227–228, 253
Fear
  blood, 215
  darkness, 189
  dental, 215
  dreams of, 189
  examination, 192
  flying, 217
  horses, 189
  injury, 215
  modeling in, 23, 183–184
  relevant vs. irrelevant imagery, 204
  sexual, 213
  snake, 174–179, 184
  swimming, 178
  urination, 213–215
Feedback, 28–31, 57, 185. *See also* Biofeedback
Fetishism, 107
Flooding, 164, 168, 204, 209–211
Frigidity, 213

Generalization, 46, 49
  assertiveness training in, 276
  aversion therapy in, 120
  respondent conditioning in, 17
  token economy from, 65, 80
  training, 41
Glass breaking, 119
Graduated exposure, 250
Group therapy, 205–207, 259–262, 274

Headache, 154
Hierarchies, 211
Homosexual behavior
  aversion treatment of, 4, 104–107
  classical conditioning in, 17
  fading in treatment of, 19
Homosexual fantasy, 105
Hypertension, 21, 30
  classical conditioning in, 17
  relaxation training in, 151–153
Hypnosis, 140, 145
Hysterical personality, 74

Imagery, 148

Imitative learning. *See* Modeling
Implosive therapy, 167, 180, 182, 204
Induced anxiety, 167
Insomnia, 157
Instructional control, 20-23
 agoraphobia in, 21
 assertiveness training in, 274
 autonomic behavior in, 21
 behavioral packages in, 247
 phobia in, 185-186
 prompts as, 21
 psychotherapy in, 20
 relaxation training in, 147
 self-instruction in, 22-23
 therapeutic instructions as, 20
 toilet training in, 250
Instrumental conditioning. *See* Conditioning, operant

Kleptomania, 119

Marital counseling, 285
Masochism, 107
Medication abuse, 73
Meditation, 146, 149, 193
Mental retardation, 53, 114-116, 119
Modeling
 assertiveness training in, 275, 278
 compulsive behavior in, 220
 fearful behavior in, 23
 overview of, 23-24
 phobia in, 183
 role-playing as, 24, 276
 toilet training in, 250
Morita therapy, 193, 233
Mourning, 218
Mutism, 41, 43

Negative reinforcement
 definition, 24
 extinction of, 51
Negative reinforcers, 24, 51, 90-94.
   See also Aversive stimuli
Neurosis. *See also* Agoraphobia;
   Anorexia, nervosa;
   Astasia-abasia; Claustrophobia; Compulsive behavior;
   Phobia; School phobia
 experimental, 3, 168-172
 extinction, application to, 51, 53-55
 reinforcement, application to, 45-48

Obesity
 aversive procedures in, 113, 243
 components of treatment, 256-262
 etiology of, 255-256
 exercise in, 261
 spouse involvement, 263
 treatment efficacy, 262-268
 treatment of, 243, 255-268, 286
Obsessive-compulsive neurosis. *See*
   Compulsive behavior
Operant conditioning. *See* Conditioning, operant
Oppositional behavior, 55
Overcorrection, 94, 119
Overweight. *See* Obesity

Pain, 157
Paradoxical intention, 192
Pavlovian conditioning.
   See Conditioning, classical
Personal effectiveness training, 272
Phobia, 8-11, 45, 51, 204-218.
   See also Agoraphobia;
   Claustrophobia; Fear;
   School phobia
Placebo effect, 150-152
Positive reinforcement
 definition, 24
 procedure, 38-42
 therapeutic application
  in neuroses, 45-48, 184
  in psychoses, 42-45, 69-73
Positive reinforcers, 24, 36, 39, 77
Practice
 behavioral definition in, 39
 generalization training in, 41
 procedure, 9-11, 38, 45
 prompting in, 40
 reinforced, 9, 39
 relaxation therapy in, 138
Premack principle, 71
Progressive relaxation, 147, 151
Prolonged exposure, 175-205

Prompts, 40
Psychoanalysis, 1
Psychoanalytic psychotherapy
  aims, 7, 64
  population treated, 64
  results, 4, 244
  similarities to behavior therapy, 11–13
Punishment, 6, 24, 27, 53, 55, 86, 89–92. See also Aversion therapy; Aversive stimuli
  complications of, 28, 95
  definition of, 27
  procedure in, 89
  side effects, 95

Rational emotive therapy, 188
Reality testing, 168
Reciprocal inhibition, 167, 181
Reflex conditioning. See Conditioning, classical
Reinforced practice, 8–11, 38–42, 184
Reinforcement
  combined with extinction, 54–57
  negative. See Negative reinforcement
  positive. See Positive reinforcement
  self, 25
  social, 73, 79
  training in, 57–58
  vicarious, 50
Reinforcers
  negative, 24, 27–28, 90–92
  positive, 24–26, 36–42, 64
  sampling, 70
  schedules of, 40
  selection of, 40
  token, 64–83
Relaxation training
  applications, 149–158, 181–182, 220–221
  biofeedback in, 139
  components of, 147–148
  metronome in, 139
  physiology of, 140–144
  procedure, 135–139
  progressive, 147
  side effects, 149
  tape-recorded instructions, 138
  theoretical basis, 139–140
Respondent conditioning. See Conditioning, classical
Response cost, 77, 95, 111, 118
Response prevention, 224
  in animals, 168–171
Rogerian therapy, 11
Role playing, 276
Ruminative vomiting, 117

Sadism, 107
Schizophrenia, 42–45, 70–71. See also Anorexia; Autistic children; Delusions; Glass breaking; Hoarding behavior; Mutism
School phobia, 189
Scratching, 53, 115
Self-care, 66, 70
Self-control, 186–188, 247, 272
Self-injurious behavior, 53, 114–118
Self-instruction, 22–23
Self-monitoring, 28, 277
Self-reinforcement, 25
Senoi culture, 189
Sexual deviance, 103–110. See also Exhibitionism; Fetishism; Homosexual behavior; Masochism; Sadism, Transvestism
Shaping
  in agoraphobia, 8–11
  astasia-abasia, 48
  procedure, 25, 38–42
  social interaction, 38
  vocalization, 42
Shock. See Aversive stimuli, electrical
Shoplifting, 119
Smoking behavior, 110–113, 157
Social withdrawal, 38, 43. See also Assertiveness training
Spontaneous recovery, 17
Stealing, 28, 119
Stimulus control, 257, 259
Stimulus discrimination, 18–19
Stimulus generalization. See Generalization
Stress, 155, 167
Submissive behavior, 268–270. See also Assertiveness training

Succinylcholine, 99
Sulfureted potash, 94
Symptom removal, 7
Systematic desensitization. *See* Desensitization

Tantrums, 54, 55
Therapeutic instructions. *See* Instructional control
Therapy. *See* Behavioral therapies; Psychoanalytic psychotherapy; and Therapeutic Index
Time-out technique, 93, 101, 118
Toilet training, 248–255. *See also* Enuresis
  age of, 249
  bell and pad method, 243
  readiness for, 249, 252
  treatment components, 250–252
  treatment efficacy, 253–255
Token economy
  at Anna State Hospital, 69
  application to neuroses, 73–75
  application to psychoses, 69–73
  controlled outcome studies, 71–73
  definition, 64
  economics, 80
  operational problems with, 67–69
Transfer of training. *See* Generalization
Transvestism, 107

Verbal aversion, 93, 100
Vomiting, 54, 55, 117

Work therapy, 71

Zen Buddhism, 193

188